GEORGE GRANT AND THE SUBVERSION OF MODERNITY: ART, PHILOSOPHY, RELIGION, POLITICS, AND EDUCATION

George Grant's mystique as a political philosopher is due in part to the seemingly contradictory public stances he took through the years. His opposition to the Vietnam War and his linking of liberalism with technological progress and imperialism brought him favour among the political left during the 1960s. Then, in the following decade, his opposition to abortion earned him allies on the political right, despite his rejection of limitless capitalist growth and free trade with the United States. This collection of original essays reveals the complex philosophic, artistic, and religious sources underlying Grant's public positions of nationalism, pacifism, and conservatism.

The collection begins with Grant's previously unpublished writing on Céline. This is a bold and vigorous Grant, writing on a topic about which he is passionate and deeply informed. Grant's own work is followed by two pieces that explore his devotion to Céline. Grant's writings on Nietzsche, Heidegger, Weil, and Leo Strauss also receive special attention. Here we discover the great modern thinkers who inspired and challenged Grant, and whose writings occupied him for much of his life.

Many of the essays draw on manuscripts and notes left unpublished by Grant, thus contributing new perspectives to the ongoing discussion of his work. The volume also examines Grant's role as a teacher and his views on education, and closes with a selection of his unpublished letters on universities.

ARTHUR DAVIS is Professor of Social Science at Atkinson College, York University.

EDITED BY ARTHUR DAVIS

George Grant and the Subversion of Modernity:

Art, Philosophy, Politics, Religion, and Education

UNIVERSITY OF TORONTO PRESS
Toronto Buffalo London

University of Toronto Press Incorporated 1996
Toronto Buffalo London
Printed in Canada

ISBN 0-8020-0668-X (cloth)
ISBN 0-8020-7622-X (paper)

Printed on acid-free paper

Canadian Cataloguing in Publication Data

Main entry under title:

George Grant and the subversion of modernity: art, philosophy, politics,
religion, and education

Includes index.
ISBN 0-8020-0668-X (bound)   ISBN 0-8020-7622-X (pbk.)

1. Grant, George, 1918–1988. 2. Philosophy and civilization.
3. Philosophy, Canadian – 20th century. I. Davis, Arthur, 1939–

B995.G74G46 1996   191   C96-930787-X

University of Toronto Press acknowledges the financial assistance to its
publishing program of the Canada Council and the Ontario Arts Council.

Contents

Acknowledgments

This collection of essays on George Grant began to take shape when Peter Emberley suggested that I edit some papers given at a Grant colloquium in the summer of 1993. The participants at that colloquium, and the other authors who have been invited to contribute to this volume, have gathered to discuss their work, and many fruitful exchanges have occurred in the course of writing, revising, and editing. The intensity of the debate that came about attests to the continued importance of Grant's questions and answers to the writers involved.

Gerald Owen's wisdom and wonderful editorial talents have been indispensable to several of the papers. I thank him especially for his enormous patience and skill while working with me on my own paper. Michael Burns spent countless hours in conversation with me and in giving me editorial advice. I thank him for our instructive perennial debate. I am deeply indebted to Dennis Lee for his excellent editorial advice on my own paper. I am grateful also to Bob Davis, Sheila Grant, Louis Greenspan, David Jones, and Henry Roper for their help. Finally, I thank Ed Andrew for pressing me to write and to take up the task of editing George Grant's work.

I am grateful to the Donner Canadian Foundation for its support. I also thank Atkinson College of York University for financial support and the excellent work done by Hazel O'Loughlin-Vidal in preparing the camera-ready copy.

ARTHUR DAVIS

Note on George Grant's Unpublished Writings

When George Grant died, his study in Halifax was filled with unpublished essays, manuscripts, addresses, lectures, transcripts of radio and television broadcasts, research notes, and letters. His notebooks contain lectures on Plato, Aristotle, the Gospels, Kant, Nietzsche, Heidegger, and Weil. A large selection of this material will be included, along with Grant's published works, in the forthcoming Collected Works of George Grant. In general there are no shocking surprises in the unpublished writings, no discoveries that contradict Grant's published works. What they provide is a more complete picture than we have had, a more complete guide to his thought as a whole.

Several of the contributors to the present book draw on passages from the unpublished writings, which are cited according to the system set up by Sheila Grant and the editors of the Collected Works.

For the present book Sheila Grant has edited an unpublished essay by Grant entitled 'Céline's Trilogy.' In her preface to the essay, she describes how the text was constructed by her from drafts and fragments that Grant left behind when he abandoned a projected book on Céline in 1983.

Contributors

EDWARD ANDREW is Professor of Political Science at the University of Toronto. His books include *Shylock's Rights* (University of Toronto Press, 1988) and *The Genealogy of Values: The Aesthetic Economy of Nietzsche and Proust* (Rowman and Littlefield, 1995).

RONALD BEINER is Professor of Political Science at the University of Toronto. His books include *Political Judgment* (University of Chicago Press, 1983), *What's the Matter with Liberalism?* (University of California Press, 1992), and *Theorizing Citizenship* (State University of New York Press, 1995).

LEAH BRADSHAW is Professor of Politics at Brock University. She wrote *Acting and Thinking: The Political Thought of Hannah Arendt* (University of Toronto Press, 1989) and is writing a book on ancient and modern tyranny.

WILLIAM CHRISTIAN is Professor of Political Studies at the University of Guelph. He is co-author of *Leaders, Parties and Ideologies in Canada* (McGraw-Hill Ryerson, 1996), author of *George Grant: A Biography* (University of Toronto Press, 1993), and editor of *George Grant: Selected Letters* (University of Toronto Press, 1996).

ARTHUR DAVIS is Professor of Social Science at Atkinson College, York University, and co-editor of the forthcoming Collected Works of George Grant.

H.D. FORBES is Professor of Political Science at the University of Toronto. He has published books and articles on Quebec and Canadian politics including *Nationalism, Ethnocentrism and Personality: Social Science and Critical Theory* (University of Chicago Press, 1985), and edited *Canadian Political Thought* (Oxford University Press, 1985).

SHEILA GRANT is co-author with her late husband, George Grant, of 'The Language of Euthanasia' and 'Abortion and Rights' in *Technology and Justice* (Anansi, 1986).

NITA GRAHAM was a student of George Grant and a lifelong friend and intellectual associate.

LOUIS GREENSPAN is Professor of Religious Studies at McMaster University and director of the Bertrand Russell Editorial Project. His books include *The Incompatible Prophecies: An Essay on Science and Liberty in the Political Writings of Bertrand Russell* (Mosaic Press, 1978). He is co-editor of *Fackenheim: German Philosophy and Jewish Thought* (University of Toronto Press, 1992).

GERALD OWEN is managing editor of *Books in Canada*.

LAWRENCE SCHMIDT is Professor of Religious Studies at Erindale College, University of Toronto. He edited *George Grant in Process: Essays and Conversations* (Anansi, 1978).

Chronology

1918   Born in Toronto on November 13 to William Grant and Maude Parkin.

1927   Enters Upper Canada College in Toronto. Graduates in 1936.

1935   Father dies.

1936   Enters Queen's University to study history. Completes Honours BA in 1939.

1939   Awarded Ontario Rhodes Scholarship. Enters Balliol College, Oxford, to study jurisprudence.

1940   Works as Air Raid Precaution Officer on the London docks in Bermondsey during the Battle of Britain.

1941   Tries to join the Merchant Marine but contracts tuberculosis. Works on a farm in Buckinghamshire. Converted after period of despair to a belief in 'order beyond space and time.'

1942   Convalesces in Canada.

1943   Works under Dr E.A. Corbett as national secretary of the Canadian Association for Adult Education. Works with Jean Morrison on the journal *Food for Thought* and the radio program *Citizens' Forum*.

1945   Returns to Balliol to study theology. Influenced by A.D. Lindsay, Austin Farrer, and C.S. Lewis. Meets Sheila Allen.

1947   Marries Sheila Allen. Begins work at Dalhousie University as Professor of Philosophy. Begins association with Professor James Doull, 'who taught me to read Plato.'

1948   Daughter Rachel born.

1950   Son William born. Awarded DPhil degree for dissertation entitled 'The Concept of Nature and Supernature in the Theology of John Oman.'

1952   Son Robert born.

1954   Daughter Catherine born.

1957   Daughter Isabel born.

1959   Son David born. Delivers a series of nine talks on CBC Radio's *University of the Air*.

1960   Publishes *Philosophy in the Mass Age*, a revised version of the nine radio talks. Accepts and then resigns a position at the newly founded York University in Toronto. While in Toronto writes for Mortimer Adler of the Institute for Philosophical Research in Chicago.

1961   Contributes 'An Ethic of Community' to *Social Purpose for Canada*, a book published to coincide with the founding of the New Democratic Party. Accepts a position as Associate Professor of Religion at McMaster University.

1963   Writes first essay on Simone Weil (unpublished). Mother dies. Appointed Fellow of the Royal Society of Canada.

1965   Publishes *Lament for a Nation*. Addresses the International Teach-In at the University of Toronto.

1966   Publishes a new introduction to *Philosophy in the Mass Age*, indicating an important change of mind.

1969   Publishes *Technology and Empire*. Delivers Massey Lectures on the CBC, which are published as *Time as History*.

1970   Reassesses *Lament for a Nation* in a new introduction to the book.

1971   Begins work on 'Technique(s) and Good,' a proposed book.

1974   Delivers Josiah Wood Lectures at Mount Allison University, which are published as *English-Speaking Justice*.

1976   Begins work on 'Good and Technique,' a proposed book.

1980   Resigns teaching position at McMaster University. Accepts Killam professorship in the Department of Political Science at Dalhousie University, with a cross-appointment to the Departments of Classics and Religion.

1982   Begins work on the idea of history in the thought of Rousseau and Darwin.

1983   Publishes essay on Céline, intended as part of a proposed book on Céline and the nature of art.

1984   Retires from teaching.

1985   Publishes Notre Dame University Press edition of *English-Speaking Justice*.

1986   Publishes *Technology and Justice* (Anansi and Notre Dame University Presses). Publishes *Est-ce la Fin du Canada? Lamentation sur l'echec du nationalisme Canadien*, the French edition of *Lament for a Nation* (reprinted 1992). Begins work on a book responding to Heidegger's *Nietzsche* with a defence of Christianity and Plato.

1988   Dies in Halifax on September 27.

GEORGE GRANT AND THE
SUBVERSION OF MODERNITY

1

Introduction:
Why Read George Grant?

ARTHUR DAVIS

By 1970 George Grant was well known to Canadians as a nationalist and a staunch opponent of the war in Vietnam. His writings of the sixties had been about politics, the economy, education, and technology more than religion and philosophy. He had come to be lionized by various groups on the political left, especially members of the anti-war and civil rights movements, many of whom he converted to Canadian nationalism. He had shown his leftward leanings in 'An Ethic of Community' (1961),[1] where he had argued for social democratic policies to temper the abuses of capitalism.

As Abraham Rotstein remarked,[2] Grant spoke with great moral authority; yet few of those who appreciated his voice were aware of the intellectual sources of that authority. Readers of *Lament for a Nation* (1965) and *Technology and Empire* (1969) were given only fleeting glimpses of his religious and philosophic roots and influences. Thus some were shocked when he became an active opponent of abortion in the seventies. During that decade he gained supporters on the Christian right, while many liberals and socialists began to question their affiliation with him.

It is worth asking how the same man came to attract both the left and the right. The assembling of published and unpublished writings for the Collected Works of George Grant, along with the publication of William Christian's biography and the *Selected Letters*, make it possible to answer questions about 'the unknown

Grant.' It was, of course, the same man who opposed the war in Vietnam in the sixties and abortion in the seventies. Grant himself did not think either stand was at bottom a political question (a matter of left or right), but rather a religious one. He did believe, however, that religion and politics are deeply interwoven, and that any worthy thinking must enter the political arena, however constrained politics may have become in modern technological society. In any case, since we now have access to more of Grant's reflections, we are in a better position to assess his contribution to the continuing public debate between the left and the right about justice.

For this collection Sheila Grant has put together the fragments of a book her husband worked on in the early eighties about his love of the wartime trilogy by the controversial French writer Louis-Ferdinand Céline. The resulting essay, entitled 'Céline's Trilogy,' stands first here. In the final decade of his life Grant became enamoured of Céline's wonderfully told story of his flight from France through Germany to Denmark during the closing months of the Second World War. Grant wished to praise Céline's trilogy in public because he thought it revealed the human condition as only a great work of art can. He makes the controversial claim that Céline should not be excluded from the canon because of his anti-Semitism or his alleged madness.

The essay is an intimate and heartfelt one, written for pleasure rather than out of philosophic duty. Nonetheless, Grant raises in it questions of great importance and considerable difficulty concerning the relation of art, philosophy, and morality in Céline's work. Grant's essay on Céline tells us something essential about Grant's vision of the way things are. And further, Grant addresses the question of how we should respond to a story that, while it may tell us about the way things are, was written by an artist who was also an anti-Semite. Gerald Owen and Edward Andrew offer their different responses to this unusual essay by Grant.

The diversity of the pieces in this collection draws attention above all to the surprising breadth of Grant's influences, which both included and reached beyond Christianity and Plato. In the late forties and fifties Grant argued for the study of Karl Marx and Sigmund Freud, both of whom were usually excluded from the North American university curriculum as too subversive. In the sixties and seventies he wrestled with the thought of Leo Strauss,

Friedrich Nietzsche, and Martin Heidegger before it was fashionable in Canada to celebrate the subversion of modern thought and practice carried out by those thinkers.

Grant did not believe he was called to original thought, but rather to a search for truth with help from the thought of others. Above all he wanted to share his search with students and the Canadian public. He never made a systematic attempt to reconcile the tension in his thought between the claims of the ancient and modern thinkers who influenced him. In his lectures on Simone Weil he told students that he cleared his mind by concentrating on what the great thinkers asserted elementally. Some have suggested[3] that his thought therefore lacks a centre of its own, that he patched together the ideas of others and did not reconcile the resulting contradictions. His work is, so the argument goes, an unresolved composite of Strauss and Heidegger, or perhaps of Plato (as interpreted by Weil) and Nietzsche. Others, meanwhile, have insisted that he was kept on a consistent and unified philosophic path by his commitment to justice.

The story of Grant's assessment of the modern technological world is told in part through his complicated responses to three major modern thinkers. His desire to understand what we have become in the modern world led him into an intense engagement first with Nietzsche and then with Heidegger. Both are modern thinkers who, in different ways, subvert liberal rationality. The same desire led him into a complex relationship with the non-Christian Platonist and political philosopher Strauss. Grant found Strauss's critique of modernity to be, in the final analysis, insufficient, although he learned enormously from it. In the second section of this collection Ronald Beiner examines Grant's engagement with Nietzsche, Arthur Davis his encounter with Heidegger, and Donald Forbes his debt to and disagreement with Strauss.

One reading of Grant holds that he became, in his later years, 'an implacable pessimist' who rejected modern science, economics, and politics as being fundamentally mistaken. But this misses the subtlety and ambiguity of Grant's subversive stance toward liberalism and modern thought in general. Modern science and morality can be considered a giant mistake because they exclude God. But that judgment, for Grant, was in a sense beside the point, for we belong to the modern world and must ask what we think of this world with its established liberal and technological modes of thought. In the third section of the collection Louis Greenspan examines which features of our modern liberal and technological way of doing things Grant supported, and which he opposed and tried to subvert. Leah Bradshaw critically assesses Grant's position on abortion against the background of his overall philosophy and the political ideas of Hannah Arendt.

The fourth section concerns Grant and religion. Although he was a Christian who believed his thought should be 'yoked by Christ,' he did not read other thinkers from the safe distance of an already established position. Christianity, like Platonism, (which Grant thought had come close to expressing the same truth philosophically) had arisen in a pre-modern world and in a technological world needed new thought. Although he believed eternal truth was still part of the experience of modern people, despite its exclusion by modern scientific and moral thought, he rejected the option of reaching religious truth by turning away from the technological world. He wrote as he taught, with the intensity of someone seeking religious truth in the belly of the secular world, rather than as one who judges that world by a truth already spelled out. He admired Weil for her insistence that a just life can be led only in the world of necessity.

Grant's intense desire to find the truth in this world was what drew students, general readers, and radio listeners to his work. Part of the intensity came from his wrestling with the tasks of teaching and writing as a Christian in an era when Christianity no longer held sway among students and readers. Grant would never have been happy writing only for other Christians, and he learned from experience that circumspection about his faith was necessary in certain situations. Somewhat surprisingly, the resulting mix of modern and religious concerns gave strength to his public voice. It seemed that many Canadians needed such a voice as they were being drawn into a new technological world that they both wanted and feared.

Grant's faith was present at the core of all his work. But because of his desire to engage the modern world on its own terms it was present in a special, undogmatic way that was uniquely his own. Beginning the fifth section of this book and giving us some insight into the close relation between philosophy and theology in Grant's thought, Sheila Grant looks at the use he made of a thesis written by Martin Luther, from his first references to it in his Oxford doctoral dissertation of the forties, through his political writings of the sixties, and into his work of the eighties. Lawrence Schmidt writes about Grant's deep affinity with Weil, a Christian Platonist whom he called a modern saint.

The collection closes with two contributions on Grant's teaching and his responses to the universities in which he worked. In 1969 he asked, 'what is worth doing in the midst of this barren twilight?'[4] The answer in his own life was, in part, the kind of teaching he engaged in during three and a half decades at Dalhousie and McMaster. He thought he had failed as a teacher, and this sense of failure is instructive about the difficulties of teaching against the spirit of the age. Nita Graham discusses Grant's Socratic and dialectical method of teaching and the obstacles (such as the dominating presence of the spirit of modern science) that stood in its way, obstacles that still hinder the teaching of Grant's ideas. William Christian has selected and edited a group of letters that give us insight into Grant's thoughts on universities during his years as a teacher.

Grant never turned away from or sought to escape the modern world. He did, however, argue that the catastrophes of this century must lead us to reject the optimism inherent in the idea of human progress. He thought the tragedies of the twentieth century were driving most sensitive and thoughtful people away from the 'religion' of progress. He hoped this movement would take them not into nihilism but toward a deeper religious response, one that would unite modern and traditional insights.

Grant was well aware that the administrators of corporate and scientific power would continue to act as if nothing had changed. The will to master the natural and human worlds is certainly tenacious. It remains true that the prevailing doctrines of our time do not support the belief that all human beings should be treated with justice. Grant's thought was essentially a response to this catastrophic loss of the rational grounds for affirming justice. Most of his work was an attempt to convince others that there is such a loss, to define carefully just what that loss is, and to nurture that awareness of it which must precede a renewal.

NOTES

1 In Michael Oliver, ed., *Social Purpose for Canada* (Toronto: University of

Toronto Press 1961), 3–26. This book was published to coincide with the founding of the New Democratic Party.

2 *The Owl and the Dynamo*, hour-long documentary film on Grant produced by Vincent Tovell and broadcast on the CBC on 13 February 1980.

3 See, for example, Michael Allen Gillespie, 'George Grant and the Tradition of Political Philosophy,' in Peter C. Emberley, ed., *By Loving Our Own: George Grant and the Legacy of Lament for a Nation* (Ottawa: Carleton University Press 1990), 130, and Zdravko Planinc, 'Paradox and Polyphony in Grant's Critique of Modernity,' in Yusuf K. Omar, ed., *George Grant and the Future of Canada* (Calgary: University of Calgary Press 1992), 17–45.

4 George Grant, *Technology and Empire* (Toronto: Anansi 1969), 78.

ART

2

Céline's Trilogy

GEORGE GRANT

EDITOR'S PREFACE

Sheila Grant

When I began this preface, its title was going to be 'Why did George Grant write about Céline?' However, I found myself repeating the answer he himself had given. It seemed more useful, therefore, just to say why I thought it worth while to piece together Grant's notes for his unpublished and unfinished book on Céline, and present them here as an imperfect whole.

The condition of Grant's notes on Céline was extraordinary. There were often groups of consecutive typed passages, most of them quite long, one passage having six different versions. Numerous handwritten pages were included, some being the origin of the typed pages, some quite separate. There were short notes, long notes, and fragments of paper containing two or three words, none of which were assembled in any sort of order. However, the relation of the short notes to the longer pieces was often evident. Sudden changes of focus were not unusual: a philosophic discussion, for example, might unexpectedly give way to memories of childhood. At points the style would be enigmatic and concise, elsewhere rambling. This material was so entirely different in style, form, and content from everything else Grant wrote, including his manuscripts of other unfinished books, that it occurred to me that some readers might like to look at it, if only from curiosity.

The work presented here is mainly about Grant's love for the trilogy of books based on Céline's wartime experiences, D'un château l'autre (Castle to Castle); Nord (North); and Rigodon (Rigadoon).[1] Grant wrote a discursive meditation on these three books, and moved from their story to the nature of stories in general, and to some extent to the nature of poetry. He wrote as a reader, and that gave him a new freedom. He did not have to protect himself from attack by summing up the history of Western civilization in every other sentence. Never did he produce such relaxed writing, certainly not on philosophy, which always required a painful degree of discipline. The reading of Céline's trilogy gave Grant such enjoyment during the last ten years of his life that I wanted to make his account of the experience readable, despite the daunting condition of the material.

I could usually understand his brief notes, because the subject was so familiar. We had spent innumerable hours discussing both Céline and the wider questions raised by Céline's work. In all seasons but winter we would often bring our lunch to York Redoubt, an old military enclosure outside Halifax, and discuss Céline while walking the dog and watching the sea far below. It was a particularly good place for talking about Céline, the fascination his trilogy held for Grant, and the enigma of Céline's racism; also for talking about reading and stories, and about poetry and the unanswerable questions such subjects aroused. There was no hurry to find the answers. Grant never brought some of his speculations to a firm conclusion. This is evident in the rather disjointed final section of this piece, printed here with the title 'Why Am I Enraptured?'

Why did Grant not finish the book? There are several possible reasons. In 1983 he agreed to contribute an article on Céline to Queen's Quarterly, which I knew might be enough to turn him away from finishing the book. He would not listen to my warnings, and felt it was appropriate to publish something in the journal his father had helped to start. In the article he discussed Céline's anti-Semitism more fully than in the unpublished material available to me.

Another reason for dropping the book might have been that he had not made up his mind about some important matters, such as Plato's account of poetry.

The most likely reasons were that philosophy was claiming his attention, and that his energy was being depleted by bouts of ill health. He wanted to write a book on Rousseau and the idea of history, and the incomparably formidable challenge of Heidegger lay ahead. He was, admit-

tedly, a great planner of never-to-be-written books, and the one on Céline would have been a luxury rather than a duty.

I have taken three kinds of liberties in putting together this text. First, many passages that addressed the same subject were widely separated, and sometimes needed an added sentence or two to bring them together. Secondly, I added some quotations from Céline's text that had not been written down by Grant but were often mentioned to me as he read and reread the trilogy over the years. As Céline's books are not easily available, it seemed important to provide some of the passages that Grant described. Finally, I expanded some of Grant's brief notes where the meaning was clear to me from remembered conversations. This was done mostly in the last section. All the ideas in this section are Grant's, but I could not be sure of the order he would have intended. Therefore this section must be treated as incomplete.

I moved the quotation from Simone Weil from the beginning of the piece to the end, where its relevance might be better understood. All Grant had written was, 'might begin with S.W. – bread and hunger.'

INTRODUCTION

The purpose of this book is to try to state what is so enrapturing about Céline's trilogy. It could be said: what a silly thing to do in a world where two grotesque empires accumulate nuclear weapons. Surely one should be doing something more important than this, and what is more important should be evident to someone who has the luck to be a Christian. My answer would be: at all times and places the apprehension of the divine has had a lot to do with the apprehension of the beautiful. In our era of late state capitalism vast numbers of people find their way to the absolutely lovable through art in one form or another. In many cases the authenticity of that experience is inhibited by the fact that the experience degenerates into consumption of entertainment. How can it not be so in our kind of society? Without going into the extremely ambiguous distinction between high art and popular art, it is clear that much of the experience of unequivocally great art falls away into much less than it could be, when it is experienced as entertainment to be consumed. I heard the chairman of the Ontario Arts Council unite *South Pacific* to *The Marriage of Figaro* as of the same order of being. (The very greatest art can defend itself by its own weight. I remember being at Stratford, one of a huge audience of southern Ontario bourgeois and New England tourists, and we settled down for a nice afternoon's entertainment – and then *Lear* fell on us!)

In this book I want to write about literary art and its reading. We live in an era where there has never been so much printed material and yet where reading, except for technical and entertainment purposes, has declined. Whatever qualifications may be put on the work of Leavis, one surely must rejoice in the centre of his work for his country. He showed how much the substance of his community depended on the serious partaking of its own works of the imagination, and therefore also the importance of the teaching of such reading. I have spent most of my life trying to teach young Canadians how to read the great works of Western political philosophy and theology. Those works are of course related to the work of the poets – from Plato's relation to Homer to Heidegger's relation to Hölderlin. Plato called some of his most wonderful writing a likely tale. I now want to write about the reading of a very great artist, Céline, and the place of such reading in a lived existence. The fact that I am not a trained professor of literature puts limitations on my ability to do this well. There is in our day an immense proliferation of the study of literature, but ironically it comes at a time when there has been a break and confusion as to what the purpose of education should be within the new technological realism.

Writing about reading is of course only a very second-order activity, compared to the reading itself. The same applies to writing about music. I consider a day wasted in which I do not listen to one of the Mozart piano concertos. In relation to that desire, I have read such a fine book as Girdlestone's analyses of these concertos. Such books have been helpful to my enjoyment of the works. But obviously such writing is only of second order interest, and its purpose is to add to the rapture of listening. The present writing is of the same order. Beyond Céline's particular work I am going to try to say something general about the purposes of contemplating great works of art in this time of late state capitalism. It is not meant in the least blasphemously when I say that my purpose is the same as Grünewald gives to the Baptist's pointing arm in the Eisenheim altarpiece. Pointing at any artist is extremely minor compared to pointing at our Saviour, but this does not mean there is no need for such minor pointing. And perhaps pointing at a great literary work of art, may, if it leads to the reading of that work, have some connection to that highest pointing. Whether Céline's trilogy has any relation to Christianity can only be judged when the book has been read. Does the experience of the beautiful help to overcome our oblivion of eternity? A preface is just a preface, not a place for justification.

Nietzsche has written that philosophers should approach the discussion of art from the attempt to understand what it is to make it, or in his blasphemous language, to 'create' it. This seems to me simply misplaced arrogance. It arises from the belief that the philosopher is himself a creator and as a greater creator than the artist, can stand above the creation of the poets. Even if there are philosophers who can stand above the poets and tell us what it is they do, I am not claiming to be such a one. I have little idea of what it would be like to be Shakespeare or Mozart or Raphael. It would seem to me pretension itself to claim to understand their position. I simply want to try to state what it has been like for me to read Céline, and to proceed hesitatingly to make some general comments about being enraptured by the beautiful in art.

Reading any good writing is an act of trust. One must simply wade in with attention. One cannot expect to read Plato as casually as Le Carré. I remember the exact moment when I knew that Mozart was near the centre of my soul; my wife had told me and told me to listen, and suddenly I knew what she meant. I had often read Céline before I recognized the extent of his greatness. The difficulty of wading in with attention requires an act of trust that one will be rewarded. Even in the case of Shakespeare that trust may not always be guaranteed. The ability to wade in with attention declines in an electronic democracy. So people write books about the decline of the importance of print.

This book is about reading, and is written from the standpoint of a particular reader. I hope of course that in my remarks something of interest about reading in general will emerge. It is about the reading of a work of art, Céline's trilogy about his journey through Germany at the time of its conquest by the American and Russian empires in 1944–5. My first purpose is to state that the three books of the trilogy, *Castle to Castle*, *North*, and *Rigadoon* are among the great masterpieces of Western art. But such a statement runs in with other things. I found I wanted to state why this writing so enraptured me, and the corollary of that, why was it so beautiful? What were its perfections?

Of course it is another matter to write down one's thoughts on these subjects. Right through life we read writings which thrill us, enlighten us, inspire us, and we may wish to present these to and discuss them with our friends. But this does not mean that we have to write down our opinion so that it will become public. In Céline's case there was a particular reason for paying homage to him publicly: so that others might be encouraged to read the trilogy. It is very little known in Canada, and Céline's name is remembered, if at all, for the infamy of his early anti-Semitism. (I have discussed this in an article for the *Queen's Quarterly*, autumn 1983.) Now that the political storms of the 1930s and 40s, in which Céline was involved, are a little less pressing, some critics are willing to state that Céline is a fine writer of this century, and there is talk of his stylistic influence on some North American writers. But the concentration is on his two novels of the 1930s, not on the trilogy, written at the end of his life, which is the cause of my love. In a museum culture like North America there is too much analyzing and talk about art, and not enough living in its joy, producing it. But my excuse is the trilogy's exclusion from the canon.

Only twice in my life have I been so ravished with love for the works of an artist that the very substance of my soul seemed to be within these works. The first time was when I really listened to the music of Mozart in my twenties; the second when I read Céline's trilogy in my sixties. I am not denying that I have lived all my life in the supremacies of such artists as Bach and Shakespeare. At a different level I have had a long flirtation with Henry James. As a child I had gobbled up the stories about Doctor Dolittle. I speak here of that sudden ravishment which changes consciousness, no more profoundly than the long sustenance of Bach or Shakespeare, but which happens so suddenly, and therefore surprisingly, that it can be compared to love at first sight. It is the unexpected, which means that one will never be again as one was.[2]

By bringing Céline and Mozart together around an unimportant fact of my individuality I do not mean to compare them in any other way. There is certainly no need and no competence here to write further of Mozart. With Céline, as I have tried to explain, it is quite a different matter.

Reading is different from watching drama or listening to music which has already been interpreted by someone else. But the reader is at least required to be open to the intention of the writer, or else he falls into the laziness of pure subjectivity. I remember a wealthy patron of the Toronto art gallery saying fervently, 'I don't care what it meant to the artist, I care what it means to me.' On the other hand, Wanda Landowska was surely being too arrogant in her put-down of Rosalyn Tureck when they disagreed about the playing of a passage of Bach: 'Let's not quarrel. You go on playing it your way, and I'll just go on playing it Bach's way.'

It must be admitted that reading can easily become a vice. I have spent large portions of my life reading trash. Who can always do without drugs? Such reading can be like the mirror of the Lady of Shalott, confining one's experience to a safe and dreamlike vision. But great literary works are the very smashing of the mirror, the restoration to reality – or to use R.G. Collingwood's metaphor, 'medicine for the worst disease of mind, the corruption of consciousness' (*The Principles of Art* [Oxford, 1938], 336).

This of course raises the mystery as to why someone else's account should sometimes be able to restore one to reality more completely than one's own experience. Simone Weil's description of language is worth pondering here. She says that language is a mean proportional between thought and the tangible. Céline might have agreed.

What follows will not be a contribution to literary criticism, for which I am not equipped. There will be many question marks, because I do not fully understand why reading can so enrapture us. It will simply be an attempted tribute to something loved.

THE TRILOGY AS STORY

I must start by saying what kind of writing the trilogy is, what name should be given to it. We distinguish company reports from textbooks, detective stories from minutes of a meeting, treatises from dialogues, epic poetry from lyric. 'What-is' questions have been discarded in modern philosophy (particularly among its English-speaking practitioners) and definitions are pursued only instrumentally. Naming may not be the last word in understanding something, but in reading it is a help. We read different kinds of writing differently, and different people read them with different attention and skill. I am sure the president of a bank knows how to read a company report better than I do, and would read it with greater attention and skill than myself, because of the nature of his work and interests. But some pieces to which we give the greatest attention may be opaque for us, because we are wrong, or not sure, about what kind of writing we are reading. All my adult life I have tried to read Plato's *Symposium* with the greatest attention of which I am capable. Yet I was held back from understanding it because I read it as a treatise and not as a dialogue, and did not know what a dialogue was. I have watched and listened to *Don Giovanni* often, and for years came away confused as to its unity in a way I was not confused by performances of *The Marriage of Figaro* or *Così fan tutte*. When I read on the score that Mozart had named it a 'drama giocosa' I became much clearer about how one should take the whole, how one should watch and listen to Giovanni's damnation. I was enlightened.

Many people have taken Céline's trilogy as a self-justification or apology. Whether apologies be noble or base (and one must remember that the noblest bears that actual name), Céline's trilogy is not one of them. To take it as such has led to much wrong reading. It is certainly not the same genre as Newman going over and over in his limpid prose just why it was so important that he changed from being Anglican to Roman Catholic. Nor is it the same as Rousseau's account of why each time he got on top he became more godlike. Nor is it the same genre as St Augustine's wonderful account of his life, addressed throughout to God. Falsely naming to oneself can lead one astray, and therefore the attempt to name correctly may be useful to reading. Anyway, it has been required of us since Adam's great work.

Céline called his work a 'chronicle,' and he certainly knew best what he was doing. The worst trap for commentators or critics is to write as if they knew better what a great author is doing than he knows himself. (The silliest victim of that trap in our era was Freud.) I would translate Céline's 'chronique' as 'story,' however, simply because the English word 'chronicle' has a more antique and more limited sense than chronique in French. Indeed in Shakespeare's Sonnet 106, where he writes of the 'chronicle of wasted time,' he also refers to the 'antique pen' by which it was written. The French word chronique is much less antiquarian than the English word chronicle, because French in its very essence and history is so much closer to the classical languages than is English. Chronicle is defined in the *OED* as 'a detailed and continuous register of events in order of time.' This definition seems to me inadequate to summon forth all the reaches of deed and event, of humour, tenderness, and horror that make up the trilogy. Therefore I will translate Céline's 'chronique' as 'story,' but without any implication that I know better than he did.

The word 'story' arose in English as a shortening of what had come into the language from the Greek 'historia.' The Greek word had originally been used to denote certain inquiries. It referred to inquiries about events concerning which one had to get a report, by asking an old person or someone in another country. The word for 'inquiry' came gradually to mean an account of what had happened.

I am not going to try to sort out the multiform uses of the word 'story,' but simply to say what I mean by the word as a form of spoken and written communication, and why I think it is the best word to catch the essence of Céline's trilogy. The story in this sense is a marvellous part of being human.

We start to enjoy it in very early childhood, from the age of two, perhaps, sometimes making additions of our own. I remember a little later my nurse would say, 'Don't tell stories,' when she knew my account of events had been made up by the heady drives of my imagination, to save myself from the consequence of having thrown some turnips down the lavatory. But when I was sad I would ask her to tell me or read me a story, and I did not mean lies. It never entered my head that what was happening to Doctor Dolittle had been made up. When I cried at the fate of the blacks in *Uncle Tom's Cabin* she would say, 'it is only a story.' So, although my elders emphasized the lack of factual basis in a story, I could not realize this, because for the young child the factual basis or its absence is irrelevant to the richness of the experience. I remember the joy in identifying with other, more exciting lives, like that of P.J. the Secret Service boy. I say all this about my own early life because I think children's hunger for the 'story' is probably universal. The joys of identification are obviously not confined to children. There are many subtle possibilities in the story or the novel. Rousseau in his *Émile* describes the imagination as enlarging the bounds of possibility for us, whether for good or ill. Simple identification is a pleasant means of escape; but there can be further value in vicarious experience, if only to confirm our membership one of another.

For adults also there are some times and places in which the need for stories is particularly strongly felt. Early English-speaking Canada was one of those times and places. The influence of the Scots was important here. They had come to Canada when their peasant past had been smashed by the English invasion, and they had to recreate their bardic past amid the alien corn. Settled or indigenous people have fewer stories. The isolation of pioneering life fostered the story when print was expensive and there were no electronic media. It is difficult to know how much storytelling goes on now, when fast moving changes make us lose the past, when there is a breakdown of the extended family, and the electronic media proliferate; I can remember the stage as a child when our growing interest in the Rudy Vallee and Eddie Cantor Hours would cut into my mother's reading aloud of Dickens and Scott.

There was still time to listen to stories. When a little older I used to visit various elderly family friends, often in retirement homes. They might tell me first of the difficulties of their present lives – how crazy a sister-in-law was, how strict an attendant, that there was not enough to eat, that it was awful. Then suddenly they might begin to talk of their adventures in the Boer War, or how they had so loved Lady Borden, or their life in the wilds of pioneering Idaho. My mother used to tell us stories of how poor she had been as a little girl in New Brunswick, and these would pass into stories of the suffering of her ancestors when they came north, when the people down there had broken with the Crown. I hope that when I am older people will listen to my stories, and that they will be true.

Some stories were told to make a point, claiming at least a basis of fact; how lucky I was, and yet how unfortunate, not to have lived in the majestic times of my dead grandfathers; or how easily young people could be led astray by bad women. However, one discovered early that the best stories were those told with no didactic purpose, and I still hold that to be true. One did not need to be taught over and over again that Mackenzie King was a twister who loved the Americans too much. One learned that storytelling was at its best an art, and as with high art, any purpose beyond itself was difficult to define.

The greatest storyteller of my life has been a Scottish maid who told me of her youth in the slums of Edinburgh, and how she came to Canada as an immigrant to work for the wealthy in Toronto. While memory holds, can I forget her sitting there with the butter from the beets running down her chin, while she told me of rushing around the dining-room table at Government House, trying to escape the embraces of the lieutenant governor, while she cried to him the warnings of St Matthew against adultery? I suppose one could say that such a story had some didactic point: that the man who was received with such respect at my mother's tea table had a life which was quite different from the life shown there, and was difficult for his employees and for his wife. But the glory of the story was not in its didactic point, but rather in the richness of the saga of my friend's life, told with such brilliance by a woman who had no formal education because she had been sent out to work at age seven. People often say that so-and-so at some party is a good storyteller. But generally the person in question is making some point or conveying some information, if only an amusing piece of gossip. It appeared to me when young and it appears to me now that the greatest stories have no point except that they are enrapturing. We must not say that the purpose of a beautiful work of art – as, for example, *Las Meninas*, Mozart's K. 488, or *King Lear* – lies outside itself. Yet at the same time we must also say, always with the greatest hesitation and bewilderment, that it points beyond itself.

What I mean by story, as distinguished from other kinds of communication, is the telling by word of mouth (whether or not written down) of events in which the teller at least had a part, or which came down to him by word of mouth. When one hears a story there is also a storyteller. A great story must be told by someone who is more than egocentric, yet sufficiently egocentric to be taken up with the events he or she is describing. He or she must be there as an individual, and yet open to otherness. The accounts of marriage breakdowns one hears in pubs are seldom real stories, and only charity requires one to listen to them. In the way in which I use the word, the teller of the story will be an integral part of it. Even in *Doctor Dolittle* it is Stubbins, the Doctor's assistant, who tells the story. Our Scottish maid was not absent from her telling, and was not some abstract, perfect person. She was a hater of the rich, a lover of Christian virtue, who put first her right to eat, and second her right to have good shoes to save her feet. So in the trilogy Céline is always present, whether as the hero of 1944, or as the dying old writer of twenty years later, sufferer of years of persecution by the élite intellects of the left.

The trilogy is the most perfectly realized 'story' I know in print. Céline's very style of writing is the style of speech. He often said that the point of his style, with its breakdown of the classical sentence, and the three little dots, was to catch the way French was spoken by proletarian people in Paris. The whole trilogy is just Céline telling you. If Hollywood had not degraded the phrase by using it to describe the gospel of our salvation, I would call Céline's trilogy 'the greatest story ever told,' entirely realized on the printed page.

The nature of the story as a kind of communication is seen more clearly when distinguished from the novel on one side and historical writing on the other. This might take one into the hardest reaches of both literary theory and historical methodology, but as I have said earlier, I am not competent in this area. To distinguish story from history, and to say that story can be poetry, must also raise the question why the ancient philosophers said that poetry was higher than history. But that question must be delayed until I have said more of Céline's excellences. I am writing this book as a reader of literature, who has spent long sections of his life reading philosophy. Let me then plunge immediately into the distinction between events which actually happened and those which are imaginary.

When comparing story and novel, we all take for granted a difference of genre between *The House of the Dead* and *The Idiot*. One is Dostoyevsky's account of a part of his life; the other is a novel. As a reader one is immediately aware of the distinction. It is not just that between imagined events and actual events; both novel and story require imagination, but the difference is between differing acts of the imagination. In the story the imagination is linked in a more dependent embrace with particular memories. Nastasia Philipovna in *The Idiot* is summoned before us by an act less tied to particular memories. When the dead Nastasia lies covered by oilcloth, with candles at each corner, while the Prince and Rogozhin play cards at the foot of the bed, we do not believe it ever happened; yet it remains in my memory more vividly than most real scenes, although I have not read it for forty years. In some mysterious act of the imagination Dostoyevsky made a world in which these events took place. That this world can now exist for us depends entirely on the author of it. In Céline's trilogy, however, although his description of Laval stopping a riot on a railway station comes to us uniquely from his words, it is an event to which we might have other entrances. Of course the difference must not be pushed too far. The making of Nastasia Philipovna was not a creation ex nihilo.

I am sure that with all the apparatus of literary research in the Soviet Union and elsewhere, many of the connections between the character Nastasia and people Dostoyevsky knew in his life will have been traced, in a way that cannot be done in the case, for example, of Cordelia. Nevertheless, the distinction between novel and story seems to me a good one. It can be seen in Céline's own writing. *Journey to the End of Night*, although connected with Céline's life in early manhood, is clearly a novel in a way that the trilogy is not.

Without going into the immense apparatus about method which now surrounds the academic practice of history, one may say that history has something in common with the story which the novel does not have. However, they are clearly different. In the case of history, imagination must be more strictly controlled. 'When Nixon walked into the Oval Office to resign, he thought to himself etc.' is an extreme example of the wrong kind of imagination. It is obviously to be eschewed, unless Nixon is known to have stated somewhere what he was thinking at the time.

The historical novel, however, has its place as a literary genre. Who would dare chase Scott out of the canon, just because Mary Renault's and Marguerite Yourcenar's achievements have been exaggerated by bored and lazy readers? The place of the historical novel does not, however, excuse history being written like a novel.

This is not to say that the historian must be unimaginative. Von Ranke's *Innocent III* has been imagined in a noble way. But clearly the historian's imagination has to be strictly controlled in the interest of the purposes he is pursuing, and these purposes are different from those of the storyteller. Without spending time over the old chestnut whether history is an art or a science, it seems to me obvious that history is in some sense a science. At the very least one asks the historian to tell us certain things 'objectively.' To use that word literally, the historian must hold away from himself the documents which he uses, so that he can examine them with proper distance. Von Ranke's *Innocent III* may have much to do with the movement to objectivity and its transcending which is present in Raphael's and Velasquez's wonderful portraits of the popes. The historian may be a great literary artist, but he must keep the necessary distance. The great storyteller is not constrained by these purposes, but is engrossed in his own experience of past events, and the very loosing of his memories as he imagines them is what makes him a great storyteller. It is the immediacy of his imaginings as they are put into a disparate unity which delights us.

If I were to write the history of a lieutenant-governor chasing a Scottish maid around his table, I would first have to supplement my friend's story with an account of the lieutenant-governor, his wife, and his other servants. I would have to look at the structure of class relations in Ontario of the 1930s, and the history and structure of proletarian Calvinism which had made her cry forth the blessed words of St Matthew. Céline's account in *Castle to Castle* of the defeated French politicians may have been taken by some historian as evidence for lives he was writing about Laval or Pétain or Bichelonne, and the historian would also have access to the wonderful wild old man who is telling it. But the story does not enrapture us because it is raw material for a certain history, any more than Shakespeare's *Richard II* enthralls us because we learn about the victor of the Lancastrian Plantagenets.

Obviously there is overlapping and uncertainty in the simple schema novel – story – history. Is *Tristram Shandy* a story or a novel? *The Remembrance of Things Past* is certainly a novel, and yet autobiographical in that it is part of the history of Paris. One could call Boswell's *Life of Johnson* the greatest English biography, and so put it in the history basket. Yet it is also the story of a friendship told with tenderness by one partner about his friend who was a genius. (As I am always ready to question Aristotle's thought, it is well to ask, does not the *Life of Johnson* correctly contradict Aristotle's teaching about equality and friendship?) The delight in reading it does not depend on wanting to be an eighteenth-century specialist, or on any detailed knowledge of English history. At another great height, *War and Peace* is a novel and a history. I have only used this schema as a means of clarifying the nature of Céline's trilogy. It is story par excellence.

One other genre might be mentioned. Could the trilogy be called an epic? Certainly Céline's style makes it difficult to use the prose/poetry distinction in order to answer this in the negative. The rhythms are extraordinarily complex, and arose partly from watching professional dancers. The word 'epic' has been debased by the American entertainment business but it can still be used properly. The *OED* defines it as 'pertaining to that kind of narrative which celebrates the achievement of some heroic personage of history or tradition.' The trilogy is indeed a consummate narrative, and as a story of the losers in a great defeat it has sometimes been called, rather appealingly, an epic of the afflicted. It could be called an epic without heroes, demigods or God. Strictly, however, an epic cannot be written by the protagonist of the story. Also, the trilogy is in no sense a celebration – what is there to celebrate? An epic must have some public declaration in it, whereas the whole teaching of the books is 'hide yourself in this era.' This is not an epic, however much the compelling narrative and the sense of the spoken word can tempt one to call it so.

It may be asked: who cares about such naming? Isn't life busy enough and difficult enough to allow us to read the best books our tradition gives us without such cataloguing? I care because I think Céline's trilogy should be part of that high tradition, and I am afraid that it may not be, because of reasons external to its merit. Before praising its perfections, I wanted to say what it is. There is something very wonderful about any work that takes a particular genre to its completeness.

A DESCRIPTION OF THE TRILOGY

Why is this trilogy such a wonderful story? The first question to ask must be, 'What is it about?' A story of some small private incident (a maid at the lieutenant governor's) may well delight us. But a great story must be about great events. When Father Zossima bows down before Dmitri at the beginning of *The Brothers Karamazov*, we know that the novel is going to be about the relation of suffering to the salvation of these brothers. We are prepared for greatness. Céline's trilogy tells us of a high historical moment: the collapse of Germany before the Allied forces of Britain, the United States, and Russia. It may indeed be the fault of the Europeans that this is happening. Be that as it may, it is a high historical event. Céline tells us about it from the side of the losers, as Euripides does in *The Trojan Women*. To put it more generally, the subject is the final throes of a technological war that has been lost. I do not know whether Aristotle is correct in saying that war is coeval with human beings. It certainly has been central to human life so far. Here is war in its modern technological form, in both its violence and its extremity in the sense of what peoples can and will do to each other. Of course, it is not yet nuclear war. That was to be started a few months later by the Americans against Japan. But this is the story of a once great civilization being brought to its knees by the most intense technological attack up to that point.

All three books are about the same subject, the fall of German-dominated Europe, and all three see this chiefly in terms of what is happening to Céline, his wife Lili, and their cat Bébert. Their friend Le Vigan, a famous French movie-star, is with them in the first two books, but escapes to Italy at the beginning of the third. Though clearly the chronicle is a trilogy, each of the books has a separate situation, which is mirrored in a difference of mood.

In *Castle to Castle* our hero and heroine and the cat Bébert are at Sigmaringen. As the regime in France collapsed before the English-speaking armies, the Germans found a place of refuge for their leading French friends in and around an old Hohenzollern castle on the Danube. The occupants are the pro-German French who (except for a few crazies) know that they have backed the losing side and are desperately looking for some escape from the revenge which will follow from the Allies and the French 'left.' They are there in serried ranks from Pétain and Laval on down. In this 'sauve qui peut' situation, Céline moves among them as a doctor, also having the means of suicide that some of them want. Little can be saved, and the central issue is usually food. Céline was above all a French nationalist, and here he is among his own countrymen. His pictures of Laval and Pétain are wonderful accounts of political leaders who have tried greatly and lost. Pétain is dignified even in his failing prostate. This is the most difficult to read of the three books, because it is necessary to use a glossary of French politics to follow it. This breaks up the reading and makes it a lesser book than the later two. Unless one has an interest in the old French 'right,' one might be put off continuing the trilogy, and that would be a pity. This is the volume which of the three is most nearly a history.

In the second book, *North*, the Célines are mostly in a small Brandenburg town where they have been sent on their arrival in Germany. They listen and watch and smell the burning of Berlin by the Western air forces, and know that the Russians are getting nearer and nearer across the European plain from the east. Here there is no need for a glossary because the characters are all Germans and not public figures. Prussian aristocrats, shopkeepers, minor officials, the ragtag and bobtail of eastern prisoners, conscientious objectors building coffins – they all parade before us. The situation is very tense, because the Germans hate the refugees and particularly such famous figures as the Célines, who put them in jeopardy by association. To Céline the Germans are entirely foreigners, and therefore are described with an intense 'objective' distance, and often with contempt. He kowtows to them, flatters them, mends them as a doctor, ridicules them, makes bitter asides about what shits they are, how nobody is to be trusted, and how everybody has some hidden agenda. One of the unforgettably funny moments in the blackness of *North* is when Madam Inge leads Céline into a wood and tries to seduce him – her real agenda being to persuade him to get her some poison to kill her defective husband. Céline's comment to himself is, 'Crude stuff, my lady, crude stuff' (*North*, 274). He and Lili are aware that they may at any time be killed in some dark corner. They only survive because they have a defender in Professor Harras, President of the Reich Medical Association. He admires Céline because they have worked together on plague control. In other words, the regime has not yet entirely collapsed. The mood of *North* is very dark, yet in some ways trivial, because the primary issue is getting enough food to stay alive, and everybody lies about it. The atmosphere is again sauve qui peut, because they all know the war is lost, and want to find some haven in the conquest.

Commentators have found it strange that *North* comes second in the chronicle when it happened first in time. The explanation seems clear. Céline had written *Castle to Castle* in 1957 for two reasons. First, he needed to make some money. When he returned to France in 1950 he was deadly poor, under continued persecution (he hardly dared go outside). All his possessions and manuscripts had been stolen and his royalties confiscated. Knowing he would die before long, he worried about his wife's future. Also, having been cleared by a military court of all charges of collaboration, he wanted now to justify his actions and those of his friends who had been expurgated in the great purges of 1945–7. This was possible in 1957, because the French intellectual community was not so much under the control of the communists as it had been in 1945. In the event, *Castle to Castle* was a bit of a financial success. Therefore he expanded the story to keep himself, his wife, and his animals alive. The order of the chronicle is simply a matter of accident, determined by financial necessity. He once mentions the question of temporal order in *North* and simply says that he must be allowed to tell the story his own way: 'I'm telling you all this every which way ...

the end before the beginning! ... what does it matter? ... the truth alone matters! ... you'll catch on' (9).

Rigadoon is the last dash across a Germany in total collapse and under massive bombing. Churchill has put 'Bomber' Harris in charge, and the promise of revenge is being fully realized, even as the society falls apart. *Rigadoon* is the name of a dance for two people, and here it is danced to the music of saturation bombing. The characters who appear are the wounded and desolated civilians who are simply trying to exist in a violent madhouse. Against this background, Céline, Lili, and Bébert are making a desperate attempt, always on the point of failure, to cross Germany and escape to Denmark. There Céline has some royalties stashed away and he feels that Denmark may afford them some chance of survival. (In fact, he was put into solitary confinement, though not executed as he would have been in France at that date.) Trains are bombed almost out of existence, buildings burned to the ground, people are dying all around them. Céline is seriously injured, but staggers on in pain and hallucination. They are nearly buried in debris. Lili often has to go into danger to rescue Bébert. Céline remembers he is a doctor first and foremost, and tries to help whoever is near him. Towards the end, this includes a group of retarded children, for whom he and Lili have assumed complete responsibility. At last they escape into Denmark, through the kindness of a Swedish Red Cross doctor who stands together with another doctor. The book ends with the release of an achieved escape, but the release has a note of the sinister; in the last scene in Copenhagen they walk in a park, and some strange birds, escaped from a zoo, seem to threaten Bébert. Céline will soon be in the hole in Denmark, facing a sentence of death in France.

Rigadoon is the great climax of the trilogy – the supreme account of technological war as suffered by civilians. This extraordinary story of the chances of necessity leaves the trilogy on an ambiguous note. As in all masterpieces, the trilogy is to be understood in terms of its height – in this case the height of saturation bombing, and the chance escape to Denmark. The account of the French losers in *Castle to Castle*, and the German losers in *North*, is completed by the carnage in *Rigadoon*. The chronicle is given its momentary and chancy release.

Céline died the day he finished his masterpiece. To me this is deeply moving, as is the thought of Mozart putting down his pen for the last time, having written the wonderful opening notes of the *Lacrimosa*.

When we are told stories by word of mouth, the storytellers are always present at the moment of telling, in all that they are in their immediate being; yet at the same time they take us into a past which is not there now, and is not ours. The three books of Céline's trilogy are stories, and therefore Céline is doubly there, both as participant in the action in Germany in the 1940s, and as the world-weary, persecuted storyteller of the 1950s. Indeed in the first 125 pages of *Castle to Castle* we never reach the past in Germany. It is about his present forced retirement in the suburbs of Paris, about the cold and his need of money, the calumny against him by the literary 'left,' and the tricks of his publishers, the nuts who want to interview him, the anguish of his patients, his run in the death cell in Denmark, and his wonder at the animals. The first 119 pages of *Rigadoon* are similar. Then, when the storyteller is there in all his wild concreteness, the present suddenly drops away, and we are now with Céline and Lili and Bébert in the midst of Germany's collapse, in all its horror and comedy. The Céline who dominates now is a much less broken character, a doctor who never ceases to be a doctor in his obligation to other people's bodies. He does not have the self-pitying inwardness of the excluded outsider, and he is aware that his occasional rages about his later ruin are tiresome to his readers. His preoccupation now is with the actions necessary to the immediate situation, to survival and escape. When he is injured in an air raid, there is an unforgettable account of his hallucinations, but they are part of the story, not a self-indulgence; the old storyteller must move on from his memory of this cataclysmic experience, just as the injured man in Germany had to struggle to recover from it, and to make himself return, with Lili's help, to the necessities of the situation, back to the flames, the dying, the broken, the falling buildings.

The double time-scheme gives an unusual character to the story itself, because what is only implied in most stories becomes in the trilogy a substantial element, a sort of double identity.

Style

How are these wonders achieved? Much has been written about how it is impossible to divide substance and style, how indeed this unity is a prime mark of a great work of art, and how in literary work this is clearly illustrated in poetry (if we make the distinction between poetry and prose). All this appears to me true when I think about it as an amateur. However, I am not someone who has spent his working life understanding and analyzing literary art. This writing is about reading, and why a reader enjoys reading. Moreover in my working life as a political philosopher I am a follower of Plato, in the sense that I think understanding is higher than reason, rather than the opposite, which has generally been assumed since *The Critique of Pure Reason*. Above all I would not want to seem to analyze Céline's style in a way that might imply that I could stand above it. My gravest hesitation about Plato's thought is what he writes about the poets. Within this context, I have little right to speak of Céline's wonderful style, other than to repeat some remarks of his and to make some glosses on them.

Céline said that the purpose of his 'famous style,' with its breakdown of the classical French sentence and its ubiquitous three little dots, was to catch French as it is spoken by ordinary people in Paris, and to put it on the printed page (*Paris Review*, interview with Claude Sarraute, 1 June 1960) . He also said that the rhythms of his writing had been greatly influenced by dancing, above all by watching professional women dancers. He gave the height of this trilogy the name of a famous dance. He also said that his style required very hard work, and commented bitterly that he had to write 1500 pages to produce 250 that would be published and for which he would be paid. This careful style which conveys the spontaneity of speech seems to me perfect for the story.

There are some aspects of the style which affect the story even in translation. The almost constant use of the present tense is an obvious example. The three little dots are of course more important, though I can say nothing of the rhythms of colloquial French achieved by them. (But even in Manheim's brilliant translation, the flexibility given by them makes easier the conjunction of the storyteller in the 50s and the events of the 40s.) It also allows the digressions which properly belong to a story. He can suddenly be off on his remembrance of Sartre's persecution of him, then equally suddenly come back to the chronicle with an 'I must stop ... we were in Ulm etc.' That flexibility allows the total recall of present and past which is the mark of a great storyteller. I had a Russian relative who, if he was telling you about a government department in

Ottawa, would take you through the difficulty of getting a good meal in Panama, the eccentricities of his wife's English relatives, the mining industry in India, before you got back to the details of the bureaucracy.

The three little dots also give the opportunity for withdrawal. Between the sentences and the non-sentences there is this break in which can be given the writer's withdrawal into remembrance and thought. In *Rigadoon*, for example, at a complex and dangerous moment, Céline has to take Bébert out of his musette bag, but is trusting his cat to keep close to him: 'if he sees anyone coming he'll jump up on my shoulder, one jump ... he knows ... he's an experienced traveller ... he sure was ... he made it back here to Meudon, he's buried out there in the garden ... looks as if we'll be marching up this avenue ... arm in arm, me playing blind ...' (93). This brief withdrawal into the past tense is strangely moving. The flexibility given by the three little dots allows both the reality of the storyteller and the reality of the story to exist together.

Céline's most interesting account of what he is doing in writing appears at the end of his life, in *Rigadoon*, in the extraordinary setting of the bombing of a city by moonlight. Céline has been hit on the head, his mouth is full of blood, and his back is wet with it. But Lili and Bébert are still close to him:

there, I can tell you, we had nothing left ... our last rags and knapsacks had disappeared in the smack up! the cave-in! seven hand trucks under the torrents of bricks, two three house fronts and forged iron balconies! ... ah, moonlight! you'll never see such settings and tragedies in the movies! ... much less on the stage! ... they tell us that Hollywood is dead! ... they can say that again! how can the movies deliver after what's happened for real! ... which is why I personally can't even look at a photograph! ... to translate is to betray! right! to reproduce, to photograph, is to putrefy! instantly! ... anything that existed makes you sick to look at! ... therefore transpose! ... poetically if you can! but who tries? ... nobody! (144)

(I hope that this passage will give pause to anybody who thinks of making a movie or a TV serial out of the trilogy. The necessities of democracy and profit do not make possible the impossible. It is impossible to transpose properly what is already a great transposition.)

As a definition of transposition this passage is admittedly obscure. But it makes a complete distinction between 'transposing' and 'translating,' which is not done in the interview with Claude Sarraute. Translation betrays, putrefies, and is a reduction to an inferior medium. Transposition, as seen by Céline, lifts the subject to a richer one. It can lift prose into poetry. It is more than putting the spoken word into writing, though this is a beginning.

I call it 'little music' because I'm modest, but its a very difficult transposition, it's hard work ... Speaking of me people say 'he writes the way he talks ... everyday words ... almost in the right order ... you recognise them!' Only, you see, everything is 'transposed.' You don't get the word you were expecting or the situation you were expecting. It's transposed into the realm of reverie, between true and not-true. A word used in that way becomes at once more intimate and more precise than the same word as it is ordinarily used. (Interview with Claude Sarraute. See *Castle to Castle*, vi.)

The kind of poetry Céline achieves has what Coleridge calls the 'property of exciting a more continuous and equal attention than the language of prose aims at, whether colloquial or written' (*Biographia Literaria*, near end of chapter 14).

In the same paragraph in *Rigadoon* about translation and transposition from which I have quoted, Céline extends the idea of transposition to a non-literary context. The crusaders transposed their Christian loyalties into fighting the heathen in the Holy Land. Christians in modern France express their religious aspirations differently: '"They ceased to transpose" ... what were the crusaders for? ... the crusaders transposed themselves! ... now they get themselves ejected from their sixteenth floor in Passy by air-conditioned super-jet direct to Golgotha ... seven minutes ... get their pictures taken on the Mount of Olives ... Monsieur as Joseph ... Madame as Mary ... the children? angels naturally ... home again for cocktails ...' (144).

Prodigality

Another quality of Céline's storytelling – a matter of content rather than of style – is the prodigality of his presentation. An extraordinary range of characters are brought before us, both in the places of refuge and the journey of the escape. Ruined soldiers, factory workers, flights of children, collaborators, SS leaders, aristocrats, always the tenderness of aging women, station masters, train drivers, small and great bureaucrats, and the animals, etc., etc., etc. – taking and running, cheating and dying, loving, fearing, scheming, defecating everywhere, from Pétain on down. Here is a complex and recently triumphant society, now defeated in war, in the last moments before its actual conquest in unconditional surrender. These widely various characters play out their virtues, their fantasies, their vices, all in unique individuality. This is the art of total recall. In the hands of a bore, total recall can drive one nearly mad. When presented by an artist, it gives his art one of the marks of greatness – prodigality.

I must pause to state carefully what I mean by prodigality, and its place in the art of the novelist and the storyteller. For us it must be a pregnant word, because it is used in the English translation of one of Christ's parables. The *OED* defines it as 'lavishness to the point of waste,' therefore the word may not seem appropriate to the highest art. Who would dare to say that there is waste in Shakespeare or Mozart or Raphael? Yet what other word will do for this ability to range over vast territories of human passion and action and thought, both important and unimportant, which is the mark of great literary art? Profligacy is the word for the moral vice, and the distinction implies that prodigality is not necessarily vicious. Profuseness is a synonym and means literally the ability to pour forth. But it sounds ridiculous to say that Shakespeare or Mozart was profuse. Indeed the use of 'prodigal' in the translation of our Saviour's parable points to its meaning in the present connection. The fact that the son had pursued sensuality on a lavish scale is related to the particular joy in the father's welcome home – the joy which annoys the careful other son who had been disciplined, but not generous. An analogy may also be taken from nature. In nature there seems to be an extravagant waste which would not be the case if it had been planned by a sensible human being. Yet if we are to say against the moderns that insofar as anything is, it is good (and it appears to me that Christians must attempt to think this thought), then nature is good, and part of its goodness is its obvious prodigality – its 'lavishness to the point of waste.'

This prodigality seems to me present in the highest art. As Polixenes says in act 4 of *The Winter's Tale*, 'The art itself is nature.' Mozart's range presents us with the utterly separated worlds of

Figaro and the G minor quintet. Within one genre, the piano concerto, he writes twenty-seven works which cover extraordinary reaches of feeling and technique. There is not only amazing range in Shakespeare's plays and forms of verse, but his prodigality is in the fact that some minor character, like a gatekeeper, appears on the stage for a moment and we see the human being in the round. Of course, prodigality can be attempted in much lesser works of art. There is pleasure in the vast variety of Forsytes that Galsworthy shows us. At a much lower level, prodigality is imitated in those long historical and family chronicles which now fill up the market of a bored readership, insatiable for sustained entertainment. At their worst, the writers seem to strain like prostitutes who are forced to imitate the spontaneous motions of intercourse, yet once again, for money. Obviously true prodigality has nothing to do with strained commercialism on the one side, nor on the other with lack of discrimination. Racine has few characters on the stage, and yet his plays are prodigal in their pouring forth. Shakespeare does not put a lot of characters on the stage apart from the necessities of the work. Prodigality is the quality of achievement over a great and various range. One thing that lifts Céline's art to a higher level than that of James or Proust or Joyce is that the purity of his apprehension of character and event is realized with prodigality.

The Characters

However masterly the style of the writing, I do not deny that the success of the book – that which enables us to partake in it as a lived experience – depends on the fascination of the story being told.[3] The story of the novel, or in this case the story of the story, is what matters. And this in turn depends on the characters around which the deeds and events take place. One does not so much have to like the people as to know them, so that their deeds and suffering can be experienced, in the sense of knowing that can make their lives our own. One does not admire Catherine in *Wuthering Heights*, and at moments Heathcliff is a sadist, but we know them in the sense that I have used the word. Ulysses is not particularly attractive, but we know him as a man of phronesis, and therefore the great events of his journey matter to us. (Shakespeare's consummate political judgement puts his greatest speech on politics in the mouth of Odysseus [*Troilus and Cressida*, act 1, scene 3, 78–137].

Phronesis and tenacity in the service of loyalty are basic if one is to be great in politics.) At a lower level, Aeneas is certainly more than a bit of a shit, and yet the work holds us by the sense of the purpose he sees himself fulfilling. The Greeks could see the Trojans in their greatness; the Romans who saw them as their mythical origin could not.

Dr Destouches and his wife Lili are there in the trilogy so that we know them in this way. We have, of course, the double vision: there are the detailed accounts of what goes on in Céline's mind in the 50s, but the characters of Céline and Lili in the 40s are made known to us in a simpler and more certain way – in their actions. The primacy of action in the story can be well-illustrated by how their marriage is shown. This is one of the greatest accounts of an absolute marriage ever written. Yet nothing is said of it. Lili acts with great courage, with noble pride and skill. Because she is a dancer, she is wonderfully agile, often rescuing Bébert from awkward places, and once stopping a slow-moving train single-handed in order to get some children on board. She often warns her husband to be subtle in dealing with someone. But the absolute relation between them is never spoken about. It does not need to be. Céline had said in another connection that the shame which arises from offending modesty forbade him describing the deepest parts of his life in the way so many modern writers are willing to do.

Céline's own self-portrait is given in his actions and above all in his relations to others. It is not that of a hero. There is a lot of the man who has learned you have to go along if you are going to survive. In his earlier novel, *Death on the Instalment Plan* (*Mort à crédit*), he had described himself as a little boy who had to travel around with his uncle, who used to beat him. Whatever the uncle said, even before he had finished it, the little boy would say, 'Mais oui, mon oncle.' There is lots of 'mais oui, mon oncle' from Céline in Germany. His ambiguous relation with Harras is an example of this. Harras lives in luxury, and is at some points willing to provide food and some kind of shelter and some token employment for Céline, Lili, and Le Vigan. But Céline is clearly somewhat ashamed at accepting such help from 'this smiling, opulent Harras,' 'a Boche, hundred percent Nazi.' 'Plenty compromising, no question, but our first fatal crime was leaving our country' (*North*, 62). Céline does not have to pretend to admire Hitler – he can say anything to Harras as long as he says it in French, a language Harras greatly loves. But Céline does not quite trust that Harras will not quietly get rid of the three of them.

Céline often shows himself cheating and lying and deluding. He never sees himself as doing anything particularly heroic; he is just escaping. He is moral in that he does what he can to help people, but he is not there as a saint who would be required to give up his wife and his escape, and stop to tend all the dying and needy who surround him. In *Rigadoon*, for example, he and Lili are on a train, packed to overflowing with refugees. When in the middle of the night the train stops at a huge area of empty fields, and they see hundreds of decrepit refugees being hauled out of the train by force, they ask an acquaintance what is happening:

He didn't tell you? it's the Nietzschean technique ... Oberartzt Haupt is a Nietzschean ... natural selection! ... survival of the fittest! the cold, the snow, stark naked, it invigorates them, especially the wounded! ... the weak die and get buried ... Oberartzt Haupt's technique ... they clear the cars, they put the bodies out in the field ... and leave them there ... two days ... three days ... in the cold, in the snow, stark naked ... the ones that are able to get up are invigorated ... you can see them, even on one leg ... they start for Rostock ... then they sort them out ... some go to the hospital for surgery ... the rest are put to work ... digging pits for the dead: the ones that don't move after two or three days ... (43)

Céline makes no moral condemnation of this 'technique'; he knows he can do absolutely nothing to stop it. But he takes for granted, because he is a doctor, that when somebody in need is inescapably put in his path, he does what he can directly and clearly, but without sense of righteousness. In *Rigadoon*, for example, when a dying woman, who is in charge of a group of retarded children, can go no further, he and Lili take them over. He screams and yells at them, calling them his 'droolers' and 'slobberers,' pushing them on and off trains, rescuing them from getting lost among the rubble, sharing his bits of food with them. The distinction between what he says and what he does is particularly vivid in this context. His responsibility is categorical.

It might be argued that my feeling of knowing Céline and caring about him is just the result of a literary master's trick. Is not the trilogy finally a work of self-justification? If the story is at its core a self-justification, then my claim for it is sullied. One begins to doubt the story, for self-justifications are seldom true. Does this not take away from what seems to me central to the majesty of the work – that it is the supreme account of the truth about technological war, from the point of view of the losers who are suffering it? The essence of great art is to show truth about reality.

About this I would say two things. First, there is indeed a lot of self-justification from the Céline of 1957, and he means there to be; his wildness and rhetoric of self-pity are how the storyteller presents himself as a storyteller, and he knows how boring his paranoia and justifications can become despite their wit. This is highly articulate. But in the story of the escape from Germany he does not see himself as heroic, and he is very seldom interested in justifying anything. I do not care for Céline because he is particularly noble, or, for that matter, particularly ignoble. One has just got to know him by living with him through so many intense happenings. Let us put aside the nonsense that was once talked by American journalists against one of their Republican presidential enemies: 'you have to know him really well to dislike him.' Smart, but journalistic untruth. A follower of Plato has been taught about the interdependence of knowing and loving. (One may wish that Bacon and Darwin had learned this. But more of that later.)

Another reason I would deny that self-justification is basic to the trilogy is that Céline was too proud for it. He knew that he could confound his readers by his sheer talent. The supreme telling of his story, not the making of himself something that he was not, was the way to silence his critics.

Of course 'character' may be called a kind of hypostatization. But suffice it to say here that I do not think the self-portrait of Céline as central character vitiates the truth of the story told.

I can only speak for myself when I say that the couple and their cat who emerge in the action are lovable, in the way that all heroes and heroines must be if a story is to hold one for long. The proof of this for me is that when at the end it is touch-and-go whether they will escape to Denmark, or be swept up by the Allied army, I am as much on the edge of my seat as when I read at ten of P.J. the Secret Service boy escaping from some doom prepared by his grim opponents. From outside knowledge, I know that Céline and Lili and Bébert will succeed. Yet when they get at last into the Swedish train with their band of retarded children, I sink into relief. The only comparable relief in my reading experience was when my father handed me the book which showed that Holmes had not been killed in his last encounter with Moriarty. Now, at the age of sixty-five, I rejoice again.

Not only the central characters are given us with this purity of apprehension. An enormous gallery of people are presented to us in the most immediate way, one after another in the intricate circumstances in which they are caught. Of course, many of the people are in extremis. Germany is crumbling under massive and continual bombing, and the approach of armies from east and west is imminent. Everyone is attempting to run for cover before the conquest is complete. Therefore most of the characters are not acting as they might under easier conditions. Céline describes the desperation in *Rigadoon*. 'If you've ever passed through armies in flames, through jellied cities and empires, and desperate panting populations, offering you, oh yes! their babies, their wives, and then some ... anybody! anything! ... just so the damage! the lightning! should come down on you! and not them! not them! ... nothing will ever surprise you any more' (95).

This is a cast of losers, whether they are German aristocrats who are learning for the first time to be losers, or people who have been losers all their lives. Each is a realized individual, despite the fact that they are actors in the story, and as such are always seen in relation to Céline's desire to save himself and Lili and Bébert. However wild the situation, the people Céline encounters in the fall of Germany, whether in Sigmaringen, at the Simplon Hotel in Baden-Baden, or in the desperate journey across to the Swedish train, are unforgettable human beings who are held before us just as they are. One could cry out with Lear on the heath, 'This is the thing itself.' The completeness of apprehension and the ability to put it on the page is the mystery most difficult to fathom in thinking about literary art. The people are not there over a long introspective haul, as with Maggie and Charlotte in *The Golden Bowl*. But we know them as immediately, indeed we know them more completely because we know them in the round of the flesh and the details of the flesh in a way we never do with Henry James's characters. We know them in the completeness of realization that is achieved when Natasha, in *War and Peace*, comes into her mother's bedroom to tell of her engagement. (Such a mystery when one considers that it is a man writing of two women alone.) Céline's characters are as much before us in their independent completeness as are those in *Las Meninas*.

Of course the reader can question me, asking how do I know that this is the way people are? Am I not enraptured by Céline simply because he sees people as I see them? He feeds my prejudices. In our modern 'subjectivity' we are all entitled to see anything the way we want to see it. The fact that Céline sees people the way I see them is no reason to call his apprehension 'pure,' and assert this as central to the beauty of his trilogy. Suffice it to state my position without argument: Céline's grandeur stands or falls by the claim that he brings before us people as they are.

WAS CÉLINE MAD?

What about Céline's supposed madness? Most of the literati have been forced to recognize the power of his books, and then have put them safely into quarantine by saying that he was crazy, that he must be kept in a corner, out of the main tradition, because his art was corrupted by madness. Kind words are poured forth, saying he was not responsible for what he did or for the extremities in his books, because of his head wound suffered in 1914. (He had been wounded in Flanders, with severe head and arm injuries, resulting in a 75 per cent disability rating. At this time he was awarded high military honours.) (Note. See chronology in *Castle to Castle*.) I would be glad to be able to think that he was not responsible for his period of vicious anti-Semitism, but there is not evidence to support this. As for his 'madness' having corrupted his art, such critics ignore the very clear evidence to the contrary. We have before us in the trilogy a work of art in which the inward and the outward are most beautifully at one. With extraordinary realism the poet lays his madnesses before us as part of the story he is telling.

Before considering in more detail in what sense he might be called mad, I will mention two periods of his life which are relevant to this question. Céline had grown up in the lower reaches of the small bourgeoisie, in that class which was always trying not to be proletarianized, never having enough to eat and always having to kiss ass if they were to stay out of destitution. As he wrote in the account of his youth in *Death on the Instalment Plan* 'if you haven't been through that you'll never know what obsessive hatred really smells like ... the hatred that goes through your guts all the way to your heart.' That hatred is deeply present in all his books, and understood and ridiculed within them. In the trilogy there is no more savage anti-Semitism. His racism has spread so wide it is diluted into a kind of fantasy. He rails at every nationality, including his own. The crazy old storyteller sees the final enemy being the Chinese – the 'yellow' races – because they will genetically dominate the rest of mankind. Whatever his obsessive hatred did to his character, it did not corrupt his art, nor prevent him from seeing himself clearly. Nor did it affect the way he acted towards individuals.

Secondly, he lived through the years in Europe between 1914 and 1945, in full openness to their violence. He called himself the 'chronicler of grands guignols,' and can you be a chronicler of such without the full expression of paranoia? In 1944 he had the whole French left on his back, calling for the death penalty, with Sartre at the head of the pack. (I like to hope the plagiarist of Heidegger will be remembered as the man who worked for the death penalty for Europe's greatest writer and who, if he had succeeded, would have prevented the existence of this masterpiece.) French politics has a quality of vengeance, both from the left and the right, and the left was deep in innocent and uninnocent blood in 1944, and was baying for more. Céline was pursued remorselessly till his death, although he had been cleared of any crimes by a French military court. I am forced to the old cliché, 'to be paranoid doesn't mean you aren't being persecuted.'

Taking paranoia to be what the *OED* calls it – 'chronic mental unsoundness characterized by delusions and hallucinations' – I have to make some distinctions. 'Mental unsoundness' is nonsense about somebody who can bring the world before us with such clarity. To say it of Céline reminds me of what Dr Johnson said of Kit Smart: 'His madness is not noxious to society. I would as soon pray with Kit Smart as with any man' (*Life of Johnson*, vol. 1). Delusions and hallucinations of course. But who in the world is entirely free from these? The framework from which the German trilogy is set is given in the first 125 pages of *Castle to Castle*, and in this he describes the raging difficulty of his current forced retirement just outside Paris, in the late 50s. He lived in extreme poverty, a doctor to the poor who could very seldom pay him, still tormented by slander and persecution. (He was not a storyteller who spent his life in the Café des Fleurs.) Paranoid with resentment he was. But only a sane and great artist could so perfectly convey the paranoia.

Some commentators who write of Céline's 'madness' say that he is so utterly engrossed in his own self that what is other to the self is lost. We are told that hallucination and reality are confused and can no longer be distinguished. Let us look at one of the wildest and most detailed hallucinations, the attack of malaria in *Castle to Castle*, and see whether these criticisms ring true. Even in this fearful vision of Charon rowing the dead across the Seine, after bashing their heads in with his oar, when Lili at last finds him her figure comes through the visions with the same clarity as always, calm, not arguing, doing what is necessary, even paying some attention to the lost hedgehog, Dodard ('he doesn't ruffle his quills, he knows us'). And when Céline is safely in bed, tossing in fever, he is still worrying about Madame Niçois, his dying cancer patient, whose dressings are going to need changing. During hallucinations one does by definition confuse delirium and reality. Even a careless reader may do so at moments. But not the writer.

The other great account of hallucination (again with a clear physical cause) occurs in *Rigadoon*, when Céline is hit on the back of the head with a brick in an air raid near Hanover. It is interesting to remember that unlike the vision of Charon in *Castle to Castle*, which occurred near the time of writing about it, the Hanover air raid happened in 1944. Any of us might hallucinate if we stopped a brick; but which of us could describe our sensations twenty-five years later in utterly convincing detail? In the middle of it, the storyteller's voice breaks in speaking to his readers: ... 'telling you about it 25 years later ... I hem and haw, I'm all balled up ... too many bits and pieces ... you'll have to forgive me.' Then to himself: 'Stop spluttering ... just tell us what happened' (*Rigadoon*, 138).

In Germany Céline does not indulge in paranoia. He is too busy. In his asides from Meudon, especially when his writing is interrupted by unwelcome visitors, he does.

In this context, critics have condemned Céline for the degree of inwardness in his art, denying the wonderful combining of inward and outward that he achieves. The books are a story, and Céline is telling the story. The inward is indeed present as the storyteller of the 1950s, and also as the storyteller who was in the story. The artist is not there with the pure consciousness of the categories in the modern scientist; nor is he there as the slightly academic 'being towards death' of the existentialist. God knows he is too much involved in dangerous activity to be there as the id, ego, and super-ego of the Freudians, or the construct of behaviourist psychology. He is there as an intelligent and compassionate French doctor, taken up with the hates and loves, both private and political, which have come from his intense life. He is there as a man who very shrewdly is trying to escape being murdered by his political opponents, and who has now lived through and survived twenty years of sustained vilification in the media. He is not attempting in his art 'to see life steadily and see it whole.' If I were to use a colloquial title for this present writing, appropriate to the master of whom I write, it would be 'Up yours, Matthew Arnold.' We have been told that the saints in prayer can contemplate the whole steadily; it is reported that the philosophers can understand the meaning of the parts within the whole. But for the rest of us, seeing it steadily is not seeing it whole, and only a well-heeled bourgeois could have claimed that it was. We only see it steadily when we don't attempt to see it whole. It was inevitable that the tired, but comfortable, aesthetic pessimism of Matthew Arnold should have asserted that part of the secular creed which says that art is what gives life meaning, and so have exalted the artists. But Céline was too noble to fall into that blasphemy. To those who would call his unsteadiness 'madness' I would suggest that there is something wrong about people who are not mad in this era.

Céline was a doctor who became a great poet. His book would not be a true story if all parts of the whole were seen steadily. In terms of the universal, is not the story of somebody driven by public events – the anguish of the refugee – a universal story of the twentieth century? And is it not more universal than our story, television watchers at the protected centre of our empire? Those who write of Céline's madness would do well to consider this.

Nevertheless, when the folly of calling Céline a mad artist has been laid aside, a more difficult question remains. The professors would call it a question in aesthetics. Céline is very much a modern artist. The word 'modern' arises in the present connection because one of the great facts of modern existence has been the centrality of individuality in modern life and thought. This is manifest in nearly all modern art. It is certainly manifest in Céline's writing. To say that his writing in these books does not come forth from distorting madness is not thereby to say that the presence of 'individuality,' which penetrates all which is modern, does not make it inferior to that which came forth in eras when 'individuality' had not yet been brought 'out of concealment.' At this point the question must be left undiscussed. It must be left undiscussed here because individuality and subjectivity came into the world above all because of Western Christianity, and can only be discussed in the light of how one considers Western Christianity.

At a less profound level, however, we can observe that individuality and subjectivity are among the central concerns of the Western literary tradition. It is not accidental that Augustine, the thinker who more than any other was influential in the coming-to-be of western Europe as against the ancient Mediterranean civilization, wrote his *Confessions*. Nor does it seem to me accidental that Protestant modernness was first magnificently proclaimed by Luther, who had once been an Augustinian monk. Nor that at the height of the Enlightenment another great philosopher, Rousseau, who was to be a patron saint of much modern art, should have written another *Confessions*. We are hardly aware of Sophocles when we are enraptured by his tragedies. Even though Plato's greatest writings are perhaps dramas and not treatises, he is wonderfully unpresent in these dramas.

It is important to distinguish the sense in which Céline is entirely modern, and the sense in which he is not. The utterly modern is the utterly American, and Céline, in holding on to everything European, cannot be called that. Nor is he turfing the grave, in Bacon's sense. The last thing he wants to do is to pretty up reality. 'The thing is as it is' (Luther). Nor does he believe in the irreplaceable uniqueness of the individual, particularly as this applies to himself. Nevertheless, as hero and observer of the events in Germany and Meudon he is constantly aware of his own subjectivity, his self-consciousness; but it is part of the story, not the point of the story.

This is a very personal judgment, but I am intensely bored by Proust's self-absorption in *A la recherche du temps perdu*, whereas I am fascinated by M. de Charlus and Mme. Verdurin. I hate the self-centredness of modern art – but Céline is not like this. I quote again from *Rigadoon*: 'such dramatics! this "me me" chronicle' (143). Proust, Woolf, Joyce, Sartre in his café – can there never again in the modern world be the noble and the base, as with Lady Dedlock in *Bleak House*?

I do not know whether Céline's subjectivity is like everyone else's, but it is like mine – not in content, but in form. He was a man full of self-pity, yet not self-indulgent. He has the modern emptiness, yet is not empty. He is not describing the world as it is without God, but the world as it is whether there is God or not – a very different matter.

Another kind of modernity is often imputed to Céline. In the long journey of eighteen months there are of course many moments of high comedy, particularly in the first two books. Many writers in the United States who have learned from Céline claim that he is the originator of 'black comedy,' that is, writing which makes you laugh but excludes all felicity from itself. To me, 'black comedy' is a contradiction in terms, because there can be no sane laughter if it is not within some overarching framework of felicity. It might be argued that in *Journey to the End of Night*, and in *Death on the Instalment Plan*, there is the origin of black comedy, in that they produce a grim laughter with no framework of felicity; and for having written these Céline may be called an originator of this kind of humour. But in the trilogy he has become a greater writer of comedy – of the kind which produces more than a grim and insane laughter. The trilogy is a chronicle, not a novel, and his purpose is to tell the truth however much enlivened by his wit. There may not be much felicity, but a sane and courageous loyalty is itself a kind of felicity. This is more fundamental than his overt cynicism. Among the horrors and afflictions of civilians at the end of a war, his loyalty is unfaltering – first to Lili and Bébert, then to all the desperate people he tries to help as a doctor. For instance, at the colossal orgy at the railway station in *Castle to Castle* (187–91), Céline is trying, for fairly self-serving reasons, to rescue a teenage girl, daughter of Major von Raumnitz, and one of the 'nymphettes of Sigmaringen.' The situation is black, Céline's account of it is very funny, but it lacks the indifference which is basic to black comedy.

My conclusion is that Céline's trilogy withstands the objections I have brought forward. Neither inwardness, unsteadiness, nor blackness destroy its beauty or make it less than human. Only people who are modern liberals, and think of charity without the cross, could think Céline mad.

WHY AM I ENRAPTURED?

Still the question recurs: why does Céline's trilogy enrapture me?

Friends, who are rationalists in the sense that they want others to learn and become educated, have told me that Céline's art delights me because I learn from him what Western human beings are like in the twentieth century; if we are to think accurately or act wisely in this difficult era, we must think about what is going on, and Céline helps us to see this. I just do not think that this is so. Indeed it is true that Céline is above all an artist of the twentieth century, and as such lays before us in detail that the world is ruled by chance and necessity. But I do not think I needed Céline to teach me that, or that most other people would. As it happens, I have had much experience of the bombing of civilians. But even those who have not do not need Céline to imagine what it is like. To anyone with a modicum of sensibility, the TV can do that.[4] Nor when I say that Céline can make me cry out, 'Thou art the thing itself' (*King Lear*, act 3, scene 4), do I think that I learned that from Céline. When one says that Céline describes the human condition, one is just saying that he sees it as one sees it oneself. One does not learn it from him.

Perhaps the question should be more general. Why does beautiful writing enrapture us? It is lucky, faced with such a difficult question, to be able to start with a statement by a famous writer at the beginning of our tradition, which answers the question, though in a false and corrupting manner.

Poesy is a part of learning in measure of words for the most part restrained; but in all other points extremely licensed, and doth truly refer to the imagination; which, being not tied to the laws of matter, may at pleasure join what nature hath severed, and sever that which nature has joined; and so make unlawful matches and divorces of things; '*Pictoribus atque poetis*' etc. It is taken in two senses in respect of words or matter. In the first sense it is but a character of style, and belongeth to arts of speech, and is not pertinent for the present. In the latter it is, (as hath been said) one of the principal portions of learning, and is nothing else but feigned history, which may be styled as well in prose as in verse.

The use of the feigned history hath been to give some shadow of satisfaction to the mind of man in those points wherein the nature of things doth deny it, the world being in proportion inferior to the soul; by reason whereof there is, agreeable to the spirit of man, a more ample greatness, a more exact goodness, and a more absolute variety than can be found in the nature of things. Therefore, because the acts or events of true history have not that magnitude which satisfieth the mind of man, poesy feigneth acts greater and more heroical. Because true history propoundeth the successes and issues of actions not so agreeable to the merits of virtue and vice, therefore poesy feigns them more just in retribution, and more according to revealed providence. Because true history representeth actions and events more ordinary and less interchanged, therefore poesy endueth them with more rareness, and more unexpected and alternative variations. So it appeareth that poesy serveth and conferreth to magnanimity, morality, and to delectation. And therefore it was ever thought to have some participation of divineness, because it doth raise and erect the mind, by submitting the shows of things to the desires of the mind; whereas reason doth buckle and bow the mind to the nature of things. And we see that by these insinuations and congruities with man's nature and pleasure, joined also with the agreement and consort it hath with music, it hath had access and estimation in rude times and barbarous regions, where other learning stood excluded.' (Francis Bacon, *The Advancement of Learning*, book 2, part 4, iii)

This passage at least disproves with clarity the belief of those who claim that Bacon wrote the plays we say are by Shakespeare. Could the man who wrote this have written *King Lear* or *Antony and Cleopatra*? I start from the assertion that great art does not turn us away from the truth of what is, but towards it. But the question is: what is the truth with which it presents us, and why is that truth enrapturing? Here, at the beginning of the modern era, poetry is belittled, not only to make the poet's activity more difficult, but also the enjoyment of poetry more difficult – or even making it less possible for human beings in a technological age 'to live on earth poetically' (Heidegger). Here poetry is taken out of its proper place in the order of enlightenment. Modern mechanistic science teaches us what is true about what is; art is the business of prettying up what is, so one can turf the grave. One of the great destroyers of the tradition puts the axe of his 'ressentiment' to the root of poetry. He does this above all by brilliantly describing bad poetry and then identifying it with poetry itself. It is well to remember that Blake wrote on his copy of *The Advancement of Learning*, 'good news for Satan's kingdom.'

One can imagine how Céline would laugh to scorn the idea of his chronicle as 'feigned history,' or the suggestion that it may be 'styled as well in prose as in verse.' The writer of chronicles, the teller of stories, the supremely subtle stylist cannot be contained within Bacon's description. Third- and even second-rate literature can be. Most of us have our beloved means of escapism, whether mystery stories, historical novels, romances, or others, and these are helpful when our lives are narrow or boring or bitter. Bacon describes this kind of entertainment quite acceptably. But great prose or great poetry is a different matter, and the joy it gives, the enrapturing, has little in common with the pleasure and relaxation of our escapist entertainment. Bacon has only clarified the enrapturing by an eloquent description of what it is not.

Bacon is speaking of poetry, but more importantly he is defining the imagination whose product may be prose or verse, and whose subject-matter can be anything but reality. It may be that the delight of reading is indeed a response to the imagination of the writer, but we need a more adequate account of that imagination. One might turn to Coleridge, in *Biographia Literaria*, the end of chapter 14:

The poet, described in ideal perfection, brings the whole soul of man into activity, with the subordination of its faculties to each other according to their relative worth and dignity. He diffuses a tone and spirit of unity, that blends, and (as it were) fuses each into each, by that synthetic and magical power, to which I would exclusively appropriate the name of Imagination. This power ... reveals itself in the balance or reconcilement of opposite or discordant qualities: of sameness with difference; of the general with the concrete; the idea with the image; the individual with the representative; the sense of novelty and freshness with old and familiar objects; a more than usual state of emotion with a more than usual order; judgement ever awake and steady self-possession with enthusiasm profound or vehement.

This could as well be a description of music as of poetry – a Bach fugue as well as Milton's 'sober certainty of waking bliss' (*Comus*, line 263). It can also be applied to Céline's writing, in which a seemingly wild and fragmented consciousness can be expressed by means of a disciplined and meticulous craft.

'It blends and harmonizes the natural and the artificial, still subordinating art to nature, the manner to the matter' (Coleridge, *Biographia Literaria*, chap. 14). Coleridge does not see 'poesy' or imagination as a fanciful escape from the nature of things, but rather as an exploration of reality.[5] Nietzsche speaks for the modern when he claims that art has more value than truth; at this point Céline is nearer Coleridge.

Some Thoughts about Music

When thinking about imagination in general, music is often uppermost in my mind. Bacon also associates music with poetry, and consigns both to 'rude times and barbarous regions.' One wonders what kind of music he is thinking of.

There is not a great deal about music in the trilogy. But there is one chapter in *Rigadoon* which shows Céline transposing his immediate experience into music, for himself. I have mentioned many times the bombing of Hanover, particularly with reference to his style, and his effort, as storyteller, to transpose the terrible scene before him, including the pain of his own battered head, into words. That is the business of the old storyteller, who can only use words, and his memory, to convey it to his readers. But what Céline at that time in Hanover was doing for himself, spontaneously, was transposing the whole terrible experience into music:

I'd even call it a melody ... can you imagine? ... untrained, untalented, forced to bumble snatches of melody ... I can hear the tune in my head ... pretty sure the tune is right ... but the notes? ... the exact notes? ... were they too high or too low? ... as I've said, magnificent! as magnificent as the panorama ... symphonic melody, so to speak, just right for this ocean of ruins ... this fiery surf ... pink ... green ... and little crackling clusters ... the souls of the houses ... grotesque memories ... in snatches ... you can't have grandiose melodies without counterpoint. (*Rigadoon*, 142)

This incomplete music continued to haunt him, even after his return to Meudon: 'through myriad adventures, amusing and much less amusing moments, I kept wondering if I had my musical setting ... oh, I have no great pretensions ... three or four notes ... pleasure notes, so to speak ... that'll do' (*Rigadoon*, 145).

This is interesting. Music had never been Céline's medium. Yet when he was looking at an amazing scene of destruction, his head racked with concussion, it was music that expressed the experience for him. This is not brought in by the storyteller to convey to the readers the nature of the scene. This happened to Céline himself.

For us he transposed his experience into words – for himself, at the time, into music.

I am not suggesting that Céline was ever in his imagination attempting program music. He knew what words can and cannot do; he was not transposing words into music, or thinking of music as a kind of metaphor for language, but perhaps as a metaphor for reality. Music and story can never be reduced to each other, any more than music and poetry. But there may be something to our enjoyment of them that is common to both. (I do not mean at the obvious level of emotional or aesthetic enjoyment.) There are things in the form and structure of both that hold our attention at a basic and elementary level, irrespective of the quality of their particular content. It is of the very stuff of music that when at the beginning a theme is introduced the ear should ache, whether consciously or not, for its return. Both music and story are like a journey in which the sure object of desire is perhaps obscured, put at a distance, never entirely lost, returning in repetitions and variations and new developments, until at the end one's desire is fulfilled in some kind of return and completion. These elements are present in most music – even in a song – but most explicitly in the sonata form, the fugue, and the theme and variations. (The *Goldberg Variations* are certainly an image of human life.) Mozart told us that he heard his music altogether and at one moment. But most of us have only the moving image, and our experience as listeners and as readers, and indeed as living human beings, is grounded in temporal sequence. The growth of complexity out of an original simplicity may be an archetypal pattern of our experience, more fundamental even than the aesthetic.

But I am digressing, for it is not only at this level that I am enraptured by the trilogy. If that were the case, the journeys of Doctor Dolittle or the mysteries of Elizabeth Daly might do me as well.

So far I have mainly tried to describe Céline's late writing and the miracle of its achievement. To use Heidegger's strange language, Céline is an artist of *Dasein*. By this I mean to say two quite different things at the same time. The first is what Céline calls his 'magic lantern show,' by which he gives the reader the sense of being directly present in the midst of events. This I have tried to describe. It is enchanting enough. The second sense of Céline's Dasein is quite beyond any magic lantern show, yet it is equally the truth of 'being there.'

What I want to say is something more universal, and therefore something more opaque and difficult of expression. In reading these books I find myself saying that this is what human beings are like always and everywhere, in one respect particularly. Our purposes and passions, both great and small, are somehow in the order of necessity doomed to a kind of incompleteness in this life. I do not mean by incompleteness such things as failure, necessary deficiency, or frustration which might imply pessimism. Nor do I mean by this the obvious fact that we are beings who know we are going to die. To repeat, I mean simply that our purposes and projects and passions somehow are incomplete (it is the only adjective I can find). Of course the situation which Céline is writing about, the losing of a great war, makes this clear in an immediate way. Also Céline knew, as one who was raised poor, that this incompleteness is more present in people struggling for food than in the bourgeois who can cover the void by eating, drinking, coupling, the pursuit of ambition etc. But it seems to me that the incompleteness of all human purposes, projects and passions everywhere and always is recognized in Céline's very apprehension of human beings. The tenderness in his presentation of other people in these last volumes (even when he is raging at somebody who is set to betray him, or when he knows the ferocity of which some human being has been capable) seems to me to arise from the recognition of this universal incompleteness and therefore vulnerability, both of flesh and spirit. It is the constant presence which makes me want to cry out about his characters, 'Thou art the thing itself.'

Obviously the question arises: how does one know that this is a universal fact about the human condition? To discuss this properly would require too long a digression. It would require a discussion of the greatest accounts of this fact – that is, in the West in terms of Christianity, or in terms of the full immediacy of the first noble truth of the Buddha, that all life is sadness. How Céline would have ridiculed somebody who took his writing as a means of making obiter dicta about the truth of the great religions! Yet in terms of Céline's art something must be said about why the sense of this grave limitation in human life has been so lost in the West. The cause of this seems to me first and foremost that Western Christianity, particularly because of St Augustine's thought, so emphasized the power of God in its teaching that it forgot the truth of the weakness of God. The doctrine of the fall of man was indeed a very inadequate account of this fact. (The history of western Christianity is strange when we consider that it centred around the rite of the Eucharist, surely a celebration of the weakness of God.) When Christian belief was secularized into the doctrine of progress it gave almost unlimited opening to a belief in our own power as a means to the forgetting of our limitation. At least its forgetting by liberal Christianity is more generous than that. This fact must be expressed hesitantly because it can be so easily used to justify the impossibility of any useful politics in this era. But it does not imply the impossibility of politics, only their grave difficulties and dangers.

It is not only in other people that Céline sees the brokenness. He is very much aware of his own. He is a witness to the weakness of God and the fragility of the flesh. In Germany he became so physically weakened that he was at times entirely dependent on Lili's help. All his political passions are long since spent; there only remains the passion for survival – for himself, for Lili, and for Bébert. For the old storyteller his disaster has happened – all his hopes have been broken, many by his own fault. What matters now is to make enough money to support Lili when he is dead, and the only way to do this is by very good writing.

Mozart felt the ice around his soul, but he still had the consolations of loveliness. Céline did not. His consolations were to write his grim stories, but poverty, old age, and constant interruptions made that difficult. Lili was his consolatrix, but also his responsibility. What he saw in the eyes of the retarded children, his band of droolers – the dignity and simplicity with which his dog suffered and died – these were mysteriously beautiful, but the love they evoked was nearer pain than joy. He was indeed a witness to the tenderness of the flesh.

This is near the heart of what moves me most in Céline. But I still cannot easily describe it. He hated generalities, despised philosophy, had no use for religion, and quite consciously avoided statements about the whole. He did not find meaning in the world; the beautiful had no purpose beyond itself. If there was God, he only saw the absence. He has been called the poet of the empty tomb. One never knows out of what depths of suffering other people's vision of the whole may have come.

Why then should I be so enthralled by him? I think it is the very mixture of cynicism and love in Céline that moves me most; because both those rather conflicting attributes are used by him to express the nearest he can get to the truth of what is. This is what distinguishes him from a nihilist or a liberal. Human beings are not often very good – we are selfish and devious and broken. Céline does not talk about good and evil, nor does he confuse them. Never does he equate bad action with good. It always matters what one does, but that is to be taken for granted, like a conditioned reflex, and never thought of as virtuous.

He works as a doctor hard and lovingly, both in the emergencies of war, and home in Meudon. Because the tenderness of the flesh is his business, he takes it as an imperative that one does what one can. He has no illusions that this will amount to very much. Loyalty is also taken for granted; to his friends, to anyone who has been good to him, to his long-suffering companion Bébert. (He and Lili are so close that loyalty is not an appropriate word.) When asked for practical help all through the terrible journeys in *Rigadoon* he grumbles, and does what he can. He is without illusions. If he finds himself indulging in them he laughs bitterly. The one thing he will not say is that things are better than they are. The thing is as it is. Yet he says that he is dominated by the desire for perfection – death's cousin.

The soul only knows for certain that it is hungry. The important thing is that it announces its hunger by crying. A child does not stop crying if we suggest to it that perhaps there is no bread. It goes on crying just the same. The danger is not lest the soul should doubt whether there is any bread, but lest, by a lie, it should persuade itself that it is not hungry. It can only persuade itself of this by lying, for the reality of its hunger is not a belief, it is a certainty. (Simone Weil, *Waiting on God*, trans. Emma Craufurd [London: Collins 1959], 162)

NOTES

1 Grant's quotations from Céline's trilogy were taken from the Ralph Manheim translations published in New York by Penguin in 1975–6. The original French editions were published in Paris by Gallimard in 1957, 1960, and 1969, respectively. Gerald Owen and Edward Andrew in their essays in the present book use other editions of the novels.

2 This phrase, 'one will never be again as one was,' taken from the final words of *The Wings of the Dove*, was a favourite of Grant's. His love for Henry James was less trivial than the word 'flirtation' might suggest.

3 Grant wrote in a bracket on this page, 'note on Anschauen and Erleben.' These two German words always interested him, but they do not appear again in 'Céline's Trilogy.'

4 I think Grant would have wished me to remind readers here that this was written before the Gulf War.

5 Grant had at this time some thought of rereading Owen Barfield's *Poetic Diction*, which gives an almost ontological account of metaphor in poetry.

3

Why Did George Grant
Love Céline?

GERALD OWEN

How Céline would have ridiculed somebody who took his writing as an illustration that the incompleteness of his life points to the eternal order.
– George Grant[1]

Why did this Christian Platonist love that slummer on the lam? On the lam, what's more, from the good side at the end of the Second World War.

Most of the one article he published on Céline, which appeared in *Queen's Quarterly,* is spent clearing the ground for what he wanted to say about him. If not handled with care, it can be misleading. Having read his notes and drafts for a book on Céline, and now the coherent version put together by Sheila Grant, I find that he was not very interested in the Céline who said that Europe had ended at Stalingrad, or in the Céline who wrote three anti-Jewish books, or in any political side of Céline. He loved the Céline of his final trilogy, a man who says he was foolish to have put forward any political opinions, who is telling the story of his life on the run, of his 'disaster' (which luckily furnished him with a tragedy to write about); the story of the after-effects of his political acts – of his unpolitical scramble to survive political and military events.

One reason why Grant himself is of great interest is the unusual combination of authors who mattered to him. Perhaps 'configuration' would be better than 'combination,' because he certainly was

not aiming at a synthesis. So I mean to sketch out a kind of landscape, giving some detail to a couple of the higher hills in it, though
they do not lie side by side.

I will now switch metaphors.

It is plain that Simone Weil and Leo Strauss offered to George
Grant's mind two distinct *ways*, both Platonic. Other philosophic
ways were important to him, above all Nietzsche's and Heidegger's, but they never held his allegiance; on the whole he regarded them as daunting opponents. I believe that his allegiance
to Simone Weil was much greater than to Leo Strauss, though he
learned more about the history of political philosophy from
Strauss, and referred to him more often (or more directly) in his
published writings. But I think there was a deeper rift between
the ways blazed by Simone Weil and Céline. Céline's way was –
is – neither philosophic nor classical, but Grant did not face him
as an opponent.

LIE OR DIE

Even between Simone Weil and Céline there are a couple of odd
points of contact. One of them is a bit of monologue in Simone
Pétrement's life of her. In her labour union activity, Simone Weil
knew an ex-con with the nickname of Le Boul. Someone who knew
them both noted down a story he told in her presence. If you replace the dashes in it with what Céline called his three little dots
(his ellipses), you can see (or hear) that Le Boul's style and mood
are very like Céline's: the slang, the suffering, the spunk and relish
in the midst of suffering and disgrace, the jagged discontinuity –
but graceful tempo – of the sentences. Simone Weil listened in fascinated silence, apparently in awe and reverence.

Her quest to bear the sufferings of the poor was very different
from Céline's – or Le Boul's – handling of suffering. Like Céline,
she was a slummer; unlike Céline, she was not an intellectual or a
spiritual slummer. She subjected herself to gruelling factory labour.
Le Boul was not a slummer; to him it came naturally. But he was
not simply alien to her. And perhaps he offered something she was
missing. His liveliness while doing hard labour in a military prison
in North Africa must have perplexed her. He in turn revered her,
but she did not cope well with his attempts to be friendly, such as
when he invited her to dance with him in a bar.[2]

A couple of months after Céline's first novel was published (in 1932), Simone Pétrement quoted it to Simone Weil, in the course of a philosophic argument: 'Je me rappelle que je lui citai un passage du *Voyage au bout de la nuit*, que je venais de lire: "Il faut choisir, mourir ou mentir. Je n'ai jamais pu me tuer, moi." Je voulais lui montrer que l'amour de la vérité, quand il s'agit de la vérité sur soi-même, est au-dessus de la nature.' ('I remember that I quoted to her a passage from *Journey to the End of Night*, which I had just read: "You have to choose – to lie or die. Me, I've never been able to kill myself." I wanted to show her that the love of truth, when the truth about oneself is at issue, is above nature.')

Lying (in that speech in the *Voyage*) means hope in one's own attempts, 'a sufficient sum of delirium'; 'truth' means a 'death agony that doesn't stop; the truth of this world, it's death.' (Why bother to add 'of this world,' I wonder?) The occasion for these reflections is his recollection of 'true despair': when 'not even masturbation' provides comfort or distraction.

But the philosophic argument was a continuation of conversations a year earlier, when Simone Weil had resisted challenges by Simone Pétrement to the doctrine of their teacher Alain. Alain had taught them what I'll call (without getting into it) a pure liberal metaphysics, in which liberty is the supreme source of truth: much more than a necessary condition for arriving at truth. Simone Pétrement made her case against this on the ground of the difficulty or impossibility of accepting truth about oneself – without some force from outside, without grace. She even said that the world, or life, needs lies.[3]

Simone Weil came around later to the opinions that truth can only be attained with supernatural intervention, from outside oneself, and that truth is above nature.

But she also came around to agreeing with Ferdinand, the antihero of the *Voyage* – not about what choice to take, but about what the choices are. I do not mean that she ever mentioned Céline on this subject. But her statements are equally extreme.

On the whole, her finished writings show her more cautious side. Sounding rather like Socrates in the *Phaedo*, she says, for example, that philosophy is a death-like detachment. But she goes much further in her notebooks. These I know only through the selection called *La pesanteur et la grâce* and through Miklos Vetö's book *La métaphysique religieuse de Simone Weil*, which is largely an orderly exposition and analysis of thoughts scattered through her notebooks and other writings (but especially the notebooks).[4]

One of her extreme expressions of this thought does appear in *L'enracinement,* however: in a book that acknowledges human needs: 'Dans ce monde-ci la vie, l'élan vital cher à Bergson, n'est que du mensonge, et la mort seule est vraie. Car la vie contraint a croire ce qu'on a besoin de croire pour vivre.' ('In this world, life, Bergson's beloved life force, is only lying, and death alone is true. For life constrains one to believe what one needs to believe in order to live.')[5]

In *La pesanteur et la grâce,* she says on the face of it more positively, 'l'erreur comme mobile, source d'énergie' ('error as motive, source of energy'). But 'Tous les mobiles particuliers sont des erreurs' ('All specific motives are errors').[6]

In some versions of this theme, she is speaking about the opposition of truth and life in what we may hope are extreme cases: given the choice between dying and lying, one should choose truth and death.[7] We are not so shocked by this; we may be tempted to think we could possibly do that, if faced with the choice.

I think that Simone Weil is saying that we are always faced with this dilemma. The truth, she says, is that there is no good 'down here.' We all glimpse this, but almost all of us cover it back up with falsehood. Knowledge of the truth is a mortal wound. It ruins us as living, carnal beings.

The truth is 'beyond,' because God withdrew, withdrew from being all of being, in the very act of making the world. Necessity is the opposite of good, but down here goodness is, or at least includes, yielding to necessity: suffering and dying. Goodness is not, and does not include, becoming an agent of necessity, or its worshipper.

But the truth of death is more than saintly submission: it is true of the rest of us. Being flesh, we are all dying, we are all breakable and in the course of being broken. She is almost saying that we are as good as dead, right now.

Simone Weil may still have had the younger Céline in mind in *Attente de Dieu.* One of the covering-up, life-restoring lies is this: 'Beaucoup même se complaisent à la proclamer en cherchant dans la tristesse une jouissance morbide, qui n'ont jamais pu supporter de la regarder en face plus d'une seconde.' ('Many, who could not bear to look truth in the face for more than a second, even take pleasure in proclaiming it by seeking in sadness a morbid enjoyment.')[8]

Professor Vetö presents Simone Weil's criticism of sadness in contrast to suffering. Joy and suffering are both in contact with reality; they are paradoxically (but consequently) allies against *tristesse* and 'modern anguish.' Tristesse is a kind of pride, because it is a certainty that there is no help.[9] That may well be true of the melancholy posturing of the *Voyage*.

On another passion Céline and Simone Weil also agree. In their writings, anger appears very differently from the way it does in the *Republic* – allied with spiritedness – and even less like the way it appears in Aristotle's *Rhetoric* and (less clearly) in the *Ethics*: a passion that is accompanied by opinions of justice.

They show anger as a transfer of pain, a way of distracting oneself from one's own suffering by making others suffer – much like relieving an itch by scratching or pressing it with a fingernail.

I realized this from Frédéric Vitoux's *Céline* (not his biography but a book-length essay in a series called Les dossiers Belfond). As he says, the account in the *Voyage* of how the other passengers on a ship going to Africa choose Ferdinand as a scapegoat to relieve their boredom and their sickness at heart is striking, coming from someone who later made the Jews his scapegoats in much the same way.[10]

The anti-Jewish 'pamphlets' are a strange thing: pacifist hatred, partly rising from a well-founded fear of the next great war – not utterly unlike the anti-nuclear anger of *Lament for a Nation*. Very unlike, however: George Grant may well have exaggerated in his anger, but he did not leap into a lie, let alone into a wilfully lying fantasy as Céline did.

Before the war, Céline and Simone Weil were both defeatists. But Céline of course did not turn his fear – a fear based on genuine experience – into practical prudence, or virtuous courage, or saintly patience, or even philosophic observation. He threw himself into a ferocious anger, so openly preposterous and funny in its contempt for truth that Gide for one thought it was a satire against anti-Semitism. It wasn't. The evidence of people who knew Céline then is that he was sincere.

Frédéric Vitoux again is right to say that the comedy only makes it worse. Céline could partly pretend to stand aside from his lying sincerity, 'above' views that he had really adopted. He was trying to have it both ways: lying to himself and knowing that he was lying: giving himself to the lie – not even for any earthly gain, because he made himself offensive to Vichy and the Germans, as soon as they had apparently won.

For Simone Weil, however, the war led to further thought. I should make clear that I am not attributing George Grant's interest in Céline to that passing point of contact with Simone Weil. But it may clarify his interest in these two extremists, in the starkness of the choice they presented. He had little interest in the *Voyage*. He was of course greatly interested in Nietzsche, who 'agreed' with Céline and Simone Weil about the opposition of life and truth. But Nietzsche's is in a way too complex a case: hardly a clear exemplar of big-L Life. Céline, at least in the form of his main characters, *lives*, unlike Nietzsche, who sought for some sort of enhanced vitality in a very bookish way of life. Céline (or the main character in each book) was a 'wild and crazy guy.'

I find it striking that Simone Pétrement adduced Céline to argue that Simone Weil's early opinions made impossible demands. Although her doctrines changed, the rigorous quality of her thinking remained, and I sometimes think she still made equally impossible demands – and George Grant, according to Sheila Grant, sometimes thought the same. Perhaps Simone Weil would have agreed, but put it differently, replacing 'impossible' with 'supernatural.'

What about the older Ferdinand? I can hardly say 'maturer.' Céline did not of course turn to detachment and the quest for truth. But he was in a way detached in old age when he wrote the trilogy. George Grant says in his *Queen's Quarterly* article that he had come to some sort of tranquillity, and that he was by that time 'all political passion spent,' with 'his hopes burned out of him' – arguably an ever-so-slightly Simone-Weilish approach to truth and death.

EGOCENTRICITY

Modern, will have to sort out in what senses he is modern, in what he [is] not.

he is truly modern our modern emptiness but not empty.

– George Grant

These notes are among several of George Grant's that say Céline was a modern, but not just a modern. He does not mean that Céline was somehow an advocate of technology. At least in part, he means here by 'modern' one who places a very high estimate on the goodness and importance of individuality.[11] He himself put a lower estimate on it than most Western philosophers and intellectuals from Rousseau on – perhaps from Hobbes on. (There's an example in the first paragraph of the *Queen's Quarterly* article.)

Céline writes about himself, says George Grant, because 'he was a product of subjectivity.' So far he must mean modern subjectivity. And certainly Céline is ever-present in the trilogy. In this he is unlike Homer, Plato, all three of the great Athenian tragedians, and Xenophon and Thucydides, but like Augustine and Rousseau. 'Even although Plato's greatest [writings] perhaps are dramas and not treatises, he is wonderfully unpresent in these dramas.'[12]

Novelists are with the ancients on this. Grant says that, like Thucydides, they 'lie as it were hidden, yet disclosed, in their works.' Céline is 'not withdrawn in the way that Turgenev thought proper to the novel.' And however irritatingly, pompously repetitive Heidegger is when he tells us that truth is 'unconcealment,' I agree that unconcealment is a good description to apply to Céline. His slangy, seemingly but only seemingly spontaneous diction, is a successful imitation of someone who is present, speaking vividly and very informally, and often in the historic present.

'I know Céline better than I know certain friends.' In several drafts, Grant says something like this: 'Let us put aside the bullshit that was talked about ... President Nixon by American journalists: "You have to know him well to really dislike him." Smart but not true.'[13]

'He brings human beings before us in their wonderful individuality.'

In Heideggerian, one could say Céline presences himself. Grant says, 'To use Heidegger's strange language,' Céline 'is the artist of Dasein' – there-being, which means something like the human way of being but without any biological-physical specificity – 'as if we were as much there as himself.'[14] And he often speaks in mildly Heideggerian style of how Céline brings things before us. I don't mean that he liked Céline for being some kind of implementer of some program of Heidegger's. On the contrary, in some notes he replies to Heidegger, saying that surely the good is what is absent, what is desired and not present, at best hinted at by what is present; that the good is not 'there' (or here), but transcendent – in the baffling phrase of the Republic, beyond beingness. But he is divided on this matter; Christianity and Platonism seem to him to hold both this 'transcendental' opinion and the opposite one that all being, as such, is good.

He translates *chronique* – Céline's description of the trilogy – as 'story.' By this Grant doesn't mean narrative in general (let alone *mythos*). He means a narrative in which the actual narrator (and not an imagined one even as closely akin to the author as, say, David Copperfield) is the central character. 'What I mean by calling Céline's trilogy a story is that he has transposed that sense of story onto the printed page,' the quality, that is, of direct, word-of-mouth communication, where there is 'no didactic purpose outside the telling and the listening.' He denies that the distinction between a novel and a story rests on a distinction between imagined and actual events. Although, like Céline, 'Dostoyevsky had to summon up the remembrance of the past,' Dostoyevsky's *The House of the Dead* is a novel because of the stance of the narrator, who is not presented as someone present, as an acquaintance to whom one is listening, but as a fictional 'character' 'addressing' a reader, in a way that only a reader could be addressed. I am trying now to say something Grant did not explicitly say. But he plainly praises the personal quality of the communication – an apparent divergence from his usual depreciation of personality and individuality. Céline's 'making-present' of himself is his giving a vivid sense not just of his persona inside the story, but also of his persona as a storyteller. It is as if he were physically present as the narrator.[15]

Grant praises Céline for a perfect unity of inwardness and outwardness. I believe that his case in Céline's favour alleges that his very patent, very unclassical presence is a redemption of individuality. He often expresses his preference for Céline's egocentricity over the introspective egocentricity of other recent moderns: Henry James, Proust, Joyce, Virginia Woolf, the whole stream of consciousness school; but also as against the Rousseau of the *Confessions* and the 'consciousness of self-debate as one finds in Pierre or Raskolnikov or Emma Bovary. (He [Céline] is too busy surviving and escaping.)' With Céline it is a stream not of consciousness but of events. He is in the thick of things. 'A great story must be told by someone who is more than egocentric and yet sufficiently egocentric to be taken up with the events that are being told. The storyteller must be absolutely there as an individual and yet absolutely open to otherness.' Other drafts say, instead of 'taken up,' 'enwrapped,' 'intoxicated.'[16]

These books are plainly not studies in character – which is one of the main elements of the genre called 'novel.' Céline sometimes openly disclaimed psychologizing and characterization (and once added, 'les faits seuls existent, et pas pour longtemps'). In *Voyage*, the Céline-like character makes this point by saying you can't be a La Bruyère these days; the unconscious runs away whenever you go near it.

But this freedom from introspection is not obviously true of the paranoid and near-paranoid speech of Céline in the first half of the first volume of the trilogy, *Castle to Castle*. In fact his inner life – that is, his lonely griping – blossoms out into a hallucinatory fever. You might say that he is so very introspective that he begins to re-create the outer world. In his second novel, *Death on the Instalment Plan*, and in the third volume of the trilogy, *Rigadoon*, there is also a movement from hallucination into very present, lively memory, as if temporary madness (from malarial fever) were what it takes to re-live, and re-present. The 'inner life' in the trilogy belongs to the cranky old crank of the fifties, not to the middle-aged fugitive of the forties. So, the inner life comes earlier in the trilogy, later in the time of the world. I suspect that this is an intended movement outwards.[17]

Grant says something similar: 'In these last writings of Céline, there is a purity of apprehending other people in their completeness which seems to have come to him when his art had come to him through the intensity and density of his disaster.' In another connection he asks himself, 'If the story is a self-justification is not my claim dimmed?'[18] But the self-justification is mostly in those self-regarding preludes – at least the open self-justification.

Grant speaks of the tenderness in the trilogy, at first a surprising thing to say, in the garish light of Céline's violence. But tenderness, violence, and hatred do coexist in these books. All the violence on his own part in the trilogy is imaginary, and almost all is near the beginning of each volume. As there is a movement from inner to outer life, there is a movement from violent fantasies and hatreds toward tenderness – notably in the story of the imbecile children that is told almost at the end of *Rigadoon*. (This, by the way, apparently did not happen.) The violent fantasies are chiefly directed against his publisher, Gaston Gallimard; it is a new application of his lifelong hatred of the boss, whoever he may be.

Grant is right that Céline sometimes ridicules his own self-centredness. So that his account of Céline shows a modern who, like Heidegger, is criticizing subjectivity and trying to come to terms with it. Subjectivity is very much the main charge in Heidegger's criticism of scientism and technology – but he rejected the language of subject and object, and so did Grant, here for once following Heidegger. (Or rather he accepted Heidegger's analysis, but took it as grounds in favour of thinking in the ancient way about soul – he did not use Heideggerian terms for most of his positive opinions.)

He does say that the 'presence of "individuality" which penetrates all that is modern' perhaps makes the writing in the trilogy 'inferior to that which comes forth "out of unconcealment." It must be left undiscussed here because "individuality" came into the world above all because of western Christianity' – plainly he is thinking of Augustine – 'and can only be discussed in the light of how one considers western Christianity.'[19]

But this matter is larger than modernity, more permanent than the modern doctrines that have placed a high value on individuality because they have placed the highest value on freedom or on the pursuit of gain.

When Grant speaks of egocentricity, the influence of Simone Weil is unmistakable. It was one of her central teachings that self-centredness is a delusion of perspective, an error to which our natural sense-perception lends itself: each of us imagines that he or she is the centre of world. This folly, she says, is one of the burdens of being made of matter, not just a price of being born in the last four centuries; it is not something that any of us can simply overcome 'down here.'

Still less should a writer of a story (or chronique) pretend to overcome it. Up to a point he must wallow in it.

FRAGILITY

In the books themselves people come to us in all the sadness of their fragility and openness to accident; they come to us with a great sweetness about the idiosyncratic and foolish desires which lead us whither we would not. [We are shown the] fragility of the flesh and the brokenness of hopes.

Grant takes this theme a long way. He says that Céline is 'a witness to the weakness of God and the tenderness of the flesh.' He often uses the word 'tender' in regard to the trilogy – tender is the way human beings are 'held before us just as they are,' not as objects, but in their truth, somewhat as God sees them. The artist who does this 'is essentially one of "God's spies."' As such, Céline's art is a witness to the helplessness of God.'

'My highest claim for the beauty of [Céline's] writing is that it holds before us in pure apprehension a vast body of human beings in the midst of their losing. There are moments in the chronicle when I want to cry out with Lear about the naked Edgar: "Thou are the thing itself."' Here Grant stands in opposition not only to triumphalism, to the theology of glory, to admiration of 'winners,' but also, not so explicitly, to nuts-and-bolts, hard-facts, Gradgrindian self-styled realism. Facts are not hard.

From the sense of fragility of beings in Céline, he points onward and upward to the fragility of their creator. More than the suffering of God, this is God's weakness, a more daring thought – suffering is (or has become) compatible with tragic magnificence, with baroque agony.

He says that 'western Christianity, particularly because of Saint Augustine's thinking, so emphasized the power of God in its teaching that it forgot the truth of the weakness of God,' and goes on to say that the doctrine of the Fall was 'a very inadequate doctrinal account of this fact.' And he attributes to Céline a 'remembrance of it in a wonderfully untheoretical form' – as opposed to its prettying up by French existentialism or (worse) 'Kierkegaard's neurotic account of Christianity. At least its forgetting by liberal Christianity is more generous than that. It must also be said that this fact must be expressed hesitantly because it can so easily be used to justify the impossibility of politics in this era. But it clearly does not justify the impossibility of politics, only [illegible word] their grave limitations.'[20]

To what degree is Grant's dissent from Augustine on the theology of glory connected with his dissent from Augustine on individuality, on autobiography? The phrase 'will to power' may help explain it. The theology of glory and triumphalism is about God,

and individuality is about human beings. If Augustine is the founder of individuality, then it was originally about contrite, confess-
ing human beings. But perhaps the explanation is (a) that if the
nature of God is power, and human beings are made in God's image, then human beings are essentially beings of power – whatever
that would mean, or (b) as God's servants, saved human beings are
triumphant agents of God's power and glory, or (c) human weakness is the counterpart of God's power, as a cringing slave is to a
harsh master. Or (d) the will to power is an atheist doctrine that is
modelled on the theology of glory, applying to some or all human
beings what was alleged about God, or (e) some or all of the above.

The weakness of God is a teaching of Simone Weil's, but she
says that the world created by God is strong, that his weakness
consists in his withdrawal from being the only being, and in the
permission to govern that he has given to the hard order of necessity that he has designed; not the fall of man, but creation itself is this alienation of God from man and the world. But if we
can trust the appearances of Céline's trilogy, the world is *not*
hard and strong.

I'll risk belabouring a joke of Céline's – where he says he is giving
the details, not the big picture. He alludes (it's one of his rare references to any philosopher) to an image in Henri Bergson's *Creative
Evolution*. A hand – in Céline's version a fist – passes through iron
filings 'which are compressed and offer resistance to it in proportion as it goes forward'; it leaves the filings 'massed and co-ordi-
nated in a certain form' moulded by the hand and forearm. If the
hand is invisible, then a materialist (or mechanist) will explain the
pattern by the interaction of the filings themselves; an idealist (or
teleologist) will explain it by a plan of a planning mind; a
Bergsonian will explain it by Bergsonism. But Céline says he's not
giving the punch-of-the-fist explanation of the war, he's just describing the iron filings, as he experienced them. Perhaps his *coup
de poing* is Simone Weil's order of necessity.[21]

You would think that saturation bombing qualified as a powerful
punch. But it is true that he is not describing the RAF pilots, or the
Luftwaffe, let alone the causes of the war. Simone Weil herself furnishes an explanation for the divergent perspectives. Egocentricity
hides the order of necessity. 'Si nous nous prenons comme fin du
monde,' she says, 'le monde est chaotique et sans finalité.' (*Finalité*
is, roughly, purposiveness, teleology, Kant's *Zweckmässigkeit* –

whether egocentric or theocentric.) Necessity looks like chaos when the true order is not perceived. The iron filings do not obey any human ego, and in frustration an egocentrist dismisses events as anarchy.[22]

Grant testifies that Céline's description of aerial bombing was truer to his own experience of it than anything else he had read. And that experience was a turning point for him. In the fragments for 'History and Technology' (a projected book) he says it came on him as a loss of faith in history, that is, in human progress. Céline openly mocks progress and 'le Sens de l'Histoire,' referring to Marxists, to de Gaulle, and to anyone else it might apply to.

In one aspect of his quarrel with capital-H History, Céline is on the same side as Simone Weil: History means Woe to the Vanquished; we hear from the winners not the losers. Like Simone Weil, though in a very different tone, Céline reminds us of the numerous forgotten conquered nations.

But where she wished to partake in the sufferings of the vanquished, Céline had an urge to make himself one of the losers, not it seems from a sense of justice or from compassion, but from a desire for experience, from curiosity, and from contrariness. He was for any appeasement to avoid war, and he predicted the fall of France, but right after he was proved right in this, he concluded that the Germans would lose, at the height of their success; he was doubly a defeatist. He did not collaborate with Vichy and Germany, because he proclaimed that to be futile, but he persisted in wild slanders that were obnoxious to the Resistance and the Allies. This provides one of the contexts in which he himself speaks of fragility: talking about having everyone against him, he says, 'si fragile celui qu'a raison!' (how fragile he who is right!). Self-serving though this is, it may well be true that reason is frail.

'How the fall of civilization can be our image of the good,' says a note of Grant's on a point to be developed in his Céline book. Technology and history would have come into it, by way of these themes of weakness, of defeat, of tragedy, of losers. He does not claim that Céline tells us much that we would not otherwise know about technology, or about modern times. ('Indeed it is the number of people from the history books that makes Castle to Castle the least satisfactory of the three.') But as he often says, Céline is showing a technological civilization in collapse. I don't find any hint of vindictive, machine-smashing, anti-technological pleasure; the trilogy shows technology succumbing to the assault of technology.[23]

Céline brings forward the comic incidentals of catastrophe, like the booming demand for postage stamps that signals the fall of a regime, when all other businesses are going under (the stamps of Pétain and Hitler are about to become collector's items); like the hectic pursuit of sex; like the desire to smoke before being executed, allegedly a proof of the primacy of the desire for reverie; like his preposterous observation that revolutions always begin with thefts of bedding; like the general refusal to accept payment for anything, when it has become pointless.

He doesn't show us technology from the inside. He renders the experience of being on the receiving end of aerial bombing. He doesn't analyse much; he shows again and again how apparently solid people and things are vulnerable, brittle.

TREMBLING AND STAGGERING

In Céline, the fragility is not theological.

Under the relentless RAF, everything is vibrating, trembling – everything ordinarily solid: the earth, the walls, the floors and ceilings – and everything liquid but ordinarily still: the soup in one's bowl, the water in the pond, the muck in the pigsty. Leaves tremble as if there were a wind, when there isn't. The soil is jumping in the fields. The customary distribution between things at rest and things in motion has been altered. In the cities buildings are mostly façades, shell-like things – sometimes with one of the floors intact and still furnished, but with emptiness above and below. Sometimes whole parts of buildings are hanging out sideways from the remains. New hills have been made out of the ruins by explosions: fragile, hollow bell-shapes, of clay and debris. Upside-down streetcars and railway locomotives are – impossibly – on the tops of great heaps of debris: heavy things that have flown through the air. In harbours, huge boats stand with their sterns in the air. These real scenes are – as Céline says – about as crazy as surrealist paintings, but with the added touch of the stench of death.

The (reported) fear of the ancient Gauls that the sky might fall has come to seem reasonable. The sky is bright and white at night, full of colours, especially yellow and black, but all the others too, at one time or another. It is as if people were playfully painting upon the clouds, with their bombs and searchlights.

Machinery screeches for lack of lubricating oil. But the noise of engines supplies some cover for a little freedom of speech: you have to bellow your indiscretions to be heard by the person right beside you.

The noise of bombing, the consequent trembling of everything, and the artificially white nights make it hard to sleep. The constant vibration reaches into human souls. People are jumpy and jittery. According to Céline, they are still nervous. The always agitated nature of human beings has been aggravated – pending the next great war, the first fully nuclear war.

The universal shakiness is strikingly like the shaking of Céline and his bed in the hallucinatory malarial fevers that bring on the re-creation of his memories. The world as it appears in his 'chronicles' is not dreamlike, not unreal, but it is more vivid, more animated than the heaviness of day-to-day human life. He once said that, above all, human beings seem to him heavy. In the books they – we – are mischievous, keyed up, crazed, much more than we are heavy. But aerial bombing makes for a world quite like Céline's tempo and atmosphere, though at the same time it has a very believable monotony.

The chronologically earliest part of the trilogy is at the beginning of the second volume, *North*. Céline, his wife, their cat, and a movie-star friend of theirs are in a grand hotel at Baden-Baden, having just fled France. The assassination plot against Hitler has just failed. It is right after this that Céline begins to suffer from the staggers. He cannot walk any more without a stick. I think there is a hint at a larger parallel, that Céline is suggesting that the failure of the plot, and the consequent inevitability of the Allies' insistence on unconditional surrender, made certain what he called the end of Europe. More certain than Stalingrad. No compromise with Germany would be possible. Russia and America would divide the spoils.

Tituber, 'stagger,' is one of Céline's favourite verbs in the trilogy. It is as if there were a loss of solid, even ground, as well as a loss of the power to stand up straight. Staggering is a kind of locomotion, without the stability required to get somewhere efficiently and gracefully, but it still means getting somewhere; at least there is some sort of ground to totter and stumble across. Céline has long since stopped drinking, but this state is like the result of drinking; it is a giddiness, a dizziness, akin to the innate human *ivresse* – which means something more like light-headedness, enthusiasm, delirium, than like the waterlogged state our word drunkenness suggests. In the later part of the third volume (named after a kind of dance), Céline is not only staggering but light-headed, having been hit in the back of his head by a brick during a bombing raid on Hanover. He feels a most inappropriate but somehow also appropriate gaiety, as he, Lili, and Bébert (the cat) pass through genuine but hallucinatory scenes of Germany laid waste.

(I find it striking that both Swift and Céline seem to have suffered from Ménière's disease, which causes dizziness, noises in the ear, and a staggering gait. The loss of balance may contribute to a particular sensibility or vision. They both praised animals for being more temperate, more sane than we are.)

Lili, a professional dancer, is the opposite of a staggerer. She is an acrobat. Grant was struck by the evidence of her graceful agility in the midst of dangers, such as when she throws herself in front of a Swedish Red Cross train to get it to stop. The point of this was to rescue more than a dozen severely retarded, speechless children who have been landed on them, to get them to safety by putting them on this neutral train. These children are staggerers too, but with them unsteadiness is clearly allied with gaiety. They are resilient; their tumbling over and getting back up again are great jokes to them; they can ignore the danger from the air, and from everywhere else. They are fragile, by nature unfitted for life – for nature; they are hopeless cases, but once in motion – once Céline and Lili become their guides – they are on an outing, they are madly hopeful, or rather they are free from hopes and fears. They have something other people are missing.

I think the frailness of things is also seen in preposterous causes, and in lost causes. Sigmaringen, the German refuge for Vichy France, is a zoo of them. One of the few times I laughed aloud while reading the trilogy was when an Albigensian bishop shows up in the middle of a chaotic scene outside a clogged lavatory. (Almost another point of contact with Simone Weil!) The rickety, stage-set quality of the castle of Sigmaringen is another instance of fragility; it is precariously perched on a rock, apparently teetering in much the same way as all human beings are tottering and staggering. The unreal plans of its inhabitants are fragile because they are futile.

Live people in the trilogy are often likened to ghosts; they are as if already dead, waiting for the inevitable destruction – certainly of the way they have lived, probably of themselves.

Céline is half in sympathy with futility. An example is his portrait of Corpechot, a man who denies the importance of air power in its very face, who insists the real threat is from the Russian navy, which will come up the Upper Danube toward Sigmaringen: 'les vrais authentiques et les dingues ... la seule différence ... l'endroit qu'ils se trouvent.'

Once and only once in the trilogy Céline flirts with hopeless schemes. Pierre Laval offers him a favour in return for cyanide (with which to commit suicide if necessary); he asks to be made governor of St Pierre and Miquelon, and Laval agrees. The only favour he accepts from the Vichy types is consciously preposterous – he asserts as a joke (in the book's present) that he is still the rightful governor.

But he genuinely likes those islands. The wish behind the hope is not foolish.

Céline's picture of life under aerial bombing is persuasive because it steers well clear of the art of persuasion. He hides his anti-rhetoric by the outrageous overemphases of his digressions. But his narrative and descriptions bring out the monotonous, repetitive element in the most bizarre disasters, and the laughably boring difficulties of trying to answer ordinary needs.

Grant rightly made the important point that the story is told from the side of the losers (in a way doubly losers, as alleged French collaborators in the midst of the German collapse).[24] But Céline presents horrors without exclaiming over them, he does not ask for compassion, does not apostrophize, does not tear-jerk, does not weep. He does not openly try to make our flesh creep. He does complain, but more like a spry curmudgeon, and like a teller of tall-but-true tales.

He also doesn't beautify the strange sights of war, at least not explicitly; and he doesn't mystify them by making them into omens, or by describing them in portentous tones. A couple of times he notes in passing that the colours in the sky would be pretty in other circumstances, and he does bring out the oddness of it all with boyish excitement, but not with praise. On the whole he does not play up the accidental – and weird – beauty in war. He comes closest in observing the gaiety of the dancing, multicoloured flames, but by then he is returning to something like the hallucinatory state of the (non-chronological) beginning of the trilogy. This comes after he is hit by the flying brick in Hanover – he is in his light-headed state, with music playing in his brain.

There is a resemblance between Céline's picture of war in Germany and Grant's experience of war on the south bank of the Thames (as it appears in chapter 6 of William Christian's biography). This is true of people and things and events.

Grant felt the 'excitement' of the blitz and saw its strangeness: 'twisted steel beams'; the 'tiger-like footsteps' of the raids; the way 'High Explosive [took] the air as its ally and [did] more destruction by blast' than by itself; a man standing at a billiard table with only a trickle of blood from his nostrils to show he was dead; the sudden destruction of 'even the most intricate, delicately balanced human personality.'

Grant loved and saw the beauty and the 'many vices' of the lower-class people of Bermondsey, who 'would save any man's life and steal any man's property.' They were free of bourgeois posturing, particularly of moral edification. For example, his account of the funeral of a certain Mrs Fuller's husband ends with her saying, 'Well, 'e was a fair devil, 'e was.'

Slumming has its dangers (including its own posturings). But it can also be good for the soul. The story of Simone Weil and Le Boul goes to show that in this at least, Grant surpassed her: in his liberating friendships with people who were emotionally direct, who were directly and openly exposed to 'the order of necessity.'

LAMENT FOR TECHNIQUE

I will close with some unmetaphysical, comparatively political matters.

Céline is not on the whole a praiser of past time. But in the trilogy he does from time to time lament the days of his childhood and youth, the days before '14. Yet this is to mourn the world of *Death on the Instalment Plan*, and in that book he has scarcely any mercy for that world – at least on the surface. When Céline dwells on the turn of century, he makes it look bad, from the point of view of a child and a young man – there is no lament for a former time.

The thing that is most Grant-like about Céline's laments is that he says, in effect, there is no point locking the barn door after the horse is gone. This is his accusation against the Poujadistes, the French petty-bourgeois right of the fifties, with whom he might have been expected to agree. He has a sort of Poujadisme of despair. It is like Grant's argument that conservatism is futile in our time. But what is the horse that is gone? What is the unlocked barn?

Céline spoke – in his bizarre way – for his own class. He was, as he often reminds us, the son of a shopkeeping lacemaker (his mother), and he himself was a down-at-the-heels doctor who practised among the working class. His father was an unhappy employee of an insurance company. The hatred of bosses is the most consistent thing in Céline. On the other hand, the proud, much-clung-to independence of the shopkeeper is shown to be wretched. Customers (and patients) are depicted with hatred too. The combination of poverty with a frantic clutching onto respectability is a horrific thing. This is Céline's childhood – or the side of it he showed in his second novel.

As for his own career, I can attest to the truth of his portrait of what it is like to be a member of a supposedly dignified 'liberal' profession who is barely getting by: the attachment to independence that is mixed with despair; the jadedness and misery; the awareness of genuine need in many of the people who ask for one's services, malign though they often are; and the absurd reluctance to charge clients enough or anything at all, resulting from pride mixed with considerateness; and the often futile attempts to get rid of unpleasant clients whose confidence only seems to be increased by one's negative advice.

Grant did not belong to the petty bourgeoisie, but his sympathy for it appears in his sympathy for Diefenbaker, whom he called 'the small-town lawyer'; he disliked the urbane Pearson, whose milieu was quite close to the one he came from himself. Social Credit in Canada (both English and French) has often been likened to Poujadisme, and Diefenbaker had something in common with Social Credit in a loose sense, being prairie, anti–Bay Street, and fairly anti-statist. Grant was of course not a bible-thumper like the Social Crediters. But he disliked the contempt poured on North American fundamentalists. He disagreed with their Calvinism and with their rejection of philosophy and learning, but he thought that the condemnation of them was largely snobbish, that it hid what was good about them.

The petty bourgeoisie has the negative merit of not controlling any mammoth-like institution (by definition it lacks the organization that would allow it to do so); it lacks sophistication, the style of civilization that can hide a lack of nobility; it is attached to a morality; it is attached to a practical, not to a metaphysical or existential, freedom; it has no triumphalist aspirations.

The petty-bourgeois pride in self-reliance is nonetheless an overwhelming pride. It is often observed that there is an alliance between shyness and arrogance, and this is true of Céline. The pride that is self-esteem awarded in one's own inner court of honour is in the final account more egocentric than vanity, than showing off – than wishing to please.

Céline scorns *les gens du monde* – both the nobility and the high bourgeoisie – as show-offs: they are always on stage; unlike the haughty, allegedly silent Céline, they cannot keep anything to themselves. Many of his jeremiads are spent shouting at les gens du monde 'It's over!' This 'it' is the world of aristocratic salons and of bourgeois civility: the world of Proust. A lot of *North* is spent showing a hopeless yet uncannily preserved remnant of the age of Versailles, of Louis XIV, on the frontier of civilization in the Mark Brandenburg – waiting for 'the Tartars' – the Red Army – to arrive.[25]

Is this, as Grant puts it, a great civilization that is collapsing in the trilogy? Up to a point, yes. One must read this in. Céline does dwell on the 'noble' class in the trilogy. The closest he comes to fellow-feeling with it is when, as a former cavalryman from before '14, he feels a certain concord and admiration for the grimly, insanely quixotic ride of an ancient Prussian nobleman. But he certainly does not feel he belongs to this class, either according to the letter or the spirit.

Except, except, that he implicitly but repeatedly laments the destruction of the artefacts that the nobles possess, for which they are – were – the market. They are the bitterly resented and badly needed customers. Céline is a member by birth, upbringing, and even vocation, of the artisan class.

The fragility of beings is not the frailty of animals and human beings alone. It is shown again and again in manifold artefacts – at the Hohenzollern castle of Sigmaringen, at 'Zornhof' in the Mark Brandenburg, in a railway car that had been prepared by the kaiser for the visit of the shah. Céline does not quite lament this last, but there is a sense of its magnificence. He does not deny the necessity of pillaging, of ripping down splendid curtains in a train to keep warm on a futile journey. In fact there is a sense of fun at the destruction wrought in it by a horde of German children, as well as at the laughable sight of Vichy cabinet ministers wrapped up in ornate drapery.

Céline is struck by the repetitive work that maintains magnificent places. He seems to be attracted to the baroque, 'coquettish' workmanship that he often finds in Germany. If there is a great civilization here, it is from before the First World War. The relation of older techniques, crafts, to technology and the religion of technology is not clear, but even a pre-modern artisan would be bound to be fascinated by new machines. A petty-bourgeois craftsman may well be threatened by technological change, but he is not apt to condemn it as a whole.

Consider the extremely ambivalent portrait of Courtial that makes up the latter half of *Death on the Instalment Plan*: a con man genuinely intoxicated by technical progress, an inventor-fantasist, a small businessman with his own little magazine. This is the only boss whom Ferdinand/Céline ever admires. Of course he also despises him, but he is plainly sick at heart after Courtial destroys himself – it is a disaster when this popularizer moves into an ostensibly practical undertaking. In the trilogy Céline's laments are often for old kinds of workmanship. He likens his writing style to his mother's trade: to lacemaking, with its fine detail. Improbably enough, he enjoys comparing himself to aged spinster seamstresses. This style was put forward as a renewal of French, for the sake of renewal itself, and for the sake of the demotic speakers and speech: it was 'populist.' It was a rejection of the classical – and Christian! – sentence. Simone de Beauvoir said she and Sartre and her friends welcomed the style of the *Voyage* as a change from the marble prose of Gide, Valéry, and Alain – this last the teacher of Simone Weil. She wrote very classical prose, and deplored the anti-rationalism of twentieth century art (including the amoral content of Gide, in spite of his conventional diction). Still, she liked to think she wrote in Louis XIII prose: a style with some of the older French raciness, not yet hardened into Louis XIV classicism.

At his least Grant-like, Céline professed – in explaining his style – that 'in the beginning' is emotion, not the word. I think that this is a claim to more inwardness than he practised. It is truest of the *Voy-*

age; in an interview he denied having any 'inner life.' Once in the trilogy he claims that the word ('le verbe') kills – or rather kills hard-ons. This is an aspect of his habit of praising silence (odd in someone so prodigal of words). He accuses the French of being artists of le verbe, not of the heart – but then, he never pretends not to be French.

In defence of the *Voyage*, Céline quoted Thomas à Kempis, of all people (his source was Huizinga's *Waning of the Middle Ages*; it's not that he was reading *The Imitation of Christ*): 'Don't try to imitate the warbler or the nightingale, if you can't. But if it's your destiny to sing like a toad, go for it! With all your might! Let them hear you!' (He was not quoting literally, but the substance is true.)[26]

Probably Céline meant it when he said he was mainly a stylist. He went to great pains to make apparently spontaneous prose. His diction may well have been more important to him than life on the margins, than *la vie bohème*, or than what he mockingly calls his 'fortes pensées.' But his devotion to this *techne* necessarily implies certain opinions. A class analysis of Céline stands up to examination: he held, in an extraordinary guise, the opinions of a petty-bourgeois artisan, which, both as doctor and as novelist-'chronicler,' he was.

What has that to do with George Grant? Well, a techne of that kind is, in Heideggerian, not technology, *Technik*, but *Handwerk*. Grant did not say much about pre-technological technique. But for that very reason Céline may have represented a vista he had not pursued. Though far from artsy-craftiness – far from its moralism, from most of its morality, and from most of its explicit nostalgia – Céline stood on a neglected path and walked some distance on it.

NOTES

I am grateful for the help of the Ontario Arts Council, which made possible the research for and the writing of this paper – and for the assistance and hospitality of Sheila Grant.

1 Cf. 'Céline's Trilogy' (this volume) [hereinafter: CT], 50. Having written this paper before Sheila Grant edited George Grant's drafts and fragments, I often quote or mention phrasings different from the ones she has chosen. Consequently, my references to CT are points of comparison as much as or more than source notes. I have tried to make

some sense of some of the themes that Grant himself resolved the least – hence my recourse to sometimes rather crumbly fragments.

Sheila Grant describes, in her preface to 'Céline's Trilogy,' how she assembled the drafts and fragments to make a coherent whole.

2 Simone Pétrement, *La vie de Simone Weil* (Paris: Fayard 1973), 1:373–5, 377.

3 Ibid., 1:171–4, 299; Louis-Ferdinand Céline, *Voyage au bout de la nuit*, in *Romans* I (Paris: Gallimard 1988), 200.

4 See Miklos Vetö, *La métaphysique religieuse de Simone Weil* (Paris: Vrin 1971), 73–4, both for his account of Weil's views on the opposition of truth and life, and for his collection of citations on this matter.

5 Simone Weil, *L'enracinement* (Paris: Gallimard 1949), 313–14.

6 Simone Weil, *La pesanteur et la grâce* (Paris: Union Générale d'Éditions 1967), 101.

7 Simone Weil, *Attente de Dieu* (Paris: La Colombe 1950), 163, for example.

8 Ibid.

9 Vetö, *La métaphysique*, 100–1, with his citations.

10 Frédéric Vitoux, *Céline* (Paris: Belfond 1987), 158–9. See also 164–5.

11 CT, 42–44.

12 Ibid., 43.

13 Ibid., 37.

14 Ibid., 49–50.

15 Ibid., 18–25, 29. The point I mention about *Notes from the House of Dead* is different from the one that appears in the edited version.

16 Ibid., 21, 29, 36, 38, 41–42, 43.

17 Ibid., 29, 35, 37, 40–41, 43, 44.

18 Ibid., 36–37, 38–39, 51.

19 Ibid., 42–43, 50–51.

20 Ibid., 50–51.

21 Louis-Ferdinand Céline, *Rigodon*, in *Romans* II (Paris: Gallimard 1986), 731, 1199 (notes); Henri Bergson, *Creative Evolution* (New York: Modern Library 1944), 105–6.

22 Vetö, *La métaphysique*, 95–6; CT, 45.

23 CT, 25–26, 28.

24 Ibid.

25 Ibid., 25–26, 33.

26 Céline, postscript to *Voyage au bout de la nuit*, in *Romans* I, 1113, 1506 (notes).

4

George Grant's Céline: Thoughts on the Relationship of Philosophy and Art

EDWARD ANDREW

THE TENSION BETWEEN PLATO AND CÉLINE IN GRANT

I have been perplexed for more than a decade by George Grant's attraction to Céline's writings. One might say this perplexity is misplaced because attraction to, or repulsion from, a writer is a matter of taste. But such a statement would be entirely alien to Grant, who put forward extravagant claims about the truth as well as the beauty of Céline's work and would have thought that the 'truth' of Céline's trilogy was not subject to the vagaries of personal taste. Perhaps one might even say that Grant shared my perplexity. Of course, there is no doubt that he loved Céline. In her wonderful introduction to Grant's unpublished meditations on Céline's trilogy, Sheila Grant indicates how much enjoyment the trilogy gave Grant in the last decade of his life. George, Sheila, and their dog Arthur – mirroring the triumvirate of the trilogy, Céline, Lili, and the cat Bébert – spent a lot of time talking about Céline, the mysterious fascination of his poetry, and the enigmatic character of his racism, which George Grant thought had exhausted itself by the time Céline wrote his trilogy.[1] A psychological interpretation of Grant's views on Céline might suggest a parallel between the collapse of Grant's Canada and Tory party and the collapse of Céline's world and partisan commitment. Moreover, the trilogy's portrait of a fallen giant on the run might have been appealing to a thinker fleeing McMaster and not fully welcome at Dalhousie, who well remembered the aerial bombing of the Second World War (magically chronicled in *Rigadoon*). But psychological parallels between the Grants (and Arthur the dog), and the Célines (with Bébert), against a hostile world trivialize both the claims Grant makes for *Castle to Castle, North,* and *Rigadoon*[2] and his theory of the relationship between philosophy and art.

Grant's unfinished manuscript on Céline exhibits the mystery, enigma, and self-critical questioning to which Sheila Grant refers. Perhaps Grant was concerned about whether his love of Céline was warranted. But why should one worry about justifying what one loves? Grant was fond of Simone Weil's view that faith is the belief that love illuminates the intelligence. But love, in popular legend, is blind. A blind faith is not fitting for a philosopher, and an intelligent account of the grounds of one's love is incumbent on philosophers. Grant attempted to do just that in 'Céline's Trilogy' as well as in his *Queen's Quarterly* article, 'Céline: Art and Politics.'[3]

Also, followers of Plato, such as Grant, have been taught that beautiful poetic images are subordinate to the good discovered by philosophy. In his reflections on Céline and poetry, Grant writes that he has serious reservations about Plato's views on poetry (CT, 30). The only occasion on which Grant criticized Plato was when he discussed the latter's view of the relationship between poetry and philosophy. The point of my paper will be to reaffirm Plato's teaching against Grant's implicit criticism. Alternatively stated, I will be criticizing, from a Platonic standpoint, Grant's intoxication with Céline.

Plato thought poetry must be subject to the censorial eye of philosophy precisely because poetry is so seductive. Although Plato's assessment of poetry had none of the early church fathers' venom with respect to the seductive charm of women, Plato's *Republic* advocated the censorship of poetry for the very reason that it is so very attractive. Of all things, music and poetry sink most deeply into the human soul, and they have the power to shape conduct and character as do no other stimuli to the senses. Unlike other intoxicants, the effects of poetry do not wear off. I will be arguing that Grant, 'under the influence' of Céline, failed to see some stop signs and indeed ran some red lights.

By stop signs, I mean the indications of Céline's racism, of which Grant was only hazily aware, despite his *Queen's Quarterly* piece, where he refers to Céline's racism. By red lights, I mean not only that Grant was blind to the untruth in the master chronicler but also that Grant did not define what he took to be the truth of Céline's trilogy.

Gerald Owen has brilliantly elucidated Grant's attraction to Céline in terms of the choice of lying and dying, and why living in our graceless and God-forsaken world requires untruth. The impossibility of truth in our world perhaps suggested to Grant an otherworldly truth to anchor our turbulence in this imperfect world. Aside from this theology attributed to Céline, Grant was attracted by Céline's vitality and his willingness to expose himself to the vicissitudes of history, as opposed to writing from the privileged vantage point of a Parisian café (CT, 40–1). Céline wrote from experience, from the peril at the centre of experience. Perhaps that is what Grant meant (CT, 49–50) by Céline's truth being 'the truth of Dasein,' being there at the cutting edge of experience, not from the vantage point of some comfortable academic chair.

Concerning the 'lie or die' dilemma of vitalist philosophy, Nietzsche wrote, 'we possess art lest we perish of the truth.'[4] Nietzsche, like Plato and unlike Grant, held that art and truth were opposites. Heidegger, who shared Grant's view that the notion of an opposition between art and truth was highly questionable, asserted that Nietzsche did not think there was an inherent discordance between poetic art and philosophic truth. The discordance is not between truth and art as such, he claimed, but merely between Platonic 'truth' and art. Plato's true world is 'anaesthetic,' a freezing of the senses by the dead hand of the Good. This eternal, supersensible world is anti-natural, anti-sensual. Platonic dualism deprecates both the natural and the historical worlds as mere appearances. In celebrating art, as opposed to Platonic truth, Nietzsche, according to Heidegger, affirmed the reality or truth of this world, of sensual earthiness given form by the artist.[5] Another, and more obvious, interpretation of Nietzsche's view of the necessity of art, which Heidegger ignored, is that Nietzsche thought life was unbearable without art. According to Nietzsche art is 'life-preserving errors,' and art serves life by enhancing it or by offering an escape from it. Julian Young rightly points out that, for Nietzsche, 'art can only be of service to us by bringing, like religion, hope of another kind of life.'[6] Céline was a devotee of Nietzsche's atheist religion of art. Grant's devotion to artistic beauty, on the other hand, was connected to his 'apprehension of the divine' (CT, 13).

The difference between Plato and Nietzsche is that the former thought the forms by which we live – or which make our lives intelligible and meaningful – are discovered by philosophers, while the latter thought they were created by artists. Nietzsche declared, 'My philosophy *reversed Platonism*: the farther from true beings, the purer, more beautiful, better it is. Life in splendid appearance (*Schein*) as goal.'[7] Art is fabrication,[8] both creation and deception. Nietzsche championed Schein, which means both splendour or brilliance and illusion or deception. Schein is the antithesis of Platonic truth, a celebration of sensuous vitality over supersensible ideas. The triumph of Nietzschean aestheticism over Platonic moralism has been manifest during this century – although, like Grant, contemporary thinkers disavow the Nietzschean opposition between art and truth. Hans-Georg Gadamer, Charles Taylor, and Richard Rorty point out that most contemporaries hold that art, not philosophy, reveals or creates the deepest truths about life.[9] Grant seems close to being a child of his time when he asserts that Céline was unsurpassed in presenting the reality or truth of our time (CT, 28, 49–50).

Grant seems to be a creature of a century that celebrates the victory of the poets over the philosophers. According to Rorty, that victory means that metaphors of creation have supplemented metaphors of discovery. As a Platonist, Grant deprecated talk of 'creativity' (CT, 15) but celebrated an artist, Céline, who prided himself on his novelty and creativity. As a Platonist, Grant rejected Nietzsche's doctrines, however powerful he thought them to be, particularly Nietzsche's doctrine that creators have to be hard, without conscience, beyond good and evil. Fundamental to Nietzsche's inversion of Platonism was his view that a moral person is always uncreative. Reversing Plato's notion of the artist as mimetic, Nietzsche proclaimed, 'The moral man is a lower species than the immoral, but not a type in himself, – a copy, a good copy at best – the measure of his value lies outside him.'[10] Céline, I will argue, was a faithful adherent of Nietzsche's theory of an opposition between creativity and morality.

Céline's immoralism is unproblematic to both Plato and Nietzsche; it is problematic only to those who conflate artistic creativity and moral sensibility. Platonists in short, do not expect moral authority from artists, but non-Platonists often do. For example, George Steiner asserts that Céline presents 'the puzzle of the disassociation between poetic humanism on the one hand and political sadism on the other, or, rather, on their association in a single psyche.'[11] For Platonists there is no inherent connection between poetry and humanism. The connection between Heidegger and Nazism is more problematic for Platonists, but, as Heidegger falls outside the concerns of this paper, let me just suggest here that Heidegger's Nazism, like that of Céline, derived from a Nietzschean conjunction of poetry and philosophy, as distinct from the Platonic disjunction of poetry and philosophy. Philippe Lacoue-Labarthe observes that Heidegger came to 'the definitive revelation that National Socialism (national-Aestheticism) was the truth of the inversion of Platonism.'[12]

George Steiner is troubled, as Grant was, by the conjunction of great art and great evil in Céline, but differs from Grant in asserting that, 'To separate the novels from the prophetic and inflammatory pamphlets is not only dishonest; it is to relinquish any chance of coherent insight into this single and singular personage.'[13] Céline wrote the racist pamphlets in 1937, 1938, and 1941, after his celebrated *Voyage au bout de la nuit* and *Mort à crédit*, and before the postwar trilogy Grant loved. I agree with Ian Noble, who writes that Céline 'cannot be divided into ... convenient compartments' separating 'the good Céline (who wrote the novels) from the bad Céline (who wrote the pamphlets).'[14] First of all, the pamphlets, *Bagatelles pour un massacre*, *L'école des cadavres*, and *Les beaux draps* are between three hundred and five hundred pages long, and thus are as long as Céline's novels. They were published by Denoël and Gallimard, the prestigious publishers of the novels. Secondly, these morally repellent works have been recognized by André Gide and others as creative, stylistic masterpieces.[15] Thirdly, the repulsive racism of the pamphlets, I intend to show, informs Céline's trilogy. I say this not to reduce Céline, the great artist, to the level of a crude propagandist, but to show that great art can conflict with morality. I thus want to confirm Plato's view – at least as it can be applied to Céline – of the tension between poetic intoxication and philosophic reason, between ecstatic delirium and sober restraint. To compartmentalize Céline the racist from Céline the artist is to avoid engagement with what Plato called the enduring strife between philosophy and poetry.

THE PAMPHLETS AND THE TRILOGY

I will attempt to show in this section that Grant was wrong to separate or compartmentalize Céline the racist pamphleteer from Céline the supposed greatest artist of our time, a man who presented the truth of our technological, militarized world as no other person has done. I will not attempt to follow Gide in analyzing the fantastic novelty and consummate artistry of Céline's pamphlets but rather attempt to show that the racial metaphors and delirious hatred of the pamphlets informed the trilogy. I shall thus use material from *Bagatelles pour un massacre, L'école des cadavres* and *Les beaux draps*, as well as from *Castle to Castle, North,* and *Rigadoon*. Grant did not refer extensively to the first three works, and I think it unlikely that he knew them well, for then he would have been more alert to the racist codes of the trilogy.

Grant wrote that *L'école* was 'the most distorting' of the three pamphlets (QQ, 802). I see no basis for Grant's singling out of *L'école*, as all three pamphlets call for the elimination of European Jewry. *L'école* seems to be more preoccupied than the other two works with the Freemasons' alleged part in a global conspiracy. It also includes four photographs, and because a picture is proverbially worth a thousand words, it is worth saying a few words about the photographs. They begin with a fake group portrait purporting to show the first entirely Jewish Soviet commissariat. (We will return to this fake photograph in this essay's account of the mimetic and creative elements in Céline's art.) The second photograph represents some happy French Aryans drinking in a bar, oblivious to the capitalist-communist conspiracy orchestrated by the Jews. The third is of a malnourished black soldier, who represents the 'jewified, negrified but at least optimistic' French army. The fourth is of Lord Castlerosse smiling and leering over drinks and food at Mrs Mark Ostrer. Céline's caption does not assert that Lord Castlerosse is a Jew, but there can be little doubt that he intends his readers to think that Castlerosse's wealth, girth, and prominent nose leave no doubt of his racial origins. Céline's pamphlets frequently make the bizarre allegations that the British House of Lords is dominated by Jews and that wealthy Jews plunder the flesh of beautiful Aryan women.

Céline loved beautiful women, particularly dancers, and his favourite lover, the dancer Elizabeth Craig, left Céline for an American Jew a year before he wrote *Bagetelles*, and two years before *L'école*. In *Bagatelles*, he laments that there are 'no ballerinas for me – only for the Yids' (31) and later asserts that 'Jews are at a premium as spouses in the United States. The Jew is vicious, the Jew is rich, the Jew stuffs himself well. The Jew "negrifies," well below the nigger' (275). In short, there is no basis for Grant's assertion that *L'école* is the most distorting of the pamphlets, except that the fake photographs with misleading captions add a multimedia dimension to Céline's artistry.

Grant wrote that the French government was right to ban *L'école* (QQ, 802). The Blum government took *Bagatelles* and *L'école* off the shelves after the former had tremendous sales for two years, and the latter for one year, sales much brisker than his critically acclaimed *Voyage au bout de la nuit* and *Mort à credit*. Curiously, *Les beaux draps*, published by the Nazified Gallimard press in 1941, was banned by Bernard Payr the German superintendent of the Pétain government, even sooner after its publication. Payr thought that Céline 'always started from correct racial notions' and correctly identified the Jewish-communist enemy, but that his 'savage, filthy slang' and 'brutal obscenities' cancelled out 'the author's good intentions.'[16] The irony is that fascism moved faster to suppress fascist propaganda than did the Popular Front constitutional government that Céline so abhorred.

Grant wrote, 'Even if Céline's plea for peace at all costs between Germany and France was sensible, even if he was correct that the Jews were in favour of war between the two nations, even if he could not be expected to predict what crimes the National Socialists would come to before they were through, it is nevertheless wrong to publish such inflammatory writings against fellow citizens at any time' (QQ, 802). I would have preferred Grant to express these views in the subjunctive mood to reflect Céline's delirious subjectivity, rather than using language that acknowledges the possibility that Céline may have got his facts right. Secondly, I would have preferred Grant to specify which Jews advocated war, rather than referring, as Céline does, to an undifferentiated genus, 'the Jews.' Thirdly, I think that Grant probably did not penetrate the three pamphlets very deeply, because there is nothing that the Nazis did which Céline did not advocate.

Grant separated the pamphlets, which appeared to him morally and legally impermissible, from the novels, in which 'all [Céline's] political passions are long since spent' (CT, 51). Indeed, Grant asserts that 'In the trilogy there is no more savage anti-Semitism. His racism has spread so wide it is diluted into a land of fantasy' (CT, 40). Had Grant read the racist pamphlets, he would have known that Céline's anti-Semitism was spread so wide that it seemed fantastic. Anyone or any group Céline disliked was 'Jewish': all communists are Jews; all capitalist exploiters are Jews; all members of the English and American ruling classes are Jews; all English and American writers are Jews, including 'Lawrence, Huxley, Cohen, Wells, Cahen, Shaw, Faulkner, Passos, etc.' (Bagatelles, 197); the Catholic church, including the papacy, and especially the Jesuit order, is Jewish – 'all evangelists, since Peter through the present pope, passing through Marx, have all been Jews' (L'école, 223); homosexuals are Jewish, Masons are Jewish, blacks and Asians are Jewish, and so on. In Rigadoon Céline (responding to French losses in Vietnam in the 1950s) emphasizes the yellow peril more than the international Jewish conspiracy, but attentive readers know that in Céline's eyes these are two aspects of the same thing. Céline writes 'The nigger Jew is in the process of toppling over the Aryan in communism and robot art to achieve the objectivist mentality of perfect slaves for Jews. (The Jew is a nigger, the semite race does not exist, it is an invention of freemasons, the Jew is only the product of a cross between niggers and asiatic barbarians.)' (Bagatelles, 171).[17]

Thus when Grant says racism in the trilogy is so diluted as to be fantastic, his statement does not exclude the pamphlets that he acknowledges to be savage anti-Semitism. Before writing the pamphlets Céline wrote Mea culpa, an anticommunist book. But it lacked an anti-Semitic angle and thus 'apparently did not fire his linguistic imagination so readily.'[18] The force of Céline's political writing, and the source of his artistic imagination, was race hatred. For the Platonist, the fantastic element of, or the element of fancy in, Céline's art is what distances him from the truth.

Grant wrote that artists 'should be more than usually excused' for their racism because 'western thought and tradition lie in ruins' (QQ, 802). While Grant's explanation of this special dispensation from ordinary morality for artists may be unsatisfactory, he did at least recognize that there was something in Céline that stood in need of an excuse. Blind worshippers of Céline's artistry have accepted Céline's assertion that he had nothing for which to apologize. Dominique de Roux claims that Céline used the word 'Jew' figuratively rather than literally, referring not to a specific race or religion but as a metaphor for what is fearful in all human beings. De Roux writes, 'Such an infinitely tender sensibility as Céline's would never have tolerated the slightest racial persecution because he could not bear pain in others.'[19] In *Bagatelles* (317–19), *L'école* (25, 107–9, 222, 245), and *Les beaux draps* (115–18, 194–7), Céline called for the expulsion or death of all European Jews. He thought that democratic anti-Semitism was unfeasible while Jews controlled the electorate process, and thus averred that 'the only political slogan that matters [is] Votes for the Aryans, Urns for the Jews'[20] (*Les beaux draps*, 194). How de Roux thinks such a statement would not cause pain to others is beyond me; she seems to have the blind faith that artists are incapable of evil. Grant, like de Roux, referred to Céline's tender sensibility but, unlike de Roux, limited Céline's tenderness to people presented in his trilogy: 'The tenderness in his presentation of other people in these last volumes ... seems to me to arise from the recognition of the universal incompleteness and therefore vulnerability, both of flesh and spirit' (CT, 50).

Echoing Nietzsche, Céline declared that Jews should not be condemned as Christ-killers but as Christ-bringers who sought through Christianity to undermine the virile strength of the Aryans (*L'école*, 165, 223, 266; *Les beaux draps*, 80–1). The difference between Nietzsche's and Céline's views of the Jewish genealogy of Christianity is that the former wished to point out the folly of anti-Semitism and the latter wished to kill all Jews. For Céline, Christianity, like Judaism, is internationalist; Jewish-Christianity is antinational in the sense that it promotes revolution and class struggle, which divides nations, and in the sense that it fosters a rootless cosmopolitanism, a transnational identity. Judaism and Christianity have undermined art. Céline wrote, 'Art is only Race and Country. Here is the rock on which to build.' (*Les beaux draps*, 177). Céline begins *Rigadoon* with a reiteration of the theology of his racist pamphlets. The Catholic, Protestant, and Jewish religions are all the same: 'their only real job ... perfect agreement ... is to besot and destroy the white race' (1–2). Céline frequently repeats that 'all soldiers of the Christ child' are intent on mongrelizing 'the white man's blood' (2, 15, 25), the 'Hebrew-Christians' (25) should be called the 'League of Mongrelization' (29) or 'the Chinese in Brest': '... all churches in the same boat ... Demolition and Co. ... Hebraic, Rome, Protestant, *tutti-frutti*' (29).

Céline's equation of Jews and Jesuits is integral to the style as well as the content of the trilogy. Céline stated that his little dots, his 'little music,' were an attempt to put spoken language into writing. Following Nietzsche's view that belief in the order of grammar is belief in God, Céline told Claude Sarraute that 'I'm going to give you a little lecture on French literature – don't get sore. The religions brought us up, the Catholic, Protestant and Jewish ... well, let's say the Christian religions. For centuries French education was directed by Jesuits. They taught us to make sentences translated from the Latin, well balanced, with a subject, a verb, an object and a certain rhythm. In short, a mess of sermons.' In this sermon Céline recognized that sermons get people sore. Céline's style attempted to wash away the baleful effects of the sermonizers on experience. The Jews and the Jesuits, with their moralistic reasoning – Talmudic, Jesuitical – are the hypocrites, those who depurify Aryan experience. We shall come back to Céline's repeated references to 'little Esther Loyola,' Céline's transposition of Anne Frank, who, in Céline's view, raked in millions by faking her diary and death. The name 'Frank' sounds Germanic and bears the connotations of openness, and loyalty. 'Loyola,' Céline's transposition of 'Frank,' has the connotation of a Jesuitical lack of frankness. The unfrank, disloyal Loyolas become Céline's name for Jews. For example, in Céline's transposition of history into the story of 'the Nazi Yids' he excoriates the false dichotomy of 'over here the little Loyolas! ... over there Himmler's paid executioners!' (*North*, 200).

Céline's style is an attempt to purge the moralizing distortions imposed by Jewish-Jesuit moralizing on Aryan experience. The style of the French language has been restrained and made unnatural by Jesuitical experience: 'I come back to my grand battle against the Word. You know, in the Scriptures, it is written: "In the beginning was the Word." No! In the beginning was the emotion.' Emotion and dialectic are enemies. Emotion is the natural gallop of the horse; *logos* is restraint of motion into an artificial trot. Céline held his style to be a breaking free of the artificial restraints of logos. 'Ideas, nothing is more vulgar ... I am not a man of ideas. I am a man of style.'[21] Céline here announces not only an opposition between art and religion but also between art and philosophy. Céline took up cudgels on behalf of poetry in what Plato called the age old strife between poetry and philosophy. That is, Céline's war on Jewish-Jesuit rationalism and moralism was also a war on Platonism.

Céline followed Nietzsche in accepting an opposition between morality and creativity, but gave the Nietzschean antithesis a characteristically racial twist into an opposition between moralistic, Jesuitical Jews and creative Aryans. Jews, Céline averred, are essentially mimetic, incapable of poetry or creative innovation (*Bagatelles*, 192).[22] Communist ideas, however Jewish, were first formulated by Engels and then stolen by Marx. (*L'école*, 113) Because of their lack of taste, style, and creativity, Jews introduced standardization into production and robotic art into culture. Jews have negrified taste, reduced music and poetry to a tom-tom sensibility, transformed style into a standardized mimicry (*Bagatelles*, 188, 194). Jews introduced an alien God and morality into Aryan culture, and 'Thus the sad truth is that the aryan has never known how to love or worship the god of others, never having his own religion, the white religion' (*Les beaux draps*, 81). Jewish-Christian moralism, Céline asserts in *Rigadoon* (1–2, 10, 21–2, 25–6, 29, 183, 207, 216), has kept the white race at a disadvantage in a racist world, leaving Aryans prey to cannibalistic Africans and racist Asians. Aryan art, fuelled by an emotivity not restrained by logos, is the only hope for the white race.

Céline's adversary, Jean-Paul Sartre, who is given a physical description matching Céline's archetypal Jew, is called 'holy Sartre' or 'Jean-Baptiste Sartre,' and a plagiarist.[23] The moral man, as Nietzsche said, is a copy and a copyist. The worst thing a creative artist can say about another worshipper of artistic creativity is to call him a plagiarist. Grant followed Céline in calling Sartre a plagiarist (QQ, 803; CT, 40), although Grant meant a plagiarist of Heidegger and Céline meant a plagiarist of himself. The only time Céline copied anyone in the trilogy was to reproduce the words of René Barjavel – the production manager of Céline's publisher, Robert Denoël – who said that Céline was the only innovator of the twentieth century (*Rigadoon*, 7). Ian Noble states that Céline did not 'admit the extent to which he plagiarized' in *L'école* from anti-Semitic tracts 'or falsified the statistics given in them so as to give even greater 'weight' to the claims made against the Jews.'[24] As a Platonist I am less concerned with Céline as an uncreative copyist or plagiarist than with Céline the creative falsifier of statistics and artistic faker of photographs. If Céline praised the impressionists for painting what the photographer could not represent, Céline's faked photographs perfectly represent the mixture of *mimesis* and creativity that Plato thought was the essence of art. Grant's worship of Céline's poetic transposition – 'to photograph is to putrefy! instantly! ... anything that existed makes you sick to look at! ... therefore transpose! ... poetically if you can!' (CT, 31) – might be assessed in relation to Céline's creative fakery.

Céline's inversion of Platonic logos was a rejection of dialectic or public speech for rapturous reverie. The holy rapture that Nietzsche and Heidegger took to be the source of poetry,[25] was, in Céline's case, wholly rage or unholy rage. His argot was hate-filled words, and his three little dots arose from resentment of the Jewish-Christian moral order built into grammatical structure.

With respect to the hardness of the creator, let us consider Céline's treatment of Anne Frank in *North*. Anne Frank ('Esther Loyola') is the other, the antithesis of Céline. Céline writes, 'little Esther had the whole world with her, we had the whole world against us ... little Esther Loyola made her movie in the attics of Autredam ... nobody asked us to make any movie ... (140). At a later point in the book Céline continues, 'I see little Esther Loyola, with the whole world at her feet, begging her, imploring her, to deign to lie down in a holy chapel ... Hollywood and its millions would do the rest.' Céline states that he and his wife were in hiding like the Frank-Loyola family, 'but it didn't get us anything! hell no! ... neither a chapel nor fancy contracts ... My racial brothers are domestics ... Esther is one of those who give orders ...' (214). Creative cruelty is essential to transpose a dead girl into a live millionaire enviably situated vis-à-vis Céline himself. Little Esther Loyola raked in millions by faking her diary and death while the truthful Céline, and his fellow Nazis, suffered at the hands of Jews. His fellow Nazis are domestics, regularly subject to the orders and dominance of Jews. (The editor of this volume, Art Davis, is witness to my inability to put suitably academic words to Céline's transposition of historical reality.) Céline asserts that, if he had only lowered himself to praise little Esther Loyola, 'I'd have had the Nobel Prize, 'I'd have been rich, everyone would have adored me' (214).

Céline not only blames the victim but denies any victimization of anyone other than himself. After all, the trilogy is the chronicle of 'my disaster' (*Castle to Castle*, v). The dozens of times Céline refers in the trilogy to Joseph Juanovici – a Jew who obtained forged papers establishing his Aryan origins, and profitably produced metal during the occupation while covertly working for the Resistance – indicates that Juanovici was Céline's model of a profiteering Jew during the Nazi occupation. His frequent references to Maurice Sachs – who was persecuted in France and forced to work in a factory in Germany – 'no exception' to Céline's rule of 'Nazi Yid' collaborators, to Pierre Lazareff as 'Petzoreff, the honorary Buchenwald'; to Madeleine Jacob, who 'makes you puke that she should even exist'; to the Baroness de Rothschild dining at the Ritz in Paris with Hermann Goering and 'all the high Nazi dignitaries'; are purported examples of Céline's bizarre view that the Esther Loyolas of this world flourished under Nazi occupation. Céline reports that 'the terrible calamity of the goyim is being such jugheads, such blithering Cartesians' as to think Jews and Nazis are clearly distinct and opposing groups; the reality for the creative artist is that there were plenty of 'Nazi Yids' in close contact with, and working for, Hitler (*North*, 200).

Céline's creative cruelty was directed at all non-Aryan peoples: 'a Gypsy, I hadn't expected that! ... where'd this Gypsy come from? weren't the Gypsies supposed to be eliminated according to the Nuremberg Laws? ... highly contaminating! ... crypto-Asiatics! ... a Gypsy free and shooting the shit! might as well say the war was a waste of time! ... Hitler's New Order, let's not forget, was just as racist as the blacks of Mali or the yellows of Hankow ... we'd see what we'd see! ... luckily, we've seen nothing! ... except Monnerville King of France ... and the Gauls booted out of their supposed Empire! ... everybody can't be a racist ...' (*North*, 199–200). One might read the above as Céline's cynicism and irony about the silly policies of the Nazis, which were just as racist, Céline reminds us, as anyone else's policies, except that Céline does not seem delighted that Gaston Monnerville, a black, was president of the French senate at the time Céline was writing the trilogy. Or one might read Céline as a cynical critic of Hitlerism when he observes Gypsies left alive in Hitler's Germany, 'when according to Nuremberg they're the worst contaminator of races ... worse than the Jews,' except that Céline attempts to hand over the Gypsies to German officials (*North*, 218). Grant wrote, 'Céline does not talk about good and evil, nor does he confuse them. Never does he equate bad action with good' (CT, 52). Celine's reporting on the Gypsies must at least be considered highly irresponsible, comparable to his counsel to Ernst Jünger at the German Institute in December 1941. Jünger wrote of Céline, 'He says how surprised and stupified he is that we soldiers do not shoot, hang, exterminate the Jews – he is stupified that someone availed of a bayonet should not make unrestricted use of it.'[26]

If Grant is at all right about the absence of moral confusion on Céline's part, this absence is exhibited in his consistent lying about his role during the German occupation, whether this lying was consciously meant as a misleading self-justification or 'unconsciously reducing reality, tailoring it to the level of his personal desires and illusions.'[27] After the war Céline could write, *'the Jews should erect a statue to me for the harm I didn't do them and which I could have done them*. They persecute me, I have never persecuted them.'[28] Writing to a friend whose husband had died at Dachau, he briefly commiserated with her and then referred to his own tragedy: 'I'm going to court on March 8. You see Jews can persecute too.'[29] The people who took Céline to court, in fact, were not Jews, but were accused in his anti-Semitic tracts of being Jewish. The total absence of guilt about Jews is attributed by his biographer, Frédéric Vitoux, to 'a lack of imagination.'[30] Vitoux seems to link morality and imagination, moral obtuseness and lack of imagination. For those, like myself, less enraptured by the poetic imagination, Céline's moral blindness may derive from his projective imagination, his fevered and fanciful construction of a world totally unreceptive to the world as it is. Elsewhere Vitoux refers to Céline's tendency to 'enclose himself in his words so as not to see or hear the world, as if to reject it, which is perhaps as it should be with dyed-in-the-wool storytellers.'[31] Céline's storytelling imagination, the direct antithesis of Simone Weil's attention, may be the source of the amoral, solipsistic world he inhabited.

Céline constantly portrayed himself as a mere voyeur in the grand guignol of war, 'a platonic genocide, purely verbal.'[32] Early in *Castle to Castle* Céline writes, 'I've got nothing on my conscience. Except for one thing ... that I never ask for money! ... I've hurt my reputation more by never taking a cent from my patients than Pétiot did by cooking them in the oven!' Céline contrasts himself, who never got a cent for attacking Jews during the war, and thus has nothing on his conscience concerning Jews and ovens, with another doctor, who pretended to protect Jews for money during the war while in fact murdering them. Later in the novel Céline writes 'that I deserved to be put in cold mud for *Bagatelles*,' and that the other war criminals at Sigmaringen felt relieved that Céline, who deserved to be hanged before the rest of them, kept them some distance from the gallows (251). In *North*, Céline records the last moments of a fellow fascist propagandist: 'Hérold Paqui weeping with rage on his way to be hanged ... "they haven't shot Céline!" ... he'd have died happy' (409). Céline's fellow Nazis, then, did not agree that Céline had nothing on his conscience, nor would they have agreed with Grant's assessment, shared by the tribunal that overturned Céline's conviction as a war criminal, that artists 'should be more than usually excused.' In *Rigadoon*, Céline laments that France won't welcome home a hard-working stiff like himself when Israel welcomes its brethren home 'all so persecuted, tongues hanging out, heroes of labor, of deforestation, of the hammer, bank, and sickle' (246). Of course, Céline means that Jewish exploiters have never worked or been persecuted. By 'the hammer, bank, and sickle,' Céline is reaffirming his position in *Bagatelles*, *L'école*, and *Les beaux draps* that a capitalist-communist conspiracy, of the Rothschilds and the Trotskys, of idle rich degenerates, continued to suck the life blood from poor, hard-working Aryans. Céline needed a fictive enemy to be able to write as one of life's losers and to fuel the rage animating his creative poetry.

To summarize this section, I have attempted to show that one cannot separate Céline the racist pamphleteer from Céline the consummate artist. The anti-Semitic, and diffusely racist, views of the pamphlets inform the style and content of the trilogy. Grant thought the pamphlets were rightly suppressed under the circumstances in which they appeared. I do not think Céline's trilogy should be suppressed, but I do think *Castle to Castle*, *North* and *Rigadoon* are more morally unacceptable than *Bagatelles*, *L'école*, and *Les beaux draps*, because the former were written after the Holocaust and the latter before, because the Holocaust-denying message is untrue, and because the racist, Nazi doctrines of the trilogy are unworthy, however artfully they are portrayed. I distinguish between the legal impermissibility and moral impermissibility of the trilogy not because I share Grant's view – and that of the tribunal that overturned Céline's conviction – that artists 'should be more than usually excused,' but because I subscribe to the Millian view that works with no truth or goodness in them should be publicly accessible, if only to expose as false the contemporary prejudice in favour of artist-worship.

Grant compared Céline to other notable anti-Semites such as Dostoyevsky, Frege, and Degas, but did not make his comparison in terms of whether their anti-Semitism intruded on their work. Grant observed that 'Degas' painting has not been excluded from the canon because he was anti-Jewish' (QQ, 802). If Grant's analogy were valid, Degas would remain in the canon even if all his dancers were being fingered by men with monstrously distorted hooked noses and circumcised fingers, and Frege's reputation would be unimpaired even if he could not, because of an uncertainty about the humanity of the Jews, distinguish the logical form of 'all men are mortal' from 'some men are mortal.' As far as I am aware, anti-Semitism did not distort either Degas's art or Frege's logic, but it was central to the style and substance of Céline's trilogy.

GRANT ON POETRY AND TRUTH

In the previous section I attempted to establish that Grant did not see the anti-Jewish elements in Céline's trilogy and thus was able to erect barriers between the reprehensible racist pamphlets and the consummate artistry of the chronicles. In North, Céline referred to the last of the pamphlets as 'simply a chronicle of the times' (236). I think if Grant had had greater familiarity with the pamphlets he might have recognized the enduring anti-Jewish dimension of the chronicles. Had he done so, the Platonist in Grant might have questioned whether Céline deserved to be called the truth-teller of our times. But these remarks concern detailed interpretation of the trilogy, and in this section I propose to examine Grant's general account of storytelling and poetry.

The difference between Grant and Plato would seem to be that the former thought reason and imagination to be in harmony, while the latter thought them to be in discord. Plato did not believe beautiful poetic images were true, while Grant claimed they were. My guiding question, in my examination of Grant's view of art and poetry – or, as he would have it, of great art and great poetry – is, in what sense are enrapturing or intoxicating stories true?

Grant asserts in 'Céline's Trilogy' that ordinary works of art distort reality, as both Plato and Bacon thought, but that great works of art present (in Shakespeare's words) 'the thing itself,' or (in

Luther's words) 'the thing ... as it is.' Grant says that much of his life has been spent reading trash, which he likens to 'drugs' or to 'the mirror of the Lady of Shalott, confining one's experience to a safe and dreamlike vision. But great literary works are the very smashing of the mirror, the restoration to reality' (CT, 17). Grant is here denying that his enrapturement with Céline was, as I have intimated, a drugged intoxication, that the mirror Céline's art held up to him was narcissistic, and that Céline's art was a 'dreamlike vision,' however unsafe that delirious vision was. Great art bridges the distinction between art and nature; as Shakespeare said, '"The art itself is nature" (CT, 33). 'The essence of great art,' according to Grant, 'is to show truth about reality' (CT, 37). One might wonder whether 'truth about reality' is different from 'truth' or 'reality.' Does Grant mean more than 'the essence of art is to reveal reality'? Céline's trilogy is 'the supreme account of *the truth* about technological war, *from the point of view* of the losers who are suffering it' (CT, 37 [my emphasis]). Grant here does not seem to oppose, as Plato did, truth to opinion or perspective, reality to appearance. Truth, the thing itself, or the thing as it is, is traditionally juxtaposed to personal perspective or point of view, but Grant merges truth with the losers' point of view. The truth Céline revealed to Grant was not 'objective' truth but 'subjective' truth. Céline, as a modern artist, reveals the truth of 'subjectivity' (CT, 42–3), whereas both Sophocles and Plato are 'wonderfully unpresent' in their works (CT, 43). Grant does not know whether 'Céline's subjectivity is like everyone else's, but it is like mine' (CT, 43–4). Despite this scepticism, Grant asserts that Céline presents 'what human beings are like always and everywhere,' particularly with respect to their imperfection or incompletion (CT, 50). Céline thus demonstrates the truth about fallen human nature, the reality that human beings stand in need of redemption. (Of course, Jews do not emphasize the Fall as Christians do, because they do not think humanity needs the Christian redeemer – or, indeed, the very unChristian redeemer of Céline and Heidegger.)

Grant not only tries to tell us why he finds Céline enrapturing but also why stories have always enraptured him. The child's hunger for stories, Grant implies, is not a hunger for truth. 'Telling stories' is lying, as when Grant's nanny told him not to tell her a story about his disposal of some unappetizing turnips down a toilet (CT, 19). But when he asked his nanny to tell him a story he 'did not mean lies' (CT, 19). He meant something akin to what Céline meant by transposition 'into the realm of reverie, between true and not true' (CT, 32). This realm of reverie, between true and not true, is what Plato deprecated as a world of appearances and what Nietzsche championed, against Plato, as Schein.

Grant, referring to his childlike infatuation with stories, says: 'although my elders emphasized the lack of factual basis in a story, I could not realize this, because for the young child the factual basis or its absence is irrelevant to the richness of the experience' (CT, 19). Grant, as noted, did not perceive the Holocaust-denying message of the trilogy. I risk appearing as a moralistic nanny, or as the Duchess in *Alice in Wonderland*, when I ask whether the absence of a factual basis for Céline's story detracts from its richness. Or, to use examples of what most moved him in *Rigadoon*, would Grant have remained as enraptured with Céline's story about the rescue of the retarded children if he had known that it had no factual basis? If Grant had known that Céline invented the account of being hit on the head with a brick, and then having the hallucination of aerial bombing as *son et lumière* – which is indeed magically transposed – would he still have maintained not only that Céline's words conveyed the supreme truth of an experience of aerial bombing and also an 'utterly convincing' detailed description of 'our sensations 25 years later' (CT, 41)? Sober addition, rather than trust in Céline's 'art of total recall' (CT, 30), would have revealed to Grant that Céline had been dead for almost a decade on the twenty-fifth anniversary of the Hanover air raid of 1944. Stories are in some sense fictions, and in some sense faithful reality.

Grant is clear that storytellers are not historians, who are constrained by the facts. Although few historians would accept Grant's (and Ranke's) conception of history as 'objective' (CT, 23), they would accept his view that the historian's 'imagination must be more strictly controlled' than that of a novelist or a storyteller (CT, 23). A novelist's imagination is freer than a storyteller's, Grant tells us, because 'in the story the imagination is linked in a more dependent embrace with particular memories' (CT, 22). Stories, it would seem, stand midway between histories and novels. A novelist's imagination invents a world, whereas a chronicler gleans his material from a world remembered. The storyteller's prodigality depends on 'the art of total recall.'

A great storyteller must be egocentric, but more than egocentric. I agree with Grant that Proust's self-absorption is hard to take, while his characterizations of M. de Charlus and Mme Verdurin are fascinating (CT, 43). Grant did not see Céline's trilogy as a 'me-me chronicle' because of the prodigality of Céline's depiction of others. Yet I cannot get a sense of any character besides Céline himself in his trilogy, as I can in *A la recherche du temps perdu*. I can say little about his friend Le Vigan. He is an actor, and thus vain and inconsistent, without a centre or character to determine his roles or personae. Lili is a dancer of great grace and agility, but I get little sense of her inner life. Céline was infatuated with a series of dancers; the name Lili derived from Elizabeth Craig, the dancer who left him before he wrote *Bagatelles,* but referred in the trilogy to his wife Lucette, another dancer whom he married during the war. In the trilogy, Lili is the name of a graceful dancer and a faithful companion but we learn little of her as an individual. Of Céline's relationship to his recently married wife called by the nickname of his old lover, Grant wrote, 'This is one of the greatest accounts of an absolute marriage ever written. Yet nothing is said of it.' (CT, 35). Because Céline said nothing of it, perhaps Grant's imagination was able to project the qualities of grace in his own wife, and the qualities of his own marriage, onto the unstated 'absolute marriage' of Céline.

Grant's strongest attack is directed at Francis Bacon and at Bacon's view that imagination is distinct from reason, that poetry is distinct from knowledge, and that feigned history is distinct from true history. 'One can imagine how Céline would laugh to scorn the idea of his chronicle as "feigned history"' (CT, 46). Bacon might well have replied that one can imagine anything one likes, but truth requires some evidence to support one's imaginings or to refute the view that Céline's chronicle is feigned. Grant supports Coleridge's belief that imagination harmonizes what the Platonist opposes – reality and appearance, the idea and the image, the general and the particular, the similar and the different, reason and sense, nature and art, substance and style (CT, 47). Unlike Bacon, Nietzsche, and Plato, 'Coleridge does not see "poesy" or imagination as a fanciful escape from the nature of things, but rather as an exploration of reality' (CT, 47–8). Céline, on the other hand, proclaims in his epigraph to *Féerie pour une autre fois,* 'I loathe realities ... Down with any form of reality!'[33]

In attacking Bacon with the assistance of the romantic poets

Blake and Coleridge, Grant suggests an alliance between ancient thought, the Christian religion, and modern art against modern science and technology, the offspring of Baconian philosophy. In portraying ancient thought and modern poetry as spiritual allies in the war against spiritless technology and its domination of the globe, Grant had to face the problem that it was not just Bacon but also Plato – and indeed most philosophers – who distinguished reason from imagination, reality from fancy. Indeed, if Grant thought imagination gives us access to reality, one wonders why he thought the chronicler's imagination, as distinct from that of the novelist or poet, is constrained by his memory of actual events.

Toward the end of his life Céline told some stories about his childhood to his first wife, Edith (his second wife, if one counts his marriage to Suzanne Nebout, which was never registered in France).[34] Edith was shocked at the unreality of Céline's stories of his childhood and asked Céline to recollect to whom he was talking. After a startled silence, Céline excused himself with the statement, 'A writer has to invent his biography.'[35] Céline's storytelling may have been fascinating, enthralling, enrapturing, but may not have been a truthful chronicle of actual events.

Grant loved the musical qualities of Céline's writing, especially his transposition of the Hanover bombing into music (CT, 48). In my opinion, the narration of the bombing is the most impressive part of Céline's writing. I also love the rhythmic qualities of Wordsworth and Yeats, but I do not hold their musical poetry to be true as well as beautiful. Indeed, I cannot understand what touches me deeply in some of Yeats's poems, or why I see beauty in poems of his where I find the message to be stupid or silly. The silliness of Yeats's gyres and spooky memories does not prevent my getting goose-pimples on hearing 'hollow lands, and hilly lands,' any more than the silliness of the plot of The Magic Flute prevents my being enchanted by Mozart's music. In short, as I do not call the beautiful passages in Wordsworth, Yeats, or Mozart true, I have difficulty understanding what Grant calls the truth in Céline's virtuosity, the reality in his consummate artistry.

Grant, then, differed from Plato in holding poetic imagination to be at one with philosophic truth. He also appeared to welcome the Nietzschean liberation of art from the yoke of the Platonic good ('the best stories were those told with no didactic purpose') (CT,

20). Grant seems close to a position of 'art for art's sake,' or to the Kantian view of the purposeless purposiveness of art ('the greatest stories have no point except they are enrapturing') (CT, 21). While great art has no purpose beyond itself, 'at the same time we must also say, always with the greatest hesitation and bewilderment, that it points beyond itself' (CT, 21). Perhaps Céline's portrayal of a mad, God-forsaken world, and the imperfect creatures inhabiting it, pointed (for Grant) to another world. Grant was aware how ridiculous Céline would have thought such an interpretation of the trilogy was.

To summarize, Grant held Céline's trilogy to be beautiful, and hence true and ultimately edifying. The truth of Céline's trilogy is not the truth of Platonic *theōria*, a discovery by dialectic or philosophic conversation of a moral order not fabricated by art. It is not the truth of the natural or social scientist, with his or her rules of evidence and verification, nor is it the truth of the logician, for whom internal consistency, rather than correspondence to external fact, is the standard of truth. Céline's chronicles are not true in any sense that a historian would hold true. Céline's truth is the truth of Dasein (CT, 50). This reference to Heideggerian truth has the obscurity of Heidegger's Black Forest. But Grant was more critical, sceptical, and self conscious than Heidegger; he was honest enough to consider the possibility that the 'truth' of Céline's trilogy is that 'he feeds my prejudices' (CT, 39).

PLATO'S VIEW OF POETS

The epigraph of William Christian's biography of Grant – Wilfrid Owen's idealistic assertion that 'true poets must all be truthful' – is well chosen. One might think that Owen enjoins on poets a duty of truthfulness in that poets are not naturally inclined to truth. Grant did not see, as Plato and Nietzsche did, a tension or conflict between truth and poetry. Certainly Christian did not intend to deprecate the philosopher when he emphasized that Grant had 'a poet's imagination' and 'was as far from the bloodless rationalist as it is possible to be.'[36] In our artist-worshipping times, few readers of Christian's fine biography would hold that assessment to be insulting, or think it calls into question Grant's love of truth. Yet Plato thought poetic imagination diverges from philosophic truth. Grant's intoxication with Céline, I have been arguing, perhaps warrants an unfashionable reconsideration of the timely and timeless truth of Plato's view of poets.

Plato deprecated poetry because it appealed not to rational judgment to the irrational (lower) part of the soul, to the passions and the senses. Grant, as a believer in the Christian passion, could not unequivocally champion Platonic reason over passion. Yet Céline's poetry is a clear example of Plato's position. Céline's metaphorics of race, forged in ovens of molten hatred, highlights the tension between poetry and morality, between ecstatic delirium and sober restraint. Grant recognized that hatred is present in Céline's trilogy, but seemed to hold that it does not intrude into his art (CT, 40). Indeed, Grant emphasized the love, not the hate, in Céline's work, or at least the love that was present in the most moving passages (CT, 51). The lovableness of Céline in the trilogy, and Céline's artful ability to capture human nature, depend on 'the interdependence of knowing and loving,' as 'a follower of Plato' – Grant meant Simone Weil – had taught (CT, 37): 'One might wish that Bacon and Darwin had learned this' (CT, 37).

Where Grant and I differ is that he believed Céline's hatred was extraneous to his art, while I believe that it was both the matter and the motive of his art. Céline wrote of his argot-filled novels that 'it is hate which makes argot. Argot is made to express true sentiments of misery.'[37] I do not wish to deny that Céline was a great poet or to claim that his writings are crude propaganda and hence not art. That is, I do not wish to deny the tension between poetry and philosophy by asserting that Céline was not a true poet. It is precisely because Céline was a poet, and not just a racist propagandist, that Plato's views on poetry deserve thoughtful consideration, not the widespread condemnation characteristic of our times.

As for hatred being the matter and energy of Céline's art, Henry Miller commended Céline's unsurpassable artistry to Lawrence Durrell in 1947 with the following remarks: 'Magnificent. Ferocious. Still the best writer alive today, I do think. After they lick the Axis Powers they will have to lick Céline, it seems to me. He's got more dynamite in him than Hitler ever had. It's permanent hatred – for the whole human species. But what merrymaking.'[38] Miller, I think, understood better than Grant the source of Céline's creativity. Although Miller may have been a stupid man, he was also a writer of 'genius,' a creative artist. Miller's art usually rode on the electricity of his vibrant penis, but in one of my favourite short stories, 'The Staff of Life,' he employed Céline-like hatred against the odious American production of bread for toasters, which was a metaphor for all the world's troubles. Industrialists who read Miller's story will probably be offended by it, just as Jews are offended by Céline's writings. But whereas Miller and most of his readers are aware of the boundaries between reality and fantasy, Céline was unaware, when writing about Jews, of those boundaries.

If Plato thought enchanting poetry appealed to base passion, he also thought its power and danger lay in its reliance on sensible images rather than rational ideas. The artist conveys his or her ideas by using sensible images or metaphors. Metaphors are the stuff of poetry (CT, 49), not of philosophy. Whatever 'truth' Céline created is metaphorical, 'transposed' from the mundane world in which we live and communicate with one another.

Archibald MacLeish's poem 'Metaphor' reveals the 'truths' poets create:

When sensuous poets, in their pride invent
Emblems for the soul's content
That speak the meaning men will never know
But man-imagined images can show.[39]

MacLeish's poem illuminates Plato's allegory of the cave. The puppeteers of Plato's cave (the poets) hold forth artificial objects ('man-imagined images') before the fire, which cast shadows onto the walls of the cave and hold us enthralled. Because we can never leave the cave and discover 'the meaning men will never know,' we are contented with the sensuous images projected by the inventive poets. The world outside the cave is what is discovered by philosophers after disciplined training in the specialized sciences. Within the cave, art wins the soul's consent and nurtures the soul on artificial food.

To be sure, philosophers employ sensuous images or metaphors when they make philosophic arguments. We have only to think of Hobbes's image of Leviathan, an artificial man made by, and of, real men. Or we might think of Plato's myths of Er and of the metals, not to mention the allegory of the cave. The standard dodge of modern critics is to call Plato a poet, despite Plato's views on the distance and strife between philosophy and poetry.[40] The difference between poets and philosophers – and between unphilosophic poets such as Céline and more philosophic poets such as Shakespeare, Hölderlin, and Proust – is that a philosopher can provide a logos, a rational account of what is metaphorically present in a poetic image. Both before and after the myth of the metals, Plato reveals the tension between nature and nurture in education, opening our minds to a range of possible sources of character and intellect, and inviting us to thoughtful questioning. The allegory of the cave is preceded by a rational account of the objectives of education and the arduous process of becoming educated, and is followed by a lengthy rational exegesis of the allegory. The myth of Er is not subject to a lengthy rational account in the *Republic*. Interested readers, however, can consult the *Meno*, the *Crito*, and the *Phaedo* for a logos of the *mythos* of Er. Grant states that 'Plato called some of his most wonderful writing a likely tale,' but does not elaborate on the educative purpose of myths, the need to present philosophic teaching in sensible form to non-philosophers (CT, 14). Above all, according to Grant, Plato did not mention something that I think is crucial – that philosophers provide a rational account of the myths and metaphors they employ, and poets do not.

Céline's metaphors are not subject to rational assessment. In a 1960 interview, published in *Castle to Castle*, Céline stated that 'experience is a muffled lantern that throws light only on the bearer ... it's incommunicable ... better keep things to myself' (xix). To Grant's delight, Céline did not practise what he preached. Moreover, Grant denied that Céline's art 'throws light only on the bearer,' namely, Céline himself. In another interview Céline said emotion is what he intended to convey in his art: 'In the beginning was emotion, not in the beginning was the Word' (vi). In 'Ma grande attaque contre le Verbe,' Céline championed emotion against the scriptural and Platonic primacy of logos.[41]

Plato thought artists appealed to the irrational part of the soul and were incapable of giving a rational account of the metaphors they employed. Céline's central metaphor was the metaphor of the Jews who, he opined, 'are the born enemies of Aryan emotivity' (*Bagatelles*, 171). Jewish rationalism and moralism, he said, are the enemies of creative art; Céline's poetic metaphors are not designed to encourage debate or rational argument. One would hardly expect to debate with Céline the ideas contained in his metaphor of the Jew – the mongrelization bred by the rootless cosmopolitan, the levelling of racial cultures by world communism, the standardization and robot art encouraged by a race devoid of Aryan emotion and creativity. Here I just wish to distinguish between Plato's metaphors and those of Céline, between philosophic truth and poetic or metaphorical 'truth.' The philosopher uses metaphors to illustrate and accompany rational argument; the unphilosophic poet repudiates logos in favour of fabrication (both in the sense of creative making and in the sense of illusion or deception). *Poïesis* meant producing or making. The English words 'forging' or 'fabricating' capture the Platonic sense of lying inherent in poetic creation, in imagination undisciplined by dialectic.

Céline's transposition 'into the realm of reveries, between the true and not true' describes Plato's cave, the realm of shadowy appearances cast by the poets who present their fabricated images before the fire of desire. The fabrication of the puppets, or the poets' creations, are governed by the response of the audience in chains to the enrapturing shadowy images. (In Céline's case, the marketability of poetic images governs the process of poetic production; that is, the positive response to the hook-nosed images Céline offered his readers was oxygen to the molten hatred in which he forged and fabricated the products of his poetic imagination.) Whereas Plato sought to transpose shadowy, evanescent, and idiosyncratic opinions (between the true and the not true) into the sunlit public world of logos (where truth is the satisfactory culmination of a philosophic discussion), Céline aimed to reverse Platonism by repudiating logos, and thus to capture emotion in rapturous revery. Because the public world of speech was, for Céline, like Heidegger's public world of inauthenticity and idle chatter, Céline attempted to retire from the community of logos into the private realm of reverie and intimate emotion.

Stanley Rosen asserts that Heidegger is a bad poet and Plato a good one, but he is not clear about the criteria for distinguishing good from bad poets. He seems to agree with Grant that 'in the last analysis, there is no quarrel between philosophy and poetry.'[42] I would say that Plato is a poetic philosopher because he provides rational accounts to support his poetic images, whereas Heidegger is a mere philosophic poet because he does not offer rational arguments to support his revelations of Being. Where I would support Rosen against Grant is in Rosen's statement that 'if I cannot distinguish between reason and the imagination, then philosophy is impossible.'[43]

In this essay I have referred to Plato's opposition to the immoral teaching of creative artists, and have made use of the Nietzschean idea of an opposition between creativity and morality. In book 10 of Plato's *Republic*, however, Socrates argues that artists and poets are mimetic, that they are imitative rather than creative. The mimetic model breaks down, though, when Socrates says poets are rivals with philosophers in representing the invisible world, a world that poets cannot mirror or reproduce in their art. The difference is that poets imagine stories of the gods and the afterlife, or create enrapturing images, whereas philosophers discover ideas or forms not of their own making, through a cooperative or dialogic exercise of reasoned speech, not through solitary reveries or imaginative projections.

Céline's fake photographs provide a concrete example of what Plato meant by an artistic image, partially mimetic and partially creative. The question is, can Céline's trilogy be described as a fake photograph, partly dependent on the author's photographic memory – what Grant called Céline's 'art of total recall' – and partly on creative additions forged in his fiery imagination?

In Platonic philosophy, poiēsis as fabrication, as creative lying, as art and artifice, stands opposed to theōria, detached contemplation of a natural order. Céline presented himself as a theōros, a mere voyeur in the grand guignol of life, a merely 'platonic genocide' – that is, not a practitioner of genocide – but this self-presentation was the only Platonic dimension of Céline's poetry. In his battle against modern technology, Grant attempted to unite Céline and Plato, modern poiēsis and ancient theōria, in Christian marriage. However lofty the aim, the union appears to me to have been a shotgun wedding, but one without the prospect of offspring.

NOTES

1 George Grant, 'Celine's Trilogy' (this volume), 40, 51. Subsequent page references will use the abbreviation CT and will be enclosed in parentheses in the text.

2 I have used the Ralph Manheim translations of *Castle to Castle* (London: Anthony Blond 1969), *North* (New York: Delacorte 1972), and *Rigadoon* (New York: Delacorte 1974).

3 George Grant, 'Céline: Art and Politics,' *Queen's Quarterly* 90 (1983),

801–13. Subsequent page references will use the abbreviation *QQ* and will be enclosed in parentheses in the text.

4 Friedrich Nietzsche, *The Will to Power*, trans. W. Kaufmann (New York: Vintage 1968), 435.

5 Martin Heidegger, *Nietzsche*, vol. 1, trans. D.F. Krell (San Francisco: Harper and Row 1979).

6 Julian Young, *Nietzsche's Philosophy of Art* (Cambridge, England: Cambridge University Press 1992), 37.

7 Friedrich Nietzsche, *Gesammelte Werke* (München: Musarion Verlag 1920), 3: 318.

8 During his early years as a philosopher, when he was under the spell of Richard Wagner, Nietzsche celebrated the creative artist, but in his middle period he turned to positivism and scientism. When he reached maturity as a philosopher, positivism and scientism evaporated and were replaced by support for the poet-philosopher, the philosopher who seeks to become master of the earth by taking on the creativity of the artist. See Young, *Nietzsche's Philosophy of Art*, 148.

9 Hans-Georg Gadamer, *Dialogue and Dialectic: Eight Hermeneutical Studies of Plato* (New Haven: Yale University Press 1980), 59; Charles Taylor, *The Malaise of Modernity* (Toronto: Anansi 1991), 62; Richard Rorty, *Contingency, Irony and Solidarity* (Cambridge, England: Cambridge University Press 1989), xvi, 3, 40.

10 Nietzsche, *The Will to Power*, 205–6.

11 George Steiner, 'Cry Havoc,' in W.K. Buckley, ed., *Critical Essays on Louis-Ferdinand Céline* (Boston: G.K. Hall 1989), 203.

12 Philippe Lacoue-Labarthe, *Heidegger, Art and Politics: The Fiction of the Political*, trans. C. Turner (Oxford: Blackwell 1990), 86.

13 Steiner, 'Cry Havoc,' 201.

14 Ian Noble, *Language and Narration in Céline's Writings: The Challenge of Disorder* (Atlantic Highlands, NJ: Humanities Press 1987), 167.

15 André Gide, 'The Jews, Céline and Maritain,' and Merlin Thomas, 'Remarks on *Bagatelles pour un massacre*,' in Buckley, ed., *Critical Essays on Louis-Ferdinand Céline*, 195–7 and 226–42, respectively.

16 Pierre Assouline, *Gaston Gallimard: A Half Century of French Publishing*, trans. H.J. Salemson (New York: Harcourt Brace Jovanovich 1988), 277.

17 For other statements that Jews are mongrel crossings of Asiatics and Africans see *L'école*, 215, 227, 284; *Les beaux draps*, 196.

18 Noble, *Language and Narration in Céline's Writings*, 168.

19 Dominique de Roux, *La mort de L.-F. Céline* (Paris: Bourgois 1966) 92–3.

20 'Urnes' means ballot boxes as well as funeral urns.

21 Louis-Ferdinand Céline, *Le style contre les idées* (Paris: Gallimard 1987), 67.

22 Ronnie Beiner has pointed out to me that Nietzsche, despite his gener-
    ally philo-Semitic stance, was not above referring to Jews as a mimetic,
    uncreative people. See Nietzsche's letter to P. Gast of 31 May, 1888 in
    Selected Letters, ed. C. Middleton (Chicago: University of Chicago Press
    1969), 297–8.

23 Céline, *Le style contre les idées*, 135–42; *Castle to Castle*, 338.

24 Noble, *Language and Narration in Céline's Writings*, 184.

25 Heidegger, *Nietzsche*, Vol. 1: 92–123.

26 Frédéric Vitoux, *Céline: A Biography*, trans. J. Browner (New York:
    Paragon House 1992), 378.

27 Ibid., 460–1.

28 Ibid., 461.

29 Ibid., 331.

30 Ibid., 435.

31 Ibid., 148.

32 Céline, 'Entretien avec Albert Zbinden,' in *Romans* (Paris: Gallimard
    1974), 2: 944.

33 Quoted in Vitoux, *Céline*, 530.

34 Céline married Édith Follet in August of 1919. She divorced him in
    June of 1926, obtaining custody of their daughter, Colette. She was his
    second wife, but was sometimes thought his first, because his actual
    first marriage was a lightning one to Nebout, a dancer, in 1916 in
    London, apparently undertaken to help both parties with immigration
    problems. During the years from 1926 to 1933 Céline developed a deep
    and personal intimacy with Elizabeth Craig, an American dancer, to
    whom he dedicated the *Voyage*. He met Lucette Almansor, also a
    dancer, in 1935 and lived with her from 1936 until his death in 1961.
    They were married officially in August of 1942.

35 Quoted in Vitoux, *Céline*, 549.

36 William Christian, *George Grant: A Biography* (Toronto: University of
    Toronto Press 1993), xix.

37 Céline, *Le style contre les idées*, 144.

38 Lawrence Durrell and Henry Miller, *A Private Correspondence*, ed. G.
    Wickes (London: Faber and Faber 1963), 176–7.

39 Archibald MacLeish, *The Human Season: Selected Poems 1926–72* (Boston:
    Houghton Mifflin 1972), 135.

40 See Stanley Rosen, *The Question of Being: A Reversal of Heidegger* (New
    Haven: Yale University Press 1993); *The Quarrel between Philosophy and
    Poetry* (New York: Routledge, Chapman and Hall 1988).

41 Céline, *Le style contre les idées*, 67.
42 Rosen, *The Quarrel between Philosophy and Poetry*, 26.
43 Rosen, *The Question of Being*, 43.

PHILOSOPHY

5

George Grant, Nietzsche, and the Problem of a Post-Christian Theism

RONALD BEINER

Why would a quasi-Christian quasi-Platonist like George Grant want to have any truck with militant anti-Platonists like Nietzsche and Heidegger? Grant himself gave a full response to this question, and his remarks are worth quoting at length:

Nietzsche and Heidegger are those who have thought through most clearly what is happening in modernity, and thought it within the acceptance of the basic assumptions of that modernity. The negative side of that thinking-through is their assessment of what is wrong about Christianity and Platonism – why human beings thought they were true in the past, but why no sane person should do so now. Somebody such as myself, inescapably bound to Christianity, must try to understand what it is to think at a superlative level, with Christianity put aside root and branch.[1]

Why they need to be read is that they are the two thinkers who have most completely thought through the modern western project from within it. To use Marxian language, they are the modern project conscious of itself. As it seems to me that the great task of philosophy now is to think through the modern project to its fundamental assumptions, then we must study those thinkers who can help us.[2]

Surprisingly, given Grant's emphasis on the importance of a philosophic encounter with those towering thinkers of modernity,

Grant's published writings on Nietzsche[3] offer little in the way of a sustained engagement with Nietzsche's texts. Rather, they consist mainly of what one might call 'cultural polemics,' a form of writing at which Grant so clearly excelled. But for all their rhetorical power, they fall well short of a distinctively Grantian reading of Nietzsche. Grant merely puts together Strauss's image of Nietzsche as a radical historicist with Heidegger's image of Nietzsche as the arch-philosopher of technological mastery. Somewhat more helpful are the lectures on Nietzsche delivered by Grant in 1969–70 and 1974–5, which offer a basis for constructing a theoretical dialogue between Grant and Nietzsche.[4]

NIETZSCHEAN MODERNITY

For Grant, Nietzsche is the supreme thinker of radical modernity. What does modernity mean for Grant? No account of modernity can overlook the following basic characteristics: first, a privileging of the future over the past; secondly, an affirmation of technology and of mastery over nature; thirdly, an affirmation of radical freedom (affirming that which is posited by human creativity as opposed to deferring to what is already given); fourthly, an acceptance of cosmopolitan deracination, that is, of the dissolution of particularistic communities of experience necessary for genuine human rootedness; and, most important of all (certainly for Grant), an affirmation of secularism and liberation from the (obedience-demanding) claims of the transhuman. These form the core constituents of the master-ideology of modernity, of which liberalism and Marxism represent mere ideological offshoots. Now it is certainly true that each of these five characteristics applies in some measure to Nietzsche, but none of them applies to him unreservedly. The more closely one examines Nietzsche's thought under each of these five rubrics, the more one has reason to qualify Grant's description of Nietzsche's position as unambiguously modern. Grant makes a less than generous effort to do justice to the complexities of Nietzsche's position. In fairness to Nietzsche, and in the service of a more serious Grant-Nietzsche dialogue than Grant himself ever undertakes in his writings and lectures, I want to spend the rest of this essay looking at various Nietzschean texts, with the intention of beginning the task of attending to some of these complexities.

Nietzsche's Anticonservatism

In one of his notebooks Grant alludes to the important section in *Twilight of the Idols* ('Skirmishes of an Untimely Man,' §43) in which Nietzsche thoroughly rejects conservatism of any kind: 'Nietzsche [believed] that all political reactions or conservatisms were futile. All merely backward-looking positions are doomed, according to Nietzsche.'[5] This is indeed central to what defines Nietzsche's modernity: one must go *forward*. Our situation, however grim, can only be resolved by being pushed in a more radical direction. This applies especially to Nietzsche's diagnosis of 'the death of God': there is no turning back.[6] But does Grant actually disagree here? If the death of God means the open acknowledgment that the cultural energies of Christianity within the civilization of the West have irreparably exhausted themselves, then Grant surely *agrees* with Nietzsche that God is truly dead in this sense. He takes Nietzsche's slogan to be a true description of our situation in the contemporary world. In another significant entry in one of his notebooks, Grant remarks, 'I don't want simply to write as if I were trying to take people back to Platonism – what a hopeless thought.'[7] Isn't this a rather decisive concession to Nietzsche?

In any case, Nietzsche's privileging of the future over the past is by no means unqualified. When Nietzsche writes in the preface to 'The Advantage and Disadvantage of History for Life' that while he himself was a child of the present age, he could attain the 'untimely' experience to carry him beyond this 'only so far as I am the nursling of more ancient times, especially the Greek,' this is hardly the voice of modern progressivism. Nietzsche's rejection of progressivism is explicitly stated in §4 of one of his last books, *The Antichrist*: 'Mankind does *not* represent a development toward something better or stronger or higher in the sense accepted today. "Progress" is merely a modern idea, that is, a false idea. The European of today is vastly inferior in value to the European of the Renaissance.'[8] There will be more on this theme throughout this essay.

Nietzsche's Commitment to Technological Mastery

Like Heidegger, Grant sees Nietzsche's philosophy as the climax of Western technological thinking, and thus he says the following about Nietzsche: 'In his work, the themes that must be thought in thinking time as history are raised to a beautiful explicitness: the mastery of human and non-human nature in experimental science and technique, the primacy of the will, man as the creator of his own values, the finality of becoming, the assertion that potentiality is higher than actuality, that motion is nobler than rest, that dynamism rather than peace is the height.'[9] Grant might have hesitated before putting forward this Heideggerian picture of Nietzsche as the thinker of unbounded technological domination had he attended to the following passage in the *Genealogy of Morals* (third essay, §9): 'measured even by the standards of the ancient Greeks, our entire modern way of life, insofar as it is not weakness but power and consciousness of power, has the appearance of sheer *hubris* and godlessness; for the longest time it was precisely the reverse of those things we hold in honor today that had a good conscience on its side and God for its guardian. Our whole attitude toward nature, the way we violate her with the aid of machines and the heedless inventiveness of our technicians and engineers, is *hubris*.'[10] Admittedly, it is not self-evident that Nietzsche regards hubris, ancient or modern, as necessarily a vice; nonetheless, this is surely not the voice of someone who unreservedly worships the triumphs of modern technology.[11]

Nietzsche's Affirmation of Radical Freedom

We come now to the central issue: Nietzsche's exaltation of the human will, his releasing of it from submission to any transhuman standards. Here it is indeed undeniable that Grant has ample reason to find the basic categories of Nietzsche's thought distressingly modern, for Nietzsche elevates the human will to a status unprecedented in Western thought. He takes his bearings neither from nature nor from history but rather from the sheer creativity of the will in emancipating itself from natural and historical constraints. It hardly seems necessary to refer to a great many texts. Consider, for instance, *The Will to Power*, §1011: 'we have to realize to what degree we are the *creators* of our value feelings – and thus capable of projecting "meaning" into history'; or §495: 'The joy in shaping and reshaping – a primeval joy! We can comprehend only a world that we ourselves have made'; or §605: 'The ascertaining of "truth" and "untruth," the ascertaining of facts in general is fundamentally different from creative positing, from forming, shaping, overcoming, willing, such as is of the essence of philosophy. To introduce a meaning – this task still remains to be done ... On a yet higher level is to *posit a goal* and mold facts according to it.'[12] Reading such passages one could easily get the impression that Nietzsche's ideal is the absolute sovereignty of the willing individual, as though Nietzsche were committed to a wildly exaggerated version of liberalism.[13] But this would be radically mistaken, for in fact Nietzsche's intention is at the furthest extremity from the liberal freedom that encourages individuals to choose their own purposes. As Nietzsche rightly insists, 'My philosophy aims at an ordering of rank: not at an individualistic morality' (*The Will to Power*, §287). Although there is certainly a great quantity of hyperindividualistic rhetoric in Nietzsche, his ultimate project is the cultivation or 'breeding' of entire cultures. What is required for this purpose is the very opposite of freedom, as liberal modernity understands it.

The Nietzschean emphasis on radical willing has the effect not of opening horizons so that we may will what we choose, but the very opposite: of closing horizons, so that whole societies regain the sense of cultural purpose that modernity inexorably disrupts. Thus he writes in *Beyond Good and Evil*, §188, 'there should be *obedience* over a long period of time and in a *single* direction.' He goes on to say, '"You shall obey – someone and for a long time: – *else* you will perish and lose the last respect for yourself" – this appears to me to be the moral imperative of nature.' In the same context he bitterly condemns the anarchists for demanding *laisser aller*; any 'natural' morality (as opposed to the 'unnatural' morality of Christian-derived modernity) 'teaches hatred of the *laisser aller*, of any all-too-great freedom, and implants the need for limited horizons.' This paradoxical consequence – that the Nietzschean liberation of the will requires a severe constraining of freedom[14] – comes out very well in a crucial text, *The Will to Power*, §144: 'Moralities and religions are the principal means by which one can make whatever one wishes out of man, provided one possesses a superfluity of creative forces and can assert one's will over long periods of time – in the form of legislation, religions, and customs.' In Nietzsche's view modernity is the name for precisely that form of social organization (or social disorganization!) that is utterly incapable of such legislation. Thus he writes in *Twilight of the Idols*, 'The whole of the West no longer possesses the instincts out of which institutions grow, out of which a *future* grows: perhaps nothing antagonizes its "modern spirit" so much. One lives for the day, one lives very fast, one lives very irresponsibly: precisely this is called "freedom"' ('Skirmishes of an Untimely Man,' §39). He adds that 'we moderns, with our anxious self-solicitude and neighbor-love, with our virtues of work, modesty, legality, and scientism – accumulating, economic, machinelike – appear as a *weak* age' ('Skirmishes of an Untimely Man,' §37).[15] Are these sentences that could have been written by an unreserved celebrator of modernity? Admittedly the Nietzschean emphasis on *willing* the civilizational possibility of premodern institutions is radically modern: one might formulate the paradox by saying that Nietzsche offers a stridently modern vocabulary in defence of a rabidly antimodern way of life. But it remains the case that no one who reads §§37, 38, and 39 of 'Skirmishes of an Untimely Man' could conceive of Nietzsche as being in any sense a defender of modernity.

The core of Nietzsche's way of thinking concerning the will (that is, the Nietzschean dialectic of freedom and constraint) is given decisive expression in *Beyond Good and Evil*, §262: modern freedom *relaxes* the bow, whereas Nietzsche wants urgently to *tighten* the bow.[16] *The Will to Power*, §961, makes the same point: 'The significance of protracted despotic moralities: they tense the bow.' 'Freedom' as defined in accordance with the Nietzschean conception of the will is the antithesis of liberal freedom, and therefore the antithesis of freedom as modernity conceives it.

Nietzsche's Cosmopolitanism

That Nietzsche (to his great credit!) vehemently rejects nationalism does not imply that he embraces its opposite, modernizing cosmopolitanism.[17] To be sure, he describes himself as a 'good European,' and it is easy to misinterpret this in a cosmopolitan light, as if Nietzsche were anticipating the faceless Eurobureaucracy that we associate with Brussels in the 1990s. But nothing could be further from Nietzsche's intentions. His project, rather, is the willing of a new pan-European nation that can subsume the cultural and religious energies that circulate within the boundaries of Europe (hence the multinational cultural inventory that Nietzsche supplies in *Beyond Good and Evil*, part 8). One way of describing this project would be to say that it aims at a *more ambitious* nationalism; what

Nietzsche rejects are the *petty* nationalisms that fragment Europe. By contrast, a *grander* nationalism that integrates Europe into a single cultural-political will is not at all inconsistent with Nietzsche's vision.[18]

Consider in this regard Nietzsche's analysis, in §§16–17 of *The Antichrist*, of the distinction between national gods (gods that embody a people's pride, its sense of thankfulness, its belief in itself) and cosmopolitan gods (gods that, having lost their organic link to a particular people, are consigned to a condition of rootlessness, a sort of divine tourism). Nietzsche is wholly and uncompromisingly on the side of the former, and therefore praises the Old Testament God who adheres to his chosen people, and condemns the New Testament God whose cosmopolitanism is the mark of his decadence. Far from praising cosmopolitanism (which Nietzsche rightly conceives of as a *Christian* legacy), Nietzsche means to deliver the most severe reproach to Christianity when he declares that 'Christianity was not "national."'[19] It is according to the same 'national' standard that Nietzsche proclaims his overwhelming partiality for the Old Testament: 'I find a people' ('ich finde ein Volk') (*Genealogy of Morals*, third essay, §22). Good European he may have been, but he was no defender of cosmopolitanism.

Nietzsche's Atheism

As important as the preceding themes are to Grant's critique of Nietzsche, the real key to Grant's account of Nietzsche's modernism is his conception of Nietzsche as someone who uncompromisingly rejects the entire tradition of Western theism.[20] Therefore my purpose in the remainder of this essay is to explore the ambiguities in Nietzsche's stance towards the theistic legacy of the West.

When one considers all those aspects of Nietzsche's thought that set him most at variance with the modern spirit – his presentation of himself, in the preface to 'The Advantage and Disadvantage of History for Life,' as someone who has drawn from his experience as a philologist the great benefit of remoteness from modernity; his steadfast rejection of the Enlightenment; his Burckhardtian distaste for the commercial-technological frenzy of modern life[21] – it becomes impossible for us to go along with the statement by Grant (which more or less sums up Grant's Heideggerian reading of Nietzsche) that Nietzsche 'saw modernity with the greatest clarity

... and welcomed what he saw.'[22] If the 'welcome' that Nietzsche supposedly extended to modernity appears dubious to us, our scepticism about Grant's reading applies especially to the question of Nietzsche's stance toward religion in the face of modernity's dissolution of a civilization based on theism.

THE PLACE OF THEISM IN NIETZSCHE'S *UMWERTUNG* OF MODERNITY

In his Nietzsche lectures of 1974–5 Grant states that nobody ever ridiculed with greater acuteness than Nietzsche the modern ideologies (liberalism and socialism) that arose from the secularization of Christianity, although 'he did not do so in the service of a pious way of thought – but in the name of an even greater [that is, more radical] modernity.' In particular, Grant remarks, Nietzsche radicalizes rather than challenges the West's turn toward atheism. Hence the language of values, the language that typifies Nietzsche's thought, 'is unequivocably an atheistic language.'[23] In Grant's view Nietzsche's (successful) championing of the language of values suffices to establish him as the spearhead of radical modernity – as the spearhead of radical modernity, moreover, defined in terms of the civilizational triumph of atheism. I think it is a reasonable acknowledgment of the power of Heidegger's reading of Nietzsche to say that there is an important measure of truth in this view. But it is not the complete truth about Nietzsche's stance toward modernity or theism. To begin with there are three major challenges to its hermeneutical adequacy. For one thing, Nietzsche states, quite unequivocally, that theism is practically-politically superior to atheism. Secondly, Nietzsche affirms, with equal unequivocacy, the practical-political superiority of Catholicism to Protestantism. Finally, Nietzsche's general standard for evaluating Christianity is not post-Christian modernity but rather a range of *pre*modern religions: Hinduism, paganism, Judaism, and Islam. (Clearly, modernity is not the standard precisely because it *is* post-Christian – that is, thoroughly infiltrated by Christian value-perspectives.) Nietzsche judges each of the premodern alternatives to be practically-politically superior to Christianity, whether in its more modern Protestant version or its less modern Catholic version. It is hard to see how anyone who is committed to the three propositions just mentioned can be a radical proponent of modernity in Grant's sense of the term, or how Nietzsche can be conceived as a wholehearted champion of modern atheism. But again, Nietzsche does clearly endorse all of the three propositions.

Let us examine the relevant texts. For my purpose, the crucial Nietzschean text is *The Will to Power*, §151: 'Religions are destroyed by belief in morality. The Christian moral God is not tenable: hence "atheism" – as if there could be no other kinds of god.' What is implied in this text? Atheism is not the inevitable product of the maturation of the species, as imagined, for instance, in some Enlightenment scenario of a liberation from ignorance or a leap into truth; rather, atheism is caused by *Christianity*, that is, by the wrong kind of theism. Moreover, if, as Nietzsche thinks, certain decisive features of Christian theism have been responsible for the outcome of atheism in the West, this is not something for which Christianity deserves to be *congratulated*; on the contrary, it obliges us to render a damning judgment against Christianity. According to Nietzsche's view (as I interpret the text), Christian theism makes inevitable a *descent* (not an *ascent*) into atheism – a descent from which it is necessary to rise to new theistic possibilities. Christianity is, because of its moralism, a religion-destroyer, a force destructive of our 'God-inventing spirit' (as Nietzsche refers to religion in *The Will to Power*, §1062). To recover the 'god-forming instinct' (§1038), Christianity must be abolished. If we could but pry ourselves away from the assumption that our god must be a *moral* god, we could liberate our human creativity for the spawning of new forms of theism. '[H]ow many new gods are still possible!' Nietzsche twice exclaims in §1038. The creative well that is the source of culture-nourishing divinities has dried up, thanks to the Christian drought, and needs to be replenished.[24]

It is important to be aware that Nietzsche does not simply condemn Christianity as such; he is also concerned to rank competing versions of Christianity. If one conceives of Nietzsche as a prophet of radical modernity, it comes as an astonishing surprise that he ranks Catholicism as decidedly superior to Protestantism. Yet the more one reflects on Nietzsche's actual judgments on modernity, the more this makes sense. The decisive texts here are §§87–9 of *The Will to Power*. In §87 Nietzsche writes, 'Decline of *Protestantism*: understood as a halfway house [als Halbheit] both theoretically and historically. Actual superiority of Catholicism ... Protestantism simply doesn't exist any more.' In §88 he again refers to Protestantism as a 'halfway house' ('etwas Halbes').[25] In §89, he writes, 'Can one even imagine a spiritually staler, lazier, more comfortably relaxed form of the Christian faith than that of the average Protestant in Germany?' That Nietzsche criticizes Protestantism as spiritually stale, lazy, and relaxed would seem to imply that he would approve of a version of Christianity that would be less relaxed, less lazy, more spiritually robust. His reference, in §87, to the 'actual superiority of Catholicism' ('tatsächliches Übergewicht des Katholizismus') may carry the same implication. If Nietzsche thinks that Christianity is a bad thing, shouldn't he *welcome* a version of the Christian faith that is stale and spiritually exhausted?[26]

As Grant reminds us, for Nietzsche there is no going back; one must thrust forward. For Nietzsche, certainly, going back from Protestantism to Catholicism is no solution at all to our predicament. But in going forward one can learn from past possibilities, and Nietzsche's utmost aim is to derive maximum instruction from what the religions of antiquity have to teach us. Indeed, the further one retreats from late-Christian modernity, the more valuable becomes the instruction one hopes to gather from the various religious traditions. (This is not to say that Nietzsche doesn't think we have much to learn from Christian experience: his sometimes hysterical outbursts against Christianity often fail to do full justice to the complexity of his relationship to the Christian legacy.) Nietzsche is therefore committed not only to a hierarchical ranking of different varieties of Christianity relative to each other, but also to a hierarchical ranking of Christian theism in general relative to non-Christian and anti-Christian (including pre-Christian) theisms. The most obvious alternative to Christianity is, of course, paganism, and Nietzsche gives us plenty of reasons to think his ultimate goal is a recuperation of pagan possibilities. His later writings contain repeated invocations of the Greek god Dionysus. In *The Will to Power*, for example, he addresses his preferred readers as 'we pagans' (§1034), and says his task is 'To demonstrate to what extent the Greek religion was higher than the Judaeo-Christian' (§1042). But as we will see in the next section, Nietzsche's ambitions as a theorist of civil religion are not exhausted by the project of recovering pagan horizons.[27]

There is ample evidence of Nietzsche's favourable attitude toward Jewish theism (or at least a version of it) relative to Christianity.[28] His determination to side with the ancient Jews against the ancient Christians is very sharply expressed in *Genealogy of Morals*, third essay, §22, where he exclaims, 'I do not like the "New Testament," that should be plain ... The *Old* Testament – that is something else again: all honor to the Old Testament! I find in it great human beings, a heroic landscape, and something of the very rarest quality in the world, the incomparable naïveté of the *strong heart.*' Nietzsche's rejection of the Christian appropriation of the Old Testament is expressed even more sharply in *The Antichrist*, §45: '*Impertinent* rabble! They compare themselves with the prophets, no less.'[29] And, as discussed above, Nietzsche argues in *The Antichrist*, §§16–17, on the basis of the principle that 'A people that still believes in itself retains its own god,' that the God of Israel, as the god of a people, is far superior to the Christian God, which is a cosmopolitan, and therefore unnatural and unhealthy, god. Nietzsche's ranking is summarized in *The Will to Power*, §145, where religions are categorized primarily on the basis of a class analysis. The religions unfolded in the lawbook of Manu, in the lawbook of Mohammed, and in the older parts of the Old Testament are said to be affirmative (*ja-sagende*) religions; those unfolded in the New Testament and in Buddhist texts are said to be negative (*nein-sagende*) religions. The reference to 'the older parts of the Old Testament' indicates a crucial complexity in Nietzsche's evaluation of the Hebrew Bible. Notwithstanding Nietzsche's very generous statements in appreciation of the Old Testament relative to the New, there are, of course, many passages in *The Antichrist* and elsewhere in which Nietzsche's judgments on the Jewish contribution to Western theism seem just as harsh as his judgments on the Christian legacy. As §145 of *The Will to Power* clearly implies, there is a simple solution to this puzzle, for Nietzsche makes a sharp distinction between the 'heroic' books of the Old Testament, which for him express an aristocratic warrior-creed comparable to Hinduism and Islam, and the later books of the Old Testament, which for him reflect the hegemony acquired by the priests. The story of this crucial transformation in Jewish history is told in *The Antichrist*, §26, where Nietzsche writes that 'in the hands of the Jewish priests the great age in the history of Israel became an age of decay; the Exile, the long misfortune, was transformed into an eternal punishment for the great age – an age in which the priest was still a nobody ... *From now on* all things in life are so ordered that the priest is indispensable everywhere.'[30] It is this 'hijacking' of Judaism by the priests that turns the Hebrew religion into a proto-Christian phenomenon. This, then, explains the tension in *The Antichrist* between those passages in which Nietzsche strongly endorses the Hebrew Bible and those in which he harshly condemns it.

Where all this is leading, clearly, is toward legislating a post-Christian regime, and everything in *The Antichrist*, as well as in his other writings that analyze the various religions, is intended as preparatory to such a post-Christian regime. As Nietzsche puts it in *The Will to Power*, §361, 'I have declared war on the anaemic Christian ideal ... not with the aim of destroying it but only of putting an end to its tyranny and clearing the way for new ideals, for *more robust* ideals.' (In §1051, however, the tone is less conciliatory: 'to *overcome* everything Christian through something supra-Christian, and not merely to put it aside.') In §§20–3 of *The Antichrist* Nietzsche offers a distinction between two kinds of nihilistic religion: Buddhism, which represents the end-point of a civilization that has exhausted its energies, and whose nihilism (a kind of tranquillizer for old age) is excusable; and Christianity, which serves to domesticate youthful Europe's barbarian energies, and whose nihilism is therefore *not* excusable. Weary civilizations are permitted to drug themselves to sleep, but Christianity lacks this excuse. Yet at the end of §22 Nietzsche concludes this analysis of Buddhism with the following astounding claim: 'Christianity finds no civilization as yet – under certain circumstances it might lay the foundation for one [es begründet sie].' Surely he doesn't mean that Christianity furnishes an adequate basis for a substantial civilization. What he means, what he must mean, is that a resolutely anti-Christian thinker such as himself can survey the rubble left by Christianity, with a view to erecting on this inert base a radically different *post-Christian* civilization.

NIETZSCHE'S THEOCRATIC POLITICS

The Antichrist does not itself present a civil religion, but rather supplies the standards of evaluation that a suitably post-Christian civil religion (*Thus Spoke Zarathustra?*)[31] would have to satisfy. Sections 16–17 of *The Antichrist* teach us that national deities are superior to cosmopolitan deities. Sections 59–60 teach us that unabashedly masculine warrior-religions are superior to religions of feminine love and benevolence.[32] Sections 20–3 teach us that even among the nihilistic religions, a ranking is necessary: forms of nihilism, such as Buddhism, that express the twilight of a great civilization are superior to a form of nihilism (Christianity) that opposes itself to still vibrant civilizations and drains them of all vitality. (Related to this is the vampire theme of §§49, 58, 59, and 62.)[33] Further important clues to Nietzsche's theocratic or civil-religion teaching are offered in §§56–7 of *The Antichrist*. In §55 Nietzsche states that what is common to *all* religions, healthy as well as decadent, is lying: whether one looks at paganism, Confucianism, the religion expressed in the law of Manu, Islam, or Christianity, the universal law is that the priest lies. Platonic theology is the same, but it distinguishes itself from the others in claiming explicitly the right to lie; indeed, in asserting the necessity of a 'philosophic-priestly rule' based on lying. But at the beginning of §56 Nietzsche emphasizes that he has no objection to lying as such: 'it is a matter of the *end* to which one lies.'[34] Here, Nietzsche's preferred model of a well-functioning civil religion seems to be found in the Hindu lawbook of Manu. It hardly seems likely that Nietzsche's choice of the Hindu caste system as his privileged alternative to Christianity is merely coincidental. Yet in a parallel discussion in the section entitled 'The "Improvers" of Mankind' in *Twilight of the Idols*, Nietzsche appears to be far more critical of the Hindu laws; and in several sections of *The Will to Power* (notably §§142–3), he is more critical still (although in other sections, such as §145, he seems less critical). We seem to get a solution to this puzzle in *The Will to Power*, §116: the lawbook of Manu made no mistake in dividing society into castes; its mistake was to place the *priests* at the apex of the social pyramid, and to give *them* the power to rule all. In this respect, as Nietzsche insists in §§142–3, it had a disastrous influence on other religions, for it established the universally imitated model of a priestly regime.[35] Nietzsche's prescription, as announced in §116, is to *retain* the Hindu caste structure but to invert its content, with *priests* as the new chandala class (outcasts, untouchables),[36] and 'blasphemers, immoralists, free-floating individuals of every description, artist-performers, Jews, street minstrels' at the very top.[37] This text suggests a way of achieving a perfect reconciliation between the apparent praise of the lawbook of Manu in *The Antichrist* and its apparent condemnation in *Twilight of the Idols*. Insofar as it entrenches the rule of priests, the Hindu lawbook serves as a dreadful precedent in the history of religion, one duly followed by every other religion; on the other hand, as the most radical example of a set of laws giving religious sanction to the idea of a caste-structured society, it offers the most impressive alternative to Christian egalitarianism. What appear to be contradictory judgments concerning the Hindu laws can, in fact, be rendered fully consistent. Strangely enough, there is no analogous tension in Nietzsche's judgments concerning Plato's *Republic*, for while he notes in many passages the similarities between the Hindu rule by Brahmins and the Platonic rule by philosophers (in fact, he claims repeatedly that Plato – via Asian or Egyptian sources – *borrows* his basic conception from the Hindu laws),[38] he never *credits* Plato with having legislated a caste-based politics. Rather, Nietzsche consistently focuses on one sole aspect of Plato, namely Plato's having sown the seeds of everything Nietzsche hates about Christianity.[39] This yields a very striking irony that Nietzsche has no inclination to acknowledge: while the philosophy of Plato's *Republic* is radically antithetical to Nietzsche's, its politics is surprisingly similar to Nietzsche's own politics.[40] The clearest illustration of this similarity is in fact Nietzsche's account in §§56–7 of *The Antichrist* of what he admires in the lawbook of Manu.

Nietzsche finds it impossible to discuss these questions without bringing Plato into the centre of the discussion. When Nietzsche says, 'Neither Manu nor Plato nor Confucius nor the Jewish and Christian teachers have ever doubted their right to lie' (*Twilight of the Idols*, 'The "Improvers" of Mankind,' §5), he implies that Plato's *Republic* offers a civil religion. Moreover, Nietzsche is committed to the view that Plato's civil religion is, *despite appearances*, closer in spirit to Christian egalitarianism than to Hindu hierarchy.[41] If we go back to the text with which we started, namely *The Will to Power*, §151, we can begin to see more clearly why Plato looms so large within Nietzsche's civil-religion argument. We may recall that according to Nietzsche's suggestion in §151, what killed Judeo-Christian theism was the incredibility of the notion of the biblical God as a supposedly *moral* God. Conversely, if it were possible for there to be a post-Christian theism, it would be preferable, perhaps indispensable, for the post-Christian gods to be decidedly *immoral* gods.[42] This is clearly intended as a direct inversion of Plato. In the Platonic theology at the end of book 2 and the beginning of book 3 of *The Republic*, Plato rejects Homer's gods on the grounds of their immorality – thus anticipating the Christian God, who is irreproachably moral. It is arguable that the God of the Hebrews is rather more like the Homeric gods in this respect, which is obviously why Nietzsche so ardently prefers the God of the Old Testament to the God of the New Testament.[43] In this sense, the Christian culpability for Western atheism, as Nietzsche understands it, is ultimately traceable back to Plato, insofar as Christianity gave Plato the kind of theism he wanted, namely a theism purged of gods capable of immoral conduct.[44] It is precisely this Platonic-Christian (that is to say, anti-Homeric) theism that, in Nietzsche's view, drives the West in the direction of atheism.

Nietzsche plays a more elaborate version of the same tune in §16 of *The Antichrist*. This section, while it appears to be addressed strictly to Christianity and its 'revaluation' of the Old Testament, is actually an implicit dialogue with Plato's *Republic* 377d–391e. When Socrates says to Adeimantus, 'Above all, it mustn't be said that gods make war on gods, and plot against them and have battles with them,'[45] Nietzsche responds, 'What would be the point of a god who knew nothing of wrath, revenge, envy, scorn, cunning, and violence? who had perhaps never experienced the delightful *ardeurs* of victory and annihilation? No one would understand such a god: why have him then?' When Plato insists, against Homer, that 'the god, since he's good, wouldn't be the cause of everything, and that, 'of the bad things, some other causes must be sought and not the god,'[46] Nietzsche replies on behalf of Homer, 'religion is a form of thankfulness. Being thankful for himself, man needs a god. Such a god must be able to help and to harm, to be friend and enemy – he is admired whether good or destructive. The *anti-natural* castration of a god, to make him a god of the good alone, would here be contrary to everything desirable. The evil god is needed no less than the good god.' The national god of the Hebrews is superior to the god of the New Testament for the same reason that Homer's gods are superior to Plato's god, namely that a god who knows nothing of 'wrath, revenge, envy, scorn, cunning, and violence' is humanly unintelligible, and therefore eventually discredits theism.

One could say a great deal more about Nietzsche's preoccupation with evaluating religions by analyzing their cultural-political implications. For the purposes of this essay it suffices to quote *The Will to Power*, §144: 'Moralities and religions are the principal means by which one can make whatever one wishes out of man, provided one possesses a superfluity of creative forces and can assert one's will over long periods of time – in the form of legislation, religions, and customs.' The spirit in which one embarks on this awesome enterprise is clearly stated in *The Will to Power*, §1051: 'To wait and to prepare oneself; to await the emergence of new sources ... to wash one's soul ever cleaner from the marketplace dust and noise of this age; to *overcome* everything Christian through something supra-Christian, and not merely to put it aside.' One way in which all of this can be summed up is by remarking that Heidegger's famous pronouncement, 'Only a god can save us,' echoes a recognizably Nietzschean mode of response ('waiting and preparing') to our current dispensation – except that in Nietzsche's thought this recourse to awaited gods finds a more directly political expression.

THEISM AND MODERNITY

At the risk of oversimplifying Nietzsche's theocratic or quasi-theocratic teaching in all its elusive complexity, let us try to summarize the theistic dimension of Nietzsche's theorizing. We start with the idea of a hierarchy or ranking of theistic possibilities, with Christianity at the bottom: 'The Christian conception of god ... is one of the most corrupt conceptions of the divine ever attained on earth. It may even represent the low-water mark in the descending development of divine types.'[47] Concerning the criteria that define this hierarchy, Nietzsche argues, first, that national gods are better than cosmopolitan gods; second, that immoral gods are better than moral gods; and third, that gods that are more masculine are better than gods that are more feminine. This analysis obviously presupposes the idea of constituting, first philosophically and then in practice, a *post*-Christian civilization: As we noted earlier, this, surely, is what Nietzsche has in mind with his bizarre formulation in *The Antichrist*, §22, that 'Christianity finds no civilization as yet – under certain circumstances it might lay the foundation for one.' Nietzsche's suggestion here is incredible – as if we are still awaiting the emergence of a civilization founded on Christianity! The meaning of this queer utterance is that for Nietzsche, 'Christian civilization' is a contradiction in terms (just as, for him, 'liberal civilization' and 'democratic civilization' are oxymorons). His aim, therefore, is to turn the whole inheritance of Christianity into a mere foundation-stone on which to erect a new civilization that is not only post-Christian but anti-Christian. Finally, Nietzsche's civil-religion argument teaches us, as *The Antichrist,* §19, suggests, that what most condemns Christianity is that it deactivates the 'god-creating power' of human beings. Europe has put up with the Christian God for two thousand years, and has made no attempt to dispose of him (although it hasn't lacked opportunities to do so). We await the enchanting variety of new post-Christian gods that will arise with the re-awakening of the *'creator spiritus'* that Christianity put to sleep.[48]

Why is Nietzsche so obsessed with the question of how an ancient Hindu law code managed to fashion one particular galaxy of human life? Why do two of his last books give such concentrated attention to what appears, surely, as an obsolete possibility? The answer, clearly, is that *Nietzsche* was not convinced that religions had, for all time, relinquished the capacity to steer human beings in specific directions. On the contrary, it seems evident that this was still, for him, a live option; and *only* on the presumption that Nietzsche thought civil religion could be resurrected in the West can we make sense of this dimension of his theorizing. It confers a unique energy on his efforts to render comparative judgments on the spectrum of human religions, and, having done so, to arrange those religions in a philosophically grounded rank order. Having ranked religions, one then legislates them: 'The philosopher as *we* understand him ... as the man of the most comprehensive responsibility who has the conscience for the over-all development of man ... will make use of religions for his project of cultivation and education, just as he will make use of whatever political and economic states are at hand.'[49] At the same time, 'one always pays dearly and terribly when religions do *not* want to be a means of education and cultivation in the philosopher's hand but insist on having their own *sovereign* way, when they themselves want to be ultimate ends and not means among other means.'[50] As Leo Strauss rightly points out, 'The fundamental alternative is that of the rule of philosophy over religion or the rule of religion over philosophy.'[51]

Notwithstanding Nietzsche's statement in *The Will to Power,* §116, that 'We are proud of no longer having to be liars,' if Nietzsche is committed to the view (as he states it in *The Antichrist,* both at the beginning of §56 and at the beginning of §58) that what matters is not lying but the *end* to which one lies, then (by his own account) he accepts in principle the whole project of a civil religion. He intends to modify this project in two key respects: first, one will be lying for

life-affirming rather than life-negating ends; second, one will en-
sure that responsibility for these lies will not be in the hands of a
class of priests. But in this respect Nietzsche is entirely faithful to
the modern tradition of civil religion as set forth by Machiavelli,
Hobbes, and Rousseau.[52] For each of these authors it is possible to
embrace a politics that is both 'theocratic' and radically anticlerical.
In the words of Leszek Kolakowski, modern theorists of civil religion opt for theocracy (what Hobbes labelled 'the Priesthood of
Kings') but not for clerocracy (what Hobbes labelled 'the Kingdom
of Priests').[53]

That Nietzsche is such an unremitting opponent of priestly rule
should, one might think, make him quite sympathetic to the aspirations of the Enlightenment. Of course, Nietzsche is perfectly well
aware that his own project of combatting Christianity presupposes
the contribution of the Enlightenment in loosening the grip of
Christianity on our civilization. Yet the fact that Nietzsche is an
enemy of clerocracy does not make him a friend of the Enlightenment. The clearest statement of Nietzsche's position concerning the
Enlightenment is in the preface to *Beyond Good and Evil*: 'twice already attempts have been made in the grand style to unbend the
bow – once by means of Jesuitism, the second time by means of the
democratic enlightenment which, with the aid of freedom of the
press and newspaper-reading, might indeed bring it about that the
spirit would no longer experience itself so easily as a "need."'[54]
According to Nietzsche, what bent the bow of the European spirit
in so magnificent a fashion was 'the fight against the Christian-ec-
clesiastical pressure of millennia.' But rather than crediting the Enlightenment with having participated in this epic anti-Christian
struggle, he does the opposite: he accuses the Enlightenment of
trying to see to it that the fight against Christianity has only the
most feeble and mediocre outcome – mere democracy. And the fact
that Nietzsche is so critical of the Enlightenment means at the same
time that he is less than happy with the cultural price we pay for all
the science, rationalization, and technological progress that define
our modernity (however much he may nonetheless appeal, in de-
nouncing Christianity, to the authority of science). If Nietzsche had
to choose between living in a disenchanted world that had been
thoroughly rationalized by science, and living in a world where
religious myth and mystery continued to furnish durable horizons
within which human beings could have a meaningful existence de-

fined for them, there seems little doubt that he would choose the latter. To repeat what was quoted earlier, 'it is a matter of the *end* to which one lies.'

As we observed above, Grant's claim is that Nietzsche 'saw modernity with the greatest clarity ... and welcomed what he saw.' This claim is very difficult to square with the descriptions typically employed by Nietzsche to characterize modernity, for instance in §§1–4 of *The Antichrist*. In §1 Nietzsche defines modernity as 'lazy peace, cowardly compromise': '"I have got lost; I am everything that has got lost," sighs modern man.' In §7 he refers to 'our whole unhealthy modernity,' and in §38 he writes, 'to leave no doubt concerning what I despise, whom I despise: it is the man of today, the man with whom I am fatefully contemporaneous.' While Nietzsche is prepared to forgive the lunacies of past millennia ('I am careful not to hold mankind responsible for its mental disorders'), what he finds utterly intolerable is 'modern times, *our* time. Our time *knows better*.'[55] For Nietzsche, not unreasonably, one cannot separate modernity from the political legacy of liberalism, egalitarianism, democracy, humanitarianism, and so on. Furthermore, all these political fruits of the rationalist Enlightenment are inseparable from the legacy of Christianity. In that sense, being radically anti-Christian entails being radically antimodern. And all the quotations from *The Antichrist* that have just been cited bear out the fact that this antimodernism is indeed integral to Nietzsche's self-conception.

Here it is important to take note of an important difference between what Nietzsche means by the concept of modernity and what Grant means by it. For Grant, crucially influenced in this respect by Heidegger, modernity is viewed as a frenzied engine of willing. Nietzsche, by contrast, sees modernity, shaped by Christian humanitarianism and Enlightenment rationalism, as defined by a woeful incapacity to will something grand, or at least significant. Indeed, modernity is unable to will anything at all: judged by the standard of power, modernity stands for impotence, not omnipotence. Therefore, as Nietzsche sees it, to genuinely liberate the human capacity for willing, one must *transcend* modernity; that is, create a *trans*modern civilization that might well restore some of the defining characteristics (hierarchy, reverence for the ancestral, rootedness in centuries-long tradition) of the *pre*-modern civilizations that Nietzsche admired. Far from being *anti*conservative,

Nietzsche thinks unprecedentedly radical measures are needed to rescue us from *modernity's* anticonservatism.

CONCLUSION: REJOINING THE DIALOGUE

Having attempted in the previous sections to mount the strongest possible challenge to Grant's Heideggerian reading of Nietzsche, let us now try to shift the weight of the Grant-Nietzsche dialogue a bit, and turn some challenges back on Nietzsche. But before we do that, let us make due acknowledgment of the fact that Grant, especially in some of his later Nietzsche lectures, offers some crucial concessions to the sort of reading of Nietzsche presented in this essay, namely a reading that highlights the *anti*modernist strain in Nietzsche's thought. Grant's 'standard' view, let us recall, is that 'Reason in its deepest modern account of it teaches us to be atheists ... Nietzsche seems to me the height of modern reason and he sees it as unequivocally atheist.'[56] In his 1974–5 Nietzsche lectures, however, Grant presents a more subtle view than we get from his usual view of Nietzsche as an unmitigated radical atheist: 'unlike the hope of liberalism and Marxism he is quite clear that the popular atheism of the West is leading to a much lower type of man than was produced by the theism of the past.'[57] And further, 'Nietzsche is swimming against the more obvious current of modernity in that he is perfectly clear that theistic man produced higher beings than modern atheism.'[58] This important insight actually prompts Grant to acknowledge the deficiency of his usual characterization of Nietzsche as a radical modernist: 'in the last years I have seen Nietzsche in a slightly new way, that is, not simply as the thinker who catches the very swell of the ocean of modernity, but also as somebody who is not content to swim with that current – but finds other currents than that.'[59] And in a subsequent lecture Grant gives even more decisive expression to this 'new way' of seeing Nietzsche: 'At the height of his teaching – that is, the doctrine of eternal recurrence – Nietzsche seems to be battling to pass beyond modernity.[60]

As promised, let us now conclude with some possible challenges to Nietzsche's civil-religion project. For instance, Nietzsche might be charged with violating his own strictures against decadent modernity. In §7 of *The Case of Wagner* Nietzsche tells us that the decadent is one whose style approximates 'the anarchy of atoms,' where

the part triumphs over the whole: 'The whole no longer lives at all:
it is composite, calculated, artificial, artifact.' This passage is bound
to make us think of contemporary postmodernism, with its cut-and-
splice approach to inherited cultural traditions. But isn't
Nietzsche's project of a new post-Christian synthesis, which appro-
priates elements of paganism, Hinduism, atheism, and even Christianity, proto-postmodern in just this sense? And indeed, the same
accusation might be levelled against the ersatz scripture that
Nietzsche attempts to construct in *Thus Spoke Zarathustra*. It is not
too hard to see why Nietzsche admits in the preface to *The Case of
Wagner* that 'I am, no less than Wagner, a child of this time; that is,
a decadent.' But he also tells us that as a philosopher he compre-
hended his own decadence and resisted it; what he wished for more
than anything was to fashion something that was *more* than a composite, calculated, and artificial artifact made up of bits and pieces
of old religions.

Needless to say, there is a real paradox underlying the whole
project of a Nietzschean civil religion. The more remote a particular religion is from modern horizonlessness, the more attractive
Nietzsche finds it (hence his preference for the lawbook of Manu
over the Gospels, for Islam over the New Testament, for Catholic
Christianity over Protestant Christianity). Yet the very fact that
we are in a position to survey the totality of world religions and
to judge them from an independent philosophic standpoint –
which implies detachment from any particular religious tradition
– seems radically modern. It is as if we could legislate a new religious dispensation by a sheer act of will, and of course it is this
novel aspect of Nietzsche's 'theism' that greatly disturbs Grant.
This is what distinguishes Nietzsche's paradoxical modern-
ism/antimodernism: one must embrace modern voluntarism in its
most radical aspect in order to will something radically antimodern.[61]

It would, of course, be possible for Grant to object that his view
of Nietzsche as the spearhead of radical atheistic modernism remains perfectly valid unless Nietzsche actually *believes* in the theism he propounds, rather than simply proposing it as an object of
political invention, or as a vehicle for the will to power of post-
Christian founder-princes. Consider here Nietzsche's view, expressed in *The Will to Power*, §972, that Mohammed's only mistake
was to *believe in* the theism he so successfully established as the

basis for a new regime. All the better if one can do what founder-princes such as Numa or Mohammed did *without belief*. Grant would clearly have a point in raising such an objection. The problem with Nietzsche's 'theism,' according to this Grantian objection, is that the reduction of theism to the limitless creativity of *Übermenschen*, or of prophets of new religions, is precisely what *characterizes* Nietzsche's radical modernism, rather than serving to mitigate it.[62] Nonetheless, I don't think this invalidates the claim (the one I am attempting to advance in this essay) that serious qualifications need to be attached to the vision of Nietzsche as an uncompromising modernizer. On the contrary, there are equally good grounds for seeing Nietzsche as conducting, in alliance with Burckhardt, a kind of cultural war *against* modernity.[63] It is in Nietzsche's Burckhardtian hostility to modernity that we can locate the deepest meaning of his statements (which, relative to Grant's interpretation, appear highly perplexing, perhaps incomprehensible) that theism is superior to atheism, that Catholicism is superior to Protestantism, that Judaism and Islam are superior to Christianity, and that theocracy is superior to Enlightenment.

NOTES

1 Larry Schmidt, ed., *George Grant in Process: Essays and Conversations* (Toronto: Anansi 1978), 67.

2 Ibid., 66.

3 See George Grant, *Time as History* (Toronto: CBC 1969); idem, 'Nietzsche and the Ancients: Philosophy and Scholarship,' in *Technology and Justice* (Toronto: Anansi 1986), 79–95; idem, Review of Werner J. Dannhauser, *Nietzsche's View of Socrates, American Political Science Review* 71, no. 3 (September 1977), 1127–9.

4 I am very grateful to Arthur Davis for making available to me all the unpublished material by Grant cited in this essay. Because the lecture notes are sometimes quite rough, I have made some very minor changes in punctuation in the interests of clarity.

5 Grant, Notebook F 1978/79, typescript, 4. Cf. Grant's 1974/75 Lectures, 2nd Half: Lectures on *Beyond Good and Evil*, typescript, 4, where he classes together Marx and Nietzsche as 'modern thinkers who are oriented to the future – as against those who are oriented to eternity.' On the same page Grant states, 'my chief purpose in teaching has been to expound what modernity is.' In this context, modernity is conceived

as the thrust toward a contentless future, with the consequent loss of eternity.

6 Grant, 1974/75 Lectures, 2nd Half: Lectures on *Beyond Good and Evil*, typescript, 8: Nietzsche 'is a modern in that he proceeds to thought from the prejudices of the modern era – the central one being of course God is dead.'

7 Grant, 'Heidegger notes,' typescript, 10.

8 Walter Kaufmann, ed., *The Portable Nietzsche* (New York: Penguin 1976), 571. All references to *The Antichrist, Twilight of the Idols*, and *Nietzsche contra Wagner* in this essay are to this edition. Where I have amended Kaufmann's translations, this has been noted.

9 Grant, *Time as History*, 44. It may be worth pointing out that Grant borrows the phrase 'time as history' from Heidegger. See Martin Heidegger, *An Introduction to Metaphysics*, trans. Ralph Manheim (New Haven: Yale University Press 1959), 38; idem, *Einführung in die Metaphysik* (Tübingen: Max Niemeyer Verlag 1953), 29: 'die Zeit als Geschichte.' However, the meaning that Grant attaches to 'time as history' is radically different from what it signifies in Heidegger. In its Heideggerian meaning, 'time as history' (as opposed to time as 'velocity, instantaneousness, and simultaneity') connotes a more profound relationship to time than modernity makes available, and an experience of 'historicity' whose loss is a spiritual catastrophe. 'Time as history' in its Grantian meaning, on the other hand, represents the oblivion of eternity, and therefore refers to our being under the spell of modern historicism, a spell that we would do well to banish if we could. This inversion by Grant of what 'time as history' means for Heidegger casts considerable light on Grant's relationship to Heidegger.

10 Walter Kaufmann, ed., *Basic Writings of Nietzsche*, (New York: Modern Library 1968), 549. All references in this essay to *Genealogy of Morals, Beyond Good and Evil*, and *The Case of Wagner* are to this edition.

11 Technological domination is also central to Leo Strauss's reading of Nietzsche, which emphasizes the project to conquer chance to which Nietzsche commits himself in *Beyond Good and Evil*, §203. Cf. *The Will to Power*, ed. Walter Kaufmann and trans Walter Kaufmann and R.J. Hollingdale (New York: Vintage 1968), §§898, 979. And see 'Note on the Plan of Nietzsche's *Beyond Good and Evil*,' in Strauss, *Studies in Platonic Political Philosophy* (Chicago: University of Chicago Press 1983), 184–5, 189–190 (this article was first published in 1973 and Grant cites it in his 1974/75 Nietzsche Lectures, 1st Half: Book I, typescript, 18).

12 Cf. Grant, *Time as History*: 'We must live in the knowledge that our purposes are simply creations of the human will and not ingrained in the nature of things. But what a burden falls upon the will when the horizons of definition are gone' (30); 'Most men, when they face that their purposes are not cosmically sustained, find that a darkness falls upon their wills. This is the crisis of the modern world to Nietzsche' (31).

13 Something like this notion is implied in the connection that Grant draws between Nietzsche and Kant: 'Now Nietzsche's will to power is the opposite of Plato's eros, and it comes from Kant's will, with its lack of need ... For Kant the sovereignty of the human individual presupposes the absence of poverty or need.' Grant, Notebook K: Kant 1977–78, typescript, 3.

14 At least a severe constraining of freedom *as moderns understand it*: see *Twilight of the Idols*, 'Skirmishes of an Untimely Man,' §§38, 41.

15 *The Portable Nietzsche*, 543, 540. Cf. 544, where Nietzsche distinguishes between modern and premodern institutions (for example, marriage and the family) according to whether society can or cannot 'affirm itself as a whole, down to the most distant generations.' Cf. also 543: 'In order that there may be institutions, there must be a kind of will, instinct, or imperative, which is anti-liberal to the point of malice: the will to tradition, to authority, to responsibility for centuries to come, to the solidarity of chains of generations, forward and backward, *ad infinitum.*'

16 It should be noted that in both *Beyond Good and Evil*, §262, and *Twilight of the Idols*, 'Skirmishes of an Untimely Man,' §38, Nietzsche refers to 'aristocratic commonwealths' such as Venice or the cities of Greek and Roman antiquity as exemplary in this regard.

17 On this point Grant does indeed acknowledge the complexities of Nietzsche's thought. In his 1974/75 Nietzsche Lectures, 1st Half: Book I, typescript, 23–4, Grant poses the question of whether Nietzsche is cosmopolitan or anti-cosmopolitan, and rightly concludes that there is no simple answer: a '*European* cosmopolitanism' is clearly something of an oxymoron.

18 Hence, in *The Will to Power*, §104, Napoleon is extolled for 'conceiving Europe as a political unit.'

19 *The Antichrist*, §51: 'Das Christentum war nicht "national," nicht rassebedingt.' The context is Nietzsche's rejection of the thesis that Christianity arose out of 'the decline of race' (that is, as a product of the national decline of the Romans): 'Sie drückt *nicht* den Niedergang einer

Rasse aus.' The point here is that Christianity gathers together the weak of all nations, rather than expressing the decadence of one particular nation. In Nietzsche's judgment cosmopolitan decadence is far more calamitous than mere national decadence.

20 The clearest expression of Grant's standard view is in the notes for his Nietzsche seminar of 1969–70, typescript, 1: 'Reason in its deepest modern account of it teaches us to be atheists ... Nietzsche seems to me the height of modern reason and he sees it as unequivocally atheist.' See also the 1974/75 Nietzsche Lectures, 1st Half: Book I, typescript, 13: 'Nietzsche: the first great explicit right-wing atheist' (whereas prior to Nietzsche, the right wing had been defined by devotion to 'the throne and the altar').

21 As regards the last of these points, consider *The Will to Power*, §33, where Nietzsche cites the following among the reasons for the advent of European nihilism: 'that diminution, sensitivity to pain, restlessness, haste, and hustling grow continually – that it becomes easier and easier to recognize this whole commotion, this so-called "civilization," and that the individual, faced with this tremendous machinery, loses courage and submits.' Cf. §1051: 'to wash one's soul ever cleaner from the marketplace dust and noise of this age.'

22 Grant, 1974/75 Nietzsche Lectures, 1st Half: Book I, typescript, 2.

23 Ibid., 4.

24 Heidegger has made sure that we can't fail to recall *The Antichrist*, §19 in this context: 'Almost two thousand years – and not a single new god!' This, in turn, makes one think of Machiavelli, *Discourses* 2.5, according to which the passage of two millennia makes it reasonable to expect a change of religion.

25 On Protestantism as a *Halbheit*, cf. *The Portable Nietzsche*, 654–5. For a similar judgment concerning Protestantism as a compromise with modernity see Heidegger, *Nietzsche*, vol. 4, *Nihilism*, ed. D.F. Krell and trans. F.A. Capuzzi, (San Francisco: Harper & Row 1982), 99. However, it is not typical for Heidegger to condemn the Protestant Reformation, let alone to do so with the consistent venom that Nietzsche expresses on this question. Indeed, we know from Heidegger's pupils that the young Heidegger was intellectually infatuated with the young Luther: see Karl Löwith, 'The Political Implications of Heidegger's Existentialism,' in R. Wolin, ed., *The Heidegger Controversy* (Cambridge, MA: MIT Press 1993), 172–3; Hans-Georg Gadamer, 'Erinnerungen an Heideggers Anfänge,' *Dilthey-Jahrbuch für Philosophie und Geschichte der Geisteswissenschaften* 4 (1986–7), 22. (It would be relevant, though, to

observe that for Heidegger, who struggled to break free of his Catholic upbringing, Luther would have been liberating in a way that he obviously wouldn't have been for Nietzsche, who was brought up as a Lutheran.)

26 Cf. *The Antichrist*, §10: 'Definition of Protestantism: the partial paralysis of Christianity.' At the end of §61 of *The Antichrist*, Nietzsche refers to German Protestantism as 'the most unclean kind of Christianity that there is.' If Protestantism is the most unclean kind of Christianity, then again it follows that Nietzsche regards Catholicism as theoretically superior.

27 Karl Löwith, in a very illuminating article on 'Nietzsche's Revival of the Doctrine of Eternal Recurrence,' highlights the pagan antecedents of that doctrine, but also shows why Nietzsche's version necessarily stands, owing to its Judeo-Christian aspect, outside the pagan horizon. As Löwith presents him, Nietzsche is a thinker who desperately wants to resuscitate paganism, but, *malgré lui*, is precluded from doing so by his involuntary debt to the biblical tradition. See Karl Löwith, *Meaning in History* (Chicago: University of Chicago Press 1949), 214–22 (esp. 220–2). (The title of the book seems to refer back to *The Will to Power*, §1011.)

28 Perhaps the most dramatic illustration of Nietzsche's overwhelming partiality for the Old Testament is the fact that it is only by detecting an affinity between Luther and the Jewish prophets that he can bring himself to say something positive about the Reformation. See *Nietzsche contra Wagner* in *The Portable Nietzsche*, 668.

29 Cf. *Beyond Good and Evil*, §52.

30 *The Portable Nietzsche*, 596–7 (my italics). Nietzsche has a similar story to tell about Hinduism. In *The Will to Power*, §145, he distinguishes between a good stage of the religion, when power belonged to the warrior caste, and a bad stage, when power shifted to the priests. Exactly parallel to his account of the Old Testament, this thesis accounts for Nietzsche's similarly ambivalent judgments in regard to the lawbook of Manu.

31 This is what is suggested by Nietzsche's reference to the eternal recurrence in *The Will to Power*, §462, as a substitute religion. Cf. Grant, 1974/75 Lectures, 2nd Half: Lectures on *Beyond Good and Evil*, typescript, 22: 'Zarathustra a founder of a new religion beyond Christianity. A new Bible – a new ironic bible parodies the Bible while overcoming it or claiming to overcome it.'

32 Cf. *The Will to Power*, §145.

33 Hence the relevance of Nietzsche's argument in *The Antichrist*, §51, that Roman antiquity was not a spent force, undone by its own decadence ('the scholarly idiocy which upholds such ideas even today cannot be contradicted harshly enough'). Rather, it was 'vampirized' and subverted by Christianity. As Nietzsche puts it in §59, 'Not vanquished – merely drained.'

34 The italics are Nietzsche's, although omitted by Kaufmann.

35 The most ambitious statement of this thesis occurs in a letter to Peter Gast (31 May 1888) in which Nietzsche relates that he has been reading the lawbook of Manu in a French translation, and describes its impact on him:

> This absolutely *Aryan* work, a priestly codex of morality based on the Vedas, on the idea of caste and very ancient tradition – *not* pessimistic, albeit very sacerdotal – supplements my views on religion in the most remarkable way. I confess to having the impression that everything else that we have by way of moral lawgiving seems to me an imitation and even a caricature of it – preeminently, Egypticism does; but even Plato seems to me in all the main points simply to have been well instructed by a Brahmin. It makes the Jews look like a Chandala race which learns from its *masters* the principles of making a *priestly caste* the master which organizes a people ... The Chinese also seem to have produced their Confucius and Lao-tse under the influence of this *ancient classic of laws*. The medieval organization looks like a wondrous groping for a restoration of all the ideas which formed the basis of primordial Indian-Aryan society.

> This letter is found in Christopher Middleton, ed. *Selected Letters of Friedrich Nietzsche* (Chicago: University of Chicago Press 1969), 297–8.

36 The chandalas are outcasts or untouchables by virtue of being of mixed caste. Strictly speaking, the chandalas are not a caste but a subcaste, that is, beneath or outside of the fourfold caste system of priests, warriors, farmers, and servants. See Louis Dumont, Homo Hierarchicus (Chicago: University of Chicago Press 1970), 52–3, 66–71, 284 n. 32f. For regulations concerning relations between the castes, see *The Laws of Manu*, trans. G. Bühler (Delhi: Motilal Banarsidass 1964), 13–14, 24–8, 399–430. For regulations concerning the chandalas see 92, 119, 141, 183, 192, 343, 404–5, 407–9, 411, 414–15, 425, 466–7, 496. Nietzsche's quotations in *The Antichrist*, §56, correspond very roughly to V:130, V:133, and V:132 on page 192 of the Bühler edition; presumably he is quoting from memory. In any case, Nietzsche is conspicuously overgenerous in

praising the 'tenderness' of Manu's teaching concerning women (see the Bühler edition, 195–7, 327–32).

Nietzsche frequently uses the term 'chandala' to characterize Judeo-Christian religion. This appropriation of Hindu vocabulary is obviously a deliberate strategy within his Machiavellian project of a 'revaluation of values.' It is difficult not to feel a chill going up one's spine when one considers that in the 1930s the Nazis, too, appropriated Hindu vocabulary in order to pursue *their* revaluation of values.

37 The German reads, 'die *Gotteslästerer*, die *Immoralisten*, die Freizügigen jeder Art, die Artisten, die Juden, die Spielleute.' I have revised Kaufmann's translation; the context stresses disreputableness, which Kaufmann's rendering doesn't fully convey.

38 In addition to the letter cited in note 35 above see *The Will to Power*, §143.

39 See, for instance, *The Portable Nietzsche*, 557–8: 'Plato ... so pre-existently Christian ... Plato ... made it possible for the nobler spirits of antiquity ... to set foot on the bridge leading to the cross.' See also *The Will to Power*, §427: 'preparation of the soil for Christianity.'

40 One place where Nietzsche *does* acknowledge how much he shares with the politics of Plato's *Republic* is at the end of his early essay, 'The Greek State.' Consider, also, *The Gay Science*, §18, where Nietzsche encapsulates the politics of the ancient philosophers as a broadening of the slave class to encompass as a slave everyone who is not a philosopher. Is this not a way of characterizing Nietzsche's own politics?

41 According to Grant (Nietzsche Lectures, 1974/75: Book I, typescript, 20), Nietzsche combines the radical voluntarism of modernity with the anti-egalitarianism of the ancients, and this produces a deep tension in his thought. But one can turn this argument around, insofar as one finds in Grant himself precisely the opposite combination, namely the egalitarianism of post-Christian thought joined to the theocentric philosophy of Plato (as one does as well, of course, in Simone Weil). For this reason, it might be possible to explore the tensions that this generates in Grant's thought.

42 For further elaboration of this thought see *The Will to Power*, §§1034–8, and also §1011. In §1034 Nietzsche makes it perfectly clear that his own preference would be for pagan gods. But insofar as one must have something like the biblical God, Nietzsche argues in §1037 that such a god should at least be defined, not surprisingly, in terms of his power, rather than of his goodness or wisdom. Cf. Hobbes, *Leviathan*, chap. 31.

43 This is what Nietzsche implies when he writes the following: 'A great

moralist is, among other things, necessarily a great actor ... And indeed, it is said that the moralist imitates in that no less a model than God himself: God, the greatest of all immoralists in practice' (*The Will to Power*, §304). The context suggests that what Nietzsche is referring to here is Machiavelli's description of God as the 'tutor' (*precettore*) of Moses in chapter 6 of *The Prince*.

44 Cf. *The Will to Power*, §438: 'Moral fanaticism (in short: Plato) destroyed paganism.'

45 *The Republic of Plato*, trans. Allan Bloom (New York: Basic Books 1968), 56.

46 Ibid., 57. Cf. 58.

47 *The Antichrist*, §18. Cf., for instance, *The Will to Power*, §200: 'Christianity as the most fatal seductive lie that has yet existed ... the most disgusting degeneration culture has yet exhibited.' Cf. also *Beyond Good and Evil*, §62: 'Christianity has been the most calamitous kind of arrogance yet.'

48 See, for instance, *The Will to Power*, §1038, and the end of §1005. In *Beyond Good and Evil*, §53, Nietzsche distinguishes between 'the religious instinct' and the theistic manner of satisfying this instinct, but it is not entirely clear what this means.

49 *Beyond Good and Evil*, §61.

50 Ibid., §62.

51 Strauss, *Studies in Platonic Political Philosophy*, 176.

52 See my article, 'Machiavelli, Hobbes, and Rousseau on Civil Religion,' *The Review of Politics* 55, no. 4 (fall 1993), 617–38.

53 Leszek Kolakowski, *Modernity on Endless Trial* (Chicago: University of Chicago Press 1990), 179. For Hobbes's version of the distinction between theocracy and clerocracy see *Leviathan*, chap. 35, and cf. *Philosophical Rudiments concerning Government and Society*, chap. 16.

54 For other passages in which Nietzsche invokes the same metaphor see *Beyond Good and Evil*, §206, §262, and *The Will to Power*, §961.

55 Cf. 'One should be more severe toward Protestants than toward Catholics and more severe toward liberal Protestants than toward those of strict belief. The criminality of being a Christian increases in so far as the Christian approaches science.' This passage is from the 'Decree against Christianity,' quoted by Gary Shapiro in his article 'The Writing on the Wall: *The Antichrist* and the Semiotics of History,' in Robert C. Solomon and Kathleen M. Higgins, eds., *Reading Nietzsche* (New York: Oxford University Press 1988), 212–13. Shapiro's article represents something quite rare in the field of Nietzsche scholarship,

namely an attempt to take *The Antichrist* seriously as a philosophic text, and it sheds much light on various dimensions of the work, such as Nietzsche's relationship to nineteenth-century theological philology. For another very important reading of *The Antichrist*, see Peter Berkowitz, *Nietzsche: The Ethics of an Immoralist* (Cambridge, MA: Harvard University Press, 1995), chap. 4.

56 See note 20 above.

57 Grant, 1974/75 Nietzsche Lectures, 1st Half: Book I, typescript, 11.

58 Ibid.

59 Ibid. Considering the date of these lectures, Grant's phrase 'in the last years' might refer to his reading of the Strauss article cited above in note 11, which presents Nietzsche (I think rightly) as a paradoxical theist-atheist, rather than an out-and-out atheist.

60 Grant, 1974/75 Nietzsche Lectures, 2nd Half: *Beyond Good and Evil*, typescript, 14.

61 To Nietzsche's paradoxical modernism/antimodernism corresponds his paradoxical atheism/theism. Cf. Strauss, *Studies in Platonic Political Philosophy*, 179.

62 As the powerful example of Machiavelli shows, one doesn't have to be a philosopher of late modernity in order to believe that religions are this-worldly products of the political creativity of founder-princes. Consider, for instance, the proto-Nietzschean doctrine of *Discourses*, 2.5, that the revolutionary introduction of new religions is 'due to men,' not 'due to heaven.'

63 An excellent treatment of Nietzsche's debt to Burckhardt (hardly a defender of untrammelled modernity!) is available in Richard Sigurdson, 'Jacob Burckhardt as Political Thinker' (Ph.D. diss., University of Toronto, 1991). Of particular relevance to the themes of this essay is Sigurdson's discussion of Burckhardt's critique of the Protestant Reformation at 303–15.

6

Justice and Freedom: George Grant's Encounter with Martin Heidegger

ARTHUR DAVIS

George Grant struggled with Martin Heidegger throughout the seventies and eighties.[1] In the course of that struggle he continued to engage with a question that had occupied him since the fifties, a question that, he believed, had not yet been addressed adequately by any contemporary political thinker. This question can be phrased as follows: How can we accept the modern discovery – that we are free to shape nature and ourselves – without forsaking the insight of the older moral and political tradition – that we are shaped or fitted for a justice which does not depend on our wills?

Grant was led to a strange, apparently contradictory, double claim. He believed we have been put beyond good and evil (as he thought Heidegger had maintained, following Nietzsche); but at the same time, he said, we are not beyond good and evil (a point that he, as a Platonist and a Christian, felt compelled to affirm). If we shy away from either of these truths, he argued, we close ourselves off from part of our experience. To opt for only one or the other would mean failing to see the whole of our political reality.

Grant apparently believed not even Simone Weil or Leo Strauss had found complete solutions to the conflict between ancient and modern thought. He assumed that the job is still ahead, that we do not yet have a way of thinking through the conflict of modern freedom with the classical and Christian moral limits. He was arguing that a defence of justice at this time requires both Heidegger's understanding of our historical fate – that we are living inside and shaped by the empire of capital and technology – and also Plato's understanding – that we are enfolded in and claimed by an order that transcends time: meaning that, as human beings, we are fitted for being just.

Grant's work is striking and thought-provoking, therefore, because he was deeply committed to *both* these claims, refusing to give in to the enormous pressures to slide one way or the other.

His task, Grant decided in the eighties, was to prepare for a Platonic confrontation with Heidegger, one modelled on Heidegger's confrontation with Nietzsche in the *Nietzsche* volumes. Grant characterized the Plato/Heidegger confrontation in a carefully worded statement contained in a short piece he called 'Confronting Heidegger's *Nietzsche*':

To put it barely: the very clarity of Heidegger's incomparable thinking of historicism, from out of his assertion that human beings are only authentically free when they recognize that they are thrown into a particular historical existence, meets here the clarity of Plato's insistence that thought, at its purest, can rise above the particularities of any historical context, that indeed philosophy stands or falls by its ability to transcend the historical. Describing this as the central theoretical division in all western thought is perhaps a mere expression of my struggling uncertainty as to who misses what in this greatest of confrontations.[2]

The book he intended to write about 'who misses what' did not get written, but we can reconstruct the argument between Plato and Heidegger that was taking shape in Grant's mind, for we now have available his unpublished as well as his published work,[3] along with William Christian's biography, to help us in this effort.

Those who did not know Grant (and some who did) may well ask whether a mixture of Christian Platonism and Heideggerian existentialism[4] is credible. In one possible reading of Grant's thought, he started out as a left-leaning existentialist in the fifties but eventually turned back toward a purer adherence to the ancient truth, having seen the error of his progressive ways. This would mean that he backed away from the modern world, and came to believe the best we can hope for is to protest against and delay the inevitable triumph of technological modernity. This reading of Grant would cite as supporting evidence his retractions, written in the mid-sixties and later, of earlier Hegelian and existential statements.[5] His attack on Heidegger (though it was mixed with praise) would serve as the final case in point.

Another possible reading suggests that Grant was indeed far too existentialist, and therefore a thinker whose Platonism cannot be taken seriously. Grant, as Platonist, said he was searching for rational support for 'the hunger and thirst for justice,' but perhaps this search never got beyond nostalgic yearning, as was said of his *Lament for a Nation*. If this was so, his apparent agreement with Heidegger – that traditional politics has been eclipsed in technological society – would demonstrate that he cannot be considered a Platonic *political* philosopher.[6]

Against these readings I suggest that Grant's struggle with the apparent opposites of Platonism and existentialism yielded an important insight into the task of philosophy (and into the problems of present and future politics). The purpose of this essay is to examine the nature and genesis of that insight. I will also argue that Grant believed Plato must be rethought in the face of modern technology, and must be combined with a special reading of Heidegger. Grant's question was, who misses what in this greatest of philosophic confrontations? I will first try to draw out his answer to this question by looking at his struggle with Heidegger and Nietzsche. Next, I will examine his encounter with Heidegger in the seventies and eighties. In the seventies Grant led seminars and produced writings on technology in which Heidegger was front and centre. In the eighties he set out to 'justify Plato against what Heidegger says.' I will close this essay with some brief comments on the Heideggerian and Platonic elements in Grant's politics.

WRESTLING WITH HEIDEGGER AND NIETZSCHE

Grant often spoke of Heidegger and Nietzsche in the same breath, as though they offered essentially the same views on the important matters of religion and morality. He believed Heidegger accepted the doctrine that we are beyond good and evil, and on that score he opposed both thinkers as one. But he was also aware of Heidegger's critique of Nietzsche and his encounter with Heidegger was clearly different from his encounter with Nietzsche. For the most part Grant had come to terms with Nietzsche and had reached a settled position on the philosopher by the mid-seventies. He felt he knew where Nietzsche stood and why he opposed him. With Heidegger, on the other hand, he remained ambiguous. Right to the end he was still learning and being astounded by elements of Heidegger's thought. Heidegger became for him the more important combatant (and illuminator), because Heidegger had experienced the full blooming of modern technology and had moved after the Second World War toward a less Promethean (though still anti-Platonic) stance.

Grant confronted both Heidegger and Nietzsche as formidable challengers of the validity of his faith. What he spoke of as his conversion as a young man in England in 1941 had led him to a belief that there is an order beyond space and time, an order that sustains us and places us within moral limits. He was convinced that Heidegger agreed[7] with Nietzsche's attack on such a belief. Nietzsche attacked Socrates and Plato – and Christianity, which he called Platonism for the people – for pretending out of weakness that we are guided by an eternal order inherent in the nature of things. It is clear that Grant felt his own faith, as well as the authority of his religious and philosophical mentors, was on the line. He knew his conversion had come at a time when he was deeply shaken and in despair. In dark moments it seemed possible that he might have deluded himself, reaching out for what he merely wished were true.

Nietzsche's relentless attack struck home in one important respect – it exposed to Grant his own human frailty:

Oh the botched and the bungled, am I entirely that? Because I am the botched and the bungled I nevertheless do not want to live as N. says – by sheer instinctive will – nor do I think morality and religion is for me simply the desire to put off my botched and bungled self into another world – it is rather that even if I am botched and bungled I still want to give myself – as I feel Mozart does – to the forces of the world – be they just nature or be they God's – give myself, take part in them.

What Nietzsche has made me really admit is that I am one of the botched and the bungled.[8]

Grant was deeply affected by the element of truth in Nietzsche's condemnation of the Western tradition, and he was profoundly moved by Heidegger's argument about technology and the response we must make to it. Grant believed he would not have been able to reach the true strength of Plato and Christianity without the deep illumination of the modern that those thinkers provided. Nietzsche argued that Christians rejected and downgraded time, and also the earth and the body that belong to time. But Grant knew that he loved the earth, the body, and the world of time and change, however much he hated the affliction suffered by human beings, and however much he insisted that we must restrain our passions. He did not think being a Christian and a Platonist must mean defending revenge against time, the earth, and the body. Rather, a way needed to be found to hold together the love of God and the love of time and the earth.

'DIGESTING' HEIDEGGER'S ACCOUNT OF TECHNOLOGY

The encounter with Heidegger became the main event in Grant's intellectual life during the early seventies. He had decided that Heidegger understood modern technological science in relation to the decline of religion and morality in a way that another of his formative thinkers, Jacques Ellul, though a Christian, did not. At this point Grant began to face the danger that he would be engulfed by the ocean of Heidegger. But there was no turning back once his own questions had drawn him in. What he had to do was swallow Heidegger whole, digest him with Christian Platonism and egalitarianism, and thereby transform Heidegger's thought into his own.

I introduce the metaphor of one thinker digesting another to draw attention to the *critical* way Grant absorbed and transformed Heidegger's account of the relation of science and technology. I want to challenge the view that he took it in uncritically, and merely grafted onto it an inconsistent Platonic-Christian morality.

In 1971 and 1972, and again in 1976, Grant worked on two books (never published) about the exclusion by technological society of 'the old idea of good.' 'At its barest,' he said in his notes, 'the ancient language of "good" came down to two platitudes: human beings should sometimes care for others and not only for themselves; humans should sometimes control instinctive appetite. Whatever else was at issue for those who lived with such language, it was considered out of the question for these "shoulds" to be debated. For to debate them was to step outside morality.'[9] The two books were to be called, respectively, 'Technique(s) and Good' and

'Good and Technique.' The essay entitled 'The Computer Does Not Impose on Us the Ways It Should Be Used,' revised and published in 1986 as 'Thinking about Technology,' is the only published work that resulted from these efforts. Some large drafts and sets of notes from the period have survived, however, to complete the picture we already have of his work on technology.

Grant shared with Heidegger the view that the contemporary world had to be understood by thinking about it as essentially technological.[10] Heidegger had demonstrated brilliantly that the technological spirit informs modern science, rather than the reverse. This insight completed Grant's understanding of the revolution of the fifteenth and sixteenth centuries that had spawned modern science. Heidegger gave him a better understanding of the paradigm of knowledge that dominates our era. Grant pointed out in 'Thinking about Technology' that our sciences are now rightly called 'techno-logy' because they unite in their project the Greek words for making (*techne*) and knowing (*logos*). A new form of knowing (and producing) things had emerged, which assumed a change in our relation to nature and to God. Grant accepted Heidegger's help on this, as he had earlier accepted the help of Ellul and others.

Grant differed from Heidegger, however, in drawing attention to the fact that modern science allows no place for a concept of justice based on the way things are in nature and in human nature. If we are only accidents in an implacable universe, Grant argued, there is no reason for us to be just. (For Heidegger, the concepts of nature and human nature as well as the Platonic concept of justice were part of the 'metaphysical' thinking we need to overcome.)

An important and subtle digestion of Heidegger by Grant was occurring at this point. Heidegger argued that modern science in its representation of things does not let the earth, the sky, human beings, and the gods be what they are. (This fourfold designation was Heidegger's way of naming all that is.) Instead, modern science 'summonses' things, before a tribunal as it were, and interrogates them for their reasons or grounds for existing. Similarly, technological knowing does not allow human beings to be thoughtful and poetic producers, but instead commands them to marshal themselves and the natural world for technological projects. Up to this point in Heidegger's account Grant was all unqualified praise. He absorbed him critically, however, at the point where Heidegger argued that the concept of justice in Platonism and Christianity was part of the problem rather than part of the solution. Grant could see that the concept 'justice' *was* part of the problem because it had been progressively reduced by modernity to mere subjective judgment. But he would not take that one step further to say that Plato's thought *is properly and exhaustively interpreted* when it is seen as the foundation of subjective metaphysics, and hence something that must now be overcome.

From Heidegger's lecture about technology Grant accepted the claim that the usual sense of the word 'technology' – that it consists of instruments made by us for our use – though 'correct,' stops short of a true understanding of the ruling forces of our era. We are not independent subjects who can make decisions about the use of the techniques at our disposal. We cannot simply manipulate them and fine-tune them from a position of self-sufficient neutrality. That way of seeing ourselves is itself as much a product of technology as are the techniques themselves. Grant's way of making this point was to say 'we can hold in our minds the enormous benefits of technological society, but we cannot so easily hold the ways it may have deprived us, because technique is ourselves.'[11] Here Grant was transforming Heidegger. When Grant spoke of technological society depriving us, he was referring to the loss of that guidance which is *specifically about good and evil*. And the loss, for Grant, must not only be *embraced* (à la Heidegger), but also *contested*. This double vision was the new stance that Grant arrived at. He said our historical destiny is not the whole of what is given. We still know certain acts are wrong because of the way things are.

Evidence of Grant's critical digestion of Heidegger can be found by looking at the questions the two men used to study technology. A comparison of these questions shows how Grant could be very close to Heidegger and also decisively different from him. Grant made Heidegger's lecture on technology[12] the focus of his graduate seminars in the seventies. But the question he chose to guide his students was profoundly un-Heideggerian: 'What does technical civilization portend for good and evil?' Heidegger's own question had put 'freedom' rather than 'good and evil' at the centre of concern: 'We shall be questioning concerning *technology*, and in so doing we should like to prepare a free relationship to it. The relationship will be free if it opens our human existence to the essence of technology.'[13]

Grant defiantly interjected the question about good and evil into the Heideggerian discussion, where freedom held sway. This defiance takes us to the heart of his stance. His questions led him deep into Heidegger's territory of modern freedom, and *there* he held up the banner of his Platonic-Christian faith and morality. He was driven by the conviction that neither historical freedom nor eternal good could be evaded or compromised.

I have found Grant's lectures on Kant helpful in understanding his interjection of good and evil into Heidegger's account of technology. In 1974 and 1978, during the period when Grant was writing his works on technology, he led graduate seminars on Kant that kept the questions raised by his long struggle with Nietzsche and Heidegger always in the foreground. Kant fascinated Grant because he was the emancipator of modern subjectivity who simultaneously upheld an eternally based morality.[14]

By the seventies Grant had come to see Kant's contribution differently than he had in the fifties. For years he had taught his students Kant's defense of practical reason and egalitarianism. With help from Nietzsche he now saw that Kant was the 'delayer'[15] of the full consequences of the radically subjective teaching that he, Kant, had espoused. Kant was the supreme justifier of human subjectivity and the moral thinker who 'erased the good.' In place of a good that is given to human beings in nature and by God, Kant substituted critical philosophy, the categorical imperative, and the autonomous good *will*.

Grant was aware that the modern situation forced moral thinkers (and actors) to defend morality as if it belonged in a different category or compartment from science; he was aware, too, that those who turn back to the older account of truth have failed to come to grips with the modern account of truth in science. Nietzsche was right, he thought, to call Kant the delayer of the complete arrival of modernity. Kant, Grant said, did not 'cross the Rubicon to the new account of justice which is required of the new account of truth proceeding from the new account of reason.'[16] In other words, Kant, defended morality in the manner suggested – as if it belonged in a different category than science. We are autonomous subjects but we experience the command of practical reason that requires us to act according to the moral law. Kant was, according to Grant, 'turning back' from the consequences of the new doctrine of truth endorsed in his own account of science.

Unlike Nietzsche, Grant applauded this tactic of delay and turning back. But he also saw that it failed to anticipate the power of the new sciences. With the rise of the new scientific paradigm of knowing, morality had been weakened, perhaps fatally. Though similar to Plato's transcendent good that comes to us from beyond being or beyond nature,[17] Kant's moral law as self-legislation had been freed not only from nature but also from God. People eventually found themselves in circumstances where scientific *facts* were distinguished from subjective moral *values*. According to Grant, the language of values was first made the language of morality by Nietzsche because he *had* accepted the consequences for justice of the new doctrine of truth. Thus we now see ourselves as the creators of our moral horizons as well as of our scientific ones.

Heidegger took a step past Nietzsche when he rejected the language of values, calling it the final example in Western thought of subjective 'metaphysics.' Grant waged a similar battle with the language of values.[18] But Heidegger also rejected the language of good and evil as the historical precursor of values language. On the one hand he spoke in the 'Letter on Humanism' about a primordial ethics emerging once again through a renewal of meditative thought and art, but on the other hand he agreed with Nietzsche that we are no longer bound by the traditional moral precepts that emerged from Greek, Hebrew, and Christian beginnings and became part of the Western tradition. When our connection to the roots was lost, he argued, the branches lost their healing power. According to Grant, Heidegger was saying that we must, to move on, accept that we are beyond good and evil, that the Platonic-Christian moral tradition and its secular descendents have lost their efficacy. Grant asserted that 'we are living in the era ... [of] the absolutely profound theoretical breakdown of the Western world. This is illustrated by the fact that the greatest contemporary philosopher, Heidegger, certainly doesn't believe there is such a thing as morality.'[19]

More accurately, Grant should have said Heidegger didn't believe in a classical and Christian approach to morality. After the war Heidegger argued that our political efforts no longer could or should be restrained by the old moral bonds. But Heidegger proposed an alternative approach.[20] What might stop us from destroying the earth and ourselves was something different from morality in the form it has been handed down to us. It was what he called responding thoughtfully and poetically to what it is to be in this time. If we learn to respond appropriately to the whole of Being as it addresses us in this time, he said, we may eventually begin to produce things differently in the world, in a manner more at home with that whole. In the modern world, we produce in a way that treats every human being and every thing as 'standing reserve' for technological projects. The old morality as much as modern science, he was convinced, stands in the way of new guidance. The claim that we already know what is good blocks our ability to listen to the novelty of what is now happening.

One point I want to draw out of this discussion is that both Heidegger and Grant believed that the pre-eminent task for contemporary thinkers was to rethink the foundations of modern science. Science, they argued, has for the most part forgotten its own genesis, and morality-as-values is the thought-poor complement of science. It is my opinion that Grant believed Heidegger had begun the illumination of the foundations of science, though in a problematic way. The question for Grant therefore became: as we take up the task of rethinking science and technology, how can we learn from Heidegger without accepting that we are beyond good and evil? How can we continue the job Heidegger began, without joining him in a root-and-branch rejection of the Platonic elements of the moral tradition?

To conclude this part of the discussion: Grant knew we could learn from Heidegger's illumination of who and what we are. Heidegger's thought was advanced modernity conscious of itself. But Grant also saw the need *to recast Heidegger as we learn from him*, to digest him carefully. Though Heidegger brilliantly illuminated what is going on, he was not right about technology because he was not right about justice. The proper way to encounter Heidegger was, for Grant, the same as the proper way to encounter the modern world.

Grant knew we cannot merely impose on ourselves the classical concept of justice, making it merely a kind of moral appendage to the modern concept of truth. He also knew that he himself was not capable of the monumental task of thinking the truth of modern technology together with the ancient view of justice. But he saw that it had to be attempted nonetheless. What he could do was try to convince others that such a direction was the right one. He began by challenging the reading of Plato at the heart of Heidegger's thought.

RETHINKING THE CONFRONTATION
BETWEEN PLATO AND HEIDEGGER

I want to argue here that Grant's strength lay in a refusal to compromise either the eternal or the historical truth, as well as his insistence that we cannot rest with those truths remaining in contradiction.

His first call for a synthesis (a call he later thought naïve) was the suggestion in 1959 that we need a careful theory in which the idea of 'limit' includes within itself a doctrine that sees history as the sphere for the overcoming of evil.[21] The second came in 1974 when he was teaching and writing about technology: we must think the truth of modern science together with the concept of justice as what we are fitted for.[22] The final call came in 'Confronting Heidegger's Nietzsche' (1984), when Grant said a defence of Plato was needed to prepare for a *genuine confrontation* between Heidegger's 'consummate' historicism and Plato's philosophy of eternity.

In the 1984 essay Grant argued that Heidegger was wonderfully open to other thinkers, including Plato. But even Heidegger's brilliant reading missed part of the meaning of the doctrine of 'being as idea.' As Grant saw it, Heidegger's majestic attempt to think eternity and history together remained in the end profoundly historical. He argued that Heidegger viewed Plato from within Heidegger's own discourse. We can take this as saying also that modern thought fails to acknowledge the whole of our experience. It misses specifically what Plato knew about existence. Historical thought misses that aspect of existence which is true in any time and place. The prevailing modern discourse, because of the way it is constituted, excludes any sense that our existence is more than historically particular. It therefore cannot see that we are part of an order which is more than historically generated:

it must be ... said [that] the exposition of what Plato is stating in these passages is inevitably expressed by Heidegger from within (the very preposition seems presumptuous) what he thinks thinking to be. At this point it is hard to clarify the implications of this sentence. Suffice it to say that on the one hand I must avoid any implication that what Plato is saying can be laid before others from out of some neutral stance of 'objectivity.' Nobody is clearer than Heidegger that the account of one philosopher by another cannot be simply a matter of 'objective' scholarship. Whatever else may be true of philosophy, it transcends the stance of 'objectivity.' On the other hand, to state this must not cloud the fact that what Plato is saying in these passages is, in the very moment of its exposition by Heidegger, placed within the Heideggerian universe of discourse.[23]

Grant knew there was no way to jump out of the modern world or to go back to the ancient world. 'I don't want simply to write as if I were trying to take people back to Platonism – what a hopeless thought,' he wrote when preparing to defend Plato against Heidegger.[24] His agenda was a modern one, like Heidegger's. But because his experience of modern existence was different from (as well as the same as) Heidegger's, he thought he was able to see that Plato's idea of the good was indispensable in a way that Heidegger did not see.

For Heidegger the ultimate question was what he called the question of what it is to be. This question included not only our human existence but also the whole of what governs, determines and sustains the way things are. The question of what it is to be must be an open response to the whole destiny of the age. The questioning may not be guided and limited by a metaphysical first principle or ground assertion. Heidegger claimed that Plato did not ask, what it is to be, without preconceptions. Plato's idea of the Good, said by him to be 'beyond being,' was, for Heidegger, a metaphysical preconception that meant Plato was turning away from the question 'What is it to be?'. The Platonic assertion, according to Heidegger, set the pattern of Western subjective metaphysics that humanity must overcome.[25] But Grant argued instead that Plato raised the most important question of philosophy when he asked about living the good life, and encountered 'Goodness itself' in the course of that asking.[26]

Heidegger's philosophic project, Grant believed, helped to illuminate the 'Platonic' and 'metaphysical' genesis of nihilism, but only up to a point. Grant thought Heidegger blocked humanity's recognition of the claim of good and evil. To bring the Platonic and Heideggerian claims together, Grant argued, it was necessary to hold fast to both and to bring them to bear on each other. Grant held, as well, that we must not slide into a too-easy synthesis that belittles one or the other side of this strange duality that is our fate in the modern world.

CONFRONTING HEIDEGGER'S PLATO

I have found in Martin Heidegger ... an interpretation of Greek philosophy which is very similar to some of the remarks I have been making this year ... that western thought has floated out upon a great tide of nihilism, and the origin of that nihilism is what happened to philosophy somewhere between the time of Parmenides and Plato.[27]

Grant made these remarks in 1958 to students in his Dalhousie seminar on Plato, after a reading of Heidegger's essay entitled 'Plato's Doctrine of Truth.' He did not at that time add a defence of Plato's idea of the Good. In 1958 he agreed that Platonism had played a decisive part in the origin of 'nihilism.' In Heidegger's work nihilism meant that truth had become subjective or propositional rather than ontological. The Western understanding of 'truth' had evolved from a Platonic beginning to the modern account that truth is created freely by human beings, as opposed to being something that is given to them.

Then, in 1984, in the important but little-known essay called 'Justice and Technology,'[28] Grant attacked Heidegger for missing the meaning of Plato's idea of the Good. Returning to 'Plato's Doctrine of Truth,' he argued that Heidegger had defined Platonic justice formally, abstracting it from the pain-filled content of people's attempts to live good lives:

When Heidegger defines good as used by Plato simply formally, as what we are fitted for, he does not give content to that fitting as Socrates does when he says that it is better to suffer injustice than to inflict it. Heidegger describes Plato's doctrine of truth so that 'being' as 'idea' is abstracted from that love of justice in terms of which 'idea' can alone be understood as separate. Good itself is 'beyond being.' This is why I take even Heidegger's wonderful account of technology as having been written within that loss which has come with 'technology.' It is in this sense that I finally take Heidegger as an historicist, although the most consummate of the historicists.[29]

I want first to look at the question of Grant's apparent 'reversal' of his 1958 position. What may look like an about-face, I want to argue, is a result of two different but *complementary* goals in a consistent position. We may ask whether Grant would have retracted his 1958 remarks had they been brought to his attention in 1984. I think he would certainly have regretted the limitations of his existential concerns in the fifties and his failure at that time to say what was wrong with Heidegger's account. But I don't think he would have taken back the basic point about the role of Platonism in the coming of nihilism, assuming it could have been integrated into (rather than contradicted by) his defence of Plato in 1984.

The two different responses to Heidegger only appear contradictory. The 1984 response was simply a change of emphasis, like others that show up in the retractions and addenda Grant appended to earlier works. In 1985, for example, he retracted his 1955 broadcast on Sartre.[30] In the retraction he expressed regret that he had praised as a philosopher and artist someone he had come to think of as a shallow intellectual and a plagiarist of Heidegger. For my purposes it is sufficient to note that, even in the 1985 attack on Sartre, he was not dissociating himself from existential philosophy (such as the early work of Heidegger, which he referred to in the 1985 essay).

It is vital for an understanding of Grant's thought to insist that he did not abandon his 'modern' existential and anticapitalist convictions in the mid-sixties when he lost hope for a relatively easy reconciliation of modern and ancient thought. He had been drawn to Marxism and existentialism in his early years at Dalhousie because thinkers such as Marcuse and Sartre were challenging the established order and urging resistance to economic and scientific oppression. Though he became more critical of those thinkers for other reasons in the sixties, he never lost the conviction that we are called to try to resist evils in the world.

Grant's two different responses to Heidegger's account of Plato are consistent. A distinction may be made between Platonism as it shaped the Western tradition and Plato's thought as it may still be interpreted. In the Western tradition Platonism did indeed play (along with Christianity) a key role in the coming of subjectivity. Grant agreed with Heidegger on that point, but said Plato's thought remains to be interpreted anew by each generation.[31] Grant both learned from Heidegger and diverged from him significantly on the interpretation of Plato. In any case, he believed the Good belongs to what endures, not to what has died. In 1958 Grant joined Heidegger in diagnosing the problem of subjectivity. In 1984 he announced his intention to defend the Plato who had been missed in the historical account.

'PLUNGING INTO THE MODERN' AND 'HOLDING UP' PLATONISM

Grant responded to modern existence by plunging into it as it thinks itself to be, not by backing away into a religious faith apart from it.[32] By 'as it thinks itself to be' he meant primarily that we moderns are oblivious of eternity. And he said he wanted to *hold up the ancient religion against the modern,* having taken the plunge and faced what we are now. He used these phrases when he told his students in a course on Plato and Augustine in 1974 about his method of teaching the truth of Socrates and Christ in a world where a different account of morality prevails: 'Now the second way of living in modernity as a believer is to plunge oneself into the modern directly and simply so engross oneself in the modern by taking its parables – not as parables, but as what those who use them think them to be – a true account of what is, a world in which there are no parables, because no eternity – and therefore hold up the ancient religion against the modern.'[33] The other method of living in modernity as a believer – simply asserting the older truth as superior to the modern one – didn't get beneath the surface, he thought, though it was perhaps safer. His method, as he knew all too well from his own encounters with Nietzsche and Heidegger, was difficult and dangerous: 'The advantage of the second, negative method is that one is aware of the superficiality of the first method [teaching from within the ancient religion and trying to show the inadequacy of the modern approach]. Its great disadvantage or danger is to the person who practises it – because it may lead the person concerned to madness, or to reclusiveness (the inability to live in the modern) – one or the other, not both.'[34]

The metaphor of plunging into the modern is not a spatial one, as if we could begin 'outside' the world and then plunge down into it; rather, he was saying we have to open our eyes to who and where we already are. As members of this world we are put beyond good and evil, but at first we delude ourselves that morality still endures as values, and that we can use values politically to control the direction of technological society. It takes a plunge to get past that delusion, to the point where we realize that the modern world has dealt a body-blow to morality – and to politics. In his notes from the seventies Grant wrote that 'not to be in doubt is to abstract oneself from the modern.' He could not teach as if the world had not put his students – and himself – beyond good and evil. In this he was holding firmly to one side of his double vision.

Grant thought the confrontation between Plato and Heidegger posed crucial questions. Does our existence in our technological world still include the claim of good as revealed and thought by Christianity and Plato, even though the science and morality of this world have turned away from it and assume we are beyond it? Or is Heidegger right, following Nietzsche, that we must embrace the move beyond good and evil, because Plato and Christianity, in giving shape to our sense of good and evil, also gave birth to the very subjectivity that is now our modern problem? Grant certainly answered yes to the first question. But he also knew a way had not yet been found to support the claim of good in a world that had answered yes to the second. Our thoughts and actions must come to terms with where and what we are.

Grant's opposition to subjectivity did not mean that he decided that human beings are not or should not be free. He did decide that freedom comes from accepting what is given. When we break with the classical tradition we have inherited and 'shape our own truth,' we still do so within the limits of what is given. But Heidegger, as I have said, also thought freedom comes from accepting what is given. Grant's disagreement with him was about what it is that is given. We have been put beyond good and evil as part of our destiny as modern people, Grant argued. But that did not mean for him that we are beyond good and evil in the sense that we are no longer fitted to be just. This was a crucial distinction for Grant. He acknowledged the power of the modern world to make morality subjective at the same time that he denied we actually are beyond good and evil.

Grant wrestled throughout his years of teaching with the difficulty of 'holding up' the ancient religion against the prevailing freedom-dominated thinking. In 'A Platitude'[35] he suggested a promising opening, but did not develop it explicitly in his later work. The modern language of freedom, he said in 'A Platitude,' is sometimes used to express a vision of a positive good, because that language has become the only possible medium for what we as human beings still revere. The civil rights movement in the American South during the sixties might have been a case he had in mind. The anthems of the movement, such as 'Oh Freedom,' many of which were rewritten hymns, were about the deprival of a positive way of life, not just about the removal of restrictions. Perhaps the language of good (or at least what it expresses) is not as dead as a surface view of language would make it appear. Perhaps the language of freedom is not as antithetical to obeying the good as Grant came to believe. Heidegger made an attempt to work through modern subjective freedom toward obedience and guidance. Even though Grant was right that Heidegger failed to honour the good sufficiently in that attempt, I think the opening remains a promising one.

Can the matrix of human nobility include both reverence and freedom? Grant seemed at times to say no. But I believe that his thought directs us toward answering yes – though we have yet to find the way. We still may have the capacity to learn reverence for what is other than ourselves, for the earth and for each other. Grant did not take us into a way of thinking that combines Heidegger and Plato. But he did insist that the job had to be tackled, and he drew our attention to the failure of others to complete it. He let us know that the work is still ahead of us because it hasn't been done – not by Heidegger, not by Strauss, and not even by Weil.

GRANT'S POLITICS AFTER HEIDEGGER

I have argued that Grant did not change from leaning left and being pro-modern to leaning right and becoming antimodern. He did say, for example, that 'It is by looking at modernity in its greatest power that one is perhaps able even slightly to escape its power.'[36] But it is worth pointing out that he wished to escape modernity's power insofar as it denies that we are subject to good and evil. He did not mean to reject everything about the modern world, including his own liberal and left-wing convictions. Though his objection to subjectivity was admittedly a substantial one, he continued to defend the right to dissent and to believe we should try to change the inequalities of the world. This complex stance toward various facets of modern politics was what made Grant the unusual political animal that he was.

Don Forbes and Sam Ajzenstat have described Grant's political stance very well.[37] He was part conservative, part socialist, and part liberal in his response to the special circumstances of Canada struggling to survive inside the American empire. I want to add that his politics remained remarkably consistent from the fifties to the eighties. In 1985, for example, he declared that 'North American capitalism has been a ferocious and terrible thing in the world ... A society whose whole end is making money is not going to be a good society.'[38] In *Philosophy in the Mass Age* (1959), he applauded Marx and the Marxists for drawing attention to the evils of capitalism and for insisting that something must be done about them. But he also criticized the Marxists for denying 'the infinite' and for paying insufficient attention to individual freedom and individual rights. He was a strong defender of the practical traditions of English-speaking liberalism, though critical of liberal philosophy for its failure to see how modern subjectivity has weakened morality. He defended conservatism as a noble practical stance, but argued in the introduction to 'Religion and the State' that the important questions we must face as members of a technological society cannot come into view if 'clouded by a "conservative" hope.' And finally, Grant's nationalism, though passionate, was tempered by his commitment to a universal good. We must move, he said, from the love of our own to a love of the good, a good that is not determined solely by the particular time and place in which we live.

Like Heidegger, Grant was driven by the need to reconstitute political thought in the new circumstances of technological society. It was pre-eminently for the sake of a genuine politics that Heidegger turned to the question of what it is to be and Grant to the question of what it is to live a good life. It would be misleading, therefore, to claim that either man backed away from politics in his later thought. Neither became gnostic or quietistic. Grant argued that 'useful politics' had become 'gravely difficult, but not impossible.'[39] The liberal, socialist, and conservative political positions were, like nationalism, falling short of the task at hand because their thought had been outstripped by the modern world. Political regimes of every kind were being drawn ever more tightly into the power of the prevailing forces of capital and technology. But Grant staunchly denied that this diminishing of politics should lead to inaction. He did not wish to encourage 'the flaccid will which excuses the sin of despair in the name of necessity.'[40] Rather, the political task was to expose the ignoble delusions that were leading to catastrophe. And that is where Heidegger could be helpful, provided a defence of Plato against him could be kept in the foreground.

Heidegger's radical thought addressed the failure of traditional politics in a way that liberalism and socialism did not. He came closer to understanding the destruction of nature and the estrangement and homelessness of human beings under the rule of capital and technology. Heidegger's politics was about 'the encounter between global technology and modern man.'[41] This statement, though it was made by Heidegger in 1935, could have been applied just as easily to his politics of the later 'poetic' period, when he stepped back from political judgment. Both his catastrophic support of the Nazis and the later withdrawal to political 'silence' were motivated by a desire to find an adequate political response to technology.

Grant was more respectful (though also critical) of inherited politics, and he was less hopeful about the political future. I think, however, it is right to say he too was trying to find a politics that was an adequate response to the new technological world.[42] Both men were horrified by the tragedies of the century of planetary technology and were, as a result, shaken loose from their faith in progress. They both felt, as I have said, that liberalism and socialism were unable to respond adequately to the tragedies of the twentieth century. Heidegger learned after 1933 that National Socialism was also not the answer.

The inadequacy of existing political regimes and ideas 'drove them deep'[43] in their search for the strength to engage capital and technology. The important differences between Grant and Heidegger on morality and politics, both philosophically and practically, should not obscure the similarities in their desire for an adequate politics.

Grant's differences with Heidegger are nonetheless vitally important. They pertain to the immediate political demands that continue to press on us while we seek a new politics. They also pertain to the limits within which the search is carried out.

However fragmented the single-issue political struggles of Grant's time had become without the guidance of an overall position or direction, it was evident to him that the need to protest, to resist, to defy the established order was as pressing as ever, as was a passion for justice at a time when true justice was no longer a part of what people considered 'justice.'

Heidegger did not move from political engagement in 1933 to a later quietism. Nor did Grant believe Heidegger had become a quietist. It will not do to pretend that Heidegger had nothing practical to offer and that his alleged quietism was the reason for Grant's rejection of him. Silence is practical when it replaces misguided words. Grant agreed that silence was needed to replace inadequate solutions and to prepare the way for genuine thought about what was happening in the world. We are learning what is needed as we see the failures of current regimes and policies.

Grant's disagreement with Heidegger was more specific than an attack against silence as such. He wished to assert forcefully that the search for an adequate politics – and our actions along the way – are not free from the claim of good (though the spirit of the age puts us beyond it): 'This seems to me the great difficulty of being a modern: that at one and the same time one must know what it is to say that the modern era is the night of the world and also know that we must not live as if good were evil and evil, good – that is not to know something of justice. An extraordinary difficulty.'[44]

Grant believed Heidegger's Nazi connection, properly interpreted, could reveal 'the whole question of the destiny of modernity.'[45] Heidegger looked for something stronger and more alive than the inherited tradition. But that revolutionary move in his thought meant, after the War, that he had to be silent about the terrible actions of the Nazis. The silence was ominous – but not because Heidegger the man approved of anti-Semitism or recommended genocide. There is no doubt in my mind that he did not. But whatever the truth or falsity of the accusations against him, the silence was ominous because this greatest of modern thinkers had decided that he would be betraying his thought-path by pretending that we have grounds to condemn *any* actions, including his own. He argued on one occasion that 'the questions are so difficult that it would be contrary to the meaning of the task of thought to step up publicly, as it were, to preach, and to impose moral judgment.'[46] For Grant this stance was anathema. He took from it the conclusion that modern thought at its height is led to be able to say nothing about how it is best for men to be together – it is led to have to be able to be silent before the most important question for man – what is the best public life for man.'[47]

Grant agreed with Heidegger that a politics based on 'half-measures' (Christian, democratic, constitutional) cannot understand what modern technology is, and therefore will be deluded about political possibilities. He argued, however, that we must make judgments to support the best and prevent the very worst. When, for example, the state carries out torture (perhaps in the name of its citizens' security), or judicially condemns innocent people for some larger purpose, or pursues a 'morally disordered' economic policy that increases poverty and inequality, we are required to say no publicly. The fact that there will always be deep disagreements about what is good and what is evil (Vietnam? abortion?) does not justify backing away from the necessity that we make judgments as best we can, and act on them.

In full recognition of the modern situation Grant insisted that individual human beings are still required to oppose evil, no matter what public or private goal the evil in question is supposed to serve. Heidegger thought a revolutionary break with legal and moral restraints was necessary to confront growing technological tyranny. For Grant, this break with restraint draws attention to the limits of historical thought, even at its greatest. We must oppose such a break, as we must protest and try to prevent the evil actions committed by existing regimes in the name of order, security, and economic necessity.

Grant was, I think, speaking on behalf of all who protest and struggle – as Christians, conservatives, liberals, socialists – against increased inequality and the loss of liberty, however they name what they are doing and thinking. They must persevere, he argued, even when they find that their protest has less and less bite. They also need to strive to free themselves from the illusion that the technological package-deal we have embraced can accommodate a justice that is not consistent with it.

Strangely, it was Grant's refusal to propose a specific synthesis of the ancient and the modern that gave him what Abraham Rotstein called his moral authority,[48] and allowed him to address such a broad range of questions about technology, Canada, the university, and the war in Vietnam. Heidegger's approach was different. He would have objected to having his thought called a synthesis; he tried to take thought to a place where a split had not yet occurred, and therefore where no synthesis was needed. But he did try to unify what Plato had kept separate as eternity and time. And when he rethought, in a new (and old) unity, what had been thought as eternity and time, he was forced to fall silent on the question of good and evil.

Grant travelled along Heidegger's thought-path and also took up Heidegger's challenge to search for a better one.[49] I have tried

to show that Grant believed we need Heidegger's thought –
about science and technology, about the darkness it entails, about
poetry, and about the healing that is growing in the midst of danger – to open ourselves to the world we are in. Grant urged us to
bring Heidegger's insight together with the demands of living a
good life, demands that he thought could be illuminated by a
newly appropriated, purified Plato and Christianity. The search
therefore continues for a thought-path that combines the truth of
freedom with obedience to the demands of justice as what we are
fitted for.

NOTES

1 At the time of his death in 1988 Grant was still working on his complex
   and ambiguous response to Heidegger. He wanted to praise Heidegger, and to urge others to learn from Heidegger's account of the
   modern world. But at the same time he knew it would not do to neatly
   sever Heidegger's morality and politics from Heidegger's account of
   science and technology, tempting though it might have been to
   embrace the latter while rejecting the former. Grant was moving
   instead toward a more difficult, and ultimately more compelling point:
   that Heidegger was right as well as wrong about morality and politics.
2 Grant, 'Confronting Heidegger's Nietzsche' (unpublished, 1984) 10.
3 Grant's published work includes statements on Nietzsche and Heidegger and on Plato and Christianity: See Grant, *Time as History* (Toronto:
   CBC 1969); the conversations in Larry Schmidt, ed., *George Grant in
   Process: Essays and Conversations* (Toronto: Anansi 1978); Grant, 'Faith
   and the Multiversity,' 'Thinking about Technology,' and 'Nietzsche
   and the Ancients: Philosophy and Scholarship,' in *Technology and
   Justice* (Toronto: Anansi 1986); 'George Grant and Religion: A Conversation Prepared and Edited by William Christian,' *Journal of Canadian
   Studies* 26, no. 1 (spring 1991), 42–63; Grant, 'Justice and Technology,'
   in Carl Mitcham and Jim Grote, eds., *Theology and Technology* (Lanham,
   MD: University Press of America 1984), 237–46. The unpublished material includes several lectures on Nietzsche and Heidegger and on Plato
   and Christianity, most of which were delivered during the seventies;
   letters collected by William Christian; and notes on Heidegger's
   Nietzsche from the seventies and eighties.
4 Though Heidegger opposed the use of the term 'existentialist' to
   describe his thought, I am arguing here that it is nonetheless appropri-

ate, as long as it is not given Sartre's meaning of radical freedom and humanism.

5 See, for example, the new introduction to George Grant's *Philosophy in the Mass Age* (Toronto: Copp Clark 1966); the introduction to 'Religion and the State' in idem, *Technology and Empire* (Toronto: Anansi 1969) 43–5; Grant's 1985 retraction (as yet unpublished) of his 1955 CBC broadcast on Sartre, which was published in *Architects of Modern Thought* (Toronto: CBC 1955), 65–74; and the 1988 addendum to 'Two Theological Languages' in Wayne Whillier, ed., *'Two Theological Languages' by George Grant and Other Essays in Honour of His Work* (Lewiston, NY: Edwin Mellen Press 1990), 16–19.

6 See, for example, Michael Allen Gillespie, 'George Grant and the Tradition of Political Philosophy,' in Peter C. Emberley, ed., *By Loving Our Own: George Grant and the Legacy of Lament for a Nation* (Ottawa: Carleton University Press 1990), 123–31.

7 In a 1988 interview Grant said 'conversion came to me at the worst stage of the war. Now many people might say – Heidegger would say this so it's not a foolish remark – that this was just a way of looking for a safe, other world because I couldn't bear this world,' See 'George Grant and Religion: A Conversation Prepared and Edited by William Christian,' *Journal of Canadian Studies* 26, no. 1 (spring 1991), 42–63.

8 This passage is from Grant's notes for 'Good and Technique,' 1976. I would like to thank Ronald Beiner for locating several passages in Nietzsche, including the 'botched and bungled' quotation. Nietzsche said: 'O you dolts, you presumptuous, pitying dolts, what have you done? Was that work for your hands? How have you bungled and botched my beautiful stone! What presumption!': *Beyond Good and Evil: Prelude to a Philosophy of the Future*, trans. Walter Kaufmann (New York: Vintage Books 1989), §62.

9 This passage is from Grant's notes for 'Techniques and Good,' 1971–2.

10 'Indeed it is central to my way of thinking that the essential way to ask the question of the whole these days is to ask it through technique. The question of the whole appears to us most clearly in asking the question about technique': Grant, Lecture on 'Political Philosophy and Its Relation to the Tradition,' Notebook M (1972).

11 Grant, 'A Platitude,' *Technology and Empire*, 137.

12 Martin Heidegger, 'The Question Concerning Technology' in D.F. Krell, ed., *Basic Writings* (New York: Harper and Row 1977), 287–317.

13 Ibid., 287.

14 In an unpublished letter written to R.D. Crook on 19 July 1965, Grant

tried to answer the question whether the distinction between necessity and good really leads to the fact-value distinction: 'Of course, this account of the moral judgement for Kant had to go with the possibility of science – and that for Kant meant a nature freed from purpose. Therefore reason commanded us rather than nature giving us the law.'

15 See, for example, Friedrich Nietzsche, *The Will to Power* ed., Walter Kaufmann and trans. Walter Kaufmann and R.J. Hollingdale (New York: Vintage 1967), §101.

16 'Now it seems to me that this is what is so fascinating about Kant. As much as anybody he lays before us the new essence of truth in which humanity as subject installs itself as sovereign over all that is and in which humanity understands itself as autonomous legislator to master all that is and to enact what the world will be like – but then at the height of that new system of representation – namely in the question of justice, he does not cross the Rubicon to the new account of justice which is required of the new account of truth proceeding from the new account of reason. He offers the categorical imperative, that morality is the one fact of reason; he offers a fundamental equality of persons – that is, an account of justice which comes out of the older account of truth which was based not on the first principle of subjectivity – but on the eternal order': Grant, Kant seminar manuscript, 1978.

17 'I think (but am not sure) that there is in Plato a much greater understanding of the suffering of man than in Aristotle. The transcendence of the forms ... does appear to me very similar to Kant in the sense that the good by which we act comes to us somehow from beyond nature – call it if you will by that hated word supernaturally – and demands the death of worldly desires. All the psychological or sociological reductions of that position in the name of accusing it of repression, aberration and perversion does not seem to me to get around its appeal for two reasons: (a) the meaning of the whole does not seem to be understandable in the light of evil in an immanent way; (b) the question of the meaning of the whole cannot easily be put aside either existentially or scientifically': Grant letter to Crook, 19 July 1965.

18 See, for example, 'The University Curriculum,' in Grant, *Technology and Empire* , 118–27.

19 Larry Schmidt, 'An Interview with George Grant,' *Grail* 1 (March 1985), 41.

20 Heidegger's advocacy of thought and poetry was essentially an alternative to the Platonic, Christian, liberal, and socialist approaches to justice. But, in addition, he did address the meaning of the Greek root

word for 'justice,' *dike*. There is, for example, his work on the idea of justice in Parmenides. But since there is no evidence that Grant engaged with that part of Heidegger's work, it will not be included here in the more general discussion of Heidegger's proposed alternative to classical justice.

21 George Grant, *Philosophy in the Mass Age*, ed. William Christian (Toronto: University of Toronto Press 1995), 102–3.

22 'The great theoretical achievements of the modern era have been quantum physics, the biology of evolutionism, and the modern logic ... These are the undoubtable core of truth which had come out of technology, and they cry out to be thought in harmony with the conception of justice as what we are fitted for': George Grant, *English-Speaking Justice* (Toronto: Anansi 1978), 54.

23 Grant, 'Confronting Heidegger's Nietzsche,' 10.

24 Notes on Heidegger's Nietzsche from the seventies and eighties. Another fragment from Notebook V of the 1970s reads, 'If modern thought is ambiguous for us in having made technology and not therefore able to judge it, ancient thought is ambiguous for us in having been dead before technology.'

25 Heidegger wrote, 'Was Plato therefore the first to think in values? That would be a rash conclusion. The Platonic conception of agathon is as essentially different from Nietzsche's concept of value as the Greek conception of man is from the modern notion of man as subject. But the history of metaphysics proceeds on its path from Plato's interpretation of Being as *idea* and *agathon* to an interpretation of Being as will to power, which posits values and thinks everything as value': Heidegger, *Nietzsche*, vol. 4, *Nihilism*, ed. D.F. Krell and trans. F.A. Capuzzi (San Francisco: Collins 1991), 166. Heidegger thought Plato had played a decisive role in the changed meaning of the Greek word for truth (*aletheia*) by shifting the meaning from unconcealment to correctness of judgment. He later retracted his claim, made in 'Plato's Doctrine of Truth,' that Plato was the first to endorse such a shift. Paul Friedlander agrees with Heidegger's etymological account of the development of the meaning of aletheia but points out that the sense of 'correctness' appears as early as Homer. Heidegger's basic point remains, however. A fateful shift in the conception of truth occurred, and Heidegger argued that humanity's task was to remember and rethink the more original meaning of unconcealment in relation to the change to correctness of judgment. The teaching about being as idea or form, he thought, and especially the idea of the good as separate from being,

had placed humanity firmly on the road that led eventually to modern subjectivity and to ethics as 'values.' Grant, on the other hand, argued that Plato used the word aletheia to incorporate both correctness and unconcealment, with the emphasis shifting according to the context.

26 Grant preferred to translate the phrase usually rendered as 'the Idea of the Good,' as 'goodness itself.' In a lecture on Plato in 1979–80, he said that 'In *The Republic* Socrates talks of the *idea tou agathou,* which some people translate by 'the idea of the good.' But the word 'idea' has been changed by modern subjectivism – your idea, my idea, etc. I think therefore you get what Plato means when you translate it "goodness itself."'

27 Lecture notes from Grant's Dalhousie University Philosophy 7 seminar on Plato, 1958–9. The lecture continued as follows: 'For Parmenides, being and awareness were one, and according to Heidegger human existence was rooted in that oneness ... For the pre-Socratics truth was what Heidegger calls the unhiddenness of Being. In the *Republic* of Plato we find, as against this first and greatest insight, the beginning of a less profound and misleading conception. In the analogy of the cave, for instance, with its shadows of imitations of real things, in the Line, with its parallel hierarchies of Knowns and Knowers, and in the very conception of the idea itself – the seeing, the appearance which is cut off from the flow of our perceptions – we have the beginning of the lie: Truth comes to belong not to Being but to propositions.'

28 Grant, 'Justice and Technology.'

29 Ibid., 244. The quoted passage is preceded by the following: 'Heidegger's call to thought is to think beyond "technology" in this night of the world. But – and what a "but" it is – the ontology he is moving towards is one which excludes the one thing needful – namely, justice in its full and demanding purity ... In ["Plato's Doctrine of Truth"] he is criticizing Plato's account of "being" as "idea," because it is the foundation of the definition of truth as correctness, and therefore is the foundation of the age of metaphysics ... It is a remarkable writing. However, what is so singularly absent is any discussion of the *politeia* or the virtues, in terms of which "the Sun," "the Line," and "the Cave" were written. The extraordinarily powerful and painfilled language used by Plato concerning the breaking of the chains, the climb out of the cave into the light of the sun and the return to the cave, are all related to the virtue of justice and its dependence upon the sun. This is absent from Heidegger's commentary. From his translation and commentary one would not understand that in the Sun, the Line, and the

Cave, the metaphor of sight is to be taken as love. That which we love and which is the source of our love is outside the cave, but it is the possibility of the fire in the cave and of the virtues which make possible the getting out of the cave.'

30 See note 5 above.

31 I think Grant would have readily endorsed Stanley Rosen's statement in *The Question of Being* that 'My "reversal" of Heidegger is at the same time a reconstruction of the spirit of Platonism, a spirit that must renew itself in each generation, like a firebird that is reborn from the ashes of refutation': Rosen, *The Question of Being: A Reversal of Heidegger* (New Haven: Yale University Press 1993), ix.

32 Grant's sometimes dramatic and extreme statements about Heidegger – both positive and negative – are a result of the difficulty of his plunge into modern thought and his fierce holding up of the Christian Platonic morality against it. When he praised Heidegger on science, he spoke of 'staggering illumination,' giving the misleading impression that he accepted him on science and technology without reservation. But on questions of morality, Heidegger, in sharp contrast, often became the devil. Grant tended to focus on the specific element of Heidegger's position that he opposed (in particular the alleged agreement with Nietzsche that we are beyond good and evil). He then declared his absolute opposition, obscuring his partial agreement with Heidegger on religion. On Heidegger's relation to Christianity, for example, Grant said theologians had been seduced by his anti-Christian thought. But I believe this question is, at a minimum, more difficult than that statement implies. I also think Grant knew this but sometimes exaggerated dramatically to make a point.

33 Grant, Lecture from undergraduate course on Plato and Augustine, 1974.

34 Ibid.

35 Grant, *Technology and Empire*, 141–3.

36 'How does one then ever move out of the circle of our present destiny? Seeing modern assumptions laid before me at their most lucid and profound in Nietzsche and Heidegger has allowed me (indeed only slightly) to be able to partake in the alternatives of Plato. It is by looking at modernity in its greatest power that one is perhaps able even slightly to escape its power': Schmidt, ed., *George Grant in Process*, 67.

37 See H.D. Forbes, 'The Political Thought of George Grant,' and Samuel Ajzenstat, 'George Grant on Liberal Self-Destruction,' *Journal of Canadian Studies* 26, no.2 (summer 1991), 46–68 and 69–71, respectively.

38 Speaking about the technological paradigm of knowledge that he
   called 'the great civilizational destiny of the modern West,' Grant said,
   'I think it is now clear that the great economic machine through which
   that paradigm has been put into the world is capitalism. One has to
   look at capitalist civilization with very suspicious eyes. These days
   people are all praising capitalism to the skies, but I think one should
   look at that. I have very little sympathy in any way for communism, or
   socialism as a total regime. But I think that North American capitalism
   has been a ferocious and terrible thing in the world, and I think we
   should face that ... A society whose whole end is making money is not
   going to be a good society': Schmidt, 'Interview with George Grant,'
   34–47.
39 Grant made a careful distinction in 'Céline's Trilogy' about the possibilities and limitations of 'useful' politics. He was talking about our
   vulnerability as human beings and the incompleteness of our purposes
   and projects. The western tradition has emphasized the power of God,
   he said, while forgetting the weakness of God. The belief in the power
   of God has been secularized in our time into a belief in unlimited
   human power, forgetting our own 'grave limitations.' Grant said, 'This
   fact must be expressed hesitantly because it can be so easily used to
   justify the impossibility of any useful politics in this era. But it does
   not imply the impossibility of politics, only their grave difficulties and
   danger': Grant, 'Céline's Trilogy' (this volume), 51.
40 George Grant, *Lament for a Nation* (Toronto: McClelland and Stewart
   1970), xi–xii.
41 See Martin Heidegger, *An Introduction to Metaphysics,* trans. Ralph
   Manheim (New Haven: Yale University Press 1987), 199.
42 Grant observed in his notes from around 1980 that 'Heidegger writes
   outside politics because it has been broken in him. I also must write
   outside politics, but that is not outside the ethical in the sense of the
   good as more than resolution. Writing public but not political. Outside
   politics and yet in it.' Grant also remarked that he had to face the fact
   that Heidegger was more 'historically hopeful' than he, though Heidegger's hope went hand in hand with a rejection of the tradition of goodness.
43 I have borrowed this phrase from George Steiner. I think it is appropriate for Heidegger's thought as a whole, (even though Steiner used it to
   describe Heidegger's use of language: 'We are to be slowed down,
   bewildered, and barred in our reading so that we may be driven deep':
   Steiner, *Heidegger,* 2nd ed., (London: Fontana 1992), 9.

44 Grant, Graduate lecture on Plato's *Phaedo*, 1979–80.

45 'How could this amazing unfolder of the nature of modernity, this person who can illuminate the philosophic past, how could he opt for National Socialism at the political level? This is much more than an historical question about Europe in the 1930's. If one uses it as an oyster knife to open up his brilliance, the whole question of the destiny of modernity can be revealed': Grant in Schmidt, ed., *George Grant in Process*, 66.

Grant condemned Heidegger for continuing to praise National Socialism in the fifties. (Heidegger published his *Introduction to Metaphysics* in 1953, leaving in, without comment, a now-famous phrase written in 1935: 'the inner truth and greatness of the national socialist movement (the encounter between modern man and global technology).') Grant thought the Third Reich had committed great crimes *as a matter of principle* (unlike, for example, the crime of the saturation bombing of Dresden), and should not have been praised after the war, even indirectly by praising the National Socialist movement. Grant was suggesting that the bombing of Dresden was not essential to the Allied regimes in the way that the extermination of the Jews was to the German regime, though it can be argued that civilian terror and revenge became essential principles of the Allied war strategy in the later years of the war.

Grant also remarked in his notes that 'a case could be made' for national Socialism in Germany in the thirties, given the country's situation at the time, and the other options available to the Germans.

46 Heidegger added later that 'it would be asking too much of thinking to have it set about giving instructions. By what authority could this take place? In the realm of thinking there are no authoritative assertions': 'Only a God Can Save Us,' interview with Heidegger in *Der Spiegel*, trans. Maria P. Alter and John D. Caputo and published in *Philosophy Today*, 20 (1976), 297, 283.

47 Grant, Notebook M, 1972–3, 5.

48 *The Owl and the Dynamo*, hour-long documentary film on Grant produced by Vincent Tovell and broadcast on the CBC on 13 February 1980.

49 Heidegger cast his central thesis in the form of an invitation in his 'Letter on Humanism' published in 1949. It was a general invitation to join him on the path of his thought or to find 'a better one': 'Ob der Bereich der Wahrheit des Seins eine Sackgasse oder ob er das Freie ist, worin die Freiheit ihr Wesen spart, möge jeder beurteilen, nachdem er selbst versucht hat, den gewiesenen Weg zu gehen oder, was noch

besser ist, einen besseren, das heisst einen der Frage gemässen Weg zu bahnen.' ('Whether the region of the truth of Being is a blind alley or whether it is the free [das Freie] wherein freedom saves its essence, each may judge after he has tried himself to go the pointed way, or better, to go a better one, which means to pioneer a way appropriate to the question.'): Heidegger, *Wegmarken* (Frankfurt: Klostermann 1967), 174.

7

George Grant and Leo Strauss

H.D. FORBES

THE PROBLEM OF INTERPRETATION

George Grant's writings from the 1960s contain some remarkable tributes to Leo Strauss. No one familiar with both writers can help noticing the real similarities between them, despite their obvious differences. But how should these similarities and differences be understood?

Grant and Strauss found much to question about 'modernity.' Both stood apart from the professional philosophers of their own time, sharing an antipathy to the assumptions governing the modern republic of letters. Yet both were quite realistic about practical conservatism. They avoided the bromide that 'human values should control technology,' and devoted themselves instead simply to understanding what 'values' have in fact controlled it and perhaps must always do so. Beyond the undeniable threats of war and pollution, both were concerned about the fate of education – and about the educational role of government – in a worldwide technological society. Both turned to the classical political philosophers, and to Plato more than Aristotle, for a deeper understanding of the nature and problems of the modern world. Grant's well-known forebodings about unlimited technological progress seem to have been based on Strauss's argument for the superiority of ancient political thought to modern political thought.

The purpose of this essay is to clarify Grant's relation to Strauss and thus the differences between them. I will focus on Grant's writings from the mid-1960s, particularly his most widely read book, *Lament for a Nation*, which was published in 1965, and his essay about Strauss and Alexandre Kojève, 'Tyranny and Wisdom,' which was published in 1964.[1] Grant called the disagreement between Strauss and Kojève 'the most important controversy in contemporary political philosophy' – a judgment that shows at the very least his ability to stand apart from the conventional opinions of his academic and political milieu. Why did he attach so much importance to a rather arcane controversy between two rather obscure writers? What was it in Strauss's thought that so impressed Grant? What reservations did he have about it?

The impact of Strauss on Grant is sometimes explained by saying that Strauss put an end to Grant's 'Hegelian phase.'[2] Grant, it seems, had taken Hegel to be the greatest of all philosophers. He had credited him with understanding all that was true and good in the Greek world, and then with synthesizing it with Christianity and with the freedom of the Enlightenment and modern science. Hegel had thus clearly shown what it means to believe in divine providence. One need only quote from the introduction to the 1966 edition of Grant's *Philosophy in the Mass Age* to demonstrate the merit of this interpretation. As Grant himself said, Strauss liberated him from his uncritical admiration for Hegel. But this formula – that Strauss showed Grant the limitations of Hegel – will be most helpful to those who already know Hegel's system. For those who do not, it may be like trying to take one's bearings from a landmark, the location of which is unknown. In this essay, therefore, I will adopt an approach that stresses what Grant says about North America rather than about Hegel. I will present Grant's encounter with Strauss in such a way as to shift the emphasis from Hegel and the problem of history to Socrates and the problem of virtue.

GRANT'S LAMENT

Grant used to protest against being described as a pessimist, but there is something remarkably dark and gloomy about his writings from the 1960s. The decade seems to have been a time of anguish and perplexity for Grant, well symbolized, perhaps, by the black cover of *Technology and Empire*. Does the darkness or 'pessimism' of

Grant's writings have anything to do with his discovery of Strauss? Was he perhaps both seduced and repelled by Strauss's analysis of modernity and inclined to dramatize his own predicament?

In the introduction to the 1966 edition of *Philosophy in the Mass Age*, Grant concludes with a tribute to Strauss: 'As the greatest joy and that most difficult of attainment is any movement of the mind (however small) towards enlightenment, I count it a high blessing to have been acquainted with this man's thought.' A few pages earlier, however, he says that 'the serious entry into the human past is a prodigious event in the life of any individual,' for if it is motivated by more than just scholarly mandarinism, it means recharting all the moral landmarks by which we normally take our bearings. In particular, it means putting into question 'the faith that all human problems will be solved by unlimited technological development' – 'it is a terrible moment for the individual when he crosses the Rubicon and puts that faith into question.' When a North American loses his faith in progress, it 'is equivalent to the loss of himself and the knowledge of how to live.'[3] Technique is our god, and to lose faith in it is to experience a crisis of faith.

Grant's most widely read statement of this 'crisis of faith' is *Lament for a Nation*, a 'defence of Mr. Diefenbaker' that becomes an attack on modern liberalism. At the book's turning point Grant has a surprisingly lengthy discussion of Strauss's interpretation of the history of political philosophy. He agrees with Strauss that its recent history may be divided into two main periods.[4] But he takes sides against Strauss insofar as he treats Strauss's 'two waves' interpretation of modern political philosophy as an ideology that helps to hide from Americans their true role in the world.

According to Grant the United States is not, as Strauss suggests and as conservative Americans like to think, the guardian of traditional Western values against their suppression or perversion in the political thought and practices of the Eastern empires. Rather the United States is (as liberal or progressive Americans like to think) 'the most progressive society on earth and therefore the most radical force for the homogenizing of the world.' Indeed the United States is the 'heart of modernity,' the very 'spearhead of progress,' and its liberalism is the purest expression of the modern belief in open-ended progress.[5] In a dynamic empire spearheading the age of progress, no true conservatism is possible – not even the unconservative conservatism of allegiance to American traditions. The practical Americans who call themselves conservatives are at best old-fashioned liberals sincerely committed to the principles of the Founding Fathers: 'They stand for the freedom of the individual to use his property as he wishes, and for a limited government which must keep out of the marketplace.'[6] But according to Grant even this older liberalism/conservatism was a spent force by 1964: 'Goldwater's cry for limited government seemed as antediluvian to the leaders of the corporations as Diefenbaker's nationalism seemed to the same elements in Canada.'[7] Future 'conservatives,' as they twist conservatism into a façade for class and imperial interests, will be, like their liberal rivals, essentially defenders of whatever structure of power is necessary to keep technology dynamic and to contain its social effects.[8] So those who denounce the United States as a conservative country are wrong. American power should be resisted, not because it strengthens reaction and blocks progress (the usual critical line), but because it actually promotes the social and economic development of backward countries and the realization of a world order based on freedom and equality.

Readers of *Lament for a Nation*, puzzled by Grant's rather unconventional anti-Americanism, have often been satisfied to interpret the book 'psychologically,' as an 'Anglo-Saxon lament.' It cries out at 'the disappearance of Canada'; it mourns 'the end of Canada as a sovereign state'; and it concludes with what seems to be a veiled expression of the author's wish to die.[9] All of this is hard to understand, because Canada had not disappeared in 1965, and the political events discussed in the book seem unable – even to its author – to justify all his grief. Surely there must have been more on Grant's mind than just the difficulties of an accident-prone prime minister whose Cabinet and caucus had split over a very complicated and ambiguous question of foreign and defence policy, and whose government had been repudiated in the ensuing general election. Behind Grant's 'pessimism' most readers have seemed content to detect distress about the loss of status suffered by 'Anglos' in Canada as a result of the collapse of the British Empire and Britain's loss of power vis-à-vis the United States.[10] Only a few commentators have shown much interest in the arguments from political philosophy that Grant insisted were the real reason for his 'pessimism.'[11]

The foundation on which Grant built his argument about 'the defeat of Canadian nationalism' was evidently a novel theory

drawn from Strauss about the superiority of ancient political philosophy. Canada's disappearance will be ultimately due, Grant
says, to the acceptance by Canadians of the modern liberalism best
expressed in the politics of the United States. Because nearly all
Canadians think that modernity is good, nothing important distinguishes Canadians any longer from Americans: 'The power of the
American government to control Canada does not lie primarily in
its ability to exert direct pressure; the power lies in the fact that the
dominant classes in Canada see themselves at one with the continent on all essential matters.'[12] In particular, Canadians share the
modern liberal and American dedication to the building of a universal and homogeneous state:

The universal and homogeneous state is the pinnacle of political striving.
'Universal' implies a world-wide state, which would eliminate the curse
of war among nations; 'homogeneous' means that all men would be equal,
and war among classes would be eliminated. The masses and the philosophers have both agreed that this universal and egalitarian society is the
goal of historical striving. It gives content to the rhetoric of both Communists and capitalists.[13]

If this goal is reasonable, then Canadians should support it, and
Canadian nationalism should be treated as a misguided parochialism: 'Only those who reject that goal and claim that the universal
state will be a tyranny, that is, a society destructive of human excellence, can assert consistently that parochial nationalisms are to be
fought for.'[14] Relying, it seems, on Strauss's authority, Grant appeals to the authority of the ancients: 'The classical philosophers
asserted that a universal and homogeneous state would be a tyranny.'[15] But how can this interesting and debatable claim be explained? Grant notes only that its elucidation would require a
lengthy metaphysical discussion of time and eternity. Were the ancients right to think that changes in the world take place within an
eternal order that is not affected by them: 'This implies a definition
of human freedom quite different from the modern view that freedom is man's essence. It implies a science different from that which
aims at the conquest of nature.'[16]

Readers of *Lament for a Nation* are apt to be guided in their confrontation with these rather obscure remarks by a deep-rooted assumption that is questioned by Grant, namely that modern thought

is superior to ancient thought because it comes later and is based on more history or experience. This assumption – which may just be a way of begging the question, since the issue is whether modern assumptions are true or false – tends to hide a problem that is not easily explained. It is perhaps best to begin, as Grant does, by recognizing that a case can be made for modernity: 'Has it not been in the age of progress that disease and overwork, hunger and poverty, have been drastically reduced?'[17] Modern natural science certainly seems to have progressed beyond ancient natural science, and modern philosophy claims to have made a similar (if much less striking) advance over ancient philosophy. In fact, as Grant points out, the distinctively modern accounts of human nature and destiny were developed from a profound criticism of Plato and Aristotle. Writers such as Machiavelli and Hobbes, or Rousseau and Hegel, believed they had overcome the inadequacies of ancient thought while maintaining what was true in the ancients. Plato and Aristotle became, from the perspective of these later philosophers, merely a preparation for the perfected thought of their own age. Yet as Grant also points out, those who originated the specifically modern accounts of human nature and destiny were themselves just 'particular men in particular settings.' Do their claims to stand apart from or above the social and historical influences on their thought have any better foundation than the similar claims made by ancient writers? Our tendency to give them more credence than we give the ancient philosophers may have no better support than a naive and uncritical belief in progress: 'Plato and Aristotle would not have admitted that their teachings could be used in this way [as a preparation for later thought]. They believed that their own teaching was the complete teaching for all men everywhere, or else they were not philosophers. They believed that they had considered all the possibilities open to man and had reached the true doctrine concerning human excellence.'[18] To be sure, Grant continues, ancients such as Plato and Aristotle had very little sense of history as a long-term process moving toward some kind of salvation for mankind (as did Hegel and Marx, for example). Rather, as Strauss understands them, they were struck by the immediate social and political impediments to philosophy and by the permanent tension between philosophy and politics. But perhaps this awareness was precisely what made them superior to modern thinkers.

Philosophy can be defined in a variety of ways, as Grant observes, and not all ancient philosophers were in agreement about human excellence and its relation to society.[19] Philosophy is sometimes distinguished from dogmatism, even if philosophers always seem to have a rare confidence in their ability to think abstractly and to transcend the most common or reputable opinions of their time. Must philosophers also claim to be able to enunciate principles true for all time? Plato and Aristotle, too, had predecessors whose teachings they regarded as open to improvement. Why should the right they asserted to correct their predecessors, including Socrates, not be shared with their successors? Perhaps the issue here is not so much 'historicism' as 'excellence.' Perhaps our own 'ancients' – Machiavelli, for instance – need correcting in the light of more recent experience ('the tragedies and ambiguities of our day').[20]

In the end Grant refuses to draw any conclusion about the relative merits of ancient and modern thought. By linking 'the defeat of Canadian nationalism' to the idea that mankind may be saved by building a free, peaceful, prosperous, and democratic world state (under the direction of world leaders such as Kennedy and Eisenhower), Grant reduces the appeal of such salvation for Canadians. But he acknowledges that Canada's disappearance may be necessary for the attainment of this higher political objective. And whether its attainment would be good or bad, he does not claim to know: 'I do not know the truth about these ultimate matters.'[21]

After 1965 Grant's reactions to the war in Vietnam dominated his comments about the United States. In his 1967 essay, 'Canadian Fate and Imperialism,' he writes about the profound alienation he feels from 'the dominant world religion,' 'the religion of progress.' There is a certain thrill, he admits, in rebelling against everything that one's compatriots hold dear, but there is also a cost: 'Man is by nature a political animal and to know that citizenship is an impossibility is to be cut off from one of the highest forms of life. To retreat from loyalty to one's own has the exhilaration of rebellion, but rebellion cannot be the basis for a whole life.' The defence of the remaining vestiges of Canadian sovereignty (to keep Canadian forces from fighting in Vietnam) is worth the effort of practical men, but the small practical question of Canadian nationalism has to be seen in the larger context of the fate of Western civilization: 'By that fate I mean not merely the relations of our massive empire to the rest of the world, but even more the kind of existence which is becoming universal in advanced technological societies. What is worth doing in the midst of this barren twilight is the incredibly difficult question.'[22]

My suggestion is simply that Grant's dark depiction of our situation, like his loss of optimism about the effects of a technological society on the individuals who comprise it, can best be understood by looking more closely at his encounter with Strauss. Grant may well have done some Anglo-Saxon lamenting, and his thinking was certainly entangled with his reactions to political events, but fundamentally was he not confronting Strauss's argument about the superiority of ancient to modern philosophy?

ANCIENTS AND MODERNS

Grant apparently discovered Strauss's writings in 1959 or 1960.[23] The context for his discovery was the need he had described at the end of *Philosophy in the Mass Age* (which appeared in 1959) for a deeper knowledge of both ancient and modern philosophy. The ancient idea of moral law, he had written, must be reformulated in a way that fully recognizes the modern idea of the freedom of the spirit. The independence proper to morality must be reconciled with the dependence proper to adoration and obedience. Similarly, the ancient conception of nature as a timeless framework for our limited freedom (and for our admiration) must be reconciled with the modern understanding of history as the imposition of our unlimited freedom on nature, understood now as the infinitely malleable, which has meaning only in relation to our domination of it: 'What doctrine of nature will be adequate to express that nature is a sphere for our timeless enjoyment and yet also a sphere which we must organize, that it has meaning apart from our ends and yet is also part of redemptive history?'[24] The needed synthesis 'may perhaps arise,' Grant had written in conclusion, but only from close attention to what both the ancients and the moderns have taught: 'One of the tragedies of modern society is that those of the ancient persuasion have a rich and comprehensive knowledge of Greek philosophy and the Christian commentary thereon, while often lacking any close knowledge of the moderns; on the other hand, those who see the modern problems often have only scanty knowledge of the relevance of ancient philosophy. It must be insisted that the true relation of freedom to law can only be thought by those who have immersed themselves in the history of philosophy.'[25]

Now whatever else may be said about Strauss, it must be recognized that he was a scholar of remarkable gifts and exceptional dedication to the recovery of ancient thought. He had done what Grant said needed to be done: he had immersed himself in the history of philosophy, starting from a close knowledge of the most important moderns.

Two further commonplaces about Strauss help to clarify his importance for Grant. First, Strauss had revived the old quarrel between the ancients and the moderns, that is to say, he had challenged in a new way the conventional view that modern thought is superior to that of the ancients. He had done this, secondly, by emphasizing or rediscovering the permanent tension or opposition between philosophy and society, symbolized by the death of Socrates. The great theorists of the Enlightenment had claimed, in effect, that philosophers are to be understood as leaders of conventional opinion: philosophic criticisms of conventional opinion are meant to change it. Strauss had presented philosophers as more reclusive and less public-spirited. Since the death of Socrates they have known that they need to conceal their criticisms of convention. The genuinely philosophic thought of real philosophers is likely to be found, therefore, hidden between the lines of their writings. Inattentive readers will see in their works only edifying elaborations of conventional opinions; more careful and thoughtful readers will see attempts to shake off those opinions.

There is obviously no possibility of providing here any systematic discussion of Strauss's voluminous writings on politics and philosophy.[26] Yet there can be no understanding of their impact on Grant's thought without at least a brief summary of Strauss's unconventional account of the development of political philosophy. Strauss divides its history into two main periods. In his view Machiavelli is the pivotal figure. Before Machiavelli, philosophers had been united in believing that man's perfection lay in the highest development of his reason, which was to be attained by living a life of study and contemplation. The good society, they taught, was one that provided a secure and encouraging framework for such a life: 'The goal of political life is virtue, and the order most conducive to virtue is the aristocratic republic, or else the mixed regime.'[27] Since the sixteenth century, philosophers have followed Machiavelli in rejecting the classical scheme as unrealistic. Perhaps more public-spirited than their predecessors, modern philosophers have deliberately lowered the goal of political life in the hope of making the attainment simply of a decent or liveable political order more likely. They have denied that man is naturally directed toward virtue, emphasizing instead the importance of power, glory, comfort, and security. These selfish motives, they have taught, can be relied on to sustain a properly constituted political order. Legislators must therefore cease to take their bearings from theories about the natural end of man. The common good must not be defined in terms of the cultivation of virtue. Instead, virtue must be made relative to the common good: it must be understood as the habits required for or conducive to the attainment of the objectives that most individuals and all societies actually pursue: 'Virtue is nothing but civic virtue, patriotism or devotion to collective selfishness.'[28]

Strauss challenges this modern consensus, not in the name of revealed religion, but in the name of the correct interpretation of ancient philosophy. He denies the existence of a continuous rationalist tradition from Socrates and Plato through the later Greek and Roman writers to moderns such as Kant and Hegel. The ancient philosophers, he argues, were not the dreamy innocents that modern Machiavellian historians of philosophy have tended to make them. They had little or nothing to learn from Machiavelli about the problems of public and private morality.[29] They were every bit as 'realistic' as he was. They differed from him mainly in not entertaining such extravagant hopes for the progress of mankind, and thus their politics were much more moderate (they did not aim as high as Machiavelli did), and they did not believe that any good would come of making it easy for nonphilosophers to see that practical morality is relative to changing circumstances.

Strauss evidently provided something close to what Grant was seeking. Both, one can say, returned to the ancient philosophers in the hope of finding in ancient rationalism a tenable alternative or corrective to contemporary moral and political philosophy. Strauss succeeded in restoring the respectability of the ancients for hard-headed modern thinkers. He did not patronize them as children of their times, after the fashion of easygoing historicism, but instead he defended a tough interpretation of their teaching. He treated them as thinkers who had risen above their times and correctly anticipated what we have come to know – the grave practical and theoretical problems of progressive practical science and popular enlightenment. By clearly restating the natural right teaching of the ancients, in opposition to modern contractualism (natural rights) and historicism, Strauss clarified Grant's intuition that we are not our own: he provided a clear alternative to the reigning view that we stand, individually or collectively, beyond good and evil. Both denied that will expressed in law is the source of virtue and vice. Both affirmed the existence of objective eternal standards by which we are measured and defined. Unlike Grant, however, Strauss praised only the ancient rationalists such as Plato. In seeking an alternative to contemporary moral scepticism, Strauss evidently tended to emphasize differences (for example, between Plato, Augustine, and Kant) where Grant emphasized similarities.[30] And Strauss, in restoring ancient natural right, seemed to embrace the puzzling Socratic dictum that virtue is knowledge. Grant, on the other hand, while recognizing how difficult it is to think human beings ever pursue anything except what they believe is good, was perplexed by the problem conventionally stated in terms of tempta-tion, sin, guilt, remorse, and forgiveness.[31] The difference can be clarified, oddly enough, by an ancient discussion of tyranny and Strauss's interpretation of its contemporary meaning.

ON TYRANNY

Following the Second World War many felt that liberal democracy, whatever its practical successes, rested on shaky intellectual foun-dations. Attacks from both left and right had weakened belief in its fundamental principles. The ideas in terms of which it had once been promoted – scientific reason, the freedom of the individual, equal natural rights, moral and material progress, and so on – had become questionable for many who reflected deeply on modern science and society, and it was no solution simply to urge a return to the certainties of the past. How long could the institutions of liberal democracy be expected to stand if they rested simply on pious traditionalism or uncritical national feeling? Many had an uneasy suspicion that moral, political, and technological progress might require undemocratic forms of rule.[32]

Grant had discussed dictatorship in passing in *Philosophy in the Mass Age*. He had written that being a dictator is as unnatural as committing incest. Both are horrible because they are contrary to what is demanded of us as human beings: 'Dictatorship is not only wrong because it affects the convenience of other people, but also because it affects the dictator himself: to be a dictator is to fail in fulfilling one's manhood. It does not belong to the order of being a man to rule other men at one's own whim.'[33]

The one lengthy discussion by Strauss of dictatorial or despotic rule is his first 'Straussian' book, *On Tyranny*, which is a very detailed analysis of Xenophon's short dialogue 'Hiero or Tyrannicus.'[34] The dialogue recounts an imaginary conversation between two historical figures, the Syracusan tyrant Hiero I and a visitor to his court, the poet Simonides of Ceos, who had a reputation for wisdom and greed. The poet asks the tyrant to compare the life of a tyrant with that of a private citizen. Who has the more pleasant life? After some hesitation, Hiero explains all the disadvantages of tyranny for the tyrant. He lives in fear; the delicacies he enjoys are not really gratifying; he has no true friends, only flatterers; the honours he receives are hollow; his situation compels him to associate with base and slavish companions while he oppresses or kills the noblest citizens. The real disadvantages of tyranny thus stand in stark contrast to its reputed advantages. It is really a snare, the only escape from which is suicide. Man is evidently not made to rule over others against their will and without the restraint of laws.

Simonides is not very impressed, however, by Hiero's litany of complaints. A passion for honour and praise, he suggests, is what distinguishes real men from mere beasts and the vulgar multitude. The burdens of tyranny may be heavy, but its rewards are sweet for real men, since rulers are honoured above all others. Ordinary people are naturally grateful – *genuinely* grateful – for any attention or marks of esteem they receive from their social superiors, so rulers are in a position to get more real honour (and pleasure) from others than private citizens can. To avoid the hatred of their subjects, tyrants need only delegate the actual execution of the harsh measures that are admittedly inseparable from ruling human beings. The conversation between the tyrant and the poet ends with Simonides making a number of practical suggestions for the transformation of tyrannical rule into a more stable if not more lawful rule of willing subjects. By following this advice, it seems, and by directing his attention to the glory and prosperity of his city vis-à-vis other cities – and not just to his own superiority vis-à-vis other citizens – Hiero can reap rewards from tyranny that will more than repay its burdens. In the end the reader is left wondering whether tyranny deserves its ill repute. Neither the tyrant nor his city, it seems, need suffer from tyrannical rule. Autocratic, even somewhat despotic rule may sometimes be defensible. Simonides has the last word on tyranny, and it is a more favourable word than the standard teaching on tyranny associated with the Socratic tradition in philosophy.[35]

PHILOSOPHY AND POLITICS

In 1948 Strauss published his fascinating interpretation of Xenophon's little dialogue, which I have so briefly and perhaps misleadingly summarized. Strauss dispels any impression the inattentive reader may have acquired that Simonides's last word is Xenophon's last word, or that Simonides's failure to make any moralistic criticisms of tyranny implies any refusal on the part of Xenophon to judge its value. The fundamental problem of tyranny, apart from its undemocratic and unjust or unlawful character, seems to be shown by the unhappiness of the tyrant. A life devoted to winning the recognition of others, whether as a tyrant or as a legitimate ruler, or merely as a free and equal citizen, may be a life directed to the wrong goal. The pursuit of recognition may be a well of unhappiness.

Strauss sent a copy of his book to his more famous friend Alexandre Kojève, whom he regarded as an outstanding authority on modern thought. The result was Kojève's review essay, 'L'Action politique des philosophes,' which then provided the basis for Strauss's 'Restatement.'[36]

Both writers treat Xenophon's dialogue as above all an invitation to reflect on the relations between wisdom or philosophy and political power, whether tyrannical or lawful. Strauss emphasizes the differences between the ways of life of the philosopher, who seeks truth but lives with doubt, and the ruler, who seeks honour and must at least pretend to know things he does not know. Both lives are characterized by high ambition, or an intense desire for the recognition of one's superiority by others, but the philosopher is content with the admiration of a very narrow circle of competent judges, while the ruler, according to Strauss, craves the love of every citizen. Kojève denies this difference and all that follows from it regarding the ranking of the two ways of life. Strauss and Kojève agree however, that the relation between philosophers and rulers is generally filled with tension or conflict: both are necessarily involved in educating the young, so they meet as competitors for their loyalty. Strauss stands for the ancient solution to this problem; Kojève for the modern one. Esotericism confronts enlightenment.

Grant plunged into the controversy with a synopsis of Kojève's historical account of the relation between philosophy and politics. Contrary to the view that philosophers belong in ivory towers, Kojève taught that progress in philosophy depends on the successful practice of wise tyrants, while the latter depend on the instruction provided by philosophers, who best understand the meaning of actual historical situations. Alexander the Great, for example, was indirectly a pupil of Socrates. More recently, Lenin and Stalin were pupils of Marx, who learned from Hegel, and so on. The shortcoming of ancient philosophy, according to Kojève, was its inability to overcome class conflict. It was capable of overcoming only the 'racial' or 'ethnic' divisions of mankind – by treating them as 'conventional' rather than 'natural.' Nature as understood by the ancients provided no basis for overcoming the differences between social classes. Only the Semitic religions (Judaism, Christianity, Islam), with their idea of a unity based on a free 'conversion' open in principle to all mankind, could rise above the pagan opposition between mastery and servitude. This essentially religious idea of human unity on the basis of human equality has become in recent centuries the core of a practical political program. It has been brought down to earth by modern critical philosophy. Great leaders are now surmounting both national and class divisions, and thus working out mankind's salvation in this world, by constructing a worldwide democratic state that will do away with the scourge of war and guarantee the equality and rights of all individuals.

Public-spirited philosophers today have the task, it would seem, of advising politicians how best to attain this supreme political ideal, the only political order that can fully satisfy everyone's desire for recognition. Practising politicians are too busy for very much reflection, so they are sometimes baffled by the novelties they confront – things like nuclear and bacteriological weapons, the population explosion, urban sprawl, communications satellites, racial mixing, jumbo jets, and so on. How do these developments fit into history as the story of mankind's achievement of freedom? According to Kojève rulers need instruction about the 'contradictions' of the historical situations in which they find themselves. Philosophers must guide them in using these contradictions to work toward the abolition of poverty and oppression. Conversely, philosophers need the political experiments, so to speak, that only audacious rulers can provide. The validity of a philosophic interpretation of a given historical situation is tested by political practice: 'If philosophers gave Statesmen no political "advice" at all, in the sense that no political teaching whatever could (directly or indirectly) be drawn from their ideas, there would be no historical *progress*, and hence no History properly so called. But if the Statesmen did not eventually *actualize* the philosophically based "advice" by their day-to-day political action, there would be no philosophical *progress* (toward Wisdom or Truth) and hence no Philosophy in the strict sense of the term.'[37]

Grant agrees that Kojève's interpretation of history accurately describes the goal toward which contemporary politics is above all directed: 'Indeed the drive to the universal and homogeneous state remains the dominant ethical "ideal" to which our contemporary society appeals for meaning in its activity. In its terms our society legitimizes itself to itself.'[38] Grant follows Strauss, however, in questioning whether Kojève's Hegelian 'ideal' fully deserves the respect it now generally gets. If it does not, then current efforts to realize it can hardly be considered evidence of the impact of *philosophy* on politics. The universal and homogeneous state may still come into being, but philosophers may find themselves at odds with the ideas about human nature on which the effort is based, as Kojève himself (Strauss says) seems to think:

This end of History would be most exhilarating but for the fact that, according to Kojève, it is the participation in bloody political struggles as well as in real work or, generally expressed, the negating action, which raises man above the brutes. The state through which man is said to become reasonably satisfied is, then, the state in which the basis of man's humanity withers away, or in which man loses his humanity. It is the state of Nietzsche's 'last man.' Kojève in fact confirms the classical view that unlimited technological progress and its accompaniment, which are the indispensable conditions of the universal and homogeneous state, are destructive of humanity.[39]

Strauss goes on to say that those who still long for noble action and great deeds may be driven into revolt against such a state, even if their revolt is 'nihilistic' (because not enlightened by any positive goal): 'While perhaps doomed to failure, that nihilistic revolution may be the only action on behalf of man's humanity, the only great and noble deed that is possible once the universal and homogeneous state has become inevitable.'[40]

Strauss's deeper objection to Kojève's argument, Grant notes, has to do with the classical assumption 'that it is in thinking rather than in recognition that men find their fullest satisfaction. The highest good for man is wisdom.'[41] This is a teaching that the authorities in a universal and homogeneous state would apparently have to deny and even suppress, in the interest of affirming the equal dignity and political rights of all citizens.[42] Philosophy as the attained wisdom of such a state might well be held in high esteem, but philosophy in the ancient sense of the love of wisdom, rooted in a hatred of the lie in the soul, would be persecuted and perhaps destroyed. Thus on classical assumptions about human nature, Grant concludes (with Strauss), that the universal and homogeneous state, were it to be realized, 'would be a tyranny and indeed the most appalling tyranny in the story of the race.'[43]

Now, contemporary readers of Strauss's detailed analysis of Xenophon's *Hiero* are likely to wonder whether it can possibly throw any light on modern, twentieth-century tyranny, let alone the novel tyrannies of future centuries. Surely tyranny has different forms in different historical circumstances. Do our criteria for tyranny not change with our changing assumptions about morality, so that they are in a sense subjective and relative? (Americans had different reasons for calling George III a tyrant than they had for calling Stalin one.) Strauss deals with this objection or reservation at the outset, by conceding immediately that there is indeed an essential difference between the tyrannies of the ancient world and those contemporary regimes, usually called dictatorships, whose tyrannical excesses have surpassed 'the boldest imagination of the most powerful thinkers of the past.'[44] Yet in making this concession, he insists that 'one cannot understand modern tyranny in its specific character before one has understood the elementary and in a sense natural form of tyranny which is premodern tyranny.'[45] And it should be clear, even from my brief summary of Strauss's commentary, that he is able to raise and discuss questions of the greatest practical relevance. The readers of his book and his exchange with Kojève are led to rethink a possible 're-enactment of the age-old drama' of tyranny and wisdom in the new circumstances of universal empire, modern natural and social science, democratic constitutionalism, and popular enlightenment.[46]

Grant does not question the value of what Strauss has done. He does not let the obvious objection – 'how could the ancients understand something which did not exist in their day?' – deflect him from considering the controversy between Strauss and Kojève about the political role and responsibility of philosophers. His summary of their controversy leads him to make two critical comments.

First, he observes that Strauss offers little by way of textual evidence to support his contention that the ancient philosophers deliberately and with good reason turned away from the development of a natural science directed to the conquest of nature. Perhaps the ancient philosophers turned their backs on technological advance without ever having clearly understood what they were doing, or from a dim suspicion (as some Marxists allege) that its development would undermine the aristocratic social order favourable to themselves. Perhaps Strauss, eager to construct a consistent alternative to modern thought, read more into the few passages he cited than is reasonable. Grant notes that modern technology has clearly alleviated some suffering, and this has to be taken into account in any evaluation of it, whatever its relation to ancient philosophy: 'No writing about technological progress and the rightness of imposing limits upon it should avoid expressing the fact that the poor, the diseased, the hungry and the tired can hardly be expected to contemplate any such limitation with the equanimity of the philosopher.'[47]

Secondly, Grant observes that Strauss says little about the relationship between the history of philosophy and biblical religion. More specifically, he says very little about 'the connection between the religion of western Europe and the dynamic civilisation which first arose there, the spread of which has been so rapid in our century.'[48] Hegelian claims to have synthesized the Greek morality of honour-loving masters with the biblical morality of freedom-loving slaves may be indefensible, as Strauss argues, but there may still be some important connections between the modern, Bible-inspired understanding of nature and human destiny, on the one hand, and the orientation of modern science and philosophy to practical reform in the world, on the other hand. Strauss's reticence on this fundamental point is surprising, Grant observes. Given Strauss's intention of restoring classical social science, and his awareness that its eclipse was related to 'the triumph of the Biblical orientation,' it is perhaps untenable.

These critical comments point to Grant's fundamental reservation about Strauss's thought, which has to do with Strauss's implicit definition of virtue or human excellence as consisting simply in the perfection of one's own understanding. Such perfection may normally be a harmless (if somewhat unsocial) aspiration, or it may sometimes threaten social cohesion and thus require a certain secrecy, even some hermetical precautions, but it must be distinguished from efforts to overcome self-centredness through love of others or attention to the voice of conscience. Strauss praises the wisdom of Xenophon – cooly able to hold before itself, without moralistic rancour, cruelty, greed, lust, vanity, brutality, and injustice – but he does not interpret him as saying that tyrants should listen more carefully to the call of conscience or that they should sincerely devote themselves to the good of their subjects, even if this means risking their power or their lives.[49] An increase in virtue seems to depend simply on an improvement in understanding. Xenophon seems to be suggesting that our apparent concern for the good of others is in reality the consequence of our need for their honour or flattery. From this perspective, those who willingly risk torture and death on behalf of some great cause are far from being noble examples of the human (or any more-than-human) ability to put the good of others ahead of one's own selfish interests: they are spectacular examples of the perverse hold that the craving for praise or recognition has on 'real men.'

PRACTICAL PIETY

Strauss always presented his interpretation of ancient philosophy through a contrast between ancients and moderns. With respect to the 'moderns' – the liberal or progressive political theorists of the past three or four centuries – Grant's position seems to have been from the outset quite close to that of Strauss. Both regarded modern liberalism as in some complicated way a dangerous mistake, the bad practical effects of which can be remedied only by returning to the moral philosophy of the ancient world and somehow synthesizing ancient and modern doctrines. In his writings about Spinoza, Hobbes, Locke, and Rousseau, Strauss investigated the foundations of modern liberalism far more thoroughly than Grant ever did, but what he found, it seems reasonable to suppose, is more or less what Grant always suspected was there to be found. What must have surprised Grant, and what evidently upset an earlier way of thinking, was Strauss's way of setting Athens in opposition to Jerusalem. Plato was for Strauss a 'political philosopher,' not the mystical or religious thinker others have found in the dialogues. Strauss, one can say, emphasized the difficulties in any synthesis of classical rationalism with biblical morality that would permit one to say, with St Augustine, that 'Plato knew the whole of Christian truth, except "that the word became flesh."'[50] In his interpretations of ancient authors, Strauss implicitly elevated intellectual above moral virtue and suggested that any self-sacrificing morality must ultimately be mute or 'illogical,' however loudly it may proclaim itself in the world. In contrasting ancients and moderns, he was always silent about Christianity.

Grant seems also to have been surprised and impressed by what Strauss said and did about the tension between philosophy and society. Grant had written a great deal about education in the 1940s and 1950s. Much of it was harshly critical of 'progressive education' for putting 'adjustment' and 'success in life' ahead of intellectual insight: 'Where the purpose of the old education was to free men so that they were out of the cave, the purpose today is to equip them to be successes in the cave.'[51] Whenever he spoke or wrote about education, Grant seemed to assume that a true moral philosophy, properly taught, would be the solid foundation of social health. Strauss clearly attached as much importance to education as did Grant, and he shared the same high conception of the educator's vocation, but he had a much more modest idea of what is possible in practice. He held that true education is always at odds with politics, not just in modern America. In the nature of things we always live (practically speaking) in an inverted world, where the kings, who are not philosophers, organize education. To complain of this is only to reveal that you are still held by the Enlightenment hope that philosophy can replace religion. According to Strauss, 'opinion is the element of society,' and he was prepared to respect opinions he did not share.[52] As Grant put it, 'he is a philosopher, and not one of those who consider it their function and their joy to "enlighten" the majority by undermining their trust in the main religious practice which is open to them.'[53]

Whether that religious practice is now mainly 'religious' or 'political' is among the questions raised in 'Religion and the State,' which Grant published in 1963.[54] The article deals with the controversy at the time about the proper place of religious education in the public schools of Ontario. Should some form of Christianity be taught or should there be no formal religious instruction? The first option would imply public acceptance of the idea that Canada is a Christian country, while the second would recognize the equality of all religious groups and the right of the individual to work out his or her own religious opinions.

Grant begins his analysis of the controversy by noting that the word 'religion' is ambiguous. Should it be used to refer to those systems of belief (whether true or false) that bind together the lives of individuals and give them whatever consistency of purpose they may have? Or should it be used only for those systems of belief that include reference to a 'higher' divine power? The more restricted, more conventional definition would have the awkward implication, it seems, of denying both Buddhism and Scientology the status of religions. Grant adopts the broader sense of the term: 'I would describe liberal humanists or Marxists as religious people; indeed ... I would say that all persons (in so far as they are rational beings) are religious.'[55]

Grant then repeatedly insists, throughout the article, on the religious (dogmatic and faith-full) character of modern liberalism. What is at issue in the controversy about schools, he argues, is not *whether* religion should be taught, but *which* religion should be taught: 'It is perfectly clear that in all North American state schools religion is already taught in the form of what may best be called "the religion of democracy."'[56] The real question is only whether the necessary inculcation of the democratic faith should be supplemented by some reference to the deity. Does public morality depend on the widespread practice of piety in the more traditionally religious sense? If so, does this mean that Christianity, the religion of the majority, has a right to be the religion taught in the state schools? Grant concludes that it would, if the majority and the 'dominant classes' of Ontario were in fact Christian. The majority still may be, but the dominant classes are not. Many among them still go to church (they see the need for a moral and religious tradition in their society, in particular for their children), but they have no interest in theological questions (which they regard as merely the vested professional interest of the clergy) and no real belief that 'revelation of a decisive nature has once and for all been given.'[57] Only the partisans of 'the religion of progress, mastery and power' are able to take a more consistent position in the controversy: 'Assuming their religion to be self-evidently true to all men of good will, they are forceful in advocating that it should be the public religion. They work for the coming of the universal and homogeneous state with enthusiasm; they await its coming with expectation.'[58]

Grant dissents from this religion of progress, not by questioning the right of its clergy to indoctrinate the children, but by decrying the practical effects of their indoctrination:

Has the secular state, and the religion of progress which dominates its education, led to widespread happiness in North America in the last forty years? How can we escape the fact that the necessary end product of the religion of progress is not hope, but a society of existentialists who know themselves in their own self-consciousness, but know the world entirely as despair? ... Surely the basic problem of our society is the problem of individuals finding meaning to their existence. The most important cause of the psycho-pathological phenomena, which are becoming terrifyingly widespread at all echelons in North America, is just that human beings can find no meaning to their existence. Neither the Freudian nor the Marxian descriptions or therapies can account for or cure these new psycho-pathologies.[59]

Now, one could of course object that Grant's 'pessimism' here as elsewhere will not appeal to the dispassionate observer. Even if Freud or Marx cannot cure our current discontents, perhaps Prozac can. For present purposes the important thing to see is Grant's obvious lack of respect for the secular beliefs he defines as the current public religion. One cannot easily find any similar impiety in the writings of Leo Strauss.

CONCLUSIONS

The starting point of Grant's life and thought was the liberal pragmatic Protestantism of the Canadian middle and upper classes be-

tween the world wars. Grant's later writings are devoted above all
to clarifying what is true and false in that heritage. As a young man
he knew close up the horror of modern scientific warfare and was
torn between his revulsion from it and his feeling of obligation to
throw himself into the making of history. Out of the conflicts
within himself and the torment of others he suddenly recognized
'that we are not our own.'[60] In his studies he turned from law and
politics to philosophy and theology, hoping to find in a better understanding of Christianity, a better account of justice and the other
human virtues than what was provided by modern secular liberalism. He seems to have undertaken these studies on the assumption,
well grounded historically, that Christianity and Platonism are
closely related. His experience had led him to think we need an
understanding of ourselves, not as 'free' and 'our own,' but as
measured and defined by a natural order we can know through
reason, in the ancient sense of 'theory' or 'contemplation.' After
much reading and reflection, he chanced on Strauss's writings.[61]
Strauss interpreted the ancient philosophers as teachers of 'natural
right.' There are no laws written in the stars, but there is one right
way of life – a way of life that is best by nature, not by choice or
convention.[62] This natural way of life – love of wisdom – is not one
that can be known by many, however, and beyond defending it,
political philosophy has little to say about good and bad that is of
much interest. In practice political philosophy is 'conservative': its
politics and morality are relative to circumstances.[63] Facing a tyrant
like Hiero, it tries to be helpful in a modest way. In the circumstances of a modern liberal democracy like the United States, it can
be seen as an attack on the foundations of public life or as a defence
of them.[64]

To demonstrate that the encounter with Strauss (and Kojève) was
a turning point in Grant's life would require a far more detailed
discussion of Grant's thought of the 1940s and 1950s than can be
attempted here, or is perhaps possible given the limited evidence
available. But assuming that it was such a turning point, I have
tried to throw some light on the questions it involved. Undoubtedly
it had something to do with Kojève's 'atheistic' clarification of
Hegel's interpretation of 'divine providence.' Grant's attraction to
Hegel, strong as it may have been at one time, seems to have ended
with his study of the Strauss-Kojève controversy.[65] More importantly, as I have suggested, Grant's discovery of Strauss involved

the clarification of a possible contrast between Platonism and Christianity.

Strauss certainly helped Grant, as he has helped others, to think more clearly about justice and human virtue. In reading Strauss one feels oneself in the presence not just of great intellectual clarity and splendid scholarship, but of good moral health. There is no cynicism or bitterness; no hypocritical pretence of universal benevolence; and no moral hypochondria. But one may wonder whether there is much interest in normal human selfishness or self-love, except as they block access to truth, being at the bottom of the conceit that one already knows everything important.[66] The possibility that they may be the sickness at the root of social evils and injustice gets surprisingly little attention. Nor does one find much illumination of the experience Grant associated above all with Simone Weil, that 'the intelligence is enlightened by love.'[67]

When thinkers of this calibre disagree, what are weaker minds to do? Strauss provides a helpful analogy for the problem I am left with after reading Grant and Strauss. Having in mind, it seems, the conflict between classical rationalism and Christianity, Strauss writes that we may be unable to tell which of two distant mountain peaks shrouded in clouds is the higher, but we can still tell the difference between a mountain and a molehill.[68] In other words, even if we cannot rationally determine which of two contending models of virtue has absolutely the highest value, we need not let our moral faculties be paralysed by any fact-value distinction that would put Jezebel or Hitler on the same moral plane as Socrates or Christ. Grant would surely agree, though he was more inclined to pursue his studies on the assumption that the distant peaks are parts of the same mountain.

NOTES

For comments on an earlier version of this essay I am grateful to Sheila Grant, Clifford Orwin, and Gerald Owen, as well as to the editor of this volume, Arthur Davis.

1 George Grant, 'Tyranny and Wisdom: A Comment on the Controversy between Leo Strauss and Alexandre Kojève,' *Social Research* 31 (1964), 45–72, which is reprinted with a brief introduction in *Technology and Empire* (Toronto: Anansi 1969), 81–109. Other important references to

Strauss in Grant's writings include *Lament for a Nation* (Toronto: McClelland and Stewart 1965), 60–3, 95; the introduction to the 1966 edition of *Philosophy in the Mass Age* (Toronto: Copp Clark 1966); *Technology and Empire*, 19; and *Time as History* (Toronto: CBC 1969), 48. See also William Christian, *George Grant: A Biography* (Toronto: University of Toronto Press 1993), 203, 223–7, 249–51, 292–4, and the various remarks about Strauss in Larry Schmidt, ed., *George Grant in Process: Essays and Conversations* (Toronto: Anansi 1978), especially 64–5, 75–6.

2 Joan E. O'Donovan, *George Grant and the Twilight of Justice* (Toronto: University of Toronto Press 1984), 9–11, 50–60, 68–80, 161–6. Cf. Schmidt, ed., *George Grant in Process*, 64. For other discussions of Grant and Strauss see Barry Cooper, 'George Grant and the Revival of Political Philosophy,' in Peter C. Emberley, ed., *By Loving Our Own: George Grant and the Legacy of Lament for a Nation* (Ottawa: Carleton University Press 1990), 97–121; Yusuf K. Umar, 'The Philosophical Context of George Grant's Political Thought,' in Yusuf K. Umar, ed., *George Grant and the Future of Canada* (Calgary: University of Calgary Press 1992), 1–16; Werner Dannhauser, 'Ancients, Moderns and Canadians,' *Denver Quarterly* 4, no. 2 (1969), 94–8; Wayne Whillier, 'George Grant and Leo Strauss: A Parting of the Way,' and Ian G. Weeks, 'Two Uses of Secrecy: Leo Strauss and George Grant,' in Wayne Whillier, ed., *'Two Theological Languages' by George Grant and Other Essays in Honour of His Work* (Lewiston, NY: Edwin Mellen Press 1990), 63–81 and 82–93, respectively.

3 Grant, *Philosophy in the Mass Age*, v–vi, vii. Cf. Grant, *Technology and Empire*, 36–7.

4 Grant, *Lament for a Nation*, 60. Grant also seems to accept the larger scheme that contrasts 'ancients' with 'moderns,' and skips over almost two thousand years of Cynics, Stoics, Epicureans, Skeptics, Roman philosophers, church fathers, and medieval scholastics.

5 'To modern political theory, man's essence is his freedom. Nothing must stand in the way of our absolute freedom to create the world as we want it. There must be no conceptions of good that put limitations on human action': Grant, *Lament for a Nation*, 56.

6 Ibid., 64.

7 Ibid., 66. Cf. David Frum, *Dead Right* (New York: Basic Books 1994).

8 'The impossibility of conservatism in our epoch is seen in the fact that those who adopt the title can be no more than the defenders of whatever structure of power is at any moment necessary to technological change. They provide the external force necessary if the society is to be

kept together. They are not conservatives in the sense of being the custodians of something that is not subject to change. They are conservatives, generally, in the sense of advocating a sufficient amount of order so the demands of technology will not carry the society into chaos. Because they are advocates of nothing more than this external order, they have come to be thought of as objects of opprobrium by the generous-hearted': Grant, *Lament for a Nation*, 67.

9 Ibid., 2, 88, 97. Cf. Dennis Duffy, 'The Ancestral Journey: Travels with George Grant,' *Journal of Canadian Studies* 22, no. 3 (fall 1987), 99–100, which is the only attempt I know of to make sense of the final line of the book, which is from Virgil's *Aeneid* and reads, 'They were holding their arms outstretched in love toward the further shore.'

10 With some justification, according to Grant: 'Nothing can so much drive one to philosophy as being part of a class which is disappearing': Schmidt, ed., *George Grant in Process*, 63. See Robert Blumstock, 'Anglo-Saxon Lament,' *Canadian Review of Sociology and Anthropology* 3 (1966), 98–105, and R.K. Crook, 'Modernization and Nostalgia: A Note on the Sociology of Pessimism,' *Queen's Quarterly* 73 (1966), 269–84, where Grant is driven to 'pessimism' rather than to philosophy. 'Many simple people (particularly journalists and professors) took [the book] to be a lament for the passing of a British dream of Canada': Grant, *Lament for a Nation*, xi.

11 Grant, *Technology and Empire*, 140.

12 Grant, *Lament for a Nation*, 41, 54.

13 Ibid., 53.

14 Ibid., 85–6.

15 Ibid., 96.

16 Ibid.

17 Ibid., 94.

18 Ibid., 95. In a footnote to the quoted passage, Grant acknowledges his dependence on the writings of Strauss and expresses the hope that 'nothing in the foregoing misinterprets the teaching of that wise man.'

19 In an essay for the Royal Commission on National Development in the Arts, Letters and Sciences (the Massey Commission), Grant defined philosophy in a way that many of his professional colleagues found unsatisfactory: 'The study of philosophy is the analysis of the traditions of our society and the judgment of those traditions against our varying intuitions of the Perfection of God. It is the contemplation of our own and others' activity, in the hope that by understanding it better we may make it less imperfect': Grant, 'Philosophy,' in *Royal Commission Studies: A Selection of Essays Prepared for the Royal Commis-*

sion on National Development in the Arts, Letters and Sciences (Ottawa: King's Printer 1951), 119. Cf. Fulton H. Anderson, 'Introduction,' in John A. Irving, ed., *Philosophy in Canada: A Symposium* (Toronto: University of Toronto Press 1952), 2–5. In the ancient world not all of Socrates's followers were as reticent about their opinions and desires as Plato was; some (Diogenes, for example) were notoriously open about them.

20 Grant, *Lament for a Nation*, 95.

21 Ibid., 96. Cf. Grant, *Technology and Empire*, 33–5.

22 Grant, *Technology and Empire*, 77–8.

23 Schmidt, ed., *George Grant in Process*, 65. In a letter to Murray Ross written on 14 April 1960, Grant remarked that 'the philosopher I admire the most in North America is Leo Strauss at Chicago.' In 1962 it seems that he sent Strauss a draft of 'Tyranny and Wisdom' for his comments. See Christian, *George Grant*, 203, 223, 225. There is no evidence of any Straussian influence in *Philosophy in the Mass Age*, which was published in 1959, nor in 'An Ethic of Community,' which was published in 1961. The first clear evidence is in 'Religion and the State,' which was published in 1963. 'Tyranny and Wisdom' was published in 1964. It shows a clear grasp of the main lines of Strauss's thought and a remarkable appreciation of the importance of one of his most recondite scholarly publications.

24 Grant, *Philosophy in the Mass Age*, 110–11.

25 Ibid., 107, 111.

26 For introductory surveys of Strauss's thought see Allan Bloom, 'Leo Strauss: September 20, 1899 – October 18, 1973,' in *Giants and Dwarfs: Essays 1960–1990* (New York: Simon and Schuster 1990), 235–55; Nathan Tarcov and Thomas L. Pangle, 'Leo Strauss and the History of Political Philosophy,' in Leo Strauss and Joseph Cropsey, eds., *History of Political Philosophy*, 3rd ed. (Chicago: University of Chicago Press 1987), 907–38; and Thomas L. Pangle, 'Editor's Introduction,' in *The Rebirth of Classical Political Rationalism: An Introduction to the Thought of Leo Strauss* (Chicago: University of Chicago Press 1989), vii–xxxviii. Two features of Strauss's work that make it difficult for any commentator to summarize his thought are his insistence on the necessary 'esotericism' of philosophers and his practice of expressing his own thoughts indirectly, through detailed expositions and explanations of the writings of others. 'For these reasons among others, a discussion of Strauss's work unavoidably gets weighed down by many more citations and conditionals than is customary': Victor Gourevitch,

'Philosophy and Politics, I,' *Review of Metaphysics* 22 (1968), 63. For a recent detailed examination of many points that are important in any comparison with Grant see Kenneth Hart Green, *Jew and Philosopher: The Return to Maimonides in the Jewish Thought of Leo Strauss* (Albany: State University of New York Press 1993).

27 Leo Strauss, *What Is Political Philosophy? and Other Studies* (New York: Free Press 1959), '0.

28 Ibid., 42.

29 'As a matter of fact, there is in the whole work of Machiavelli not a single true observation regarding the nature of man and of human affairs with which the classics were not thoroughly familiar': Ibid., 43.

30 Cf. George Grant, 'Pursuit of an Illusion: A Commentary on Bertrand Russell,' *Dalhousie Review* 32 (1952), 103, and *Philosophy in the Mass Age*, 20–1, 28–30, 39–40, 47–8, 104.

31 For an early discussion by Grant of the relevant contrast between the classical language of ignorance or lack of understanding and the biblical language of rebellion and perverted wilfulness, together with an important addendum written just before the end of his life, see Grant, 'Two Theological Languages,' in Whillier, ed., *'Two Theological Languages,'* 6–19. For a somewhat later statement of Grant's view of the practical consequences of the Protestant denigration of reason that underlies the contemporary North American mixture of biblical and scientific language, see Grant, 'The Uses of Freedom: A Word and Our World,' *Queen's Quarterly* 62 (1956), 515–27. Cf. Grant, *Lament for a Nation*, 41 n. 12.

32 See Frank H. Underhill, 'Some Reflections on the Liberal Tradition in Canada,' in H.D. Forbes, ed., *Canadian Political Thought* (Toronto: Oxford University Press 1985), 230–40, for a typical expression of the uneasiness of the time. Underhill's essay was originally published in 1946. Cf. Grant, *Philosophy in the Mass Age*, 4–10, and Strauss, *Thoughts on Machiavelli* (Glencoe, IL: The Free Press 1958), 290–9. The power of the judiciary in modern democracies shows that undemocratic rule need not, of course, be simply 'undemocratic.' Similarly, a regime giving considerable power to lawyers, bureaucrats, businessmen, economists, statisticians, pollsters, journalists, and other experts, as well as to 'charismatic' politicians, within a constitutional system of checks and balances with a very attenuated sense of popular sovereignty, might be regarded as quite democratic.

33 Grant, *Philosophy in the Mass Age*, 35. See also Grant, 'An Ethic of Community,' 22.

34 Leo Strauss, *On Tyranny: An Interpretation of Xenophon's 'Hiero'* (New York: Political Science Classics 1948). For a description of this as the first 'Straussian' book see Bloom, *Giants and Dwarfs*, 126. See also Bloom's description of Kojève as 'the most thoughtful, the most learned, the most profound of those Marxists who, dissatisfied with the thinness of Marx's account of the human and metaphysical grounds of his teaching, turned to Hegel as the truly philosophic source of that teaching': 269. Xenophon's definition of tyranny as lawless rule over unwilling subjects is relevant here: Xenophon, *Memorabilia*, 4.6.12.

35 Cf. Plato, *Republic*, and Aristotle, *Politics*. A good many ancient and modern philosophers have, of course, been entangled more than just accidentally with tyrants, for example Edmund Burke with George III.

36 The original book, along with a translation of the dialogue, an expanded version of Kojève's article, and Strauss's 'Restatement,' was published in French in 1954 and in English in 1963. References below will be to the edition of *On Tyranny* edited by Victor Gourevitch and Michael Roth (New York: Free Press 1991), which restores the final paragraph of Strauss's 'Restatement' and adds the surviving correspondence between Strauss and Kojève going back to 1932. Strauss's letter of 22 August 1948, which deals with Kojève's recently published *Introduction à la lecture de Hegel*, anticipates some of the key points made in the 'Restatement.'

37 Kojève in Strauss, *On Tyranny*, 174–5.

38 Grant, *Technology and Empire*, 88–9. This seems to be Strauss's view as well, though he never says so so clearly.

39 Strauss, *On Tyranny*, 208. Cf. Grant, *Technology and Empire*, 92: 'The universal and homogeneous state, far from being the best social order, will be (if realized) a tyranny, and therefore within classical assumptions destructive of humanity.' For a recent discussion of this theme, which emphasizes its Nietzschean derivation, see Francis Fukuyama, *The End of History and the Last Man* (New York: Free Press 1992).

40 Strauss, *On Tyranny*, 209.

41 Grant, *Technology and Empire*, 94. See Strauss, *On Tyranny*, 189–94, 209–10.

42 'To retain his power, [the Universal and Final Tyrant] will be forced to suppress every activity which might lead people into doubt of the essential soundness of the universal and homogeneous state: he must suppress philosophy as an attempt to corrupt the young. In particular he must in the interest of the homogeneity of his universal state forbid

every teaching, every suggestion, that there are politically relevant natural differences among men which cannot be abolished or neutralized by progressing scientific technology': Strauss, *On Tyranny*, 211.

43 Grant, *Technology and Empire*, 95. Cf. Strauss, *On Tyranny*, 211.

44 Strauss, *On Tyranny*, 22–3, 177–8.

45 Ibid., 23.

46 Ibid., 211.

47 Grant, *Technology and Empire*, 103. Cf. Grant, *Lament for a Nation*, 94.

48 Grant, *Technology and Empire*, 106. Grant adds, 'This is the civilisation which in the opinion of both Strauss and Kojève tends towards the universal and homogeneous state.' Cf. Grant, *Philosophy in the Mass Age*, 44, and Schmidt, ed., *George Grant in Process*, 142–7.

49 'A comparison of the *Hiero* with Isocrates' work on the tyrannical art (*To Nicocles*) makes perfectly clear how amazingly little of moral admonition proper there is in the *Hiero*': Strauss, *On Tyranny*, 93.

50 Grant, 'Two Theological Languages,' 12.

51 George Grant, 'The Teaching Profession in an Expanding Economy,' (unpublished address, c. 1955).

52 Strauss, *What Is Political Philosophy?* 221 ff.

53 Grant, *Technology and Empire*, 109.

54 George Grant, 'Religion and the State,' *Queen's Quarterly* 70 (1963), 183–97, which is reprinted with a new introduction (in which Grant says that reverence rather than freedom is the matrix of human nobility) in *Technology and Empire*, 43–60. There is no discussion of this article in Christian, *George Grant*, but I assume that it must have been written about the same time as or just after 'Tyranny and Wisdom.'

55 Grant, *Technology and Empire*, 46.

56 Ibid., 49.

57 Ibid., 57.

58 Ibid.

59 Ibid., 58.

60 Schmidt, ed., *George Grant in Process*, 63. Cf. 1 Corinthians 6.19.

61 For a clear and detailed account of the first forty years of Grant's life see Christian, *George Grant*, chaps. 1–13.

62 'According to the classics, the highest good is a life devoted to wisdom or virtue, honor being no more than a very pleasant, but secondary and dispensable, reward': Strauss, *On Tyranny*, 190. See also Strauss, *What Is Political Philosophy?*, 90–4, and Strauss, *Natural Right and History* (Chicago: University of Chicago Press 1953), 126–30, 151, 162–4. Cf. Strauss, 'On Natural Law,' in Thomas L. Pangle, ed., *Studies of Platonic*

Political Philosophy (Chicago: University of Chicago Press 1983), 137–46,
which is a synopsis of *Natural Right and History,* and suggests that natural law is to natural right as astrology is to astronomy.

63 'In what then does philosophic politics consist? In satisfying the city
that the philosophers are not atheists, that they do no desecrate everything sacred to the city, that they reverence what the city reverences,
that they are not subversives, in short, that they are not irresponsible
adventurers but good citizens and even the best of citizens': Strauss,
On Tyranny, 205–6. Cf. Grant's comment on the 'Great Society' in John
Irwin, ed., *Great Societies and Quiet Revolutions* (Toronto: Canadian
Broadcasting Corporation 1967), 76: 'I think you can live perfectly well
in a tyrannical regime. I am just saying that the technological era is
coming and is going to be a tyranny.'

64 'Strauss's purpose is not to undercut liberalism practically but to find a
theoretical solution to the problem posed by its having already been
undercut. The opposite impression may underlie much of the political
hostility to his work': Nathan Tarcov, 'Philosophy and History: Tradition and Interpretation in the Work of Leo Strauss,' *Polity* 16 (1983), 9.
Understandably, those who defend against unperceived threats are
sometimes accused of creating those threats.

65 Cf. Schmidt, ed., *George Grant in Process,* 64.

66 Cf. the comment on Plato's *Laws,* 730c–732d, in Leo Strauss, *The Argument and Action of Plato's 'Laws'* (Chicago: University of Chicago Press
1975), 67–8.

67 George Grant, *Technology and Justice,* (Toronto: Anansi 1986), 38. On the
importance of Weil for Grant see Schmidt, ed., *George Grant in Process,*
65, 106–9, and Christian, *George Grant,* chap. 16.

68 Strauss, *What Is Political Philosophy?,* 23. Cf. Strauss, *Natural Right and
History,* 67–76.

POLITICS

8

The Unravelling of Liberalism

LOUIS GREENSPAN

George Grant was, if anything, a man who sought to be understood. Almost all of his most important articles were written for magazines such as *Canadian Dimension* rather than for learned journals, and most of his books were produced by Anansi and other publishers that catered to the general public rather than by university presses. As far as possible he used plain language and was on many subjects blunt and outspoken. Yet much that he wrote remains puzzling, subject to rival interpretations, and has given rise to a secondary literature in which scholars argue vigorously over Grant's place in the political spectrum. It is as if Grant was the opposite of what he seemed: not an advocate of straight talk, but a lover of the esoteric and a purveyor of the enigmatic.

This contentiousness among scholars exists in part because Grant's work has been appropriated by thinkers and writers with different agendas. The left, for example, has appropriated Grant's anti-imperialism and his considerable polemic against the corporate empires that are devouring the indigenous cultures of the globe. But the left ignores his insistence on the role of religion in society, and especially his passionate rejection of the judicial decisions that have permitted free abortion. The right, on the other hand, views him as a religious thinker and notes his warnings that abortion is a blight on society. At the same time, however, the right ignores his alarms concerning the menace of corporate greed. Some writers on Grant praise the nationalist and ignore the Christian, while others praise the Christian and ignore the nationalist. Most of Grant's admirers think of him as a man for some seasons but not for all.

Much of Grant's work is concerned with liberalism, its history, its role in society, and its fate in the modern world. His writing on liberalism is as vivid as his writing on any other subject, and yet, as one enters into its logic and its spirit, one soon realizes that there is a complexity to his writing that is belied by the vividness of his prose. Each passage is translucent, but when many passages are combined, the subtlety, depth, and sometimes enigmatic character of his views begin to emerge. In part this is because he writes simultaneously as a political activist engaged in the problems of the moment and as a philosopher surveying the whole from a vantage point far above the maddening din. And it is also because he is interested in presenting ideas in their dramatic confrontations with one another rather than providing exhaustive definitions of each.

We do not find anywhere in Grant's work the textbook definition of liberalism[1] as a creed founded on principles such as the separation of church and state, the primacy of the individual, the rule of law, and so on. Grant brings in such principles as they are needed. *Lament for a Nation* contains juicy passages describing clashes between Kennedy and Diefenbaker, in which Grant makes Kennedy the slick, suave villain who speaks for the liberal homogeneous empire, and Diefenbaker the stubborn local hero who speaks for kinship and tradition. This is Grant writing as a political combatant. Yet when Grant writes as a philosopher, Kennedy and Diefenbaker merge. Both become representatives of the liberalism that descended on the human race in the seventeenth century.

What, then, is the source of Grant's critique of liberalism? Can it be located in politics, in philosophy, or in a combination of the two?

When we consider the political milieu within which Grant came before the public in the 1960s, a milieu that had been dominated by liberal orthodoxy since the end of the Second World War, it is easy to see how Grant was seen as a maverick and an outsider. The liberal orthodoxy of the era celebrated scientific rationality (as embodied, for instance, in the study of nuclear physics) and the emerging positivism of the social sciences. It was an outlook that looked forward to the convergence of different societies and polities into a world without ideology. Grant, on the other hand, called for myth, for the celebration of the particular (that is to say, nationalism), and for a rediscovery of ancient wisdom. It is no wonder that his friend, the artist Alex Colville, dedicated to Grant his design for a coin that showed a wolf baying at the moon.

Today we are enfolded in the political world of a conservative Zeitgeist. Some see Grant as one of the prophets of this world, a prophet bearing the paradoxical title 'a conservative ahead of his time.' Grant's conservatism shared with the present's a taste for a relentless critique of liberalism, and a profound concern about the ruinous consequences of sexual hedonism. At times Grant seemed to gravitate toward a pro-American stance, for instance when he spoke enthusiastically of the Reagan administration's opposition to free abortion. But there is little doubt that Grant would have been as uncomfortable with the conservative Zeitgeist of our day as he was with the liberal Zeitgeist of his. Like many liberals Grant trusted the state more than he trusted the corporation. The term 'conservative revolution' would have made little sense to him, and the notion, which so captivates contemporary conservatives such as Mr Gingrich, that private enterprise and technological expansion are the best guarantors of a traditional *Sittlichkeit* that embraces public ethics and family values, would have been abhorrent to him. Had Grant been invited, as he well might have been, to address a Christian Coalition prayer breakfast, he might have spoken on one of his favourite themes – the impossibility of conservatism in a technological society.

Grant was out of step with every form of conservatism, even that of the Straussians, whom in many respects he admired and identified with. The leading Straussians were also prominent and enthusiastic Cold Warriors, and Grant was not. He believed the Americans were as much to blame for the crises of the Cold War as the Soviets, and that the Soviets never match American dynamism and American power. One of Grant's heroes was Charles de Gaulle, especially for his opposition to America.

Grant was commonly identified as a Tory traditionalist, a United Empire Loyalist who defended traditions that were being besieged by technology. There is much truth in this, but it was true more of the manner in which he presented himself than of his philosophical outlook. More and more he became attached to archaic forms of Christianity and critical of the entirety of western culture, and hence the bearer of a more radical outlook than is generally noticed.

Philosophic speculations, not nostalgia for the Canadian past, came to dominate his view of liberalism.

The philosophic principles that informed Grant's critique of liberalism have been described in various ways. Yusuf Umar, in his essay entitled 'The Philosophical Context of George Grant's Political Thought,'[2] argues that Grant can best be understood by looking at his commentary on the debate between Leo Strauss and Alexandre Kojève on the nature of tyranny. Grant had argued that the debate revolves around a deeper controversy about the difference between ancient and modern philosophy. Leo Strauss declares himself for ancient philosophy because, though elitist, it recognizes the difference between the citizen bound to the state and the philosopher who is attuned to an order above the state. Modern philosophy is realized, as Kojève rightly declares, in the liberal idea of the universal and the homogeneous state. This, according to Strauss and Grant, is a tyranny of sameness. Liberalism is then a homogenizing force that appeals to 'freedom as not merely a good but the highest good,'[3] so that 'the triumph of liberalism, according to Grant, is the triumph of the universal and homogeneous state,'[4] and hence of tyranny.

Umar's is a good account of one aspect of Grant's approach to liberalism. Umar implies that Grant's politics on the ground, for example his support for Canadian nationalism, was, in effect, support for whatever offered resistance to global homogenization. But Umar leaves open a number of questions. First, how is the universal homogenizing state a tyranny? Umar agrees with Grant and Strauss that it makes unequals equal. But so long as the principle of freedom survives – as indeed it does – this is far from persuasive. In one very shrewd passage, Umar notes that 'it was obvious to [Grant] that [the universal homogenizing state] would fall sooner or later because it did not truly apprehend that the essence of modern man is freedom.'[5] Only the liberal empire that recognizes freedom will last. How, then, can it be a tyranny?

For Arthur Kroker, Grant's significance lies in having shown that abstract liberal individualism, whatever its intentions, results in an alienated culture. In his book *Technology and the Canadian Mind*, Kroker writes that Grant condemned the liberal world as a chilling, barren dystopia in which free but empty individuals bang their heads against an iron cage that is bereft of all solace and human content. At the end of the book, however, he makes a curious but suggestive criticism when he argues that Grant's Christian vantage point imposed limitations on his ability to cope with technology. The argument is curious because after spending forty eloquent pages effusively praising Grant for his depiction of the technological world as a closed system of despair, Kroker then reprimands Grant because 'In Grant's world, justice is never inserted into history ... he refuses to submit his faith ... to the test of historical struggle.'[6]

But if Grant's Christianity remains magisterially above the world, there must also be some problem in his description of the world. Indeed, I will argue that his descriptions of modern liberalism and of modern politics are problematic precisely because they are penetrated by this magisterial Christianity.

What seems to me incomplete in both Umar's and Kroker's accounts of Grant, where liberalism is located in abstract principles above the world, is that they ignore Grant's sense of modern history. To say, without further comment, that Grant took an implacable stand against liberalism, is to ignore the problem of Grant's recognition of the moral strength of liberalism in the twentieth century. It is true that in Canada opposition to liberalism (in the broadest sense of the term) is a conceit, since every alternative contains some element of liberalism. In Europe the alternatives to liberalism have been the nightmares of fascism and Stalinism. Grant recognized this. He praised, as aspects of the good, the principles of freedom and consent of the governed upheld by liberalism. He even went so far as to remark that 'At the practical level it is imprudent to speak against the principles, if not the details, of those legal institutions which guard our justice.'[7]

The paradigm of Grant's most mature and most characteristic criticism of liberalism is found in *English-Speaking Justice*, the published version of the lectures that he delivered at Mount Allison University in 1974. In that year the war in Vietnam was coming to an end, and American liberalism was, in his view, showing signs of deterioration if not collapse. The American polity was devouring itself over the war, a process accelerated by the publication of the top secret Pentagon Papers. Grant had supported the Nixon administration but his support had unravelled because of the Watergate scandal. A few years earlier, in 1970, John Rawls had published *A Theory of Justice*,[8] a work that Grant regarded as a significant loosening of liberalism from the sources that had given it strength. And in 1973 the United States Supreme Court had issued its landmark judgment *Roe v. Wade*, which permitted abortion in the first three months of pregnancy, a decision that, as we shall see, Grant regarded as a watershed.

In *English-Speaking Justice* and in all of Grant's later works one finds an ambivalent approach toward liberalism. Grant shows appreciation for the achievements of liberal civilization but also alarm at the possibilities that seem to be opening up. Liberalism is not merely, as it was in his works of the sixties, the perpetrator of the horrors of technology and the will to mastery, but also their victim, as though there were a liberalism of Cain and a liberalism of Abel.

In *English-Speaking Justice* Grant writes as an insider and as an outsider. His perspective is complex. It is the perspective of the Platonist who sees liberalism from a transcendent height, as well as of the Hegelian who enters into the spirit of liberalism and observes the manner in which it unfolds, marking especially the moment when it gives birth to contradictions and, in a negative dialectic, begins to unravel. Above all in *English-Speaking Justice* there is Grant's Christianity, which defines the contradictions and shows where liberalism has strayed from God's essence. The liberalism that emerges in his writing is not simply the reservoir of satanic energy that Grant describes in earlier works but something more like a prodigal son who has strayed from his Christian parents, entered into alliances with bad company – contractualism, science, technology – and discovers that he has become so bankrupt that he is at the mercy of violent companions.

THE FIRST DIVIDE

Grant opens *English-Speaking Justice* by reminding his readers of the blessings of the liberal heritage: 'the institutions and ideas of the English-Speaking world at their best have been much more than a justification of the progress in the mastery of human and non-human nature. They have affirmed that any regime to be called good, and any progress to be called good, must include political liberty and consent.'[9] Such appreciations appear throughout the book. In a later passage he writes, 'Indeed any sane individual must be glad that we face the unique event of technology within a long legal and political tradition founded on the conception of justice as requiring liberty and equality'[10] A little later he says, 'Asian people often have advantage over us in the continuing strength of rite; our advantage is in the continuing strength of right.'[11] But the book is structured to reveal the draining of these energies and strengths. In the very first chapter Grant warns of the spiritual death of contractualism. The second chapter is an extended analysis of Rawls's theories of justice. There Grant contrasts Rawls's contractual theory of liberalism with the theories of Locke and Kant, which still connect liberal freedom either to a theory of how things are (Locke) or to an absolute, namely the good will (Kant). Grant's criticism of Rawls, it is important to note, is not that of Rawls's conservative critics, who reject his arguments in support of the welfare state. A close examination of *English-Speaking Justice* reveals Grant the Social Democrat, or, as he was called in the 1970s, Grant the Red Tory. He warns of the menace of corporate expansionism and praises English-speaking liberalism for insisting on equality as well as liberty. Concerning Rawls's emphasis on fairness for all, Grant comments, 'surely any decent human being will agree that liberty and equality are at the heart of political justice.'[12] He acknowledges that Rawls's theory is but a new version of the old welfare-state 'Rooseveltian liberalism.' He criticizes Rawls from the left – for not recognizing the power of corporations, for not bringing forth 'a doctrine of the common good strong enough to control these mammoths,'[13] and for not acknowledging that *A Theory of Justice* 'was written when his country was embarked on a savage imperial adventure.'[14]

Grant, then, does not criticize the egalitarian content of liberalism, but warns that its roots are decaying. The cosmic religious vision that sustained the vision of the free individual is being replaced by visions of self interest and by contractualism – the cement is cracking. The real weakness of Rawls's book, Grant argues, is that it does not ground its social ideal in the iron foundations of a true philosophy or religious vision.

Rawls's weakness, Grant argues, is symptomatic of a weakness that began at the dawn of modernity. Following Weber and Tawney, Grant sees in early Calvinism the first of liberalism's deadly alliances. When Calvinism embraced the idea of the autonomous individual 'it crossed the Rubicon.' From thence came scientific secularism, contractualism as defined by Rawls and others, and now the deadly embrace of technology. Grant's description of liberalism's decline echoes Plato's passages on the decline of the ideal republic and Hegel's remarks on phenomenology.

As his first example of the contradictions in liberalism Grant points to *Roe v. Wade*. This decision, Grant declares, has exposed the rot of liberalism. But the significance of Grant's arguments does not reside in the fact that he is opposed to abortion, for many people of the right and of the left are 'pro-life' rather than 'pro-choice.' Grant's argument is not merely that the abortion decision is to be opposed, but that it marks a defining moment in liberalism.

Grant's language emphasizes with unmistakable clarity the crucial importance of this moment. He opens the climactic last chapter of *English-Speaking Justice* with the words 'English-speaking contractualism lies before us in the majority decision of the U.S. Supreme Court in "Roe vs Wade" ... In that decision one can hear what is spoken in modern liberalism more clearly than in academic books ...'[15] Moreover, 'however liberal this decision might be,' the decision 'raises a cup of poison to the lips of liberalism.'[16] In *Roe v. Wade* liberalism has crossed a divide into territory from which it cannot return.

The defining moment is found in the Court's decision that the fetus is not a person during the first trimester. That such a momentous decision has been taken by a court is for Grant an unprecedented invasion of the realm of the sacred. We have, according to him, taken a giant leap down the slippery slope. If fetuses are not persons, what is to stop the state from deciding that a week-old infant, a two-year-old child, or a seventy-year-old man or woman is not a person 'in the true sense.' In this decision the liberalism of Abel has become the liberalism of Cain.

Grant's criticism of *Roe v. Wade* exposes the nerve centre of his critique of liberalism but also his critique's most questionable claim. He has certainly selected an issue that presents a crisis for liberalism. But is abortion a 'contradiction' in the Hegelian sense of an event or crisis that poses for one form of thought, religion, and so on a problem that it cannot resolve from within the resources of its own discourse? Hegel, for example, believed the reality of individualism was beyond the boundaries of the conceptual world of the Greek city-state, and Marx thought the modern corporation was outside the conceptual world of liberal individualism. The Greek city-state produced a contradiction (the individual) and liberal individualism produced a contradiction (the corporation).

I do not wish to discuss here the substance of the abortion controversy or even explore the question of its impact on liberalism in great detail because this is the subject of another essay in this volume. But I want to ask whether abortion has unravelled the entire discourse on liberalism. Abortion is a crisis but not only for the reasons that Grant gives. It is a crisis because it pits two rights, that of the fetus and that of the mother, against one another. There are cases, such as when a young woman is raped by her father, in which the priority of these rights is far from self-evident. But the question I am addressing is whether abortion can be adequately debated within the vocabulary of liberalism. Grant's questions about the limits of personhood are surely the most important questions that can be raised about abortion. But his questions are well within the canon of liberalism. Hence it is difficult to see why the abortion controversy forces the unravelling of liberalism.

WILL TECHNOLOGY END LIBERALISM?

One of the most important problems in Grant's thought is the relationship between the practical and the theoretical. Grant was an active opponent of many liberal policies because of his philosophic opposition to liberalism. But his practical activities, such as his opposition to euthanasia and his defence of Canadian nationalism, were formulated in ways that liberals could easily accept. Grant might have argued at the time that this was merely a stratagem, that the true basis of his argument lay elsewhere, but in the examples just mentioned there was no evidence that Grant's liberal vocabulary was strained beyond endurance.

Abortion, as we have just seen, is one supposed contradiction within liberalism discussed by Grant in *English-Speaking Justice*. The second is the contradiction between political liberalism and technology. In *English-Speaking Justice* Grant notes that contemporary liberalism is characterized by 'the sustaining faith in a necessary interdependence between the development of technological science and political liberalism.'[17] He goes on to warn, however, that 'it is not difficult to point to facts which suggest that technological development does not sustain political liberalism.'[18] Throughout the volume and in other writings he indeed has little trouble finding facts that demonstrate the incompatibility between political liberalism and technology. Grant is particularly concerned with the menace of the new medical technologies and their ability to create new life and to individuals, indeed to annihilate the very possibility of individuality. Grant's fear that the dystopia that faces us will be more medical than Orwellian led him to praise 'One Flew over the Cuckoo's Nest' as a great film.

One of the primary dramas of ideas throughout the book is the tension between the growth of technology and a liberalism for which contractualism is becoming more and more central. By contractualism Grant means a society that has cast off the binding cement of kinship and religion that holds it together. Contractualism is the view that 'the good society is composed of free individuals who agree to live together only on condition that the rules of cooperation, necessary to living together, serve the overall purposes of the society.'[19] Grant adds that contractualism can be defended as 'the only model of political relations adequate to autonomous adults.'[20] When he adds that contractualism is a system of relations between calculating, self-interested individuals, it is clear that the state envisaged is itself a corporation writ large, except perhaps that some private corporations are larger than most states. In such a conception, the basic loyalties to the state, loyalties that would make one ready to die for one's country, seem as inappropriate as a readiness to die for the betterment of McDonald's hamburgers.

In Grant's view, as liberalism becomes more contractual it confronts the expanding power of technology, a power that reduces people to cogs in a machine, a power that renders the liberal concept of the free individual as an anachronism and an absurdity. When Grant wrote *English-Speaking Justice* he anticipated that technology would grow stronger and the individual weaker. The facts that impressed him the most were the expansion of dictatorships in the newly industrializing Third world, and the proliferation of medical and biological instruments of control in DNA research and other areas of genetics. The manipulation of the human essence was for Grant the crucial sin of modernity. In *English-Speaking Justice*, however, Grant's fundamental concern is with the power of science's language and concepts rather than with the logic of technology. We will see shortly, that Grant does not contrast a benign science with a malevolent technology but instead regards the foundational assertions of science as the source of technology's tyranny.

Grant's finest work on technology is his essay 'Thinking About Technology.'[21] This text is a contribution to one of the most persistent themes in the writing of social philosophers on modernity, namely the conflict between free subjectivity and modernity as rationality, the tendency within modernity to liberate the individual as well as to build an iron cage. Grant's essay contains echoes of Marx, Heidegger, and Orwell. He tells us (this is 1978) that IBM 'will in the next thirty years be a larger unit than the economy of any presently constituted national state.'[22] One extensive section of this essay offers a discussion of the idea that 'the computer does not impose upon us the way it should be used.' Grant's method is reminiscent of Marx's approach toward the concept of 'commodity' in the famous first chapter of *Kapital*. Marx begins with a simple object and then presents an analysis that transforms the simple object into a social object that reveals and presupposes a type of society, namely the class society of liberalism and capitalism. Grant, likewise, begins with the computer as a simple neutral instrument that is in our care. But a moment's reflection tells us that having this simple instrument means having a certain kind of society. Grant does not make the mistake of those who have decided to abandon the twentieth century by retreating into the wilderness with a Sony Walkman and a stock of birth control pills. The very tools people use presuppose the world that makes them. Grant concludes 'that computers are not neutral instruments, but instruments which exclude certain forms of community and permit others.'[23]

The computer, moreover, not only excludes certain types of social structure but also imposes a 'paradigm of knowledge.' This paradigm is based on mathematical and scientific forms of knowledge that classify and homogenize. The consequences of this paradigm are far-reaching, for it permits only certain types of political order. According to Grant, 'The three dominant alternatives are capitalist liberalism, communist Marxism and national socialist historicism.'[24]

Grant's conclusion, then, is that the statement 'the computer does not impose upon us the way in which it should be used' reflects an illusory relationship between us and the computer, one that presupposes a world of subjects, presented with objects that are there for our disposal. It conceals how we are at the disposal of the computer. Grant's revelation that the 'subject' is an illusion, an epiphenomenon of technology, would delight the postmodernists.

In this analysis, then, the advance of rationality (in Weber's sense of instrumental rationality) is incompatible with the freedom of the subject. Technological advance is a zero-sum game. The more technology, the less subject; the less subject, the more meaningless is liberal freedom. When we adopt new technology, Grant advises, we should consider closely the price we must pay.

What is the significance of this analysis for us today? And has anything happened since Grant's passing that would call into question the correctness of his fears about technology.

With regard to the first question, we must be careful to bring his teachings about technology into careful focus. In providing dark warnings about technology Grant does not depart from liberalism or even contribute anything new. From the beginning of the industrial revolution liberal writers produced a succession of literary dystopias that can be considered the precursors of Grant's. The first generation of liberals feared industrial civilization. John Stuart Mill's celebrated phrase, 'better Socrates dissatisfied than a pig satisfied,' was a response to the promised bliss of industrial development. Huxley and Orwell, among others, presented nightmarish scenarios concerning humanity's technological future. All of these writers, however, were well within the liberal tradition.

What is it, then, that makes Grant – who claims to write from outside the traditions of liberalism – different? One way of approaching this question is to examine the difference between Grant and other writers in the liberal tradition, for example between Grant and Russell in the latter's *Prospects of Industrial Civilization*. Russell's book warns us that industrialism can be our undoing, although at most it will bring us into a constricted world resembling Weber's 'iron cage.' Russell, therefore, balances the shortcomings of industrial civilization against its benefits. He warns that the alternative to industrialism is brutish subsistence labour for the entire human race. He argues that there is a possibility (but only a possibility) that industrialism will produce freedom and high culture. Thus we press forward with vigilance against its dangers and attempt to nurture its considerable promise. Maintaining this strategy is for Russell the central challenge of the contemporary world.

Grant, too, insists (and the complexity of his view is often ignored) that industrialism is both dangerous and necessary. The passages in Grant's writings about the horror of life without technology are as vivid as anyone's. Grant insists, moreover, that technology arises from impulses toward the good. But he insists that liberal freedom in its secular scientific form cannot cope with technology. He insists that technology under the auspices of liberalism must be destructive.

But Grant's account of the collision between liberalism and technology raises the same doubts as his account of the collision between liberalism and abortion. There is, to be sure, a crisis, but has he provided the conclusive demonstration of a contradiction – that is, of a problem that cannot be solved within a liberal framework? Does his account of the logic of technology beg the question of whether liberalism has reached a logical impasse? Has Grant the Christian plunged into a gap in the way that theologians sometimes do when they perceive a disturbance in the sciences?

What has happened since the appearance of Grant's writings on computers that might affect his analysis of liberalism? In *English-Speaking Justice* Grant writes, 'it must be stated that our justice now moves to a lowered content of liberty.'[25] Yet since the late 1970s, when Grant wrote those words, the communist tyrannies have collapsed, other tyrannies are on the defensive, women and racial minorities have made gains toward being recognized as social equals of everyone else, and the danger of nuclear war has subsided. There is, of course, much to be pessimistic about, but in technological society, as in every other society, it is much easier to proclaim the forces of doom than to discern the balance of failure and success.

Since Grant wrote 'Thinking About Technology,' the technology of computers and global communications has advanced in such a fashion that the older pessimistic predictions of the inevitability of Orwellian centralization have been challenged by more complex scenarios, some of them, admittedly, just as pessimistic. Our world is one where political giants rise and fall, where the danger of disintegration from nationalism and other localisms is just as great as the danger from centralization. Grant's warning about IBM may still be apt (or perhaps can be transferred to Microsoft), but it must be remembered that IBM came to the brink of collapse several years ago. We live in a world where the small can frustrate the ambitions of the great, where the universal homogeneous empire is so fragile in the Balkans, and where mighty corporations live in terror of fifteen-year-old hackers. Orwell's Big Brother could easily be deceived by many of the subscribers to *Wired* magazine. Any new dystopia will have to be designed like a futuristic Jurassic Park, where the clash of monsters devouring one another and themselves being devoured by fleas leaves room for the people underfoot to survive and even flourish.

In 'Thinking about Technology' Grant argued that the principles and affirmations that comprise scientific rationality are not only disembodied mental processes in the minds of scientists. Following Hegel, he believed that ideas also have earthly embodiments. For example, scientific rationality is embodied in technological products such as the computer, but it is also embodied in distinct political forms. The forms that Grant discerned as the political embodiments of scientific rationality are liberal democracy, National Socialism, and Communism. For Grant these reflected the scientific world view, just as in medieval times the hierarchies of feudalism had reflected a Christian theology. Moreover, just as medieval theology has excluded certain types of political order, as, for example, democracies of free and equal citizens, so modern scientific rationalism excludes political orders other than those that Grant named. This is the meaning of his insistence that by adopting scientific ways of thinking we have accepted some forms of living and excluded ourselves from others. Scientific thought, Grant argued, is a closed system which has definite borders and horizons.

But do Grant's examples disclose the logical social boundaries of the system? Are Nazism and Communism equal (not morally, to be sure) as manifestations of the logic of scientific rationality? Do these three societies exhaust the social possibilities of scientific rationality? In my view, Grant's vision was too wide because neither Nazism nor Communism survived within the scientific world view. Nazism was technologically and economically competent, but declared itself to be antimodern and antiscientific, and indeed had a number of fatal shortcomings from a scientific point of view. Communism crumbled, in part because it could not cope with the developments of global mass media. Liberal democracy alone survived and for a time some of its celebrants declared an end to history. This optimism of course was short-lived, but still the civic societies of liberal democracy have thus far proved to be the most durable shelters from the storms of scientific and technological change.

In another sense, paradoxically, the possibilities within scientific rationality seem to be wider than those of just liberal democracy. Since the 1970s technological society has witnessed something else that Grant did not anticipate, the proliferation of religious fundamentalisms that have moved into the centre of its activity. Contrary to one of Grant's predictions, fundamentalists love computer science. All of the world's major religious texts and the commentaries on them can be found on CD-ROMs that are studied by devout and traditional congregations. Even native Indian groups have purchased laptops and established interactive networks. Grant pointed to a historical togetherness between liberalism and technology, but perhaps we are moving toward a world where liberals agonize over, and religious fundamentalists celebrate, new advances in computer science. Then, perhaps, the choice will be between the agonizing liberals in the universities and the rabbis, priests, ayatollahs, and shamans in cyberspace.

FAITH AND MODERNITY

English-Speaking Justice is a work whose underlying structure is Sophoclean. *Oedipus Rex* begins with a problem, namely the plague at Thebes and the search for its cause. The drama unfolds as Oedipus unravels layer after layer of deception until the discovery of the final sin. *English-Speaking Justice* also begins with a problem – the prospect of a disastrous encounter between liberalism and technology – and also unfolds as it uncovers layer after layer of contradiction – the weaknesses in Rawls's contractualism, the *Roe v. Wade* decision, the autonomous self of Calvinism in which liberalism as a moral system continues to unravel. Eventually it reaches the final contradiction, which Grant describes as primal. It is a contradiction that we have kept from ourselves for centuries, a self-concealment that has allowed us to function but from which we can no longer escape:

For the last centuries a civilisational contradiction has moved our Western lives. Our greatest intellectual endeavour – the new co-penetration of *logos* and *techne* – affirmed at its heart that in understanding anything we know it as ruled by necessity and chance. This affirmation entailed the elimination of the ancient notion of good from the understanding of anything. At the same time, our day to day organisation was in the main directed by a conception of justice formulated in relation to the ancient science, in which the notion of good was essential to understanding of what is.'[26]

Grant is saying that the universe which is disclosed to us by modern science is one that is ruled by chance and necessity, that it is a universe in which neither justice nor morality is embedded in the order of things – an order that offers no clues about what 'we are fitted for.' Our life-world, in other words, is necessarily cut off from nature. We are like those colonists in the fifteenth and sixteenth centuries who came to the wilderness of the New World and established a kind of civilization that did not belong there. Elaborating on his concept of the order of things, Grant maintains that all the virtues of modernity – liberty, equality, democracy – have been looted from an ancient order of things, for modernity has no capacity of its own to sustain a moral order. Dr Mengele and all the scientists of the concentration camps for whom the inmates were merely there to provide knowledge were paradigmatic expressions of modernity stripped of all that is filched from the past.

This is the heart of Grant's critique of secular liberalism. It is simple and has been repeated in countless works of theology and even in sermons. Grant, however, draws out its most radical consequences.

The contradiction between a moral language that implies the good and a scientific language in which the good has no place, implies that once the West adopts the scientific outlook it drinks a cup of poison that causes it to perish as a moral system. It implies also that the usual attempts to disassociate science from technology are ill-conceived, because it is far from true that technology is a bastard child of which science is an innocent parent. In fact, the amorality of the scientific universe, its splitting of fact and values, have opened the way for a world-devouring technology. It follows that 'the good,' in its strictest sense, is not possible in a scientifically construed world. This is Grant's stark conclusion.

One corollary of Grant's vision is that it turns Freud upside down. In *Civilization and Its Discontents* Freud argues that the world is made sick because the ghost of Christianity remains in the scientific universe. Grant argues, to the contrary, that the world is sick because science has turned Christianity into a ghost. If one remains Christian or Jewish in such a world, one is forced into a new Gnosticism in which there is a strict separation between the world in which the Kingdom of God is conceivable and the lower world, that of science and technology in which it is not. But Grant is a Christian who believes that the world was created by God and that modernity, the synthesis of freedom and rationality, must therefore be resolved in some way impossible to liberalism. But what remains enigmatic is how the solutions that faith and philosophy suggest can address the contradiction that Grant purports to have uncovered.

Grant's first solution to the enigma is Hegelian. He writes that 'it is folly simply to return to the ancient account of justice as if the discoveries of the modern science of nature had not been made. It is folly to take the ancient account of justice as simply of antiquarian interest.'[27] Some togetherness of the two must be thought. Ancient justice must be combined with the core of truth that has come out of technology. In stating that this is Hegelian I am not implying that Grant believes such a coming together is inevitable or predetermined by the logic of history. It is closer to the truth to say Grant is making an expression of faith, implying that God will not allow the satanic forces of modernity to triumph.

Grant's second solution, one that is also attractive, is a dialogue between the past and the present. He writes that 'the view of traditional philosophy and religion is that justice is the overriding order which we do not measure and define but in terms of which we are measured and defined. The view of modern thought is that justice is a way in which we choose in freedom, both individually and publicly, once we have taken our fate into our own hands.'[28] A dialogue is necessary. We will not accept 'an order where we are measured and defined'[29] unless we know who is doing the measuring and how we are defined. Without such stipulations, which are at the heart of modernity, an order in which we are measured and defined is a formula for slavery.

The difficulty here is that these last two formulae call for a dialogue between past and present, while the first, the contradiction, implies that no dialogue is possible. Where in this contradiction, as Grant has formulated it, is there a possible 'core of truth' of technology? Will science go away? Will it be reinterpreted by creationists? Can a contradiction be resolved by negating one of its terms?

Those of us who define ourselves as liberals and moderns might inquire whether there is any room for manoeuvring. We cannot address this question by drawing up lists of the costs and benefits of modernity versus the costs and benefits of the tradition. The contradiction toward which Grant has pointed us has further unacceptable consequences.

Grant's position implies that the Third Reich and the gulags were not, as some have argued, survivals of the medieval world or 'tribalism,' but were consequences of modernity. Grant is right, but for us to say this is to offer only a weak formulation of his meaning. Grant often implies that the Third Reich and the gulags are the *logical outcome* of modernity, that is, are 'explicit' modernity – modernity left to itself, without any contribution from the past. This view is a great challenge but it implies that there is little need for a dialogue between modernity and the past because there is nothing to discuss.

Having raised many questions, it is time for me to end the discussion. It has been enough to show that Grant's great eloquence sometimes conceals the disturbing complexities of his work. I have argued that the very centre of Grant's critique of modernity, and consequently of liberalism, issues from his Christian protest against a Prometheanism that has rebelled against the Almighty. In the course of giving his critique philosophic depth Grant reopens many questions. He questions the modern project and hence anticipates the antimodernist strain in our culture. He also anticipates the consequences of a wholesale rejection of liberalism. Thus the elements in his thought are in turmoil and seeking a resolution that, it seems to me, he has closed off.

I have argued that Grant has sought to bring us face to face with those issues that undermine liberalism as a viable response to modernity, and even the credibility of modernity itself. In carrying out this agenda Grant has often seemed like a Christian version of Zarathustra, declaring to unknowing multitudes that liberal humanism is dead. He has argued that these issues – the realities of widespread abortion, the proliferation of technology, and the existence of a mechanistic, scientific outlook – cannot be treated as issues that liberalism might meet by great and unprecedented efforts of thought and action. He has set out to show that these issues give rise to contradictions that undermine the very logic of liberalism. I have questioned Grant's strategy and suggested that these issues, however daunting, are not manifestations of an inner logic of negation. I have suggested that though liberalism may fail to meet the challenges that they pose, this failure will not be due to a necessary depletion of its conceptual or moral arsenal. Paradoxically, even Grant gave the liberal some reason to look within his or her own resources. When he went forth into the public realm, either against the war in Vietnam, or on behalf of the integrity of Canada or even against the decisions of the courts on abortion and euthanasia, his best arguments came from within the traditional liberal repertoire or arguments against imperialism or on behalf of human rights.

NOTES

1 For the principles of liberalism, see Stephen Holmes, *Passions and Constraint* (Chicago: University of Chicago Press 1995), 13–41.
2 Yusuf K. Umar ' The Philosophical Context of George Grant's Political Thought,' in Yusuf K. Umar, ed., *George Grant and the Future of Canada* (Calgary: University of Calgary Press 1992), 1–16.
3 Ibid., 16.
4 Ibid.
5 Ibid., 9.
6 Arthur Kroker, *Technology and the Canadian Mind: Innis/McLuhan/Grant* (Montreal: New World Perspectives 1984), 49.
7 George Grant, *English-Speaking Justice* (Toronto: Anansi 1978), 82.
8 John Rawls, *A Theory of Justice* (Cambridge, *MA*: Harvard University Press 1970).
9 Grant, *English-Speaking Justice*, 5.
10 Ibid., 81.
11 Ibid., 82.
12 Ibid., 43.
13 Ibid., 41.
14 Ibid., 42.
15 Ibid., 69.
16 Ibid., 71.
17 Ibid., 8.
18 Ibid.
19 Ibid., 33.
20 Ibid.
21 George Grant, *Technology and Justice* (Toronto: Anansi 1978), 11–35.
22 Ibid., 25.
23 Ibid., 23.
24 Ibid., 24.
25 Grant, *English-Speaking Justice*, 83.
26 Ibid., 73.
27 Ibid., 88
28 Ibid., 72.
29 Ibid.

Love and Will in the Miracle of Birth: An Arendtian Critique of George Grant on Abortion

LEAH BRADSHAW

George Grant, as we know, was a powerful and enigmatic thinker. Much has been written about the various strands of his thought, and about the way he appeals to every shade of the political spectrum. The reason for Grant's broad appeal lies in his straddling of the ancient and modern worlds, in his efforts to combine a thinking through of the intellectual ground of modernity with a commitment to a classical and Christian understanding of things. On abortion, however, Grant eschews classical categories and frames his comments exclusively within the modern context of rights discourse. On abortion Grant is an absolutist, and emphatically clear: abortion is killing. In accounting for this stance he uses entirely modern arguments, grounded in rights, to defend the entitlement of the unborn. In this essay I want to look in greater detail at Grant's position on abortion, situate it within the context of his thinking as a whole, and offer some critical reflections of my own on the abortion controversy and its profound moral implications.

I

There is no question that the abortion debate in liberal democratic societies is framed within the context of rights. We are all familiar with the stand-off in rights discourse concerning the rights of women versus the rights of the unborn. Grant immerses himself in

this debate and takes the side of the unborn. In a 1976 article entitled 'Abortion and Rights,' he asserts that 'When the argument for
easy abortion is made on the basis of rights, it clearly rests on the
weighing of the rights of some against the rights of others.' And in
his assessment of the United States Supreme Court decision in *Roe
v. Wade*, he sees a complete disregard for the rights of the unborn
that weakens the idea of rights.[1]

In *English-Speaking Justice*, published in 1974, Grant undertakes a
brilliant analysis of the history of rights theory in the English-
speaking world, which culminates in a case study of *Roe v. Wade* as
a testing ground for the faltering of rights doctrine. Grant is undeniably correct in his claim that *Roe v. Wade* proved beyond a doubt
that the right takes priority over the good in contractually based
liberal societies.[2] Grant sees that this is the inevitable consequence
of the logic of liberalism. The United States Constitution is based on
the idea that there is moral pluralism in society, and that this pluralism is justified because liberal societies must remain neutral on
the question of what is a good. People have the right to choose their
own goods, and no one has the right to deny them the choice. The
decision in *Roe v. Wade* 'speaks modern liberalism in its purely
contractual form: right prior to good; a foundation contract protecting individual rights; the neutrality of the state concerning moral
values; social pluralism supported by and supporting this neutrality.'[3]

Grant views the outcome of the Supreme Court decision on abortion as a rights struggle in which the strong prevail over the weak.
In this case the strong are women and the weak are the unborn.
Possibly because it found having to choose between the competing
rights of women and the unborn so morally repugnant, the Court
elected, Grant reasons, to see the unborn as not human. This is
what Grant in his writing on abortion in the early seventies finds so
alarming: that the Court somehow lacked the courage to face up to
its decision asserting the primacy of rights for some over others,
and instead elected to designate one group (the unborn) as not
human. He writes: 'In adjudicating for the right of the mother to
choose whether another member of her species lives or dies, the
judge is required to make an ontological distinction between members of the same species.'[4]

In arguing for the equal claims of mothers and fetuses, Grant uses
modern scientific evidence. He explicitly refers to the scientific evi-

dence that what exists in the fetus is a unique genetic code that is undeniably a human being.[5] Grant viciously attacks any account of the unborn child that tries to classify it as something other than human, or as 'potential life': 'There is no halfway house. Beings with only potential life do not suck their thumbs in the womb in preparation for the breast. It makes perfect sense to say that we are all potentially dead, but it does not make sense to say that the foetus is potential life.'[6]

Grant's meditation on abortion within the rights context causes him much anxiety. In *English-Speaking Justice* he describes how liberalism has entered an arid atmosphere where all justice seems to be a recognition of contract. On the other hand, Grant applauds liberalism and rights doctrine for their humane achievements in public policy. He lists, among those achievements, the repugnance for capital punishment and the extension to women of the 'proper equality' for which they have courageously striven.[7] Rights based societies, Grant acknowledges, have protected the weak and even given them a dignity that has not been achieved under any other political regime.

So why have liberal democracies fallen? Grant has a highly intellectual explanation for this. Rights-based societies had their original moorings in a Judeo-Christian context, and thus were informed by an intuitive understanding of that context. Grant cites the opening words of the United States Constitution: 'We hold these truths to be self-evident; that all men are created equal, that they are endowed by their creator with inalienable rights, that among these rights is life ... that to secure these rights, governments are instituted among men.' The emphasis on the Creator was actually pivotal, according to Grant, because the equality of the created was the sacred principle from which governments took their guidelines for action.

Rights-based societies are no longer situated in a Judeo-Christian context, however, but in a scientific and historicist context, and this gives rights a much crueller meaning. With respect to the scientific context, most people believe (with the scientists) that chance and accident, not purposiveness, are the framework for human life.[8] Without the conviction that all beings created by God are worthy of respect, it falls to the state to delegate rights. Justice becomes a privilege granted to some of the people, if they are the right age and sufficiently like other people.[9] Grant worries that with the erosion of the divine sanction of rights, the weakest members of the human community will now suffer. He anticipates that liberal societies will move increasingly toward dispossessing the aged, the infirm, and even the socially deviant: 'We of course do not yet kill our mentally ill, but we are moving towards ways of thought which could be used to justify such actions ... The next extension of the denial of rights seems likely to be euthanasia for the aged.'[10] If a developing baby can be dismissed as fetal tissue that is expendable without moral anguish, then Grant surmises that 'it is not fanciful to think of many more helpful euphemisms for getting rid of unwanted people.'[11] If all life is accidental and random, then it falls to those in power to create order and determine the criteria for admission to the community.

Grant does not accept that scientific evidence achieved its privileged position in a historical vacuum. The notion that life exists by accident or chance is coupled with a powerful historicist meaning that emerged in the modern world to rival the intellectual meaning of the British tradition. Grant finds this rival conception – manifested in the German tradition of Kant, Hegel, Nietzsche, and Heidegger – riveting and ultimately a much more convincing depiction of modernity than the civil Anglo-Saxon tradition of rights. If the modern liberal conception built on the legacy of Christianity, with its reverence for the uniqueness of the created, the modern historicist tradition smashed that legacy. Grant seems to see some deep truth in this smashing that he thinks was evaded by the soft liberals. Christianity was marked by its charity and egalitarianism, but it was marked equally by its emphasis on the will: 'Modern contractualism's determined political activism relates to its seedbed in western Christianity. Here again, one comes upon that undefined primal affirmation which has been spoken of as concerned with "will" and which is prior both to technological science and to revolution.'[12] Here Grant appears to identify the primacy of will in Christianity as formative for subsequent developments in science and technology. Christianity did have an activist element, namely a reluctance to accept the suffering of the world as a given. In Christianity, Grant says, 'We are called to the supremacy of practical life in which we must struggle to establish the just contract of equality.' The impetus to intervene, to do something about the world, is not modern, though as we know, Grant thinks its derailment from its divine authorization has made the activist bent of modern people a dangerous thing.

What is particularly interesting in this discussion, though, is why Grant finds thinkers such as Nietzsche so compelling in their portrait of the dissolution of Christianity. Grant credits Nietzsche with being the one who laid out clearly the contradiction we are living. Nietzsche pointed out that 'what is given about the whole in technological science cannot be thought together with what is given us concerning justice and truth, reverence and beauty, from our tradition.'[13] Nietzsche had contempt for the English moralists who had not 'discovered history' and did not understand the dominance of historicism. Kant, Grant holds, did a brilliant job of covering over the contradictions of liberal justice. Because of Kant, 'men were held from seeing that justice as equality was a secularized survival of an archaic Christianity and the absolute commands were simply the man-made "values" of an era we have transcended.'[14] These are strong words, and they are not spoken by Grant in a spirit of merely recording the words of intellectuals, but in a spirit of acquiescence. Grant thinks Nietzsche was right.

By 1988 Grant seems, at least in print, to have dropped his rights discourse. He is now fully preoccupied with the triumph of historicism and its potential effects on political life in North America. In his essay 'The Triumph of the Will,' he maintains the same rigidity on abortion, but discusses the issue in the context of fascism, not liberalism. He opens his argument by saying that the judges in *Roe v. Wade* used the language of liberalism in a purely aesthetic way. They were not really making liberal arguments, but were using the 'language of North American liberalism to say "yes" to the very core of fascist thought – the triumph of the will.'[15] The triumph of the will means something quite specific to Grant: it is the assertion of the will of the individual over all else, including the sacred and the state. In our stage of modernity, the divine ground of meaning, and the political community of meaning have collapsed like a house of cards, and all that is left is the individual with his or her desire for mastery. This is fascism.[16] Will in modern times means the 'resolute mastery of ourselves and the world.' Truth, beauty, and goodness – the three things that Grant cites as objects of veneration which ought to guide considerations of justice – have been eclipsed by the will to power. Again, Nietzsche is invoked as the person who understood this best. Will *is* power: 'To understand this modern illumination of the word 'will,' it is necessary to put aside entirely that old faculty, psychology, in which will was understood as a power of the soul, having to do with free choices. Rather, will is now considered to be the centre of our aiming or seeking, the holding together of what we want ... In the phrase "will to power," Nietzsche is not describing what we aim at – something outside the will. Rather, he is saying that will is power itself, not something external to power.'[17]

Grant's emphasis on the will to power in the late eighties, as opposed to his emphasis on the corruption of rights in the seventies, may well reflect the changing discourse of the abortion controversy, although he does not say this. What we find in public discourse in North America by the late eighties is a shift from asserting the right of women to control their own bodies (and the matter that is contained in them) to a real confrontation with the claims of women versus the claims of the unborn. There is less effort expended on trying to dehumanize the fetus, and more on defending the right of women to abortion, while acknowledging that what is being advanced is the right to terminate life.[18] Grant may have found the obfuscation of the status of the fetus enraging, but he seems to have been even more horrified at the blatant public defence of what he clearly regarded as the killing of people.

In 'The Triumph of the Will' we get Grant's fullest analysis of the condition of women under the terms of modernity. Grant says the leaders of the women's movement (not named) have adopted the language of the triumph of the will. This is presumably quite different from Justice Blackmun back in the seventies, who used the language of liberal rights. 'It is to be expected,' Grant remarks, 'that this language should become dominant among the leaders of the women's movement because they are so aware of what it is to live in modernity.'[19] The emphasis is on just how much women are participants in a modernity from which they cannot escape, and the responsibility for the will to power among women seems to be attributed by Grant far more to historical forces than to individuals. In fact, Grant uses Hegelian language to describe the situation of women in liberal democratic societies: 'In modern technological society most bourgeois women (and those who want to become bourgeois) find themselves in a sexually emancipated age, and one in which, to get any social recognition, they must work in the world. This is achieved under corporate capitalism through mastery over oneself and other people.'[20] Under such conditions abortion appears as a necessity, Grant says, since women want to be equal competitors for bourgeois recognition.

In analyzing the plight of women under conditions of modern capitalism, Grant points to the confusing legacy of Christianity and intimates how it may well have contributed to the twisted sense of the will to power that he thinks motivates the defence of abortion. The ambiguity of the feminist slogan 'biology is not destiny' is that it echoes an important Christian teaching: that at the highest levels, all people are one in Christ, neither male nor female, but equal.[21] It seems that an essential Christian teaching, intended for spiritual matters, has been secularized and thus (in Grant's mind) horrifyingly corrupted into a justification for injustice of the worst kind.

At this juncture Grant asks an extremely important question: 'At the highest levels of human life and love, gender is simply unimportant. The question is, at what levels of life and love *is* gender important, and how should this difference manifest itself?'[22] Grant answers this question indirectly. He thinks gender is important, and that it should manifest itself in women's resistance to the will to power, but not that women should have 'life and death control over beings other than themselves.'[23] Even though Grant has written extensively on the triumph of historicism, and on the lost power of any 'given truths,' such as good, truth, and beauty, to guide human conduct, he clearly thinks women ought to have the inner resources to resist the triumph of the will and to acknowledge the 'given,' the 'otherness,' of the unborn. In Grant's account, the givenness of pregnancy is specifically the providence of women, and it is the overcoming of this 'given,' more than the overcoming of any other good, truth, or beauty, that distresses him when he considers modernity. He writes of women, 'The "given" which their will needs to control is the individual members of their own species within their bodies. "Otherness" which must be dominated has always been the thing in terms of which the language of the triumph of the will arises.'[24] Women feel trapped by their gender, and they liberate themselves from this entrapment by killing, according to Grant: 'The language of the triumph of the will is a means of escaping from that trap because it frees one from the traditional restraints against killing.'[25]

In 'The Triumph of the Will' Grant sounds discouraged and defeatist. He comments at the end of it that the triumph of the will passes over into politics in advanced industrial countries when they see themselves as threatened or fading. He sees just such a 'fading' in the West, and he sees the American legal system foundering in the face of the triumph of the will. The politics of the triumph of the will he views as less and less susceptible to curtailment by reason, especially 'tired liberal reason which expresses itself only in terms of a contract.'[26]

II

There are two aspects of Grant's views on abortion that I want to address in this second half of the essay. First, I want to argue that the burden of responsibility he places on women is untenable, given his commitment to the inevitability of historicism and the triumph of the will. Second, I want to suggest a more optimistic picture of the abortion issue than Grant provides. This picture requires dispensing with the tactics of the right-to-life movement and its dependence on science (a move that Grant seemed unwilling to make, despite his disillusionment with rights talk), and a focus on what is left in our society of a public domain. In these matters, as I intend to show, the thought of Hannah Arendt is instructive.

Grant places an extraordinary burden on women if he expects that they will heed the call of the 'given' or of the 'otherness' that he alludes to in his discussion of abortion and the will to power. As we have seen, Grant is persuaded by the Nietzschean account of modernity, even if he loathes it. He of course does not live entirely in this Nietzschean world of supermen and last men, since he speaks of experiences that lie outside it. Grant knows something of good, truth and beauty, and this is why he writes with authority about the classical and Christian traditions. But he lives partly in the modern historicist reality, too, and even praises some of the developments that have grown out of that reality, notably the freedom that has been afforded to individuals to shape their own lives. He applauds the movement toward equality that has been engendered in modernity, and he mentions the courage of women who have fought for gender equality.

How exactly does Grant expect, given the secularization of Christian values and their inevitable decay into the will to power, that women will escape this historical context? He seems to believe the givenness of pregnancy ought to awaken in women intimations of the good that are specific only to them. He also seems to believe women resist the will to power better than men because they have the capacity to be mothers. Obviously this is not the case for millions of women in the liberal democracies. Grant may be right in saying that even though the goal of gender equality is a worthy one, and one that in fact originated with Christian spirituality, there are cases where gender does matter and the differences between men and women ought to be taken into account. He himself says, however, that in capitalist, contractual society, gender differences count for nothing in how success is measured. If a woman in a modern liberal democratic society has children, she has to be prepared to give herself over to this 'otherness' with love, in a climate that will demand of her that she operate according to the will to power. Grant ought to express hope when he sees that women continue to have and love children being born and nurtured under such conditions.[27] Given his own analysis of modernity, the fact that children are still being born and nurtured is more surprising than the fact of widespread abortion.

This brings me to my second criticism, which concerns Grant's depiction of rights-based societies sliding into the will to power. First let me say that Grant's understanding of rights-based societies appears to be generally accurate. The original basis of rights – that all people are equal before God – has diminished in its impact, and this has made us less kind as a society. Edward Andrew expresses this best in his book *Shylock's Rights*, where he makes the case that it is the loudest, most aggressive, and strongest who truly benefit from a confrontational and contractual culture.[28] But there are ways for the weak and the silent to get into the game. There is a lively public arena in Western liberal democracies, even if some would argue that the characteristics of the agora have been eclipsed by the clash of organized interests. The handicapped, the historically disadvantaged minorities, and the unborn have strong advocates in Western liberal states. In fact, the debate over abortion is one of the most publicized debates in North American politics. All citizens are aware at some level of the clash of rights between women and the unborn.

Grant's spectre of the will to power does not hold up under scrutiny. He actually writes in the 'Triumph of the Will' about supposed parallels between abortion in North America and genocide in Nazi Germany. The doctrine that underlay Nazism – 'the search for meaning in a universe which is known as purposelessness' – has continued to be present in the English-speaking world, according to Grant. He sees evidence of the spirit of National Socialism in the imperial designs of the Americans in Vietnam, and in the work of medical researchers to assert mastery over reproduction.[29] He draws parallels between the propaganda campaign in Nazi Germany to turn Jews into nonpersons, and the propaganda in North America to prepare the general public for the acceptability of abortion: 'With the coming of mass abortion in our society, untruths have been spread by those who do not know that they are untruths. Current scientific knowledge tells us that a separate human life is present from conception, with its own unique genetic pattern, with all the chromosomes and genes that make it human. It is the very heart of fascism to think that what matters is not what is true, but what one holds to be true. What one holds to be true is important because it can produce that resolute will, turned to its own triumph.'[30]

There has been a lot of propaganda in North America in support of abortion rights, but Grant is holding up a chimera when he continues to insist that lies are being fed to the public to perpetuate the untruth that fetuses are not human. Everyone has seen pictures of small babies in the womb sucking their thumbs. The thesis that fetuses are not human is marginal. The fact is, there is widespread public knowledge about exactly what abortion entails, and freedom of choice for women continues to be supported by a majority of the population.[31] The question that Grant should have focused on is why, when the information is widely and publicly available, and there is widespread agreement that fetuses are human, is abortion still acceptable to large numbers of people in the Western democracies? Are they monstrous people? Is this acceptance of abortion comparable to the acceptance of the genocide of millions of Jews in Nazi Germany?

If we look at the circumstances under which millions of people were exterminated in Germany, we can see that they are not comparable to conditions in present-day North America. Hannah Arendt, who wrote extensively on the Holocaust emphasizes that totalitarianism requires ideology and terror. Ideology means many different things. For Arendt, it means the deliberate repression of the 'miracle of being.' Ideologies, she writes, 'are historical, concerned with becoming and perishing, with the rise and fall of cultures, even if they try to explain history by some "law of nature."'[32] This definition may well have been acceptable to Grant, given his forebodings about how historicist accounts of modernity had corrupted common sense.[33] For Arendt, however, the critical coupling in totalitarianism is ideology and terror. The terror of totalitarian regimes is much more than traditional tyranny, for it is not simply the despotic power of one or a few men. Terror 'substitutes for the boundaries and channels of communication between individual men a band of iron which holds them so tightly together that it is as though their plurality had disappeared into One Man of gigantic dimensions.'[34] By pressing men against one another in an atmosphere of total domination, surveillance, and intimidation, terror destroys any capacity for civic life. It was under these conditions that genocide was perpetrated in Germany. We do not live under these conditions in North America.

If, in fact, we are not living under conditions comparable to those of Nazi Germany, but are living with the widespread availability of abortion, the explanation for the latter is harder. We cannot, with Grant, claim that millions of people are duped by a false sense of reality under a will to power that is sustained by ideology and terror. But, we can, with Grant, say we are living in an age that is coloured by historicism, that is flattened by the loss of traditional religious values as a civilizational glue. But we still have the human community, we still have speech, and we still have the marketplace of ideas in some form.

I think Grant's 'slippery slope' argument is misplaced. Abortion is not the first step on the path that leads toward slaughtering the infirm, the aged, and the deviant. It can be argued, in fact, that more public energy has been spent by Western liberal society to protect such people than by any previous society we know of. Concessions are made to accommodate the infirm; the aged are protected by the state from abject poverty and the depredations of ungrateful children and grandchildren; state resources are put into aiding the mentally ill and rehabilitating the criminal. We can debate the efficacy of these measures, but the fact is that as a society, liberal democracy has shown tremendous concern for the weak. What impresses me is that the weak have a *public* face. The deviant, the infirm, are not shut away in shame, as they were in the past. Also, there is the paradox that vast resources are directed toward ensuring the well-being of children. Through the aid of science and technology, babies that would have died or have suffered terrible afflictions are kept alive, helped, and permitted to lead productive lives.

All of this goes on in a setting that permits abortion, and for many this is a puzzling fact. This is where Arendt may be helpful. Arendt stresses throughout her analysis of totalitarianism that what is destroyed in totalitarian regimes is the public space – the civic space in which people are visible to one another, are compelled to confront one another. The mere fact of visibility leads to empathy among human beings. This is why the secrecy of the concentration camps and the hiddenness of medical experimentation in Nazi Germany led to such horrific consequences. For the state to operate according to the triumph of the will, people have to be pushed back into an isolated and completely privatized existence.

Arendt writes about the plight of the human being who has no community, no legal status, no visibility in a political context: 'The human being which has lost his place in a community, his political status in the struggle of his time, and the legal personality which makes his actions and part of his destiny a consistent whole, is left with those qualities which usually become articulate only in the sphere of private life and must remain unqualified, mere existence in all matters of public concern.'[35] The falling away from public life leaves a human being nothing but his or her humanity to land on, and as Arendt puts it so starkly, 'The world found nothing sacred in the absolute nakedness of being human.'[36] Arendt pursues a long discussion about how completely ineffective the so-called rights of man are when they are not attached to a public domain that can give them a specific context. Her conclusion is that rights are inherently political, despite all the language of natural or human rights. We have rights when we are recognized members of a political community. (This is why Arendt supported the state of Israel, for she felt that the only assurance of the continued existence of the Jews was for them to have statehood, within which they could acquire a political identity.)

No one is more aware than Arendt of the precariousness of attaching human dignity to political status. But she raises the troubling question, what else is there in the modern world that will give human beings their due? Like Grant, she finds that there is not enough left of the tradition of classical thought or faith to sustain rights. Except for the political protection that is afforded by the state, all we have is the power of love, and there is absolutely no way that we can enforce love as a principle of action. Arendt's meditations on this are worth repeating here: 'The mere existence, that is, that which is mysteriously given us by birth, and which includes the shape of our bodies and the talents of our minds, can be adequately dealt with only by the unpredictable hazards of friendship and sympathy, or by the great and ineluctable grace of love, which says, with Augustine, *Volo Ut Sis* (I want you to be), without being able to give any particular reason for such supreme and unsurpassable affirmation.'[37] According to Arendt's logic, a healthy public life is the one characteristic of modernity which is going to be most effective in protecting rights. She writes that 'The fundamental deprivation of human rights is manifested first and above all in the deprivation of a place in the world which makes opinions significant and actions effective.'[38] The sheer visibility of people, and of their sufferings, awakens public sympathy. This observation of Arendt's strikes me as profoundly true. There is a high degree of visibility in public life in North America, and I think that is why Grant's argument about the slippery slope, and his forebodings about the triumph of the will, do not hold up. There are advocates of euthanasia, but they are public advocates, and euthanasia is a subject of debate. Massive numbers of people are not being killed behind closed doors in the name of expediency. We have cause to worry about the power of the medical profession, and we need more public scrutiny of reproductive technology, but we understand *in principle* that public accountability is required in matters of serious moral concern.

As for the abortion question, we must conclude that it is ineluctably true that fetuses are not part of the political community, and this is why they are not protected by rights. They are not visible to the public because they are not yet in the world. They have no status as citizens, and this is their great disadvantage: not that they are not human, but that they are not citizens. I think this is why fetuses do not elicit as much sympathy in liberal democracies as do the ill, the disabled, and the criminal. The status of fetuses is completely different because they are not of this world. They are hidden within the bodies of women, where they are not yet part of the human community.[39]

The fetus is an example of Arendt's 'mere existence' (not mere existence in the sense of insignificance, but mere existence in the sense of having no particular identity as a member of any community). The fetus is subject to the unpredictable hazards of friendship and sympathy that Arendt depicts, or to the great and incalculable grace of love. Someone has to say to the fetus, 'I want you to be,' and in the present political climate there is no particular reason for such a supreme and unsurpassable affirmation. To carry a child to term and to bring it into the world in a society where the option for abortion is always there, is to engage in an act of love for which there is no political compulsion. Similarly, to mourn for aborted fetuses is to express grief at the defiance of grace, for which there is no reasonable punishment.

Grant took an intractable position on abortion: it is killing; it is killing first in the name of rights, and second in the name of the triumph of the will. Also, he saw abortion as part of a continuum of an attack in liberal societies on the weak. I have taken issue with Grant on a number of points. First, I have tried to show that Grant makes unreasonable demands on women, given his own arguments about the kind of society we inhabit. I have also tried to show, however, abortion is not killing in the name of the triumph of the will, and that we need not accept Grant's claims in that regard. Finally, I have argued that abortion is not part of a continuum that includes euthanasia and the purging of the weak.

We are still left, however, with Grant's statement that abortion is killing. Is it or is it not? We may grant that the fetus has no political status, no citizenship, no public face that would protect it in the same way that beings in the world are protected by rights defended by the state. But does the fact that the fetus has no political status mean that its extermination is something other than killing? Is the protection of life so dependent on the contingency of politics? I think these are precisely the questions we are faced with. The unborn child is outside the protection of rights because it has no political identity, and for people who think wholly in terms of rights there is absolutely nothing wrong with abortion. The same people who defend the right to abortion may well be strong advocates of the rights of children, and may, for example, oppose gender selection in the abortion process. There is no contradiction, if one understands that the criterion for judgment is membership in the political community. By choosing to abort female rather than male babies, people make political judgements about the dispensability of children. The crime is not abortion itself, but abortion induced because of a qualitative judgment about the higher civic status of males over females.[40] I would also venture to say that the tactics of right-to-life supporters have practically no effect on people who are committed to a policy of permissive abortion. The tactics are wrong because they dwell on the 'unworldly' status of the fetus, on its being human in the womb. As Arendt says, the world finds nothing sacred in the abstract nakedness of being human.

This point of Arendt's is extremely important, I think, though unbelievably harsh in some respects. I believe there is a parallel to be found in the widespread distribution of pictures of aborted fetuses and of concentration camp victims. In both cases what is being represented is so far outside the realm of ordinary 'worldly' experience that it has the appearance of unreality. When faced with such sorts of representations, the usual reaction does not tend toward great empathy or compassion, but toward denial. 'This is not me' is a much more likely response than 'this could be me.' Arendt writes about the horrors of the concentration camps *and* about the silence that descended on the survivors and on people on the outside. The experience of being in the camps was so 'unworldly,' so devoid of any identity whatsoever, that it had no possible political meaning. People are much more moved by the narrative of one person – his or her context, his or her sufferings, and so on – than they are by the brutal representations of emaciated corpses. Similarly, I think the argument could be made that the faceless, contextless fetus is far less likely to arouse compassion than the narrative of how the love of a child transformed someone's life.[41]

Where does the world find the sacred? The sacred is found through love, as both Arendt and Grant would attest. There is a hierarchy of 'goods' that has been articulated since the time of ancient Greece, and may have been altered somewhat (though I think not substantially) by Christianity. Love of one's own is fundamental; love of the polis, or political community, is higher, love of the good, or God, higher still. A really good life requires all three in proper balance, and it is the higher goods that inform the content of the lower ones. I think what we are living now is the slicing off of the highest reaches in public life: the love of the good, or God. What we are left with is the love of our own (family) and the love of the political community (manifested in the defence of rights, and also in some circumstances in nationalism). Anything that falls within the purview of the family or of the political community gets our full respect and attention, anything outside does not. The shrunken horizons of our love have led to much turmoil and moral uncertainty in the world, but as long as there is the space in liberal democratic societies for speech and persuasion, there is hope that the horizons can be expanded. If we are to discourage abortion in these societies, we have to move away from the emphasis on common humanity, on scientific portraits of small, womb-encased fetuses, and head for the high ground. We love children, and we love to have children, not because they are merely human, but because 'beginning is the supreme capacity of man.'[42] For those, like George Grant, who find abortion abhorrent, it might be better to dwell on the miraculous, world-creating capacity of the child, and less on the cellular constitution of a fertilized ovum. The birth of a child, as Hannah Arendt so eloquently said, is the miracle that saves the world.

NOTES

1 George Grant with Sheila Grant, 'Abortion and Rights,' *Technology and Justice*, (Toronto, Anansi Press 1986), 117, 119. This essay was first published as 'Abortion,' in E. Fairweather and I. Gentiles, eds., *The Right to Birth* (Toronto, Anglican Book Centre 1976). There is some thoughtful literature on Grant's understanding of rights. Samuel Ajzenstat in 'The Place of Abortion in George Grant's Thought' makes a strenuous case for why Grant thought it necessary to combat abortion from within rights discourse. According to Ajzenstat, 'Thinking about abortion helped him [Grant] to articulate a basic political paradox: the essential attitudes of liberalism not only endanger the human foetus, they are also indispensable to the possibility of protecting it': Yusuf K. Umar, ed., *George Grant and the Future of Canada* (Calgary: University of Calgary Press 1992), 75. William Mathie takes a more skeptical stance toward Grant's resistance to abortion from within rights discourse. In 'Reason, Revelation and Liberal Justice: Reflections on George Grant's Analysis of Roe v. Wade,' Mathie concludes that 'one can say that the present legal and moral treatment of abortion in dicates the insufficiency of liberalism. The moral implications of political liberalism support, if they do not generate, an individual claim to liberty which can include the right to abortion and they undermine any understanding of the family that might oppose this claim': *Canadian Journal of Political Science* 19 (1986), 463.

2 George Grant, *English-Speaking Justice* (Toronto: Anansi 1985 [1976]), 70.
3 Ibid.
4 Ibid., 71.
5 Grant, 'Abortion and Rights,' 122.
6 Ibid.
7 Ibid., 123.
8 Grant, *English-Speaking Justice*, 86–8.
9 Grant, 'Abortion and rights,' 126–7.
10 Ibid., 128.
11 Ibid., 129.
12 Grant, *English-Speaking Justice*, 76.
13 Ibid., 77.
14 Ibid., 79.
15 George Grant, 'The Triumph of the Will,' *Jeremiad* 1 (1988–9), 3.
16 Ibid., 10.
17 Ibid., 11.
18 This shift in public discourse is apparent in the philosophic writings on abortion, and in recent legal developments in Canada. See, for example, footnote 31 below for an explanation of the opinion of Justice Bertha Wilson concerning the Supreme Court of Canada's striking down of Canada's abortion law.
19 Grant, 'The Triumph of the Will,' 13.
20 Ibid., 14.
21 Ibid., 4.
22 Ibid., 14.
23 Ibid., 15.
24 Ibid.
25 Ibid.
26 Ibid., 18.
27 Allan Bloom has some insightful comments on the continuing desire of women to have children despite living in a society that makes child-bearing an irrational choice. He writes that 'Modernity promised that all human beings would be treated equally. Women took that promise seriously and rebelled against the old older. But as they have succeeded, men have also been liberated from their old constraints. And women, now liberated and with equal careers, nevertheless find they still desire to have children, but have no basis for claiming that men should share their desire for children or assume a responsibility for them. So nature weighs more heavily on women:' *The Closing of the American Mind* (New York, Simon and Schuster 1987), 114. Bloom

emphasizes that the desire that women have for children defies all the rules of the contractual, self-interested society. This point would seem to support the view that the selfless act of having children is more surprising in the modern context than the refusal to have them.

28 Edward Andrew, *Shylock's Rights* (Toronto: University of Toronto Press 1988).

29 Grant, ' The Triumph of the Will,' 13.

30 Ibid., 15.

31 In 1988 (the year that Grant published ' The Triumph of the Will'), the Supreme Court of Canada rendered its decision on abortion, which declared that Canada's abortion law was unconstitutional because it violated a woman's right to 'life, liberty and security of the person.' Canada's highest court thus came down on the side of women's rights. No mention was made in the decision of the rights of the fetus, but Bertha Wilson in her opinion called for a recognition of the state's legitimate interest in the fetus. She invited the state to regulate abortion in late pregnancy, and her reason for doing this was that it is possible for the fetus in the late stages of pregnancy to survive outside the womb. She remarked that 'This distinction between the early and late stages of pregnancy is based on the theory that the foetus should be viewed in different terms depending on the stage of the development, and that, once the foetus can live outside the mother's body, the state's interest in protecting its life can take precedence over the mother's right to terminate the pregnancy': Shelagh Day and Stan Persky, eds., *The Supreme Court of Canada Decision on Abortion* (Vancouver: New Star Books 1988), 201. Wilson's opinion was not an effort to justify abortion by declaring the fetus not human. She made it clear that the fetus *is* human, but the point at which the state steps in to defend the fetus's rights is the point at which the fetus can exist autonomously as a member of the political community, in other words, when it can emerge into the world and make itself visible and present to the community.

32 Hannah Arendt, *The Origins of Totalitarianism* (New York: Harcourt, Brace, Jovanovich 1951), 469.

33 In his essay entitled 'Nietzsche and the Ancients,' Grant criticizes historicism for many of the same reasons as Arendt. 'What gives meaning in the fact of historicism,' he writes, 'is that willed potentiality is higher than any actuality. Putting aside the petty perspectives of good and evil means that there is nothing belonging to all human beings which need limit the building of the future. Oblivion of eternity here is not a liberal-aesthetic stance, which still allows men to support regimes the

principles of which came from those who had affirmed eternity; oblivion of eternity here realizes itself politically': *Technology and Justice*, 95.
34 Arendt, *Origins*, 465–6.
35 Ibid., 301.
36 Ibid., 299.
37 Ibid., 301.
38 Ibid., 296.
39 In his review of Grant's *English-Speaking Justice*, Clifford Orwin offers an interpretation of why Justice Blackmun determined that the state has a compelling interest in protecting the fetus once it can be viable outside the womb. Orwin says that while the reasons for distinguishing between a fetus at the moment of conception and a fetus that is six months old are unclear, Blackmun's decision is a scholastic one, 'clearly inspired by medieval doctrines of "animation" according to which the foetus quickens at a certain point through the infusion of its soul [Latin *anima*]. Whereas the older distinction is ontological, however, that of "viability" – the ability of the foetus to survive outside the womb – is merely technological. As such it does not lend itself to service as a moral distinction': *University of Toronto Law Journal* 30 (1980), 106–15. While Blackmun's judgment may indeed turn on a recognition of the fact that the 'age of viability' retracts as the technology advances, and while Orwin is correct in saying that we do not make ontological distinctions among human beings based on medieval conceptions of the soul, I have tried to argue that prevailing views on 'viability' are moral in some sense. One may find that viability outside the womb is a deficient basis for determining the worth of a human being, but it is not an amoral criterion. Blackmun need not have relied on a medieval scholastic argument to produce the judgment he did.
40 The idea that human life has value only insfar as that value is sanctioned within a political context is abhorrent to many people, notably Christians who affirm that every life is a gift from God and must be treated as such. But the idea is not modern, and is not necessarily an expression of the will to power. Aristotle, for example, in his depiction of the ideal polis in book 7 of the *Politics*, lays down the conditions under which infanticide and abortion are permissible: 'Concerning exposure and rearing of offspring when they are born, let there be a law that no deformed child should be raised, but that none should be exposed after they are born on account of number of offspring, where the arrangement of customs forbids procreation beyond a certain number. A number should indeed be defined for procreation, but in cases of births in

consequence of intercourse contrary to these, abortion should be induced before perception and life arises (what is holy and what is not will be defined by reference to perception and life)': trans. Carnes Lord (Chicago: University of Chicago Press 1984), 1335b20–5.

41 The attempt by the rulers of the concentration camps to obliterate the unique identity of their victims is explained by Arendt, who says that 'Total domination, which strives to organize the infinite plurality and differentiation of human beings as if all of humanity were just one individual, is possible only if each and every person can be reduced to a never ending identity of reactions, so that each of these bundles of reactions can be exchanged for any other': *Origins*, 438. It is the anonymity of the concentration camp victim that makes him or her invisible and beyond the reach of ordinary pathos. Although Arendt does not make the parallel, I suggest that the anonymity and 'abstract nakedness' of aborted fetuses produce a similar effect.

Arendt insists that no political party, or political movement, can be built on the 'dwelling upon horrors.' In her view, 'The experiences themselves can communicate nothing more than nihilistic banalities': *Origins*, 442.

42 Ibid., 479.

RELIGION

10

George Grant and the Theology of the Cross

SHEILA GRANT

From his student days at Oxford till the end of his life, George Grant frequently quoted the twenty-first of Luther's twenty-eight theses from the Heidelberg Disputation of 1518. What did it mean to him? Why did he always use an inaccurate translation of Luther's original Latin? And why did he think the theology of the cross helped us, as Luther put it, 'to cope with the problems of Providence without either hurt to ourselves or secret anger with God?'[1]

Grant's use of Luther's thesis is a perfect example of his unscholarly but sometimes fruitful habit of employing the names of thinkers, or quotations from their works, as a shorthand for ways of thought (William Christian has noted this). As the need arose, he would take a line or two, for example, from Shakespeare or St Augustine, from Abelard or Simone Weil, or often from Henry James. He would usually remember the context, but not be in the least confined by it. The quotation would become part of his own thinking. This is what happened with the twenty-first Heidelberg thesis.

Luther wrote the Heidelberg Theses early in his career. They were first composed in Latin, and later in German. But Grant never quoted the Latin version of Thesis 21,[2] which reads,'Theologus gloriae dicit malum bonum et bonum malum. Theologus crucis dicit id quod res est.'[3] The translation he always used was, 'The theologian of glory says that evil is good and good evil; the theologian of the cross says that the thing is as it is.' The translation of the first Latin sentence is not in doubt. Luther said that his description of the theologian of glory was suggested by Isaiah 5:20. 'Woe unto them that call evil good and good evil, that put darkness for light and light for darkness.' However, the English version of the second Latin sentence is not an exact translation. Recent translations of the second sentence include, 'The theologian of the cross says what a thing is'[4]; the theologian of the cross says what is true';[5] and 'the theology of the cross calls the thing what it actually is.'[6] These all appear to be accurate versions of the Latin. Why, then, did Grant always rely on a different and inaccurate translation?

The only place I have been able to find the version Grant used is in a book he read while studying theology at Oxford. This book, *Our Knowledge of God*, which was written by John Baillie, Professor of Divinity at Edinburgh, appeared in 1939.[7] It would have been natural enough for a student to rely on such a source, and to assume accuracy from a professor of divinity. In fact, Baillie's translation suited Grant's thought better than a more exact version would have done. Grant always gave the same reference to the Latin as Baillie, but neither Baillie nor Grant mentioned the source of the translation.

Baillie quotes Theses 19 through 22, and a reading of all four helps to put the twenty-first into context:

19 He is not worthy to be called a theologian who sees the invisible things of God as understood through the things that are made (Romans 1:20).
20 But only he who understands the visible and further things of God through the sufferings and the cross.
21 The theologian of glory says that evil is good and good evil; the theologian of the cross says that the thing is as it is.
22 That wisdom which sees the invisible things of God as understood through His works altogether puffs up, blinds and hardens.[8]

With the phrase 'theologian of glory,' Luther meant to attack those, such as the Neoplatonists, who tried to reach God in his naked transcendence, but he also meant to attack St Thomas Aquinas, the most influential of the scholastic theologians. Like Luther, Aquinas did not believe God's essence was knowable by human beings. But he did believe our only way to know God is through the mediation of 'things that are made,' which can give us a kind of analogical or inferential knowledge. To Luther, as we see in Theses 21 and 22, this idea was anathema, because it did not put first the immediate knowledge given us by Christ in his sufferings. In defending the twentieth thesis, Luther insisted that 'it suffices and profits nobody to know God in His glory and majesty' (whether by direct or analogical speculation) 'unless he knows Him also in the humility and ignominy of the cross, where God is clothed with man's nature.'[9] As Luther said in Thesis 24, 'without a theology of the cross, man misuses the best things in the worst way.'

Grant was not a student of Luther, and never taught Luther's work. To get some idea of how Grant first understood the theology of the cross, we must turn to his doctoral dissertation on the Scottish theologian, and liberal Presbyterian John Oman. The dissertation, which was finished in 1950, is entitled 'The Concept of Nature and Supernature in the Theology of John Oman.' It is accompanied by an abstract whose opening sentences are relevant to the present essay: 'Nature and Supernature is the fundamental concept of John Oman's philosophy of religion. That philosophy, found in his book *The Natural and the Supernatural*,[10] should be read within the context of his "theologia crucis," which is given in his later theological writings.' This was a good way to begin, because Grant did not intend to limit himself to Oman's unwieldy philosophy, which he found unsatisfactory; a great deal of the dissertation centres around Oman's Christology, although Christology is scarcely dealt with in the *Natural and the Supernatural*, the supposed focus of Grant's concern. The tone of the dissertation is reserved and careful, but there are moments in Grant's discussion of the theology of the cross when his intensity shines through.

It is necessary for our purposes to have some account of Oman's Christology, not only because it was based on a theology of the cross, but also because it was the background of thought against which Grant first began to ponder Luther's Heidelberg Theses. Oman asserts that the cross regulates all experience. (Grant said the same thing twenty years later, when teaching in McMaster University's Department of Religion.) What is it that Oman so overwhelmingly sees when he looks at the Crucifixion? It can be summed up in the word 'forgiveness.' A perfectly good man is being executed in the most degrading way possible, and asks God to forgive his torturers because they do not know what they are doing: 'The faith which knows God's forgiveness to be real and transforming rests on Jesus, because He lived and died setting this forgiveness in the heart of human experience, and not simply proclaiming it.'[11]

Oman had been deeply moved by the Old Testament Book of Hosea, and Grant had been equally moved by Oman's very beautiful account of it, which he never forgot. Hosea could not bring himself to condemn his sinful wife, but had to forgive her because he loved her just as she was: 'He realized that no situation could ever take her out of his heart and his life. Then he knew also that the same must be true of sinful man and the mind of God.'[12] Grant never forgot Oman's emphasis on forgiveness, although the word he would later use more often was 'justice.'

So far the relation of Oman's Christology to Luther's twenty-first thesis has not been made very clear. The thesis is mentioned many times in Grant's dissertation and by Oman himself, but never quoted in full. On page 141 of the dissertation, Grant writes, 'Only in terms of the "theologia crucis" is any adequate theodicy possible.' This takes us suddenly to the very heart of his understanding of Thesis 21. Oman refers to the theologian of glory when he defines the vice of hypocrisy, which he considers to be the sin against the Holy Spirit: '"It hath never forgiveness," not because there is any sin that cannot be forgiven, but because it calls good evil and evil good, and so turns its back on the manifestation of truth ... St. Paul is taking the same view when he defines sin as resisting truth in unrighteousness ... Finally men are given over to a "reprobate mind," not only doing evil but approving of it as good.'[13] Grant was to use the Luther phrase in a similar way, though not with regard to hypocrisy. For all Oman's emphasis on God as a forgiving Father, Oman did not accept the universalist belief that all human beings will be saved. The conviction that man's essence was his freedom held him back from that. Not so with Grant, whose comment is, 'The annihilation of the insincere and the hypocrite are as difficult to reconcile with divine Providence as the annihilation of anybody else.'[14] Grant expresses extreme frustration at Oman's silence about the relation between God's love and man's freedom. This question was always of particular interest to him.

Grant makes another important criticism of Oman. It does not concern Oman's vision of what the Passion of Christ means, but rather Oman's ignoring of the difficulty and uncertainty with which we may approach it. Oman asserts that all of us are capable of responding to the revelation of the cross.[15] We therefore see forgiveness set right in the nature of things. The Father cannot be less forgiving than the Son. Oman moves confidently from the dying Son to the silent Father. He does not write of the cry of despair. Grant points out that one can interpret the Crucifixion not as a triumph but as the ending of a noble hope: 'But of course it is possible for an imaginative and reasonable man to look at Calvary and to despair ... It cannot be said that suicide is by definition irrational.'[16]

Oman has little sense of the nearness of defeat. There is, however, an understanding of the Crucifixion, common among believers, which he and Grant agree to reject, namely the interpretation of it as a terrible event that must be reversed by a triumphant miracle, the Resurrection. Oman insists on the 'theologia crucis,' while pointing out the dangers of the 'theologia gloriae,' which sees on the cross 'the King in rags, who will soon tear off his disguise and show himself in triumph.' Grant used almost the same image in his 1976 lectures on Christianity at McMaster: 'There is a ghastly way of speaking about the Resurrection in the modern world which I call the fairy-tale way. A prince is dressed in rags, and everybody scorns him. Suddenly the clothes are pulled off and he appears in his prince's costume, and everybody treats him well.'

Neither Oman nor Grant wrote freely about the Resurrection. Oman was afraid of its appearing to be a limitation on or overpowering of man's 'autonomy' (his invariable word for freedom, but without the Kantian overtones), as every miracle to some extent must seem to be.[17] Grant expressed great difficulty in speaking of it at all. He was sometimes accused of 'leaving it out.' In a lecture on revelation theology in 1974 he admitted that he could not speak of it in theological terms, and turned instead to poetry.

Both Oman and Grant believed that Christ rose from the dead. But both also believed that the Redemption, the mighty act of God, took place at Gethsemane and Golgotha. Whatever the mystery of the Resurrection, it was not the necessary reversal of a defeat. Luther did not deny all possibility of knowing God in His glory and majesty, but said that unless we start with the Passion of Christ, our thoughts about God in his glory will be empty or corrupted: 'Without a theology of the cross man misuses the best things in the worst way.'

Anyone reading Grant's doctoral dissertation will be struck by

Oman's extremely critical account of most of the Christian Churches. And anyone reading Grant's later work, in which western Christianity is continually criticized as triumphalist, may wonder whether Oman, Grant, and even Luther were trying to put forward a new kind of Christianity. But this was not so. The theology of the cross is as old as St Paul's Epistles, and has never been entirely absent. We find it in the most ancient liturgy of the Catholic Church, that for Good Friday and Holy Saturday (the latter being originally the vigil of Easter). Here, for all the rejoicing in the Resurrection, it is perfectly clear that Easter is the consequence of Good Friday, not its reversal or even its fulfilment. 'Consummatum est' was said by the dying Christ, not by the risen Christ. As Douglas Hall points out in a remarkable essay, the testimony of the past is not just the testimony of triumphalist western Christianity, whether medieval or modern: 'There is a thin tradition which, however insignificant, has never quite been overcome by the broad tradition which has informed Constantinian Christianity in its several guises. Luther named it theologia crucis, the theology of the cross.'[18]

In 1951, a few years after his work on Oman, Grant wrote a sonnet called 'Good Friday.'[19] It is worth quoting because it shows clearly in what respects Grant's thought was still close to Oman's, and where he had departed from him:

O dearest word, the very Word indeed,
Breathes on our striving, for the cross is done;
All fate forgotten and from judgement freed,
Call Him then less – Who shows us this – Your Son?
Look it is here, at death, not three days later,
The love that binds the granite into being.
Here the sea's blueness finds its true creator,
His glance on Golgotha our sun for seeing.
Nor say the choice is ours, what choice is left?
Forgiveness shows God's Will most fully done.
There on the cross the myth of hell is cleft,
And the black garden blazes with the sun.
Hold close the crown of thorns, the scourge, the rod,
For in His sweat, full front, the face of God.

The emphasis on the Crucifixion as the Redemption – 'Look it is here, at death, not three days later' – reveals that Grant was still close to Oman. Forgiveness is central. However, the assertion of universalism, and the refusal to allow freedom as man's essence, contradicted Oman. As Grant often said, 'Christ has nailed rewards and punishments to the cross.' The sonnet also shows how naturally Grant now turned to Platonic imagery: 'His glance on Golgotha our sun for seeing.'

The first time that Grant used Thesis 21 with the full significance it had for him was in a paper called 'Two Theological Languages,' which was delivered to some Protestant clergy in 1953. There may have been an earlier version, delivered in 1947, but it does not survive, so we cannot know whether Grant's use of Thesis 21 preceded the completion of his dissertation on Oman.

However much confusion can be found in the 1953 address (confusion due mainly to Grant's imputing existential meaning to biblical language), it does touch on subjects that were to be central to Grant's thinking for the rest of his life: the problem of suffering and evil, and how in the face of them one can justify the ways of God to man without smoothing away the difficulties by relying on a doctrine of Providence which says that evil is in some way good. Simone Weil expressed the dilemma incomparably in a letter to her friend Maurice Schumann: 'I feel an ever-increasing sense of devastation, both in my intellect and in the centre of my heart, at my inability to think with truth at the same time about the affliction of men, the perfection of God, and the link between the two.'[20]

The word that sums up this terrible contradiction is 'theodicy' (the two parts of which bring together the ideas of God and justice). Grant uses it quite frequently in his study of Oman, but never with such clear reference to Luther's understanding of it as in this 1953 address. Even here Luther's name is not mentioned, but Thesis 21 is paraphrased. From now on Grant will always associate the Luther quotation with the problem of evil, and with any claim that Providence can be understood by us. This is the beginning of his distrust of rational philosophies of history. Although the address is so full of mistakes as to be called laughable by Grant in his later addendum to it, his mature voice comes through.[21]

Grant introduces the subject by quoting a passage by D.M. MacKinnon, a theologian at Oxford when Grant was studying there. MacKinnon speaks of natural or rational theology: 'There is a steadfast refusal to acknowledge discontinuity in human life, to bear with its surd elements, to take those surd elements seriously in themselves, and not simply by virtue of what is expressed and achieved in and through them.'[22] Grant continues, with reference to the rational and biblical languages, to describe two ways of looking at the origin of existence:

it is impossible, (if one uses the first language) to say why infinite mind differentiates itself into finite minds; or, to use the other language, it is impossible to understand why God created the world. But here is the point – don't those two statements mean something quite different? For doesn't the first imply that the world is continuous with the infinite, while the second implies it is discontinuous with and in some mysterious way independent of the infinite? ... and isn't the idea of creation necessary if we are going to meet the problem of evil with the right agnosticism? Otherwise, without this agnosticisism, we try to answer the problem of evil, and when we do that don't we in fact say that good is evil and evil is good, rather than the very different affirmation that the thing is as it is?[23]

Here the agnosticism and mystery implied by the mistranslation are made explicit for the first time. (An accurate translation of the Latin, such as 'the theologian of the cross says what a thing is,' would have suggested knowledge rather than mystery.)

Grant then moves to the Western Christian view of Providence, and to our efforts to understand the meaning of the world, again in terms of the two different versions of our origins:

which of two things should we say? 1) Though it is difficult to understand what meaning this world has, we do, however, know in principle the kind of meaning complete insight would reach, though of course admitting that what we know in principle we cannot know in detail; or (2) that we do not know what this ultimate meaning would be, either in principle or in detail, and must simply live in hope and faith that there is such an ultimate meaning, and that we are always free for that hope to die and that faith to disappear. I think that if we say the first, we are not only being trivial about sin, we are also making God a tame confederate for our petty adventurings. If we say the second, we seem to be coming close to sheer irrationalism.[24]

Grant has not yet quite made up his mind; he is trying to balance these two different accounts of the meaning of our world. But the scales that measure the balance are the scales of justice, and one side is weightier than the other.

Hegel is not mentioned in the 1953 address, but the battle lines are already drawn. Twenty-five years later, in *George Grant in Process*, Grant says, 'What was always the thorn which kept me from accepting Hegel was those remarks in the philosophy of history, about wars being the winds which stir up the stagnant pools. That is the idea that good can come out of bad in a way that we can understand. To put it in Christian terms, it has always seemed to me that Hegel makes God's providence scrutable, and that is a teaching which offended me then and now at the deepest level.'[25]

The question arises whether Thesis 21 has anything to do with theodicy. Has Grant been wrongly connecting it with his own pre-occupations about the problem of evil? Luther did not mention theodicy in the Heidelberg Theses, but in his preface to St Paul's Epistle to the Romans he said, 'If we do not feel the weight of the Passion, the cross and the death, we cannot cope with the problems of Providence without either hurt to ourselves or secret anger with God.'[26] This idea was developed elsewhere: 'Behold God governs the corporeal world in such a way that if one regards and follows the judgement of human reason, one is forced to say either that there is no God or that God is unjust.'[27] Reason, without what is to be learned from the cross, will lead us to deny God, or worse, to hate him. I never heard Grant refer to either of these passages, but they are close to his own thought.

In 1956 and 1957 Grant was on sabbatical. He was trying to write a book about freedom, and also reading widely. His notebooks from this period contain many quotations from Hegel, and show much ambivalence toward him. To quote from notes made in 1958, 'Though I would agree with James[28] that Hegel is right to say that the philosopher is only concerned with reconciliation in thought, he must, – qua philosopher – take into his thought, and not forget, that he is not, in truth, reconciled.[29]

The three chapters of the book he was trying to write were about acceptance and evil. He had planned to write about freedom, but there is at least as much about theodicy and philosophies of history in the three chapters, and there are many echoes of 'Two Theological Languages.' In the third chapter he writes at length about Isaiah Berlin, who agrees with him about the dangers of philosophies of history. Grant says that philosophies of history, in Berlin's view, 'prevent those who believe them from seeing the facts as they have been ... this leads to a blurring of the evident facts of cruelty, pain and oppression. Gradually, good actions are not simply judged as good actions, and wicked ones as wicked, but both must be interpreted as leading to some good. Thus evil is gradually turned into good.'[30] A little later, in Notebook 4 (1958), Grant speaks to himself: 'The great question is history and you, G.P.G., have been continually right to refuse to interpret history in rational terms as so many do – see this and don't give it up.'

Did he give it up when he wrote the first chapter of *Philosophy in the Mass Age*? He was not yet entirely ready to dismiss Hegel and the doctrine of progress. Among the notes of 1956–7, he writes, 'If in my book there is a chapter upon Hegel – then say that you do not know, but this is a position.' He will not commit himself to believing it, but Hegel's position must be stated. The book referred to is of course the unfinished book about acceptance and evil, but the book that was finally written was *Philosophy in the Mass Age*. In conversations with David Cayley twenty-five years later, he said he had not known enough at the time to write anything important.

There is no reference in *Philosophy in the Mass Age* to the twenty-first thesis, but Grant does paraphrase the nineteenth thesis as 'Luther insists that no man should find his proper rest in any natural images'.[31] By the time Grant wrote the introduction to the second edition in 1966, his thought had become clear and unified. Some readers find ambiguous his statement about the Western Christian view of Providence: 'It cannot be insisted too often how hard it is for anyone who believes the western Christian doctrine of providence to avoid reaching the conclusion that Hegel has understood the implications of that doctrine better than any other thinker.'[32] This does not make clear that Grant is dissociating himself from the doctrine. However, to see the irony one has only to look at *Lament for a Nation*,[33] a book written just before Grant wrote the new introduction. At the beginning of chapter 7 Grant says he is dissociating himself from a common philosophic assumption: 'I do not identify necessity and goodness.' He then sums up the thoughts that have been developing in his mind around Thesis 21, about the progressive view of history and of Providence, which in effect glorifyies force and trivializes evil. He quotes Hegel, who said that: '"Die Weltgeschichte ist das Weltgericht – world history is the world's judgement."' Luther is not mentioned, but the theologians of glory stand out clearly. To worship history means worshipping force, seeing it as an 'ever-fuller manifestation of good.'[34] This is certainly to call evil good and good evil: 'The screams of the tortured child can be justified by the achievements of history ... As a believer I must then reject these Western interpretations of Providence.'

This thought is familiar from 'Two Theological Languages,' but Grant adds a concept that was lacking there, and was needed to dispel some of the irrationalism he feared. Plato called it 'the very real distance between necessity and the good.'[35] In holding this belief Grant is not dismissing Providence altogether. He cannot do that, because he asserts a belief in the existence of God. To say, as do Plato and Weil, that we experience a separation between necessity and good in this world, does not mean that the orders of necessity and of good do not have the same source in the Good Itself. The distinction is not final. But under our human condition we cannot understand Providence, or find it 'scrutable.'

For Grant this concept throws some light on the problem of evil. But it is not a solution. How far can one clarify one mystery by means of another? In the last chapter of *Philosophy in the Mass Age* he had asserted that the distance which divides the necessary from the good 'must be faced in any proper discussion of moral law.' Six years later in *Lament for a Nation* he states it as his own settled belief. Not till his last writings, 'Faith and the Multiversity' and 'In Defence of Simone Weil,' does he write about it more explicitly.

It is impossible in this space to explore further so difficult a subject as the distance between necessity and the good, nor am I competent to do so. As regards the theology of the cross I will quote a remark of Weil's that seems particularly relevant: 'The distance between the necessary and the good ... The great discovery of Greece ... Every attempt to justify evil by anything other than the fact that that which is, *is*, – is an offence against this truth.'[36] However awkward the translation, it is not far from 'the thing is as it is.'

Two years later, in *Technology and Empire*, Grant returns to the Heidelberg Disputation. On page 20 of the essay 'In Defence of North America,' he describes why Protestant theologians criticized the Aristotelian formulations of the medieval Church: 'that theology was attacked because it led men away from the fundamental reliance on Christian revelation. The teleological doctrine did this because it encouraged men to avoid the surd mystery of evil by claiming that final purpose could be argued from the world. Such mitigation led men away from the only true illumination of that mystery, the crucifixion apprehended in faith as the divine humiliation.' In a note he states that 'Luther laid down the whole of this with brilliant directness at the very beginning of the Reformation in some theses of 1518.'[37] He then quotes Theses 19, 20, and 21. It is the first time he has used all three in print.

It is not surprising that the attempt to know God through Christ's execution as a criminal should lead to some extraordinary paradoxes. In the teleological doctrine there is no discontinuity, and there are no surd elements. In contrast to this, as the Lutheran scholar Gerhard Ebeling describes it, 'The principle of the knowledge of God in the cross is that of contradiction. In spite of this, or in fact because of this, it is only the latter which does justice to reality.'[38]

Luther could be almost aggressively paradoxical: 'When God brings to life He does it by killing' ('de servo arbitrio'). He did not achieve the beautiful reconciliation of opposites we find in his teacher, St Augustine. Near the end of the Confessions, Augustine describes Christ the Mediator: 'In our behalf to Thee both Victor and Victim, and therefore Victor because Victim; in our behalf both Priest and Sacrifice, and therefore Priest because Sacrifice; making us out of servants to become Thy sons, by being Himself born Thy Son and becoming our servant.'[39] Weil sets forth almost the same idea: 'The mystery of the cross of Christ resides in a contradiction; for it is a voluntary offering, and at the same time a punishment to which He submitted quite in spite of Himself' ('qu'il a subit bien malgré lui').[40]

Grant himself did not search for paradox, but paradox was implicit in such phrases of his as 'the divine humiliation,' and in the idea of the hidden or absent God. Like Oman, he was always moved by St Paul's 'strength through weakness': 'The foolishness of God is wiser than men, and the weakness of God is stronger than men' (Corinthians 1:25). This theme is echoed in a prayer by Rabindranath Tagore, which Grant frequently used when taking a service for students. In Tagore's translation from the Bengali it reads, Give me the supreme faith of love, this is my prayer; the faith of the life in death, of the victory in defeat, of the power hidden in the frailness of beauty, of the dignity of pain that accepts hurt but disdains to return it.'

In the early seventies Grant was trying to write a book about what it means to say we are beyond good and evil, and whether the claim of Christianity can be heard in the technological world. In his notes Luther was seldom quoted, although there was the line, 'The gospels are the cradle of Christ – see Luther – enough for me.' Harvey Cox, a popular progressive Anglican theologian,[41] was dismissed without further comment, as 'a theologian of glory.' Thesis 21 had become part of Grant's vocabulary, and by this time, as Bruce Ward remarks, '"theologian of glory" could be applied [by Grant] to any teaching that ends in asserting that evil is good and good evil.'[42]

Grant did not write or talk much about the Crucifixion itself. In a lecture on Nietzsche he explained why he preferred to avoid doing so. Although Gethsemane and Golgotha were the events by which all other events must be judged, they had been spoken about too often, too badly. Grant said it is usually better just to say 'see,' 'look.' However, as a professor of religion at McMaster, he did sometimes have to teach directly about Christianity. In a 1976 lecture course for first year students he wrote, 'The central symbol of Christianity has always been the cross. Clearly in some sense the Resurrection takes place on the cross ... Christ says on the cross "it is consummated." Marriage is consummated, sexually fulfilled. On the cross justice is consummated – because the absolute absence of justice is met with justice.' In the same lecture Grant said (as he often did) that the greatest commentary on this was not in words, but in music – Bach's *St Matthew Passion*. 'Much better than words – the great art which combines most profoundly the abstract and the erotic.'

At the end of a lecture on revelation theology Grant had to speak of the Resurrection: 'What this course has taught me to pay attention to is Paul's great words – Christianity is foolishness to the Greeks and a scandal to the Jews ... Now to say some things about the Resurrection. It must not be thought apart from the cross. Read Luther comment carefully [he quotes Thesis 21] ... Now that, I think, is the dominating principle with which to think of this matter. The second thing is to read the accounts.' In his lecture notes Grant puts a lot of weight on Thesis 21; in the actual lecture he presumably included some interpretation of it.

On the subject of the Resurrection it is interesting to look at a letter Grant wrote to Simone Pétrement asking her about Weil's understanding of that event: 'I would be unable to put aside what is given us on this matter in the Gospels. Nevertheless I have little sympathy with the major interpretations of this doctrine in the west since Augustine ... On this matter, (although not on others) I am held by what Luther writes, although taking it in a Platonic sense.' He then quoted Theses 19, 20, and 21. Pétrement wrote back with great appreciation of the theses, which were new to her, and assured Grant that they were an expression of what Weil herself had believed. What did Grant mean by 'a Platonic sense'? Perhaps something close to what he meant when he referred to himself as on the Hindu wing of Christianity. He did not understand Christianity as an exclusive sect, of which one is in or out, but rather as an account of the way things are. The life and Passion of Christ were historical events, but not only historical. What they revealed of the nature of things is true for all times and all places. As Weil says, 'Any man, whatever his beliefs may be, has his part in the Cross of Christ if he loves truth to the point of facing affliction rather than escape into the depths of falsehood ... Wherever there is affliction there is the cross.'[43]

The perfection that blazes forth from the Gospels does not make worthless other ways to seek the good. The matter is summed up on page 42 of 'Faith and the Multiversity': 'what was given traditionally in the word "good" was not confined to Christians. The majority in the classical Mediterranean tradition would have so used it – Epicureanism being then a minority. A similar conception is in the Vedanta. Christianity's particular call was not to this language, but to the fact that Christ declares the price of goodness in the face of evil.'

In the early eighties Grant started to write a book on Céline's trilogy. Not even Grant would call Céline a theologian of anything. However, in the last part of Grant's unfinished work (published in this volume as 'Céline's Trilogy') the meaning he took from Thesis 21 is implicit: 'It seems to me that the incompleteness (it is the only adjective I can find) of all human purposes, projects and passions everywhere and always is recognized in Céline's very apprehension of human beings. The tenderness in his presentation of other people ... seems to arise from the recognition of this universal incompleteness and therefore vulnerability, both of flesh and spirit.'[44]

Grant then questions how one knows this to be a universal fact about the human condition, and asks why this limitation in human life has been so lost in the West. He suggests that the cause is Western Christianity having so emphasized the power of God that it forgot the truth of the weakness of God: 'When Christian belief was secularized it gave almost unlimited opening to a belief in our own power as a means to the forgetting of our limitation.' A little later Grant says this about Céline, as he appears in the trilogy: 'Céline does not talk about good and evil, nor does he confuse them. Never does he equate bad action with good ... the one thing he will not say is that things are better than they are. The thing is as it is.'[45] The very word 'thing' may have had a special significance for Grant. Many times in his notes on Céline he quotes *King Lear*, 'Thou art the thing itself.' Seeing Edgar as a naked madman in the storm, Lear universalizes Edgar's condition: 'unaccommodated man is no more than such a poor bare forkt animal as thou art' (act 3, scene 4). Another of Grant's favourite quotations was from an Abelardian hymn for nones: 'Est in re veritas, Iam non in schemate.' Roughly translated, it means 'Truth is in the thing, not in its outward form.' He was moved by the use of these words in Charles Williams's novel *The Place of the Lion*.[46]

The essay 'Faith and the Multiversity' was not published till 1986 in *Technology and Justice*, though most of it had been written in the late seventies. This essay was greeted by many as the first time Grant had asserted his Christianity. His beliefs are indeed made plainer in it but there are also echoes of *Lament for a Nation* and *Technology and Empire*.

On page 44 of 'Faith and the Multiversity,' Grant writes about certain Christians who turned away from the teleological science of medieval Christianity: 'The more representable the purpose of the whole was said to be, the more this natural theology became a trivializing, a blasphemy against the cross.'[47] This theology is called 'natural' because it was based on the belief that God's purposes for us could be understood by looking at the things that are made. This belief produced a medieval science that claimed to understand the final purposes of everything in nature. In this essay, the Protestants who had turned away from natural theology are the same theologians descr̄bed in *Technology and Empire*, where Theses 19, 20, and 21 are quoted. Grant says that to claim that final purpose can be argued from the world encourages us to avoid 'the surd mystery of

evil,' and leads us away from 'the only true illumination of that
mystery, the crucifixion apprehended in faith as the divine humiliation.'[48] Late in 'Faith and the Multiversity' Grant describes those
who failed to turn away from this natural theology: 'It seems true
that western Christianity simplified the divine love by identifying
it too closely with immanent power in the world. Both Protestants
and Catholics became triumphalist, failing to recognize the distance
between the necessary and the good. So they became exclusivist
and imperialist, arrogant and dynamic.'[49]

The word 'blasphemy' is used frequently in 'Faith and the Multiversity,' with the consequence that any ambiguity it may have had
in Grant's earlier writings is clarified. The belittling of suffering
and evil by those who deny that 'the thing is as it is' was always to
Grant a belittling of reality, a belittling of the cross. Among his last
written notes were the words, 'Blasphemy against the cross is central to me.'[50] In 'Faith and the Multiversity' blasphemy is at issue
when the argument moves from what we can know of purpose in
the world to what we can know of beauty:

If the intelligence is enlightened by love, and love is said to be the apprehension of otherness as beautiful, then the question must arise whether
this definition is not the kind of blasphemy of which I have been writing.
Is it not saying that the beauty of the world gives us a representable purpose for the whole? Is it not just the kind of distortion which turns us
from the facts of the world so that we seem able to affirm what is contradicted by the evident experience of living? Through it are we not led
to assert that evil is good and good is evil, and so lose what is essential
to any love of truth – namely the continual recognition that the world
is as it is?[51]

In the next pages Grant affirms that beauty does not in fact lead to
this blasphemy; it no more gives us a representable purpose for the
whole than history does. When we are enraptured by the beautiful
we can say that it seems purposiveness itself. But can we ever represent that purpose to ourselves?

This denial of representable purpose implies a considerable agnosticism; better to assert mystery than to blaspheme. Later in the
essay Grant reminds us of a deeper and more general agnosticism:

Of course, for both Christianity and Platonism, goodness itself is an ambiguous mystery. In Christianity God's essence is unknowable. In *The Republic* it is said that goodness itself is beyond being. Both Christianity and Platonism have therefore often been ridiculed as final irrationality. If the purpose of thought is to have knowledge of the whole, how can we end in an affirmation which is a negation of knowing? It is, above all, these agnostic affirmations which bring Christianity and Platonism so close together. Without this agnosticism humans tend to move to the great lie that evil is good and good evil. In Christian language the great lie is to say that providence is scrutable.[52]

In this passage it is clear, as nowhere else, that Grant's affirmation of necessary agnosticism went far beyond the Heidelberg theses. Luther's theologian of the cross must have known *what* the thing *was* ('id quod res est') – Grant did not. What Grant did know is expressed in the phrase of apparent simplicity, mistranslated from Luther's Latin – the thing is as it is.

Grant, nevertheless, was not an agnostic at all on certain matters. He never doubted that good is good, and evil its absence, and we need to know which is which, however mixed in human experience, and however limited is our understanding of both.

This certainty about good and evil made the question of theodicy all the more pressing. Grant's concentration on good, and on the problem of evil, was not a philosophic position, nor a stage in the process of reasoning. It was the result of the evident experience of living.

A philosopher is supposed to love truth. But as Weil says, 'Truth is not the object of love, but reality. To desire truth is to desire contact with a piece of reality. To desire contact with a piece of reality is to love.'[53] When Grant first encountered Luther's twenty-first Heidelberg thesis, he must immediately have understood it as affirming what is essential to any such love – the continual recognition that the world is as it is.

NOTES

1 John Dillenberger, ed., *Martin Luther: Selections from His Writings* (New York: Doubleday 1961), 32.

2 The German version of Thesis 21 reads, 'Der Theologe der Gottes unverborgene Herrlichkeit sucht, nennt das Übel gut und Gutes übel; der Theologe des Kreuzes nennt die Dinge beim rechten Namen.'

3 Martin Luther, *Werke* (Weimar: Herman Böhlau 1883), 1:362.

4 Karlfried Froelich in Dillenberger, ed., *Martin Luther*, 503.

5 R.A. Wilson in Gerhard Ebeling, *Luther: An Introduction to His Thought* (London: Collins 1970), 228.

6 Timothy Lull, ed., *Luther's Works* (Philadelphia: Fortress Press 1957), 31:40.

7 John Baillie, *Our Knowledge of God* (London: Oxford University Press 1939), 192–3.

8 Luther, *Werke*, 1:354.

9 Lull, ed. *Luther's Works*, 31:40.

10 John Oman, *The Natural and the Supernatural* (London: Cambridge University Press 1931).

11 John Oman, *Honest Religion* (London: Cambridge University Press 1941), 122, quoted in George Grant, 'The Concept of Nature and Supernature in the Theology of John Oman' (D.Phil diss., Oxford University, 1950), 165 [hereinafter: Grant, Dissertation].

12 Oman, *The Natural and the Supernatural*, 456, quoted in Grant, Dissertation, 145.

13 Oman, *The Natural and the Supernatural*, 328, quoted in Grant, Dissertation, 156.

14 Grant, Dissertation, 156.

15 Ibid., 258.

16 Ibid., 245.

17 Grant understood miracles in the Augustinian way: miracles do not happen in contradiction to nature, but in contradiction to what we understand about nature.

18 Douglas John Hall, 'Towards an Indigenous Theology of the Cross,' in Carl Mitcham and Jim Grote, eds., *Theology and Technology* (Lanham, MD: University Press of America 1984), 267.

19 *United Church Observer* 13, no. 6 (15 May 1951), 16.

20 Simone Weil, *Gateway to God*, ed. David Raper and trans. Sir Richard Rees (London: Collins 1974), 64.

21 The 1953 address appears under its original title, 'Two Theological Languages,' in Wayne Whillier, ed., *'Two Theological Languages' by George Grant and Other Essays in Honour of His Work* (Lewiston, NY: Edwin Mellen Press 1990), 6–19.

22 Quoted by Grant in 'Two Theological Languages,' 13.

23 Grant, 'Two Theological Languages,' 13.

24 Ibid., 14.

25 Larry Schmidt, ed., *George Grant in Process: Essays and Conversations* (Toronto: Anansi 1978), 64.

26 Dillenberger, ed., *Martin Luther*, 32.

27 Luther in Ebeling, *Luther*, (London: Collins 1970), 230.

28 James Doull, Grant's Hegelian colleague and friend.

29 George Grant, Notebook 4 (1958).

30 George Grant, 'Acceptance and Rebellion' (unpublished), chap. 3, p. 19.

31 George Grant, *Philosophy in the Mass Age* (Toronto: Copp Clark 1959), 144.

32 George Grant, *Philosophy in the Mass Age*, 2nd ed. (Toronto: Copp Clark 1966), vii.

33 George Grant, *Lament for a Nation*, new ed. (Ottawa: Carleton University Press 1989), 89.

34 Luther supported the use of force against the Peasants' Revolt of 1524–5. Oman, to Grant's contempt, supported British participation in the First World War. Grant agreed with Weil that 'Only he who knows the empire of might and knows how not to respect it is capable of love and justice': 'The Iliad: Poem of Might,' in Simone Weil, *Intimations of Christianity among the Ancient Greeks* (London: Routledge and Kegan Paul 1957), 53.

35 Plato, *Republic*, Loeb edition, ed. Paul Shorey (Cambridge, MA: Harvard University Press 1987), 493c. It is worth noting that Plato did not call the distance infinite. Weil sometimes did, but stressed that there is a final unity: Weil, *Gateway to God*, 37.

36 Simone Weil, *Gravity and Grace*, trans. Emma Craufurd (London: Routledge and Kegan Paul 1952), 95.

37 George Grant, *Technology and Empire* (Toronto: Anansi 1969), 21 n. 2.

38 Ebeling, *Luther*, 228.

39 *The Confessions of St. Augustine*, trans. W.H. Hutchings (London: Rivingtons 1883), 321.

40 Weil, *Gravity and Grace*, 93.

41 See Harvey Cox, *The Secular City* (New York: Macmillan 1968).

42 Bruce Ward, 'George Grant and the Problem of Theodicy,' in Whillier, ed., 'Two Theological Languages,' 96.

43 Weil, *The Love of God and Affliction*, in George A. Panichas, ed., *The Simone Weil Reader* (New York: David McKay 1977), 463.

44 George Grant, 'Céline's Trilogy,' (this volume), 44.

45 Ibid., 52.

46 Charles Williams, *The Place of the Lion* (London: Faber and Faber 1931), 103.

47 George Grant, 'Faith and the Multiversity,' in *Technology and Justice* (Toronto: Anansi 1986), 44.

48 Grant, *Technology and Empire*, 20.
49 Grant, 'Faith and the Multiversity,' 76.
50 Grant, Notes on the Good (unpublished), 1988. In the same notes he expressed his appreciation of Wayne Whillier's work in connection with 'Two Theological Languages.' Addressed to Whillier was the remark, 'Wayne, your piece raises all the great questions.'
51 Grant, 'Faith and the Multiversity,' 44.
52 Ibid., 75.
53 Simone Weil, *The Need for Roots*, trans. Arthur Wills (Boston: Beacon Press 1952), 253.

11

George Grant on Simone Weil as Saint and Thinker

LAWRENCE SCHMIDT

George Grant first encountered Simone Weil in the early fifties when he was asked to review one of her books; he continued struggling with her thought till his death in 1988. His unpublished writings on Weil bear witness to a lifetime spent trying to come to terms with a most difficult thinker. They comprise three typescripts and a course notebook. These writings are hard to understand, sometimes because they are elliptical and incomplete, and sometimes because the handwritten corrections are difficult to decipher.

The first typescript, entitled 'Some Comments on Simone Weil and the Neurotic and the Alienated,'[1] is undated but is thought to be from the early 1960s. It deals with the paradox of self-giving (kenotic) love: how does one give oneself away if one has no real self or if one has only a bungled self? The second typescript, entitled 'Introduction to Simone Weil,' was delivered as a public lecture around 1963 but was revised in 1970, apparently with the intention of publication. Many of its ideas reappear in a third typescript entitled 'Introduction to the Reading of Simone Weil,' which was likely written sometime in 1970–5. Its purpose was to persuade people to read Weil's corpus. 'Tolle! Lege!' ('Pick up and read!') was Grant's message: 'There is much that it is important for a person to read in the short span of existence and among what is of the highest importance I would assert that the writings of Simone Weil are included.'[2]

In the third typescript Grant set out to demonstrate the coherence and consistency of Weil's thought, which was obscured by the fragmentary nature and bizarre publication history of her writings. He planned 'to make a map of her writings as a whole.' Grant thought this was required because 'the circumstances of both her life and writing and of their publication make it difficult for those who wish to read her writings to find their way among the extensive volumes under her name.'[3] He wished also to relate those writings to the life of this remarkable woman, whom he considered a 'great saint.' And he intended to examine the significance of her sanctity for her thought about justice. To this end Grant hoped to describe Weil's account of the divine perfection, understanding of the human condition, grasp of human history, and analysis of practical politics. The final unpublished writing is made up of Grant's notes for his graduate course on Weil given at McMaster University in 1975–6. In these notes he continued his exploration of the themes mentioned above.

Grant never completed a book on Weil. Among his published writings all we have that focused explicitly on her thought are two relatively brief book reviews and an essay. The first review, which appeared in the *Globe and Mail* in February 1977,[4] expressed high praise for Simone Pétrement's biography, *Simone Weil: A Life*, which had been published in English in 1976.[5] The French original, *La vie de Simone Weil*, was published in 1973,[6] and Grant demonstrated familiarity with it in the class notes of 1975–6. The essay, 'Faith and the Multiversity,'[7] was written in 1977[7] and published in its final form in *Technology and Justice* in 1986[8]. It did not expound or explain Weil's writings; rather, those writings informed Grant's meditation on the difficulties of articulating in the modern academy one's Christian faith (understood as 'the experience that the intelligence is illuminated by love'). The third of Grant's publications on Weil was his acerbic review of Robert Coles's *Simone Weil: A Modern Pilgrimage*, which appeared as 'In Defence of Simone Weil' in *The Idler* magazine in 1988.[9]

After 1977 there are no unpublished manuscripts on Weil. I therefore assume that Grant felt that his plan to write a book on Weil was made more difficult and less pressing by the appearance of Pétrement's book. It clearly made aspects of the biographical and historical elements of his proposed book unnecessary. Miklos Vetö's book, *La métaphysique religieuse de Simone Weil*,[10] which in the review in *The Idler* Grant acknowledged to be the most careful among many good books expounding the theoretical structure of Weil's thought, had already appeared in 1971. While not totally satisfactory, it revealed the connection between the apparently disparate elements of her account of reality and her commentary on the works of Plato. As for the relationship between the greatness of her thought and the sanctity of her life, this seemed to require, as E.B. Heaven and D.R. Heaven point out in an essay on Grant and Weil,[11] silence from someone who considered himself less than a great thinker and knew himself to be less than a saint.

The unpublished writings fill in many of the blanks regarding Grant's understanding of Weil. They help explain more clearly the reasons why in *The Idler* he referred to her as his 'chief modern teacher,'[12] and they give us some insight into the reasons why Grant was won over by her interpretations of Plato. They also make more comprehensible what he meant when he said that 'Weil belongs to ... Greek Christianity.'[13] The central importance of Weil's analysis of modern science for Grant's critique of modernity is also made plain.[14] The unpublished writings clarify, without altering substantially, the impression gained from the published comments. As such, they will help dispel the most important misunderstanding of Weil's influence on Grant only if his readers follow his advice, 'Tolle! Lege!'

When I speak of the most important misunderstanding I am referring specifically to the view that Weil's putative gnosticism played an important role in tempting Grant to an otherworldly flight from the darkness of the technological society. Barry Cooper, who is as fine an interpreter of Grant's political philosophy as Canada has produced,[15] views Weil's gnosticism as a temptation that Grant resisted:

At times modernity and technology must have seemed to him to have exhaustively symbolized reality as given. It was at these times that the gnostic appeals of Simone Weil's speculation may have been the strongest. She may have suggested to Grant a *gnosis* of escape from technology through meditation and thereby also modernity and even from reality ... George Grant may well have been tempted by the gnosticism of Simone Weil; one may even say that he took a kind of delight in escaping, perhaps with the aid of Mozart, from the ugliness and the spiritual desiccation of technological modernity. He did not, however, assent to the inanition of the soul that a serious gnostic search entails. Grant remained a thinker, one who engaged in meditation upon the urgent present of society. Not indeed to change it but to understand it.[16]

The implication is that Weil did assent to such an inanition of soul. Cooper goes on to claim that it was the political philosophy of Leo Strauss that enabled Grant to maintain a balanced consciousness.

This line of thought is taken up by Zdravko Planinc in his essay entitled 'Paradox and Polyphony in Grant's Critique of Modernity.'[17] Planinc argues, without textual justification or documentation, that 'there are two voices of Christian Platonism in Grant's polyphony. The voice of Weil is a gnostic one; the other is the voice of Christian Platonic mysticism that rejects gnosticism.' In a neat bit of a priori reasoning, Planinc claims that, for Weil,

the locus of human participation in the good is the soul. A human being is thus torn between necessity and goodness. The soul's aspiration to the good (its love of the good) requires it to leave the constraints of blind necessity and hence its own body and society infinitely far behind. It seems impossible to love necessity or one's own. And yet Weil claims it is possible. Her explanation is given in the language of Hegelian dialectic, the best possible language for expressing gnosis: 'Necessity is absolutely other than Good, is Good itself.'[18]

Planinc's only quotation from Weil (and it is drawn from the Heavens' article rather than the original text) ignores Weil's next sentence, which forms the interpretive context and reads, 'Therein lies the greatest of all mysteries.'

It would take a lengthy discussion of Weil's understanding of 'mystery' as a technical term to determine her exact meaning here.[19] But such a discussion is not necessary to demonstrate the inadequacy of Planinc's interpretation. Planinc, unlike Cooper, seems to be suggesting that Weil is a modern gnostic like Hegel. Modern gnosticism, according to Eric Voegelin, does not involve a flight from this world to another but a flight from present alienation into the future. This world is to be perfected through the creation of a universal and homogeneous state wherein the evils of labour, scarcity, disease, and war are to be eliminated through scientific research and technological development. To suggest that Weil (or Grant) were modern gnostics like Hegel is so far-fetched that it requires no refutation. And the claim that there are two voices of Christian Platonism in Grant is unfounded and implausible in light of what Grant said in the unpublished manuscripts.[20]

Cooper's charge is, however, more serious and more seductive, partially because, on the surface, it appears much more plausible. But the fact is that if we use the term gnostic in the conventional way, Weil was not a gnostic and never engaged in any gnostic quest for God.[21] It made no sense to her to speak of seeking God. In 'God's Quest for Man' she wrote, 'Notice that in the Gospels there is never, unless I am mistaken, question of a search for God by man. In all the parables it is Christ who seeks men, or else the Father has them fetched by His messengers. Or again, a man finds the Kingdom of God as if by chance, and then, but then only, he sells all.'[22] Furthermore, the so-called gnostic quest did not legitimate for her, or for Grant, a flight from the body, society, or the world; one finds repeated in Grant's published and unpublished writings a reference to the opening paragraph of Weil's essay on the theory of the sacraments: 'La nature humaine est ainsi agencée qu'un désir de l'âme, tant qu'il n'a pas passé à travers la chair au moyen d'actions, de mouvements, d'attitudes qui lui correspondent naturellement, n'a pas de réalité dans l'âme. Il n'y est que comme un fantôme.'[23] Or, as Grant put it in his *Globe and Mail* review, 'Any desire which has not passed through the flesh by means of appropriate action remains a sentimental phantom, and in saying that, [Weil] affirms that our apprehension of the most important truths depends on the justice of our lives.' In short, 'matter is our infallible judge.'[24]

Cooper bases his understanding of Weil's gnosticism not on her writings, nor on a careful reading of Grant, but on an interpretation of Grant's statements about Weil considered in the light of a conventional understanding of ancient gnosticism. He seems to assume that Weil was a gnostic, that gnostics believed such and such, and therefore that Weil believed the same. This will not do. Grant did, of course, categorize Weil as a gnostic in *The Idler*, but he did so with hesitation and for a specific purpose, that is, 'in order to make clear that it was more than accident that held her from becoming a Catholic.'[25] Grant had no intention of identifying her gnosticism with that of those who were condemned as heretics by the early Fathers such as Irenaeus in the second century of the common era.

A brief comparison of ancient gnosticism and Weil's ideas will show, I hope, how different they were. She was a gnostic Christian, that is to say a Christian Platonist, rather than a Christian gnostic like the Valentinians or the Cathars. It is true that Weil and Grant admired the Cathars but it is also true that in 1941 she admitted in a letter to Déodat Roché, the founder of *Cahier d'Etudes Cathares*, that she knew little about them.[26]

I will not enter into the debate[27] about whether the historical origins of gnosticism are to be found in primitive Christianity (as Pétrement holds,[28] in agreement with the Church Fathers) or in those (generally pre-Christian) religious movements that were a response to the changes created by the Persian, Hellenic, and Roman imperialisms before the emergence of Christianity (which is the more common view and seems much more plausible to me). Grant was not a student of gnosticism, and his views on ancient gnosticism were most likely formed by reading two lengthy articles that Pétrement sent to him after he visited her in Paris in the early sixties.[29]

Regardless of which interpretation of gnosticism is accepted, we can agree with the explanation articulated by Eric Voegelin that

Gnosticism arises from six centuries of imperial expansion and civilizational destruction ... The spiritual and intellectual lives of the peoples exposed to the events are in danger of separating from the reality of socially ordered existence. Society and the cosmos of which society is a part tend to be experienced as a sphere of disorder, so that the sphere of order in reality contracts to personal existence in tension towards the divine Beyond. The area of reality that can be experienced as divinely ordered thus suffers a severe diminution.[30]

This contraction of order led to the anti-cosmic dualism of the ancient gnostics. The basic tenets of ancient gnosticism are outlined by Hans Jonas. In the gnostic theology,

radical dualism governs the relation of God and the world and correspondingly man and the world. The deity is absolutely transmundane, its nature is alien to that of the universe which it neither created nor governs and to which it is the complete antithesis; to the divine realm of light, self-contained and remote, the cosmos is opposed as the realm of darkness. The world is the work of lowly powers which, though they may mediately be descended from Him do not know the true God and obstruct the knowledge of Him in the cosmos over which they rule.[31]

We should note that Pétrement agrees with Jonas: 'But the dualism that is rightly called gnostic does not entail the differentiation of two principles which make up the world, within the world. It is, as Jonas says, an "anti-cosmic and eschatological dualism," a dualism according to which the entire world is rejected on the one side, and the divine is found on the other side. God and world are incompatible realities here, like light and darkness.'[32]

The ancient gnostic doctrine of salvation followed from this anti-cosmic dualistic conception. The gnostics said that the spark of the divine that is as alien from the pneumatic self 'as the transcendent God is to "this world,"' is striving to be released from the bonds of the world so that it can return to the native realm of light:

The necessary condition for this is that he knows about the transmundane God and about himself, that is, about his divine origin as well as his present situation, and accordingly about the nature of the world which determines this situation. This knowledge, however, is withheld from him by his very situation, since ignorance is the essence of mundane existence, just as it was the principle of the world's coming into existence. In particular, the transcendent God is unknown in the world and cannot be discovered from it; therefore, revelation is needed. The necessity for it is grounded in the cosmic situation; and its occurrence alters this situation in its decisive respect, that of 'ignorance,' and thus is already a part of the salvation.[33]

The ancient Christian gnostic heretics (and the Cathars after them) were generally docetists: they rejected on principle the possibility of the Incarnation. They thought Christ only appeared to be human, and they felt comfortable with a fairly broad range of understandings of their gnostic saviour. For example, the Valentinians, who were criticized by Irenaeus for their doctrinal licence,[34] did not insist on defining any dogma. Generally, however, they thought Christ was not a true man with an earthly body. Such a body would have had to participate in the corruption of all matter. On this, as on many other important matters (cosmology, soteriology, Christology, and dogma), Weil (and following her, Grant) disagreed with the ancient gnostic teaching, including that of the Manicheans.

First, in her theology, Weil was neither an anti-cosmic nor a radical dualist. She asserted that there is only one God who creates the world out of love. There are not two divine principles and there is no demiurge.[35] But this does not mean that humans cannot be utterly estranged from God or that God may not seem completely absent from human life. In 'The Love of God and Affliction'[36] she acknowledged that 'affliction makes God appear to be absent for a time, more absent than a dead man, more absent than light in the utter darkness of a cell. A kind of horror submerges the whole soul. During this absence there is nothing to love. What is terrible is that if, in this darkness where there is nothing to love, the soul ceases to love, God's absence becomes final.'[37] Yet in the same article she stated that 'God created through love and for love. God did not create anything except love itself, and the means to love. He created love in all its forms. He created beings capable of love from all possible distances. Because no other could do it, he himself went to the greatest possible distance, the infinite distance. This infinite distance between God and God, this supreme tearing apart, this agony beyond all others, this marvel of love, is the crucifixion.'[38]

Secondly, for Weil God was not 'a hidden, alien, transcendent God who was remote from the necessity and suffering which obtained in the material sphere.'[39] Unlike the ancient gnostic heretics, Weil asserted not only that Christ truly suffered and died on the cross, but that God himself suffered in the very act of creation: 'God's creative love which maintains us in existence is not merely a superabundance of generosity, it is also a renunciation and sacrifice.'[40] Her kenotic conception of creation is the key to her disagreement with both ancient gnostics (who believed the creator of the universe was not the Good) and Catholics (who asserted that the creation is simply the overflowing of God's goodness which is diffusive of itself). Grant summarized this by saying that 'For Weil, creation is a withdrawal, an act of love, involved with all the suffering, renunciation and willingness to let the other be, that are given in the idea of love. For her the passion of God is at one with the creation. In this sense it is one with the teaching about Trinity.'[41] Grant's acceptance of this view (which orthodox Roman Catholics might identify with the heresy of Patripassianism) entailed a rejection of the Western Christian understanding of creation as 'an act of self-expansion.'[42] He clearly thought the latter conception culminated in the idea of God as power, which in turn legitimated modern technological rationalism. Deploring the ascendancy of technological rationalism, he recommended that we 'read carefully a thinker of consummate intelligence and love who understood that

Christianity becomes meaningless if the creating of God is detached from the passion of God.'[43]

Weil's belief in a God who participates in the suffering of creation was not a denial of the distance between God and man, or of the blind necessity that determines the totality of matter in space and time. But she said that the distance between God and man must be understood not only as separation but also as relation. 'The universe,' she wrote, 'where we are living and of which we form a tiny particle, is the distance put between God and God. We are a point in this distance. Space, time and the mechanism that governs matter is only this distance.'[44]

For Weil this distance did not mean, as it did for the ancient gnostic heretics, that the cosmos that God created, the material world that human beings inhabit, is evil. The cosmos is the result of God's 'superabundant generosity' and, as such, is sacramental. The beauty of the universe, its order and harmony, serve as *metaxu* or intermediaries[45] between the realms of the necessary and the good: they relate humanity to the eternal. Love of that beauty is one of the forms of the implicit love of God. 'The beauty of the world,' she wrote,

is the cooperation of divine wisdom in creation. 'Zeus made all things,' says an Orphic line, 'and Bacchus perfected them.' This perfecting is the creation of beauty; God created the universe, and his Son, our first born brother, created the beauty of it for us. The beauty of the world is Christ's tender smile for us coming through matter. He is really present in the universal beauty. The love of beauty proceeds from God, dwelling in our souls and goes out to God present in the universe. It is also like a sacrament.[46]

The love of the beauty of another human being was also considered sacramental by Weil. Carnal love is 'essentially the longing for the Incarnation ... Beauty in a human being enables the imagination to see in him something like an equivalent of the order of the world.'[47] The reason for this is simple: 'Beauty is eternity here below.'[48]

The other forms of the implicit love of God, the other mediators between humans and God, were, for Weil, love of the neighbour and love of religious practices. Love of the neighbour could in no way be distinguished from justice. But for Weil justice was supernatural, not contractual: 'Love for our neighbour, being made up of creative attention, is analogous to genius. Creative attention means really giving attention to what does not exist. Humanity does not exist in the inert flesh lying by the roadside. The Samaritan who stops and looks gives his attention all the same to this absent humanity, and the actions that follow prove that it is a question of real attention.'[49] This preoccupation with supernatural justice did not require a flight from the social world but an involvement with those who were marginalized by it.

Weil's writings were not those of a follower of ancient gnostic heresy for whom the 'material world was never created by God, being in fact wholly the work of Satan.'[50] Hers were not the writings of a Valentinian for whom (as Jonas puts it) 'the world is the product, and even the embodiment of the negative of knowledge.'[51] Nor were they the writings of an absolute dualist for whom 'the cosmos is contrary to life and spirit' and 'the world (not the alienation from it) must be overcome.'[52] Her writings were much closer to those of the Stoics for whom, as Jonas says, the universe had the venerability of the Greek cosmos and 'cosmic law was worshipped as the expression of reason with which man's reason can communicate in the act of cognition.'[53]

It must be stressed that Weil, even when she found herself agreeing with Marcus Aurelius,[54] was neither anti-cosmic nor apolitical. Her thought was always dominated by an incarnational principle. It was inspired not by Catharism as such but by the Romanesque renaissance, an achievement of the Cathars and the Catholics in the south of France.[55] The last year of her life was spent writing a political program for the reconstruction of France that would be required after the Allies' defeat of Hitler. Like other Christian intellectuals[56] she thought that France's defeat might open up a radically new possibility. She hoped, mistakenly as it turned out, that such reconstruction would follow a path different from that traced by the progressivism, liberalism, capitalism, and positivism that had taken the world to the abyss.

Finally, though she was clearly attracted to the gnosticism of the Manicheans and the Cathars, it was not their antidogmatism that appealed to her. As a young person she had refused to consider the question of dogma. Later, however, she acknowledged that the function of the Church as the collective keeper of dogma was indispensable. She even went so far as to say that the Church had 'the right and the duty to punish those who make a clear attack upon her within the specific range of this function, by depriving them of the sacraments.'[57] And in her article from the same period on the Romanesque renaissance, she acknowledged the Catholic Church's responsibility for the maintenance of the deposit of faith even as she condemned it for the violence it had employed in the Crusades and the Inquisition: 'Since the Cathars seemed to have carried spiritual freedom to the point of dispensing with all dogmas, a position which is not free from objections, it was quite undoubtedly necessary that the Church should preserve the Christian dogma elsewhere in its integrity like a diamond with incorruptible strictness. But a little more faith would have prevented the conclusion that this necessitated their total extermination.'[58]

Weil, then, acknowledged the need for dogma and generally supported Roman Catholicism's approach toward the enforcement of dogma. We must take at face value the words she wrote to Father Perrin toward the end of her life: 'I love God, Christ and the Catholic faith as much as it is possible for so miserably inadequate a creature to love them. I love the saints through their writings and what is told of their lives ... I love the six or seven Catholics of genuine spirituality whom chance has led me to meet in the course of my life. I love the Catholic liturgy, hymns, architecture, rites and ceremonies.'[59] Clearly, the Catholic dogma of the Incarnation posed no problem for her: 'I never wondered whether Jesus was or was not the Incarnation of God; but in fact I was incapable of thinking of him without thinking of him as God.'[60] Weil's hesitations about being baptized into the Catholic Church were, then, not based on her agreement with antidogmatic or docetist gnostic beliefs such as those condemned by Irenaeus or Clement of Alexandria.

The fact is that Weil was neither a follower of ancient gnostic heresy nor a Catholic. And if she can be classified as a gnostic Christian, it is only in the sense that Kurt Rudolph, among others, understands the authors of the New Testament to be the same. He explains what this means in the following way:

The process which is plain from the New Testament itself is twofold, the Christianizing of Gnosis, and the gnosticizing of Christianity. The result of both processes is the canonization of Christianity as an orthodox church on the one hand, and the elimination of Gnosis as a heresy on the other. ... In Paul, there is to be found an element of gnostic concepts and ideas, evidently derived from the heritage of Hellenistic Christianity and from his own experience, which makes him interesting for the history of Gnosis; he belongs to it not only as an opponent. Through him, Christianity became a religion of salvation in late antiquity, and Gnosis played its part in it.[61]

Weil did not accept the common doctrine and practice of the gnostics of the second and third centuries of the common era. She was attracted to what she took to be the spiritual origins of gnosticism, Christianity, Manicheism, and Catharism. There was, she contended, a strain of Platonic thought or of the Greek spirit that the ancient gnostics remained faithful to. It involved

the revelation of human misery, of God's transcendence, of the infinite distance between God and man. Haunted by this distance, Greece worked solely to bridge it. This was what made her whole civilization. Her mystery religion, her philosophy, her marvellous art, that science which was her own invention, and all the branches of it, these were all so many bridges between God and man ... In the minds of the best of the Greeks there dwelt the idea of mediation between God and man, of mediation in the descending movement by which God seeks man. This is the idea expressed in the notion of harmony, of proportion, which is at the centre of all their thought, all their art, all their science, and of their whole conception of life.[62]

It seems clear that Weil was not proposing a return to Platonism as an escape from the alienation of the modern world, which in focusing on the absolute autonomy of human beings had destroyed the Greek understanding of the metaxu and all the intermediaries between God and man. She realized that gnosticism of a Manichean or Catharist variety was not an option. She said, 'One cannot be in favour of the reestablishment of the Carolingian dynasty or the throne of France or an adherent of the Catharist religion or of the Order of Templars.'[63] An alternative for her was Platonic Christianity. In her last notebook she explained what this should mean: 'The bridges of the Greeks. We have inherited them but we do not know how to use them. We have thought they were intended to have houses built upon them. We have erected skyscrapers on them to which we ceaselessly add storeys. We no longer know that they are bridges, things made so that we may pass along them, as by passing along them we go towards God.'[64]

Weil's last reflections were dedicated to overcoming Western alienation by explaining why we should halt the construction of sky-scrapers and nurture our appreciation of the intermediaries. To a society committed to living in and constructing more skyscrapers this can only appear as an antipolitics. But as Mary Dietz points out, 'we must understand her despair over living in an age "when we have lost everything" as something that distances her from the human world but which also keeps her attached to it.'[65] Her attach-ment was expressed in her last writings, where she discussed the 'things that make a human life possible and must be preserved.'[66] Weil asked in one of her notebooks, 'What is it a sacrilege to de-stroy? Not that which is base, for that is of no importance. Not that which is high for, even should we want to, we cannot touch that. The *metaxu*. The *metaxu* form the region of good and evil.'[67] Her book *The Need for Roots*, the writing of which took up most of the last six months of her life, was concerned with 'the relative and mixed blessings ... which warm and nourish the soul.'[68] She was hardly engaged in a gnostic escape.

It seems equally clear that Grant did not read her books, her essays, or her notebooks to avoid the desiccation of technological modernity through some sort of gnostic flight from this world. On the contrary, he did so precisely so he could understand modernity in all of its dry horror. Grant understood the value of a study of Weil's writings in this way:

She was a person who as much as anyone I know experienced the twentieth century – knowing its wars and its intellectual assumptions, its hopes and its factories. In the full sense of the word she was incarnate in the twentieth century – that is, she knew it not only as an observer but its afflictions became her flesh. It was because all that the twentieth century has been was immediately and mediately known that she was able to transcend it and rediscover certain treasures which our world had lost for many cen-turies. Her pierced and piercing apprehension of our immediate world en-abled her to overcome that loss in ourselves so that the ancient religion can appear to us as more than an academic curiosity.[69]

A careful reading of Grant's and Weil's writings reveals that Grant was not tempted by the emptiness of the soul that charac-terizes a gnostic quest which turns its back on this world; he was, rather, inspired by the self-emptying (kenotic) spirituality that characterized the life and the thought of a thinker he considered a contemporary Christian saint. As Cooper and other writers observe, Grant did not abandon his concern for politics even as he acknowledged that political life was not ultimate. He referred to himself as a 'political philosopher within Christianity.' He analyzed the consequences of the abandonment of a concern for transcendent justice in liberal regimes. And to the end of his life Grant opposed the legalization of abortion because this was the most telling indication that, in their commitment to technological expansion, liberal regimes had abandoned such a concern. Following Weil, Grant made it clear to his readers that a simple rejection of technological progressivism without a commitment to personal and social justice could be as nihilistic as the will to power that dominates the politics of the late twentieth century.

NOTES

1 I am grateful to Peter Emberley and Art Davis for making available to me all the unpublished material by George Grant cited in this essay.
2 George Grant, 'Introduction to the Reading of Simone Weil' (typescript), 6.
3 Ibid., 3.
4 George Grant, Book Review in *Globe and Mail* (Toronto), 12 February 1977.
5 Simone Pétrement, *Simone Weil: A Life*, trans. Raymond Rosenthal (New York: Pantheon Books 1976).
6 Simone Pétrement, *La vie de Simone Weil* (Paris: Fayard 1973).
7 George Grant, 'Faith and the Multiversity,' *The Compass* (1978), 3–14.
8 George Grant, *Technology and Justice* (Toronto: Anansi 1986), 35–77.
9 George Grant, 'In Defence of Simone Weil,' *The Idler* 15 (January–February 1988), 36–40.
10 Miklos Vetö, *La métaphysique religieuse de Simone Weil* (Paris: Librairie Philosophique J. Vrin 1971).
11 E.B. Heaven and D.R. Heaven, 'Some Influences of Simone Weil on George Grant's Silence,' in Larry Schmidt, ed., *George Grant in Process: Essays and Conversations* (Toronto: Anansi 1978), 78: 'Thus in the face of this love beyond human capability and reason, Grant is silent. It is a humble silence imposed on him from without, and born of a certain knowledge that he is distant from that about which he would speak. In this distance, this imperfection, he knows that he has not the right. To do so would almost certainly violate his deepest sense of justice.'

12 Grant, 'In Defence of Simone Weil,' 36.

13 'To place Simone Weil squarely within Greek Christianity is, however, to make one fact apparent. What she says will appear extremely alien and unlikely to western Europeans and North Americans because this form of Christianity has not played a significant role in our world for many centuries. To be a western person is to think within western Christianity – Catholic or Protestant – or within one of Christianity's secular offshoots – Marxist or Liberal. Indeed, so powerful has been the west that it is possible almost to say that to be a man is almost to think in a western way. But of course Christianity was more than western from the beginning and eastern or Greek Christianity included in itself things that have been lost in the west. But in saying that Simone Weil belongs to this Greek Christianity, I am not saying that she was near to the institutionalized form, namely the Greek Orthodox Church – because I am taking Greek Christianity to be something wider than this – I include in it much that has disappeared from the world': Grant, 'Introduction to the reading of Simone Weil' (typescript), 25.

14 Grant wrote in the notebook for his class on Simone Weil in 1975–76, '"Classical Science and After" ... is a breath-taking writing – a writing of genius of the first order. I know of no modern writing – not even any of Heidegger's – which I would put as equal to it in genius, or going right to the heart of what is our present predicament' (p. 16).

15 See Barry Cooper, 'A Imperio usque ad Imperium: The Political Thought of George Grant,' in Schmidt, ed., George Grant in Process, 22–39.

16 Barry Cooper, 'George Grant and the Revival of Political Philosophy,' in Peter Emberley, ed., By Loving Our Own: George Grant and the Legacy of Lament for a Nation (Ottawa: Carleton University Press 1990), 117–18.

17 Zdravko Planinc, 'Paradox and Polyphony in Grant's Critique of Modernity,' in Yusuf K. Umar, ed. George Grant and the Future of Canada (Calgary: University of Calgary Press 1992), 12–45.

18 Ibid., 36.

19 In her essay entitled 'The Pythagorean Doctrine,' Weil made it clear that mystery is not something that takes human beings into another realm but puts them in contact with reality: 'It is number, says Philolaus, which gives things a body ... Philolaus' formula is literally true. All concise and rigorous analysis of perception, of illusion, of fantasy, of dream, of those states more or less near to hallucination, show that perception of the real world differs from the errors resembling it, only because the real includes a contact with necessity ... There is a contra-

diction here, for necessity is intelligible, not tangible. Thus the feeling
of reality constitutes a harmony and a mystery. We convince ourselves
of the reality of an object by going around it, an operation successfully
producing varied appearances which are determined by the immobi-
lity of a form which is different from all appearances, exterior to them
and transcending them. By this operation we know that the object is a
thing and not an apparition, that it has a body': Simone Weil, *Intimations of Christianity among the Greeks* (London: Ark Paperbooks 1957),
178.

20 In 'Introduction to the Reading of Simone Weil,' 7, Grant wrote,
'Simone Weil carried on in her writings a sustained commentary on the
works of Plato which returns again and again to nearly all the Platonic
writings. This commentary is found in certain short essays, in casual
fragments and in recurring entries in her notebooks ... I would like to
bring all these statements together and attempt to state what she is
saying about Plato as a whole.' Grant never did this, but when he gave
his course on Weil in 1975–6 he stated unequivocally in his notebook,
1–2, 'Her writing on Plato – in my opinion the greatest writing about
Plato of our era.'

See also the notebook on Plato's *Phaedo,* where Grant explained why
he thought Weil a greater interpreter than Strauss of Plato: 'Aristotle in
the *Politics* attacks Socrates who he said recognized only one kind of
virtue – the virtue which springs from philosophy – instead of distinguishing the philosophic virtues from the virtues of the gentleman. He
relates this to the fact that Aristotle stands with Gorgias against Socrates, because Gorgias encounters the virtues but as you will know from
the *Republic* and *Meno* Plato derives the three cardinal virtues – mod-
eration, courage, justice – from the virtue wisdom – phronesis (not
sophia). Wisdom the core of virtue and phronesis a kind of knowledge.

'Let me say no more than that I am entirely on Plato's side and that it
is because of his understanding of this that I think Simone Weil finally
a much greater interpreter of Plato than Strauss.'

21 Eric Voegelin characterizes the essential core of the gnostic system,
whether ancient or modern, as 'the enterprise of returning the pneuma
in man from its state of alienation in the cosmos to the divine pneuma
of the Beyond through action based on knowledge': *Order and History,
vol. 4, The Ecumenic Age* (Baton Rouge, LA: Louisiana State University
Press 1974), 20. Contrary to what Grant seemed to think when he wrote
his review of Coles's book in *The Idler*, Voegelin does not use 'gnosticism as a term of abuse,' as some Catholic commentators do. Voegelin

uses the term, as the above quotation indicates, as an analytical concept. He originated this usage in *The New Science of Politics: An Introduction* (Chicago: University of Chicago Press 1952); continued it in *Science, Politics and Gnosticism* (Chicago: Henry Regnery 1968) (which is the English translation of *Wissenchaft Politik* und Gnosis [München: Kösel-Verlag 1959]); and defended it in *The Ecumenic Age*. We do not know whether Grant was aware of this or, if so, what he thought of it. We do know that in the 1975–6 notebooks for his class on Simone Weil (page 19), Grant wrote that he was reading *The Ecumenic Age* and was considering it in light of Pétrement's writings on gnosticism. Regardless, it seems to me that Grant would have agreed with Voegelin (and Weil) that the enterprise 'of returning the pneuma in man from its state of alienation in the cosmos to the divine pneuma,' whether by contemplation, magic, or activist mysticism, is illicit and destroys the balance of consciousness. (I am grateful to Terry Barker, who is completing a dissertation on Voegelin, for discussing this matter with me.)

22 Simone Weil, 'God's Quest for Man,' in *Intimations of Christianity among the Greeks*, 1.

23 Simone Weil, 'La théorie des sacrements,' in *Pensées sans ordre concernant l'amour de Dieu* (Paris: Gallimard 1962) 135.

24 Grant, *Globe and Mail* Book Review.

25 Grant, 'In Defence of Simone Weil,' 37.

26 Simone Weil, *Seventy Letters*, ed. and trans. Richard Rees (London: Oxford University Press 1965), 129: 'I have long been greatly attracted to the Cathars although knowing little about them.'

27 See Berger A. Pearson, 'Early Christianity and Gnosticism: A Review Essay,' *Religious Studies Review* 13 (1987), 1–8.

28 See Pétrement, *Simone Weil*, 396: 'I have come to the conclusion that gnosticism issued out of Christianity and was an attempt to develop its Hellenic element by diminishing the element of Judaism that it conserved.'

29 Simone Pétrement, 'La notion de gnosticisme,' *Revue de la métaphysique et la morale* 65 (1960), 385–421, and 'Le colloque de Messine et le problème du gnosticisme,' *Revue de la métaphysique et la morale* 72 (1967), 344–73.

30 Voegelin, *The Ecumenic Age*, 4: 21–2.

31 Hans Jonas, *The Gnostic Religion* (Boston: Beacon Press 1963), 42.

32 This is my translation. The French reads, 'Mais le dualisme proprement gnostique n'est pas la distinction de deux principes composant le monde, interieur au monde. C'est un dualisme "anti-cosmique et escha-

tologique" comme dit Jonas; un dualisme ou le monde tout entier se trouve rejeté d'un coté, tandis que le divin se trouve de l'autre. Dieu et monde y sont des réalités incompatibles, comme la lumière et les tenèbres': Pétrement, 'La notion de gnosticisme,' 396.

33 Jonas, *The Gnostic Religion*, 44–5.

34 See Irénée de Lyon, *Contre les hérésies*, bk. 1 (Paris: Les Editions du Cerf 1982), 293–4.

35 Grant explained her position by contrasting it with that of Augustine, who 'was a Manichee who became a Christian, and in a way the founder of western Christianity. And that taught him ... [that] evil is not the opposite of good but the absence of good. And he sees that, it seems to me quite rightly, as just following Plato's teaching, which is clearer to him in the light of Christian revelation. He avoids the dualism. Now clearly S.W. does too, in the sense that evil is absence not opposite. Yet S.W. pushes nearer to a certain dualism than Augustine, and with all her attacks on Augustine – the dualism between the good and necessity. Yet we must remember that she does this while asserting the Platonic teaching that evil is an absence': Grant, Notebook for the class on Simone Weil, 1975–6, 19.

36 Simone Weil, 'The Love of God and Affliction,' in *Waiting for God*, trans. Emma Craufurd (New York: Harper 1973), 117–36.

37 Ibid., 121.

38 Ibid. 123–4.

39 Gerald Hanratty, 'Gnosticism and Modern Thought, III,' *Irish Theological Quarterly* 48, no. 1 (1981), 88.

40 Simone Weil, *On Science, Necessity and the Love of God* (London: Oxford University Press 1968), 153.

41 Grant, 'In Defence of Simone Weil,' 40. Weil spelled this out in 'The Pythagorean Doctrine': 'For in creating, God renounces being all, He abandons a bit of being to what is other than himself. Creation is renunciation by love': Weil, *Intimations of Christianity among the Greeks*, 183.

42 Grant, 'In Defence of Simone Weil,' 40.

43 Ibid.

44 Weil, 'The Love of God and Affliction,' 127.

45 'The essence of created things is to be intermediaries. They are intermediaries leading from one to another and there is no end to this. They are intermediaries leading to God. We have to experience them as such': Weil in George A. Panichas, ed., *The Simone Weil Reader* (Mt Kisko, NY: Moyer Bell 1977), 364.

46 Weil, 'Forms of the Implicit Love of God,' in *Waiting for God*, 164–5.

47   Ibid., 172.
48   Ibid.
49   Ibid., 149.
50   Zoe Oldenbourg, *Massacre at Montségur: A History of the Albigensian Crusade* (London: Weidenfeld and Nicolson 1961) 34.
51   Jonas, *The Gnostic Religion*, 327.
52   Ibid., 329.
53   Ibid., 328.
54   See, for example, Weil, *Waiting for God*, 65.
55   See Simone Weil, 'The Romanesque Renaissance,' in *Selected Essays, 1934–1943* (London: Oxford University Press 1962), 44–54.
56   One thinks here of Emmanuel Mounier and Jacques Ellul.
57   Weil, *Waiting for God*, 80.
58   Weil, 'The Romanesque Renaissance,' 52.
59   Weil, *Waiting for God*, 49–50.
60   Ibid., 70.
61   Kurt Rudolph, *Gnosis: The Nature and History of Gnosticism* (New York: Harper and Row 1987), 300, 302.
62   Weil, 'The Romanesque Renaissance,' 46.
63   Simone Weil, *The Notebooks*, trans. Arthur Wills (London: Routledge and Kegan Paul 1956): 2: 350.
64   Simone Weil, *Gravity and Grace*, ed. Gustav Thibon and trans. Emma Craufurd (London: Routledge and Kegan Paul 1952), 132–3.
65   Mary Dietz, *Between the Human and the Divine: The Political Thought of Simone Weil* (Totowa, NJ: Rowan & Littlefield 1988), 111.
66   Ibid.
67   Weil, *Gravity and Grace*, 133.
68   Ibid.
69   Grant, 'Introduction to Simone Weil,' 26–7.

EDUCATION

12

Teaching against the Spirit of the Age: George Grant and the Museum Culture

NITA GRAHAM

From the time George Grant's writings first received public attention, his life and thought have provided material for teaching and research, or as some would prefer to put it, scholarship. During his life he responded vigorously to questions about and criticisms of what he had written, said, and done. Without his enlivening presence, however, there is now the danger that his work will be relegated to the 'museum culture' or the mausoleum. Museum culture was Grant's term for studies that no longer have any vital meaning for us in our daily lives[1] and, in his words, are increasingly 'concerned with filling out the details of the past (setting Thucydides right as the saying goes).'[2] In such a culture Grant's work is liable to be taken up from an antiquarian interest, with a subsequent loss of its particular meaning.

Grant's inclusion as a living presence in the university curriculum meets with several obstacles. These obstacles have been raised up by the very conditions about which Grant wrote, the conditions that define the curriculum itself and provide the context for Grant's statement that he had 'such a sense of failure as a teacher.' When asked whether he could have succeeded, Grant replied, 'As always, one fails through laziness and lack of attention. There is not only the failing against the spirit of the age, which I think was given, but there are all the failures that all of us know ... the spirit of modern science is going to be triumphant in the parts of the universities

that are concerned with that, but I was hoping I could say something, a No to this spirit's entry into the arts faculties ... I don't
know whether I did or not. How does one ever know anything of
that kind?'[3] To delve further into the reasons behind his sense of
failure would be to invite speculation, and it would be wrong to
claim that we might know those reasons better than he did. More
important than asking why Grant saw himself as a failure is the
question that he grappled with throughout his career, namely can
the great thinkers and artists of the past teach us in a positive way
about our lives, or are Plato, Kant, and the Vedanta worn out or not
fitted to the modern age? Those who now speak about Grant often
show that they unthinkingly accept the spirit and presuppositions
of the modern age that he challenged. Whether and how they try to
overcome their assumptions will mark them either as serious students of philosophy or as workers in the museum culture.

An initial obstacle to Grant's inclusion in the university curriculum is the failure of some critics to make a clear division between
his personality and his thought. Statements are frequently made
about 'the progress' of Grant's thought, as if there was some similarity to progress in worldly terms. Such statements are often
framed in a negative language: Grant's thought failed to progress
beyond ... etc., which suggests that he suffered from some psychological disorder or mental block – nostalgia and ancestor-worship
being two of the more striking diagnoses. Grant's reply to charges
of this sort was that 'Thought may first arise from the ambiguities
of personal history but if it is to stand fairly before the enormous
ambiguities of the dynamo it must attempt to transcend the recurring distortions of personal history. To listen for the intimations of
deprival requires attempting a distinction between our individual
history and any account which might be possible of what belongs to
man as man.'[4] It is the task of philosophy, Grant insisted, to transcend history, social as well as personal, and to attend to those
'intimations of deprival' in our lives and in our accounts of essential humanness.

Another barrier to Grant's entry into the curriculum is the methodology that prevails within the humanities. Among its practitioners are those who would deny him entry, or having admitted him
would analyze his work according to this or that critical theory.
More than four decades ago Grant's philosophy was scorned as 'no
more than an enabling device to permit him to take what he

pleases, in and out of context ... in order to create impressions while avoiding the discipline which particulars impose and ignoring communication by specified propositions.'[5] More recently, the first edition of *The Canadian Encyclopedia* appeared with an entry for Grant (in which he was called a 'brooding philosopher of apparently implacable pessimism'), but he was not mentioned in the general entry on philosophy.

This omission was attended to in a small way in the second edition,[6] but was one indication of how philosophy has been defined by many in a manner that excludes Grant. When Grant wrote about how philosophy had changed during his lifetime, he in effect described how he would be criticized: 'Indeed, in so far as philosophy moves beyond ... non-evaluative analysis, it is concerned with what is more and more seen as a series of inadequate logical formulations which can be corrected in the light of advances in analysis.'[7] A rather patronizing criticism of Grant by a proponent of the analytical approach can be found in Kenneth Minogue's review of William Christian's biography of Grant: 'Grant's thought is the kind of stimulating phenomenology which makes for good seminars and conversations without offering the prospect of technical improvement in the tools of understanding sought by contemporary professional philosophers.' Having said that 'Grant was obviously a wonderful teacher,' Minogue writes, 'It is probably impossible to teach philosophy successfully without incorporating some element of message; philosophy is the habit of understanding left when the message drops away ... How well his philosophy will wear is another question.'[8] Here Minogue defines philosophy as a medium that preferably has no message other than an understanding of the medium as a means of analysis, a technique, in which conversation, the method of dialectic, is peripheral. Having drummed Grant out of the ranks of 'professional' philosophers, he still leaves unresolved the question of how an inadequate philosopher could have been a 'wonderful teacher.' Presumably he would not say that a sloppy mathematician can be a good teacher of mathematics. For him, contrary to Plato and Grant, education has become subordinate to the demands of particular techniques for technological purposes.

Grant's thoughts on education can be illuminated by juxtaposing them to the thoughts of Northrop Frye, who is revered as an educator, critic, and scholar. Grant indeed had some 'messages' to deliver, and he often delivered them in public forums, notably at a teach-in at the University of Toronto in 1965. But according to Frye,

Teach-ins ... are entertainment of a very high quality but they are not a form of education. We cannot have education without incessant repetition and practice, drill, and going over the same things over and over until they become automatic responses.[9]

... I went through all the hysteria of the late Sixties, when there was a great vogue for teach-ins and importing people at immense expense from other countries to talk to students. Great enthusiasm was generated. What I said at the time was that these things were entertaining, and they were even quite useful, but they were not educational. Education is in the repetitive process – it is something that has to go on and on and on. Things should break into the continuum from time to time, but the continuum is the education.[10]

Should Socrates have been chastised for taking part in a symposium or for conversing with Phaedrus on the banks of the Ilissus, or with Euthyphro on the steps of a courthouse? When universities have retreated into the knowledge industry, why can a teach-in not be a place where important things are said, especially when what is said is a call to 'discipline and order and study'?[11]

When Frye speaks of education he primarily means scholarship, the exercise of what he calls speculative reason which he distinguishes from practical reason. The virtues of speculative reason are 'detachment, impartiality and suspension of judgement,' and whatever philosophic criticism others may make of this definition, its qualities, according to Frye, are those that are demanded in the sciences. On the other hand, the origin of the practical intelligence is in 'the society which is revealed to [man] by the arts and the sciences with which his education brings him into contact.' Speculative thought consists in 'identifying one's mind with a specific and highly specialized discipline,' but with respect to practical reason, much must be left to student initiative. The student must be antisocial, 'sitting on his professor's doorstep armed with questions.'[12]

At the same time, Frye the humanist describes himself as a 'bourgeois liberal,' because

the serious ideals of democracy – personal liberty, free speech, equality of citizenship and tolerance of variety of opinion – are anti-doctrinaire ideals ... It seems to me that what is called academic freedom is the key to all freedom. Once the scientist is allowed to pursue science without reference to political priorities; once the records of the past are thrown open to the historian; once the poet or novelist can write without the restrictions of ideology, I think the worst horrors of the police state will become relaxed and eventually impotent.[13]

When Frye moves from political judgments to statements about university education as a collection of separate, distinct, nonevaluative disciplines, there is a general consistency.

The bother is with the hapless students sitting on the professor's doorstep. How do they get from their education, as defined by Frye, to making any judgments at all without somehow being indoctrinated? Frye postulates two kinds of reality. There is an 'objective reality confirmed by reason and experience,' and another kind 'which does not exist to begin with but is brought into being through a certain kind of construction or creative activity.' The humanities, the arts, and religion constitute the second kind, but they 'deal *not* with external realities studied by the reason.' Yet they would serve as 'the obvious vehicles for education in concern and in social vision.'[14] When reason is separated from our vital concerns, how does Frye arrive at any political judgment? There seems to be no rational element in choosing to be a bourgeois liberal rather than a conservative or a socialist. It follows that the student is deprived of a forum for reasoned dialogue. When Frye calls for initiative and 'creativeness' he is dangerously close to an emphasis on radical subjectivity and on the power of the will, which may lead to destruction of the 'ideals' that he assumes. In the end it is not his criticism of teach-ins and their participants that is troublesome, but his placing of that criticism in the context of a vision of the ideal university, his definitions of reason and reality, and his hostility to any courses or colleges that attempt to take what he calls the 'synoptic view.'[15]

There still remains for Frye the persistent question of meaning and purpose. What is the meaning, for example, of ideals, freedom, and equality? What is the purpose of our freedom? Meaning would appear to have been replaced by 'value,' except that Frye recognizes that within each discipline values 'can be assumed, they can be argued about, but they cannot be demonstrated ... The primary criterion of value is a certain sense of genuineness.' How genuineness is recognized is not explained. After a lifetime of academic freedom and hard work he can only say,

I find myself browsing through anthologies, for example, and every so often I strike what seems to be a consistently interesting and intelligent mind. Then I want to look him up and read him in greater breadth and detail than the anthology gives me. *It is a purely random operation.* I could name a few names at random easily enough, but I would forget a lot of others. When I was about sixteen or seventeen I was excited by a great many different poets – Wallace Stevens, for one. Some of them did not stay with me. Others did. *There are no reasons I can give as a critic why some of them turned out to be more permanent.*[16]

What Grant admired about *Fearful Symmetry*, Frye's work on William Blake, was that 'full recognition is given to the fact that Blake's writings cannot be understood through the criteria of literary criticism alone, but must be judged within the wider reference of the interpretation of experience that Blake attempts ... it raises basic problems about the nature of man with which all are concerned whether they will or not.'[17] Grant was stressing that we are all affected by what we understand as human nature whether we recognize those problems that 'belong to man as man' or not. But in the modern research institution that Frye supports, there is neither place nor time for raising these basic problems without prejudging the possible outcomes of the questions. Perhaps it is not Frye's job as a literary critic to explain how his faith in the ideology of liberalism is united with scientific reason. As a teacher who writes and speaks about education he seems unwilling or unable to account for his own 'synoptic' view. If, as he says about poets, there are no reasons that may be given about 'questions of greatness,' either through the criteria of literary criticism or any criteria acceptable to the multiversity, we are left with an education dominated by historicism and the fact-value distinction. We choose our values and our purposes at will. What happens to political philosophy, and how the will is determined, are questions reduced to opinion or physiology.

This is not the isolated position of one humanist but a position occupied by the vast majority of teachers and by those who, because of their pre-eminence in one field, speak about education as a whole. The views of Minogue and Frye are illustrations of what is held, in Grant's phrasing, as 'a doctrine beyond question,' that is, the centrality of the fact-value distinction[18] in the research paradigm that governs education. It would be foolish, Grant stressed, to say that technology dominates departments of chemistry and economics but not departments of theology.

Grant warned that the supremacy of the fact-value distinction – this 'most sacred doctrine of our public religion' – puts into question '(a) whether there is any knowledge other than that reached by quantifying methods, (b) whether, as such methods cannot provide knowledge of the proper purposes of human life, the very idea of there being better or worse purposes has any sense to it, (c) whether, indeed, purpose is not merely what we will in power from the midst of chaos.'[19]

For such questions about knowledge of purpose and of better or worse, not to be shut out of the curriculum, or relegated to the mausoleum, the sacred doctrines of education must themselves be examined.

Grant often said that bringing students to an understanding of the metaphysical roots of the fact-value distinction was one of the greatest difficulties he faced as a teacher, for the language of 'values' had been so instilled in them, and traditional speech so debased, that few of them could think outside the language of technology. Grant confessed that 'it had taken him a whole lifetime to free himself from the language of modernity.'[20] He and Sheila Grant wrote that 'what makes discussion of [euthanasia] so difficult is that there is great public confusion about terminology.' Popular language, they said, 'has helped to cover up what has been happening to our society's perception of human life.'[21]

To understand the language of modernity and modernity's perception of human life, there is, according to Grant, 'no escape from reading Nietzsche who first spoke what is now explicit in modernity.' When we speak of morality as concerned with 'values,' of politics in the language of sheer 'decision,' of artists as 'creative,' of 'quality of life' as praise and excuse for the manifold forms of human engineering, we are using the language first systematically laid out by Nietzsche.[22] But 'the question of whether and how and to whom [Nietzsche] should be taught is a more complex matter,' the answer to which cannot be made by further research. Nor can we be indifferent to the consequences.

Grant's position toward Nietzsche was not value-free. As a

teacher within the philosophic and religious tradition he explicitly rejected Nietzsche's doctrine. This rejection was not arbitrary, but flowed from what thought and revelation taught him about justice when justice is loved. He described himself as one 'who in political philosophy is above all a lover of Plato within Christianity.' Thus he risked being called a dogmatist.

The complexities of teaching Nietzsche, and necessarily of teaching Plato, may be overwhelming, Grant believed. The effect of Nietzsche and Plato on badly prepared students is almost irreparable. The past as teacher having been lost to them, their susceptibility to nihilism finds no defence, and the results of superficial contact might be yet more devastating. That is why Grant posed 'the question of whether and how and to whom Nietzsche should be taught.' Nevertheless, because our 'unthought clichés' can form the basis of private and political action, the relationship between theory and practice demands serious concentration.

In writing about Nietzsche, Grant asked, 'who has been able to give a refutation of radical historicism that is able to convince our wisest scientific and scholarly friends?' We may not have an answer, but we can know from Nietzsche himself 'what Nietzsche's conception of justice is, and the consequences of accepting it.' We can ask what conception of justice is held by the directors of the 'global economy,' for example, for it is in the name of the global economy that the serious part of contemporary education that politicians take seriously is conducted. The economy is the prime 'value' in our society, other values to be added on according to taste. According to Nietzsche,

Once we possess that common economic management of the earth that will soon be inevitable, mankind will be able to find its best meaning as a machine in the service of this economy – as a tremendous clockwork, composed of ever smaller, ever more subtly adapted gears; as an ever-growing superfluity of all dominating and commanding elements; as a whole of tremendous force, whose individual factors represent *minimal forces, minimal values* ...

... Morally speaking, this overall machinery, this solidarity of all gears represents a maximum in the exploitation of man; but it presupposes those [the supermen] on whose account this exploitation has meaning. Otherwise it would really be nothing but an overall diminution, a value diminution of the type man – a regressive phenomenon in the grand style.

It is clear, what I combat is economic optimism: as if increasing expenditure of everybody must necessarily involve the increasing welfare of everybody. The opposite seems to me to be the case: *expenditures of everybody amounts to a collective loss*: man is *diminished* – so one no longer knows what *aim* this process has served. An aim? A new aim? – *that* is what humanity needs.[23]

Although these were not passages that Grant drew on, they might form part of the exposition Grant said was called for to show 'why the superman ... will be the only noble ruler for a technological age, and what he must be ready to do to the last men who will have to be ruled.' The exploitation of human resources will serve those who have passed beyond good and evil, whatever Nietzsche's 'new aim' might be, at whatever cost. This new aim has to take into account his pronouncement that 'The great majority of men have no right to existence, but are a misfortune to higher men.'[24]

The rhetoric of secularized democracy would have it that through vigilance and education our freedoms will be safe. When the faith in democracy and education is questioned, what definitions of human beings and justice do historicism and biological research provide?: 'In Nietzsche's conception of justice there are human beings to whom nothing is due – other than extermination' – or enslavement. Because of the dominance of historicism Grant knew that it was inevitable that Nietzsche would enter 'centre stage,' for he appears to release us from all constraints on the will to power. By proclaiming the expiration of limits on what human beings may do in building their future (creating quality of life) Nietzsche denies that anything is due to any human being. Because of this conception of justice, Grant attacked attempts to limit Nietzsche's influence to narrow areas of study, (for example, Nietzsche's interpretation of 'irrationalism' in Greek religion) without making explicit what the relation is of those studies to a wider understanding of the human condition: 'One should not flirt with Nietzsche as a flirtation for the purposes of this or that area of science or scholarship, but teach him in full recognition that his thought presages the conception of justice [as historically determined] which more and more unveils itself in the technological west.'[25]

Grant said that any account of knowledge of purpose, or of what 'might be possible of what belongs to man as man,' is given to us through our inheritances, which include the doctrine of revelation and our educational institutions: 'Most of us try to act from what we know or think we know. Therefore, if we are to understand society, we must understand our educational institutions.' This statement, from an article Grant wrote at the time he retired from McMaster University, introduced a summary account of his own thought on teaching and education. The title 'The battle between teaching and research,'[26] was not chosen by him, and is misleading. What he was speaking about was differing definitions of education, and their consequences.

There is no case, I believe, for teaching on one side and research on the other. That is a phoney war, when the educational principle behind each is the same. The guiding principle of our educational institutions, Grant insisted, is their definition of knowledge as evidenced in the curriculum, 'the essence of any university.' What Grant identified as the dominant 'paradigm of knowledge' is that of natural science: 'The aspiration of thought from which it sprang was, above all, the desire to overcome chance so human beings would be the controllers of nature. The effective condition for its realization was what we now call research.' Because of its achievements, research 'is at the heart and core of our lives and as such at the heart and core of our education.'

This steadfast desire to overcome chance, Grant contended, is the main animating source of scientific activity. Because the positivist scientific method embraced by the humanities could not provide answers to the 'great questions which present themselves to human beings,' Grant turned to the education that 'was carried on for centuries by the method of dialectic.' Dialectic was a 'much more erotic kind of teaching than that which has to do with knowing about objects – erotic because what is to be known about justice or God or beauty can only be known when they are loved. This is why I have such a sense of failure as a teacher.'

To sort out the different meanings of love and desire and appetite, Grant wrote elsewhere, is to enter a labyrinth. What may be said, at least, is that the desire to overcome chance leads to a different kind of knowledge than does the eros that moves us in our judgments concerning the proper purposes of human life. To speak of something as being 'at the heart' of our lives and our education is a metaphorical way of naming our desires.

The gap between what Grant said about a 'more erotic kind of teaching' and his 'sense of failure as a teacher' is striking. Some attribute his sense of failure to the circumstances of his resignation from McMaster. It is understandable that Grant should have felt isolated and depressed on realizing that the department of religion which he had helped found, and had directed so conscientiously, was to have as its focus a view of religion and its study that the department had stood against from its inception. At the time Grant said, 'if the Department of Religion just becomes another department churning out stuff and preparing people who will churn out more stuff, articles and stuff, and didn't keep before it that it was raising certain ultimate questions about human existence and, in my opinion, divine being, then I think it would just be a flop.'[27] Here Grant was spelling out his opponents' definition of educative purpose, a definition that did not justify maintaining a department of religion separate from other departments, where the stress was on research and linguistic analysis.

When we read, in Grant, about dialectics – 'sustained and disciplined conversation' – as the method of studying the great minds of the past, we recall that dialectics itself is judged by the criteria of modern scholarship. (In the words of Minogue, Grant's method of teaching philosophy 'makes for good seminars and conversation but adds no technical improvements.') What dialectics means would seem almost as difficult to grasp as the roots of the fact-value distinction. Paul Shorey, a translator of and commentator on Plato, writes that 'The full meaning of dialectics in Plato would demand a treatise. It is almost the opposite of what Hegelians call by that name, which is represented in Plato by the second part of the *Parmenides*. The characteristic Platonic dialectic is the checking of the stream of thought by the necessity of securing the understanding and assent of an intelligent interlocutor at every step, and the habit of noting all relevant distinctions, divisions and ambiguities, in ideas and terms.'[28]

Simone Weil, with her penetrating wit, may be more helpful:

The Greeks used the word 'dialectics' when thinking of the virtue of contradiction as support for the soul drawn upwards by grace. Since Marx, for his part, combined the material image of contradiction with the material image of the soul's salvation, namely the clashes between forces and the progress of production, he was perhaps right to use this word 'dialectics.'

But, on the other hand, this word, when coupled with the word 'materialism,' immediately shows up the absurdity of the idea. If Marx did not feel it, that was because he borrowed the word, not from the Greeks, but from Hegel, who was already using it without any precise meaning. As for the public, it was in no danger of being shocked; Greek thought is no longer a sufficiently living thing for that. On the contrary, the words were very suitably chosen so as to lead people to say to themselves: "that must mean something."'[29]

After some consideration of how Marx and Hegel used 'dialectics,' we are left with a method of rational discourse that may lead to the beginning of enlightenment. Dialectics, Plato tells us, is the 'coping-stone' above all other studies, which serve as preliminaries. It allows spontaneity and generates that spark of light that comes from the friction between differing answers to questions. Dialecticians make connections. The paradoxes and contradictions dialectics reveals are brought into the open. Only then can we understand our presuppositions and where they have taken us.

The dialectics necessary to examine our faith in democracy, in mankind as a machine in the service of the global economy, and in the overman on 'whose account the exploitation has meaning' (that is, to examine Nietzsche's justice), is not simply another form of research, as one exceptionally bright physicist said to me. When Grant wrote about Darwin, for example, he pointed out that what was discovered about animals 'does not itself call forth love for them.' When he wrote about Mozart, he asked about music, 'are there some works that are worth paying attention to more than others?'[30] The language of subject and object necessary to research, Grant believed, obscures by neglect any questions of goodness and beauty. How do the products of genetic research affect any love we might have for life? Can only some individually chosen definition of the 'perfect' human being determine who is to come into the world, and with what characteristics? What universities have given up on, I contend, following Grant, is the concentrated study of the 'eu' in *eu*thanasia and *eu*genics, of the 'bene' in the *bene*fits of the global economy, and of the 'beau' in *beau*tiful. The giving up is a loss, a deprival that cripples students in their search for 'education.'

Grant's enmity toward our society's dominant opinions makes

him unwelcome in the research institutions that serve our society. The evidence shows that his thought, to the extent it has been brought into the curriculum, is likely to be treated as an object within historicists' assumptions. When his work is approached in this way, he has failed as a teacher. No provocative comparison is intended by appealing to a comment Grant made about studying Plato: 'The difficulty of reading about Plato today is that one is likely to read him through the eyes of some school of modern philosophy, and this can blind one. For example, many moderns have in the last century and a half followed Kant's remark in the first Critique that he was combining an Epicurean science with a Platonic account of morality. With such spectacles how much of Plato must be excluded.'[31]

Any attempt to filter out from Grant's work what has come from Platonic thought and Christian revelation would leave only shadows. Our efforts in this direction would lack that eros toward justice which teaching (ourselves or others) requires. We would be treating Grant unjustly.

One of the more tiresome complaints brought against Grant is that he was not really saying anything new. Here we see yet another unthinking supposition: that a thinker should earn his salary by adding to the inventory of data to be warehoused in research institutions. But let Weil answer the charge as she expands on her statement that 'nothing is so interesting in philosophy as a recent discovery of an eternal idea':

The progress of science can bring nothing new to philosophy; and this for two reasons. First, science cannot be anything for the philosopher except matter for reflection. The philosopher can find something to learn from scientists, as he can from blacksmiths, painters or poets; but no more, and above all not in a different way. But the main reason is that there is not, strictly speaking, the possibility of anything new in philosophy. When a man introduces a new thought into philosophy it can hardly be anything except a new accent upon some thought which is not only eternal by right but ancient in fact. Novelties of this kind, which are infinitely valuable, are the result only of long meditation by a great mind. But, as for novelties in the ordinary sense of the word, there are none. Philosophy does not progress or evolve; and philosophers are uncomfortable today, for they must either betray their vocation or be out of fashion. The fashion today is to progress, to evolve. It is indeed something even more compulsive than a fashion. If the great public were aware that philosophy is not susceptible to progress there would no doubt be resentment at its getting any public funds. To find a place in the budget for the eternal is not in the spirit of our age. So the majority of philosophers keep quiet about that eternity which is their privilege.[32]

What *is* new, Grant wrote, is the 'unique co-penetration of knowing and making of the arts and sciences' which is technology. Grant's case against research in the humanities, and against the language which is used with it, was that they exclude the possibility of coming to grips with the newness of our situation: 'never has so much money been put into the organized study of the past and never has the past had less meaning in our lives.'[33] Were Grant's work to be presented as an object for research it would become, as he wrote about the humanities in general, 'dead for us in the sense that its meaning cannot teach us anything greater than ourselves ... This stance of command necessary to research therefore kills the past as teacher.'[34] For Grant, the need to examine the newness of our situation called for a renewal of philosophy itself, together with a purging of Western Christianity of triumphalist errors.[35]

In several ways Grant consistently asked of teachers that they be fully aware of the reasons for and the consequences of what they were saying – to speak and teach 'en pleine connaissance de cause' (in French jurisprudence the phrase means knowing all the facts of the case and the laws that pertain to them.) In writing about Northrop Frye, Grant spelled out his objections: 'Frye shows that he is judging the Bible through the eyes of modern philosophy. Why does he not then say so? ... His interpretations in terms of modern philosophy are not laid out before us *en pleine connaissance de cause*.'[36] In his own teaching Grant never let go of the attempt to understand the unity of principles with practice. When speaking to some Nova Scotia teachers in the 1950s, for example, he said that 'The job of a philosopher is to define things ... My definition of man would go behind these modern interpretations and say, as true Christianity has always said, that man is a free rational being whose destiny is to live in the light of God.'[37] At that time Grant could assume that traditional language still had some meaning for teachers in Nova Scotia. After defining education as in Plato's allegory of the cave – leading ourselves out of the chains of ignorance into the freedom of knowledge – he likened it to what Jesus meant by 'The truth shall make you free.' Grant then acknowledged that impatience may be aroused with such definitions, for they may 'seem pretty remote to your problems here, and you may say here is another of these fellows living in his ivory tower at the university and talking a lot of high-sounding nonsense to us who have good practical problems to deal with.' But, he went on to say, he wanted to show why 'ideals (that is, definitions) are important.'

That philosophic task remains the same despite profound societal changes. In 1980, having concluded that a traditional under-standing of education was hardly possible any longer, he restated the need to clarify our assumptions:

This abstruse question of educational principle may seem far away from the realities of life. Yet it is not. You cannot have a free and vibrant society unless there are free and vibrant people in it ... it is important for the health of any society that there are people in it whose sense of freedom is sustained by having thought in a disciplined way about the supreme questions of human life ... Art and religion and the passion for justice will continue, but they will be more and more *cut off from the rationality* the universities should offer them. Technological excellence plus museum scholarship are not enough. When they are considered sufficient, the mass of students will become listless. *Scholarship is a means to thought, not a sub-stitute for it.*[38]

Such statements are not likely to serve as study material in de-partments of education. Yet each sentence in this excerpt, and in a large part of the article in which it is found, could be taken as a starting point for a dialogue on education. The contrast between a vibrant society and listless students, for example, indicates a dimin-ishing, a loss of passion for justice and a weakening of the eros without which education is limited to adaptating to the demands of the dominant forces in society, and teachers are no more than ser-vants of those forces.

The listlessness that students experience is the result of finding no relation in the humanities between 'museum culture' and the popular culture: 'The first sterilizes the great art of the past; the second is democratic but at least not barren ... where are those questions going to be 're-searched,' the answers to which cannot be found in the modern sciences of nature or of history?'[39] The great questions include 'What is justice?, How do we come to know what is truly beautiful? ... Are there things that can be done that should not be done?'[40] To those can be added, What are the consequences of accepting that our answers are simply a matter of individual 'values'? What these questions require, Grant taught, is 'sustained conversation with the great minds of the past,'[41] through, that is, the method of dialectic. For Grant, the content and the form of teaching, as in Plato's dialogues and Nietzsche's *Zarathustra*, make for a unity that cannot be pulled apart.

The attention given in this essay to the barriers that exclude Grant's work from the curriculum (except as material for research) is intended not merely to promote Grant, but to show the aridity of the current methodology and language of the humanities. In a commentary on Bertrand Russell, Grant made clear what was wrong with the delegation of reason to the sciences and the cutting off of rationality from the guiding principle of human conduct – the passion for justice: 'The vast range of our particular desires does not appear simply as a chaos because reason presents us with the idea of universality as an end, in which that very unity which we call the self, and not mere separate desires, will be satisfied.'[42] Although traditional language no longer has any meaning for us, we must 'beware of using language about that loss which springs from the new forms of thought which have caused it.' The most important difficulty concerning language is that 'it must never move away from what is pressed upon us concerning justice in our daily situations.'[43] There is no turning away from the technological present. Trying to know it for what it is requires a recovery of what has been given through tradition.[44] The triumph of technology and the failure even to recognize any loss as a loss are obstacles to revitalizing the humanities for the purpose of shaking students from their listlessness.

Those who teach with some remembrance of what is given in philosophy and in the Bible may have been fortunate enough to have had teachers, such as George Grant, who joined them in conversations with the great minds. They know that a mausoleum, no matter how opulent, is still a grave, and that those who occupy the grave, not as 'living wits' but as 'flitting shades,'[45] no longer have any meaning for the living.

NOTES

1 See George Grant, 'Research in the Humanities,' in *Technology and Justice* (Toronto: Anansi 1986), 97ff.

2 Grant, 'Nietzsche and the Ancients: Philosophy and Scholarship,' in *Technology and Justice*, 87.

3 'The Moving Image of Eternity,' transcript of radio program in the CBC *Ideas* series, 1986, 18.

4 George Grant, 'A Platitude,' in *Technology and Empire* (Toronto: Anansi 1969), 140.

5 See Fulton Anderson, 'Introduction,' in John A. Irving, ed., *Philosophy in Canada: A Symposium* (Toronto: University of Toronto Press 1952), 4.

6 *The Canadian Encyclopedia*, 1st ed. (Edmonton: Hurtig 1985), 2: 776, 3: 1398–1403; 2nd ed. (1988), 3: 1660.

7 Grant, 'The University Curriculum,' in *Technology and Empire*, 125.

8 Kenneth Minogue, 'The Platonic Mission of George Grant,' *The Times Literary Supplement*, 25 February 1994.

9 Northrop Frye, *On Education* (Toronto: Fitzhenry & Whiteside 1988), 79.

10 Ibid., 208–9.

11 George Grant, 'Realism in Political Protest,' Christian Outlook 21, no. 2 (November 1965), 3–6. 'Realism in Political Protest' is the full text of a speech, excerpts from which were printed in the *Globe and Mail* (Toronto), 12 October 1965.

12 Frye, *On Education*, 72.

13 Ibid., 3.

14 Ibid., 81.

15 Ibid., 66ff.

16 Ibid., 210. My italics.

17 George Grant, 'Philosophy' (Essay Prepared for the Royal Commission on National Development in the Arts, Letters and Sciences, 1949–51) (King's Printer, Offprint 127).

18 Grant, 'The University Curriculum,' 120.

19 Ibid., 121–2. Grant rarely made lists. That he did so here highlights the importance of the questions.

20 George Grant, 'Two Theological Languages,' in Wayne Whillier, ed., *Two Theological Languages' by George Grant and Other Essays in Honour of His Work* (Lewiston, NY: Edwin Mellen Press 1990), 6–19.

21 George Grant with Sheila Grant, 'The Language of Euthanasia,' in *Technology and Justice*, 104.

22 George Grant, 'Nietzsche and the Ancients,' 90.
23 Friedrich Nietzsche, *The Will to Power*, ed., Walter Kaufmann and trans. Walter Kaufmann and R.J. Hollingdale (New York: Viking, 1968), 463–4. I have followed Grant in using 'supermen.' The Kaufmann translation has 'overmen.'
24 Ibid., 467.
25 Grant, 'Nietzsche and the Ancients,' 95.
26 George Grant, 'The battle between teaching and research,' *Globe and Mail* (Toronto), 28 April 1980 (reprinted in chap. 13 of this volume).
27 Interview with George Grant on the history of the Department of Religion at McMaster University, printed in the department's newsletter, *R & R* (1975).
28 Plato, *The Republic*, ed. J.P. Goold and trans. Paul Shorey (Cambridge, MA: Harvard University Press 1987), 2:201.
29 Simone Weil, 'Is There a Marxist Doctrine?' in *Oppression and Liberty*, trans. Arthur Wills and John Petrie (London: Routledge and Kegan Paul 1972), 191.
30 Grant, 'Faith and the Multiversity,' in *Technology and Justice*, 65 (Darwin), 46 (Mozart).
31 Grant, 'Nietzsche and the Ancients,' 91.
32 Simone Weil, 'Scientism – A Review,' in George A. Panichas, ed., *The Simone Weil Reader* (New York: David McKay 1977), 301–2.
33 Grant, 'Research in the Humanities,' 98.
34 Ibid., 100.
35 'The Moving Image of Eternity,' 26.
36 George Grant, Review of Northrop Frye, *The Great Code: The Bible and Literature*, *Globe and Mail* (Toronto), 27 February 1982.
37 George Grant, Speech on education delivered to the Teachers Institute, Bridgetown, Nova Scotia, 1950s (typescript), 5.
38 Grant, 'The battle between teaching and research.' My italics.
39 Grant, 'Research in the Humanities,' 101–2.
40 Grant, 'The battle between teaching and research.'
41 Ibid.
42 George Grant, 'Pursuit of An Illusion: A Commentary on Bertrand Russell,' *Dalhousie Review* 32, no. 2 (summer 1952), 103.
43 George Grant, 'Justice and Technology,' in Carl Mitcham and Jim Grote, eds., *Theology and Technology* (Lanham, MD: University Press of America 1984), 242.
44 In *Lament for a Nation* (Toronto: McClelland & Stewart 1965), 54, Grant showed how progressivist arguments make 'all local cultures anachro-

nistic.' Our traditions, from whatever time or place, are rendered ineffectual in the face of these progressivist arguments.

45 Homer, *Odyssey* 10.494, quoted in Plato, *Meno*, in Edith Hamilton and Huntington Cairns, eds., *The Collected Dialogues of Plato*, Bollingen Series, vol. 71 (New York: Pantheon 1963), 383.

13

Selected Letters on Universities and Education by George Grant

WILLIAM CHRISTIAN

George Grant (whose full name was George Parkin Grant) was born into a renowned family. Both of his grandfathers devoted their lives to the reform of education. Sir George Parkin started up the Rhodes scholarships at Lord Milner's request; George Monro Grant turned the struggling Presbyterian school of Queen's in Kingston into an important university. George Grant's father, William Grant, rescued Upper Canada College (a private boys' school in Toronto) from mediocrity and made it an important educational institution.

George Grant, as the following letters show, inherited the family business. He spent almost his whole life teaching or being taught. He took an undergraduate degree in history at Queen's University, where his concern for educational reform first showed itself. He tried to alert his fellow students to the kind of changes needed in university education. As he told his mother, Maude Grant, in 1938, 'I wrote a review of Hutchins's book for the Journal.[1] *I seem to practically live in the thoughts of that book ... He gives without doubt a new pride and new honour and new self-respect and new virility to the teaching profession in America.' In his review he claimed that Hutchins posed 'a challenge to the people of North America.' 'Are we going to grovel,' he wondered, 'in an unsatisfactory* status quo *or are we going to follow an intelligent educational leader like President Hutchins?'*

After he won a Rhodes Scholarship at Queen's, Grant went to Balliol College, Oxford, to study law. He was, in his own words, an 'ambitious little pragmatist,' and he meant this literally, for he admired the educational writings of John Dewey and William James. He confided to his mother that 'Passing a book shop I saw a small book of John Dewey[2] on education. They are a collection of his essays written about 1900 on education.[3] As they are general they still bear reading as a creed for progressive liberal education. I meant to read them and then send them on to you, but find that one can only send books direct from a book shop. The first essay on "His Pedagogic Creed" is the complete justification written well of Father's life. In general, it is a fine and clear expression of all that Daddy worked and strove for. As Dewey says, the educator is the greatest of all artists.'

Grant returned home to Toronto in February 1942 suffering from emotional and physical exhaustion. After he recovered he began work with the Canadian Association for Adult Education (CAAE) as national secretary. His main responsibility was to organize the Citizens' Forum broadcasts, an early experiment in the use of public radio for adult education. Although he believed universities should be 'aristocratic' institutions, catering to the best minds, he also strongly believed in the importance of adult education, and over the next decade or so he actively participated in the CAAE.

After the war Grant returned to Oxford to study for a DPhil in theology. Afterwards he taught at Dalhousie University in Halifax from 1947 until 1960. He returned in 1980 and stayed until his retirement from teaching in 1984. In the interim he accepted, and resigned from, the position of head of the philosophy department at the newly founded York University in Toronto. His resignation was principled and brave, and Grant was very discouraged because he received little support. He then went to McMaster University, and his initial years at McMaster, where he helped to create the new Department of Religion, were happy, and for a while Grant thought that it was possible to create a university within the modern multiversity. He was never under any illusions about the difficulty of his task, and the secularizing pressures in Canadian higher education ultimately proved impossible to resist. Although he had resigned from York on a great issue of principle, his departure from McMaster was motivated more by discouragement at the kind of historicist research institutions modern universities had become and by fatigue caused by the constant infighting within his department. Throughout his university career he was driven by one supreme concern – to understand the modern world philosophically, in the light of the truths of the Christian gospel.

LETTER 1 (extract)

Grant was an exceptional teacher. How? His native histrionic talent was
an asset, but more important were his belief in the importance of his
calling and his love for the students whom he taught. When Grant was
appointed to teach philosophy at Dalhousie in 1947, it was his first formal
teaching position. From the beginning he took his teaching responsibilities
very seriously.

2 October [1947]

Dearest Ould [Maude Grant],[4]
   The first lectures have been an amazing experience. To give oneself in them means three things which take all one's energy (1) A–1
preparation is necessary & often about subjects I am not trained in
& this means extensive reading & thinking. This first year I am not
going to be able to do much work but just prepare & give my
lectures (2) preparation of stories, examples that, particularly in an
elementary philosophy course of 125, is vital (3) great emotional
concentration at each hour of lecturing.

LETTER 2

In 1949 Grant returned to England to complete his doctorate. He was
determined to stand up to the powers-that-be at Dalhousie and he knew
that he had to have 'proper qualifications' to do so. While he was there his
friend and former teacher from Queen's, historian Gerald Graham, asked
him for his thoughts on universities. The following letter advances his
view of the central role that universities play in sustaining civilization.

Upper Hill Farm,
Quainton, Buckinghamshire,
England
3 June 1949

Dear Gerald [Graham],[5]
   You asked me to put down some thoughts on Canadian universities. Here they are. As they are pulled straight out of a disorganized
head, I hope you will forgive the incoherence of their ordering and
the roughness of their expression.

Universities, I suppose, should be the repositories of the tradition, where pure contemplative scholars may carry on their work of keeping the tradition explicit and where certain of the active elite of the society may come for varying periods to enrich themselves for later action by a period of contemplation. That is, of course, an unattainable ideal.

The sad thing in Canada is that it is an ideal which few want to attain.

The reasons for this lie deep. The main cause is that Canada has been forced to be a practical, pioneering country and now that that job is done it still enshrines the values necessary to accomplish that earlier job. The second main cause is the utter scorn of the contemplative life common to the scientific West. These two combined in Canada have turned our universities so far from the Greek or medieval ideals of universities, that any hope of reform within our Canadian society seems to me remote.

There are, however, several specific remedies that would, it seems to me, be a help.

(1) Fight on the part of all who teach non-technical subjects, to convince the society & to convince it ruthlessly that it cannot hope to exist if it puts its faith in techniques and not in wholeness. Of course, the lie in the soul is amongst the non-technicians, like philosophers, historians and classicists who turn their own subjects simply into technical exercises. Nobody doubts there is a substratum of necessary technique for the specialist in all these subjects. But Canadians in these fields are teaching mainly to turn out other technicians, not to produce (as for instance Greats[6] did at Oxford) men & women who learnt from their studies to be noble and educated persons.

(2) Fight against the myth of equality that clutters up Canadian universities with fine men & women who should never be there. Affirm that an advanced education must be for the few. Of course, don't choose these few by an economic criterion. (Progressive education has led Canadian high schools to place the training of the few for universities lower & lower on their scale of priorities. Who can fight for a reversal of that degraded democratic trend but the universities? And yet we don't.)

(3) This is a subsidiary clause of (2). Constant insistence on the part of scholars that they will not give in to their administrative masters and teach wholesale. Never forget & never let others forget

that too many students prevent really first-class teaching & prevent the teacher from being a contemplative scholar. This activity is the source of his teaching. I was the only teacher for 287 students in philosophy last year.

(4) A very practical fight for the scholars to have some part in the ruling of the universities. Immediately the administration will mention the *Senate*. But as Prof Innis said, where the money & the power of appointment is, there is the real power. Teachers are lackeys in Canada at the moment, to be hired & fired. The president of my university openly admitted to me that the 'presidents' were hoping for a surfeit of teachers, to make hiring & firing easy. People who are treated like slaves become slaves and there is a great deal of the slave mentality in Canadian teachers. Also, of course, businessmen in control of a university pursue many wrong ends, which scholars could help to prevent. Business is almost farthest from contemplation.

People say the president is the liaison between teachers & governors. But, of course, the governors appoint the president & kick him out if he doesn't do their bidding & they appoint men who will do their bidding. Therefore I would say that at nearly every Canadian university I know, the president supports the board against the staff. And, of course, where can you find a president who is a scholar?

I am against the solution of having a teachers' union. Many teachers advocate this. It would solve perhaps the economic question, but not the greater question of the role of the universities.

I am for *half* the board being elected by the senate. This does not go as far as the Oxford & Cambridge system of scholar-government, but it would control business-government.

Lastly I must impress that the fight for such reforms must go beyond words. Nearly ever president in Canada piously affirms his love of these ideals. Every presidential inaugural is about 'the liberal Arts,' 'the soul of our nation' etc., but two weeks after the inaugural the university money goes to a mechanical engineering building or a BA in accounting. The lie in the presidential soul is more in their wills than in their intellects. They are 'decent godless people' who want the best; as long as that best is what the businessmen want; as long as it pays; as long as it is popular at the Rotary Club or Home & School, etc. Don't watch a university president talk; watch him act. As Emerson said: What you do cries so loud, I can't hear what you say.'

Finally may I repeat. Two attitudes seem to me impossible. (1) The academic idealist who believes that in the gasping, soulless death of the West it is possible to build a real university. (2) Those who say you can do nothing. Clearly fine universities in the great tradition cannot be created in Canada; but we must try & out of that attempt something may come.

This is hopeless and incomplete.

Yours,
George Grant

PS I feel too sick to copy this out. Sorry.

LETTER 3

At Dalhousie Grant was originally the only member of the philosophy department and he had a huge teaching load. The sciences, especially physics, seemed, by contrast, well staffed. Grant believed that Canadian universities could not fulfil their critical role unless more resources were devoted to departments such as philosophy. He wrote to Dalhousie's president to press his case that philosophy deserved to play a key role in the university and that it should not be starved for resources for the sake of scientific education and research.

Dalhousie University
Halifax
29 February 1952

Dear Dr Kerr:[7]

Last week you asked for my opinion about teaching loads at the university and what could be done about them. You asked me to go away and think about the question and send you my answer. I have done so and here is my answer. As this question goes right to the heart of the problem of what universities are for, I have answered at length.

The first question is, What is a fair teaching load for a member of a university? Of course, immediately the question has to be narrowed down to this university. A small area such as the Maritime provinces cannot afford the same high ratio of teacher to student as can the great centres of Anglo-Saxon thought such as Cambridge and Yale. On the other hand, I have always believed that Dalhousie is the chief Maritime university and, therefore, should maintain a higher ratio than places like Acadia and Mount Allison.

Having placed Dalhousie in a scale of universities, what should be the scale within the university? It will obviously depend largely upon the particular task of each department. I am not fitted to iscuss those particularities. The kind of example I do know about, however, is that the Association of American Law Schools insists that every law school must abide by the standard that no law teacher lecture more than seven hours a week.

There are also certain general principles of which I am sure. First, a university is not a factory, nor is it a high school. Both these institutions are obviously valuable to society. But the laws under which they are governed are not the same as the university's laws. Therefore, the use of any metaphors from the factory or high school are misplaced about universities. It is quite easy to see that the metaphors of industrial production do not apply. It is most difficult to see the falsity of metaphors taken from the democratic school system. The university teacher is not dishing out a subject, about the limits of which he is certain. He is continually trying – or should be trying to move his mind out into the unknown. Such a task cannot be carried out by men burdened with much teaching, for it is the kind of task which requires long hours of conscientious work. I would refer you on this matter to the recent statement of the US Secretary of State.

Secondly, no society, if it desires to have educated men, can gain that end cheaply. University education, if it is to be worth anything, must be aristocratic. (Aristocratic, of course, not in the sense of birth, but of capability.) I do also know that the most aristocratic part of a university must be a philosophy department. Under the mysterious providence of God, not many men or women are intended to understand life *sub specie aeternitatis*.[8] We must grant that in their strange way those students who do may become the most important members of society. While at college they need the close and careful attention of teachers.

Of course, you are in the very difficult position of trying to carry out these ideals in Canadian society – which is a strange mixture of plutocracy and democracy. What, after all, is the board of governors but the representatives of plutocracy and democracy, deciding what they want in the way of education? And traditionally, neither the plutocratic nor the democratic spirits have been much interested in quality or contemplation. Therefore, you have the difficult function of educating the board so that they can come to see what universities are for, and not accepting their necessarily limited conception of education. This problem is made more difficult by that strange division of authority in Canadian universities, whereby academic decisions are cut off from matters of final policy.

With all this as a necessary preamble, I would answer your practical question. In any institution there will be men who do not fulfil their function properly. The head of that institution has to come to grips with that problem. But I do not think anything useful can be done except by the slow working of good will, a very careful examination of particular cases and above all a holding on to the central spiritual principle of the university. General rules about how much each teacher should teach and how many students he should teach are useless and worse than useless because they would tend toward the worst kind of competition even among the finest men. The chief thing that can be done is the greatest care in appointments.

Therefore, I have nothing immediate in the way of suggestion to make, except my complete recognition of the difficulty of your task. It is the consciousness of that difficulty that has made me write so frankly.

George Grant

LETTER 4 (extract)

Grant was asked to write an article on philosophy in Canada for the royal commission on Canadian culture headed by his uncle, Vincent Massey.[9] His criticism of Canadian philosophy departments, especially the University of Toronto's under Fulton Anderson,[10] earned him the enmity of most mainstream Canadian philosophers.

Halifax, 1952

Dearest Ould [Maude Grant],

What philosophy has to say to society is increasingly scorned and, therefore, one lives in a continual failure of communication. One of the saddest things for me is the scorn I have received from the United Church. Only the Catholics, with whom finally I have no connection, listen to me ...

As for Fulton Anderson to hell with him.[11] As Cochrane[12] said over and over, the philosophy departments in Canadian universities have surrendered their true task. They turned philosophy into technical work for the few rather than a way of life open to all. Sureness is not necessarily dogmatism and I know that it is not a question of Anderson not believing in God and I believing. I know God exists. Plato shows to those who listen that one cannot avoid that conclusion. The face of Anderson's scepticism and secularism is all around the world. Life has been too long for me and I had to learn at too great a price not to be frank about what one believes. At the personal and practical level I am always unsure and confused but at this level I know I am right, not because of the I but because the arguments are irrefutable. And nothing could be more important than this because in the next years the future of the world is tied up with those who have rational love of God. All I hate about it is the bitterness engendered and the fact that good work may be prevented by that bitterness. As to the controversy, one cannot speak wrongly when one has Plato and Augustine and Kant behind one. The issue is not really God, but whether philosophy is a practical study which can help me to live. I have not done anything about the controversy except write two articles this summer (quite unrelated) one on Bertrand Russell[13] and the other on Plato[14] which will show even farther what I mean.

LETTER 5

Determined to leave the parochialism of Halifax, Grant accepted an offer to teach at York, the new university being founded in Toronto. He never made it there. Perhaps Grant's bravest and most controversial decision was his resignation from York. As his correspondence with President Ross demonstrates, he took his responsibility as a teacher very seriously, and believed it was essential for teachers to control their own curricula.

27 February 1960

Dear President Ross,[15]

I am sorry to bother you with a letter when you have so much to attend to.

Two weeks ago the Registrar of York wrote to ask me for a paragraph about the first year course in philosophy.[16] He enclosed the paragraph from the Toronto calendar and said we were going to teach the same course as Toronto. Knowing that York was going to be under the guidance of Toronto, but not knowing that we were going to teach completely identical courses, I wrote to Professor Anderson asking him about textbooks and describing the way I would like to cover the material. I also said that as ethics was cut from general philosophy at the U of T because of the collegiate system I would like to include Plato's *Republic* in the first year. I remembered what you had said about getting youngsters to think about what makes a good life and the *Republic* has always seemed to me the greatest book on that subject (perhaps on any subject). Professor Anderson replied civilly, but forcibly, that the questions I had raised were not pertinent as York students were going to have identical courses with the U of T for at least four years and were going to write the same examinations. I write, therefore, to ask clarification about that identity.

Will the York professors have anything to do with setting the examinations at Toronto which their students write? Will we have anything to do with marking those joint examinations or will that be done solely by Toronto appointees? Identical is quite a word (and it could include York students listening to Toronto professors on tape or by microphone). Of course, what in fact matters is how these problems are worked out in a flexible and developing practice.

I quite recognize that one need of York in the next years is to have a cooperative association with Toronto and that all you do or say to anyone must turn around that need. I recognize that all your skill will be required to balance this against the need for York to be something on its own. You also may be quite confident that I will not get into any theoretical argument with the philosophy department at Toronto about how it is best to teach philosophy and will try to eliminate any acerbity in the dealings I will have with them. But I had understood when I accepted your offer that the York teachers were going to have some freedom in what they taught and how they taught it. The minimum condition of there being any freedom is for the teacher to have some say in the setting and marking of the papers of the courses he teaches. I blame myself greatly for not having discussed these questions with you in detail. My enthusiasm about the whole project meant that it just never entered my head that the new university would have the hand of Toronto so heavily upon it. To repeat, I recognize that what is important is not formulas, but how these problems are worked out in practice and how one sets out to make accommodations in good temper. But much hangs for me on how this relationship works itself out, for you can imagine that I do not relish the prospect of being *in statu pupillari*[17] to the U of T.

Please do not take this as a pressing letter as I recognize how subtle must be the job of guiding the new institution in these next months and years. Because of your burdens I have tried to make this letter short and practical and therefore have not raised questions of long range principle about the teaching of philosophy in Canada with the coming generation of youngsters. I am going to put in the mail some comments about these broader issues which you can read at your leisure (whenever that may be).

Yours,

George Grant

LETTER 6

Grant expected his resignation to raise the issue of the nature of the modern university and its relationship to Christianity. He was hurt and surprised when he received little support or sympathy. He set out his reasons in a letter to President Ross, which, unlike most of his letters, he wrote with the intention that it become a public document showing the reasons for his action.

14 April 1960

Dear President Ross,

This is just to say that after long thought I have decided it would be wrong on my part to introduce youngsters to philosophy by means of Professor Long's textbook[18] and that, as there seems no alternative to such a procedure at York, I must with regret submit my resignation to you.

As this is an important matter of academic principle I would like to state my objections to this procedure. (a) Professor Long's textbook pretends to be an introduction to philosophy which does not take sides, but introduces the student objectively to the problems of the subject. This is, however, not the case. To illustrate why it is not the case, let me take as an example the basic question of the differences between classical and modern philosophy. Professor Long's book is based on the presupposition that the assumptions of nineteenth-century philosophy are true in a way that implies that those of classical philosophy are not. As an obvious example, the book is prefaced by a quotation from Lessing which is taken as true and which implies that Plato and Aristotle largely wrote untruth. It is, of course, not my purpose here to debate the very vexed and difficult question of the quarrel between the ancients and the moderns, but simply to say that one hardly has an objective textbook when it is based on such an assumption. What makes these assumptions particularly unobjective is that they are not made explicit in the work. (b) When I say that Professor Long's book is based on an implied assumption of the truth of modern philosophy, I do not mean contemporary philosophy, but the philosophy of the late nineteenth century in Great Britain and the early twentieth in the USA. His book is oblivious to nearly all contemporary philosophy. For instance, there is no mention of Wittgenstein in his book – certainly the most influential modern philosopher in professional philosophic circles in the English-speaking world. (c) Apart from the assumptions of the book, its very method seems to me inimical to the proper teaching of philosophy. It is about philosophy; it is not philosophy. The result of this approach is to encourage sophism among youngsters – that is, it encourages them to say here are a lot of opinions about this subject and that, but it does not encourage them in the real task of trying to make true judgments about those matters.

I would like to include a paragraph about Professor Long's relation to religion and my own, because I am sure you have heard it said that I confuse religion and philosophy and that you will now hear it said that my objections to Professor Long's book come from my religion. Let me make it clear that I consider the practice of religion and the practice of philosophy two distinct human activities. I do not think that philosophy can prove or disprove Christian doctrine. My position on this matter is illustrated by the fact that the philosopher I admire the most in North America is Leo Strauss[19] at Chicago. He is a practising Jew and I would have no hesitation in saying that he is a better philosopher than any practising Christian I know on this continent. Some of my best graduate students have been practising Jews and I have had no difficulties with them on this score. Of course, though religion and philosophy are distinct activities, their relation is a philosophic question of magnitude and Professor Long inevitably deals with it. Unfortunately he does not deal with it accurately. If, for instance, you turn to what Professor Long says about the relation between philosophy and the idea of revelation in certain religions on p. 23 of this book, I do not think one could find any trained philosophers who are either believing Protestants or Catholics or Jews who would say that it is an accurate or adequate account of the matter. I did not ask that the textbooks I use should be directed towards the spread of my religion (I suggested the works of Plato and Russell, neither of whom are in any way identified with the Christian church and neither of whom are in any way identified with the true). But I could hardly be expected to use a textbook which misrepresents the religion of my allegiance. I would also point out that though Professor Long deplores the influence of faith on certain philosophers, he has no hesitation in closely identifying the claims of his faith with the facts of the case. It is in my opinion just this which above all makes Professor Long's book so poor an instrument for introducing youngsters to philosophy, most of whom will have been born since 1940 in modern industrial Canada. Professor Long's faith was obviously formed by the experience of his break with a limited Calvinism in the light of certain philosophic and scientific ideas. This was a very moving and formative experience for the English of the 1890s, for the Americans of the early 1900s and for Canadians in the 1920s, but it has little bearing on the situation of Canadians growing up in Ontario at the moment.

Some of my friends have suggested that I should get up in class and quietly say where I think the required textbook is inadequate. This would indeed be fun; but it would also be unjust. It would leave the beginners with two conflicting accounts and an exam to be faced. This might be good for the clever, but it would be radically unfair for the weaker brethren. Also I would hope that, if my teaching were good, the better students would understand the inadequacy of the book. Then they would surely ask (if I had the right relation with them) why I employed it as a textbook. To that question I would have no just answer – beyond appealing to the necessity of earning my living, my liking for my home town, etc. Such considerations would not stand up against the unflinching moral judgments of which youngsters are capable.

Professor Anderson told Professor Long to write to me about details, where his own letter covered the matter unequivocally in terms of general policy. Professor Long told me I could use other textbooks. He included a list of these which Professor Anderson would consider suitable. I do not see, however, that this makes possible any solution because if the York students have to write Toronto exams, marked by Toronto examiners, the use of an alternative textbook would cause an unfair burden on York students. Professor Long's textbook is sufficiently idiosyncratic that I do not see how students could answer questions chosen from it by studying from some other textbooks. The burden here would particularly fall on the marginal student, of which there are bound to be some at York.

I am sorry that this resignation has been left so long, but it has only become clear to me gradually in the last months the degree to which York is going to be tied to the U of T and the consequences that this would have on my teaching at York ...

If you consider there is any need for a statement about my resignation in the newspapers and if you consider that such a statement should go beyond a simple one of fact, I think that we should work it out together.

I regret that we will not be working together in the same institution.

> With all best wishes,
> George Grant

LETTER 7 (extract)

> Dalhousie University
> 5 June 1960

Dear, dear Derek [Bedson],[20]

Sheila and I were so touched at your letters and at your phone call and at your speaking to Archbishop Barfoot.[21] Loyalty to persons is a lovely quality; but even more at the moment what concerns me is what you also have with us – a common sharing about the problem of the church and its rightful place in education. The reason I wrote to you about this whole business is not only to help me get a job, but because I want Christians outside the universities to know what gates of evil these secular universities can be. Educated Christians have a traditional respect for universities because they founded them and it is therefore hard for them to recognise that universities can be sources of evil as well as good. I am sure that the church has to face this problem and that above all the Anglican church has a tremendous role in facing this in a Catholic way and yet not in the exclusive way that the Roman church so often does. This is why I am particularly glad that you spoke to Barfoot and so glad to hear of his concern for St John's[22] ...

As for St John's it would interest me greatly – much more than the possibility you mentioned over the phone. My reason is the following: in the body of Christ there are many functions all necessary to that body, but mine is theory – theology and philosophy – and I am determined to stick to that function rather than to go into administration. I would be willing to do administration in a theological college because that would be serving an end which is related to my thought, but this administration of large secular institutions is largely having to pander to the pushing aims of the boom world ...

Love,
George

LETTER 8 (extract)

Farnham Ave.
Toronto
1 January 1961

Dear Derek [Bedson],

This is just to say that I have accepted the appointment at McMaster University ...

What I will be doing is to teach Christian doctrine to non-divinity undergraduates. This dept. of religion is really introducing the faculty of theology back into the university in a big way in a Canadian university – the very thing that has always been my dream. Paul Clifford who is Dean of Men and heading the new department is a very pleasant man – Balliol '38. More than his pleasantness, he and I are in substantial agreement as to what we should be doing. Though I was very grateful that Sibley[23] offered me a job I was much less close to him as far as the religious ends of education and would have had to teach within the kind of limits he lays down. I have had too long at Dalhousie been careful to draw the line between philosophy and Christianity – and I want now to be able to speak directly. It has not been philosophy but Xian doctrine that has got me through the necessitudes of life – and I think there is a crying need for young people to know what Xian doctrine is. The choice was between doing that and being near you and after long debate we chose the former ...

Love and as always thanks for your friendship,
George

LETTER 9 (extract)

Although Grant was happy in his early years at McMaster, and had great hopes for his new department of religion, he was worried almost from the beginning about the movement toward secularization in Canadian universities.

McMaster University
24 January 1964

Dear Rhoda and Doug [Hall]:[24]

Just a note of ill-typed greeting from the battlefields of McMaster. Your depressed note of December met such a responding note in our hearts. What a queer era it is to live in and how much queerer it is going to get. I see your point about the United Church and its residence, but I am sure that the first thing is that people such as yourselves be in them, but then such people are hard to find. As for the great big, mass universities, God knows. They are going to be fantastic places and hard for youngsters to survive humanly within them. I sit on the colleges division of the Anglican offices and, except for a few young people, the church has no idea what is happening in the world, which is the first step before it decides what it should do. The sheer failure to see what is happening is staggering ...

LETTER 10 (extract)

As he had explained to Murray Ross a decade earlier, philosophy meant nothing if it did not tell human beings how to live their lives. The modern

university treated ethics, both implicitly and explicitly, as a private deci-
sion without public consequences. Grant's sister, Charity, resigned in
protest from her position as dean of women at University College, Univer-
sity of Toronto, because she considered the university to be promoting
moral laxity. Grant supported her action.

[1970]

Dear Charity [Grant],[25]

I am sure that what you are doing between students and staff is at the essence of the university; because in the midst of the chaos that modern universities have become, the only really important activity left is that some of the young people get some sense of it being a human place in which there are at least a few sane older people who live their lives with some moral cohesion. This is why I limit myself so strictly to the department of religion and yet even there I find it becoming a place caught between cold mechanism at the top and foolish ideology from some of the students. I was luck- ier than you that just at the time when the sins of the multiversity were coming so wildly home to roost I was not at the centre of the storm like you but in a fairly decent haven: (a) in a simpler, more proletarian university than yours and (b) having been driven out of any hope of taking part in administration, after the difficulties of my experience at Dalhousie and with York. But I admire greatly the courage and sense of morality that you have shown at the heart of the storm and just because neither of us have been able to talk properly to the other in the last years, I want to express that admi- ration for your courage. I have faced the storm in part through what this era has produced in my immediate family and the sense of my inadequacy of dealing properly and adequately with the tur- bulence with which the children are faced. The great and central sadness for me in that (as indeed for Sheila also) is that it is uncer- tain that we have been able to help the children to apprehend the light of Christianity.

LETTER 11

After almost twenty years at McMaster, Grant finally decided that he
could no longer stand its emphasis on historical and scientific research.
He decided to return to Dalhousie. Grant's resignation from McMaster,

unlike his earlier resignation from York, was attended by considerable controversy.

14 March 1980

Dear Dean McIvor,[26]

This is just to say that I am resigning from McMaster as from the end of this academic year.

My reason for doing so is that for the last decade the Arts Departments have been developed in the light of a principle which can only lead to their increasing sterility. The dominance of 'research' is an appropriate principle for those parts of the university concerned with the progressive sciences. This principle cannot produce an account of knowledge adequate to an Arts Faculty. As there is no evidence that this principle is going to cease to be dominant, I am going to a university more open to a broader meaning of the term.

Let me express my admiration for yourself.

George Grant

Since there was considerable controversy at McMaster about his reasons for leaving, Grant decided to clarify his position in a short piece published in the Globe *and* Mail *(Toronto) on 28 April 1980. Though not a letter, it is included here because it contains an important assessment of the role of universities. The somewhat misleading headline was supplied by the* Globe *editor.*

THE BATTLE BETWEEN TEACHING AND RESEARCH

George Grant

Dr. Grant, an author and professor of religious studies at McMaster University, unhappy with the stress on research over teaching, is leaving for a post at Dalhousie University.

Most of us try to act from what we know or think we know. Therefore, if we are to understand society, we must understand our educational institutions.

In the Sixties a great change took place in the universities of Ontario. They were expanded in numbers, size and wealth by the

Government. Like most things in Ontario, this change was initiated because of what was happening in the United States. This change should be associated with the name of President John F. Kennedy.

The question was asked in terms of Sputnik: Can it be possible that U.S. education has fallen behind that of the Soviet Union? If so, we must immediately do something about it. Beyond this response, there was also the nobler positive affirmation: Let us see that everybody in society can reach his highest potential through education; let us expand the frontiers of knowledge; let us build a noble technological society of highly skilled specialists who are at the same time people of vision.

It came to be believed that the university would become central in building a humane and liberated technological society. Ontario naturally followed the continental pattern and established a great network of universities.

The new university system came into existence at a time when the account of knowledge which had dominated the Western world for three centuries had reached its height of influence. Every civilization has produced its own account of what constitutes knowledge, and has been shaped by that account. Such accounts spring forth from a particular aspiration of human thought in relation to the effective mans for its realization. Our dominant account of knowledge in the West has been positive and progressive science. The aspiration of thought from which it sprang was, above all, the desire to overcome chance so human beings would be the controllers of nature.

The effective condition for its realization was what we now call research. Research is the method in which something is summoned before the court of human reason and questioned, so we can discover the causes for its being the way it is as an object. Research made its appearance on the public scene of history when Galileo ran balls down an inclined plane. Now research is applied to everything from matter to human beings, from modern society to past societies.

The amazing achievements of research are before us in every lived moment – in the achievements of modern medicine and communications, of modern food production and warfare. If one ever has doubts about the goodness of many of its achievements, it is well to remind oneself of penicillin. It is at the heart and core of our lives, and as such at the heart and core of our education.

Yet there are great questions which present themselves to all thinking human beings and which cannot be answered by the method of research. What is justice? How do we come to know what is truly beautiful? Where do we stand toward the divine? Are there things that can be done that should not be done? One just has to formulate these questions to see they cannot be answered by research. Yet thinking people need to be clear about such questions and therefore they cannot be excluded from the university.

Education about these questions was carried on for centuries by the method of dialectic. Dialectic just means conversation – sustained and disciplined conversation. It takes place between students and students, between students and teachers. It takes place by means of the spoken and the written word. (If one writes an essay for a teacher, one is having a conversation with him.)

We have to talk with the great minds of the past. To think deeply about justice requires sustained conversation with Plato and Kant. This method of dialectic demands a different form of education from that required when the product pursued is research. It is a much more erotic kind of teaching than that which has to do with knowing about objects – erotic because what is to be known about justice or God or beauty can only be known when they are loved.

This is why I have such a sense of failure as a teacher. The older forms of education took place in Arts faculties. But the research paradigm of knowledge is becoming so powerful in those faculties that the tradition of dialectic is gradually being driven out. Energetic professors soon came to know that prestige is to be gained from research, and therefore pursue it. The reward system of the institutions teaches young professors that if they are to get on they must produce. This not only turns them away from the business of teaching, but it also turns them away from educating themselves in a broader context. What was necessary for the traditional form of education was to become an educated human being through a sustained life of study.

Obviously there is need of research in the humanities. Who could not be glad that C.N. Cochrane from Toronto wrote the great book *Christianity and Classical Culture*? But Cochrane was not first and foremost a specialist; he was first an educated man who looked at the ancient world from out of his long life of sustained self-education.

Of course, in the older Ontario universities such as Queen's and

Toronto the tradition of dialectic has more continuance. This is also true of Trent, which was modelled on the Canadian pattern of the colleges at Toronto. But in the universities whose ethos developed in the 1960s, the dominance of the new paradigm of knowledge becomes stronger and stronger.

It is around this question of principle that the large influx of U.S. professors into our universities should be understood. Germany was the country where universities were first oriented around research. U.S. higher education was more influenced by the German pattern than by any other source. Flexner is the man most associated with that influence. On the other side, dialectical education was stronger in England than anywhere else, largely because of the powerful influence of Oxford and Cambridge. Canadian higher education was more shaped before 1945 by English influences than by any other. The influx of U.S. professors in recent decades has brought a powerful push toward the research-oriented university. The nature of that influence does not turn on the particular nationality of particular people. No decent human being should judge another solely in terms of the accident of where he was born, but the problem still remains. The influx of U.S. professors brought with it certain German ideas which have greatly cut across many of our traditions.

When I was growing up in university circles in the 1930s, it was taken for granted that Canadian universities were probably better (at least different) from their U.S. counterparts. Since 1945, Canadian confidence in its own traditions has continually weakened, because of our belief that the U.S. model is determinative.

This abstruse question of educational principle may seem far away from the realities of life. Yet it is not. You cannot have a free and vibrant society unless there are free and vibrant people in it. Obviously there are large numbers of free people in Canada who have no contact with higher education. Their freedom has other sources. Nevertheless, it is important for the health of any society that there are people in it whose sense of freedom is sustained by having thought in a disciplined way about the supreme questions of human life.

When our Arts faculties are centred around research they produce a culture which is essentially a 'museum culture.' Museums are places where we see past life as objects – as flies in amber. We do not see them as existences which light up our existence.

Never has so much money been spent on the organized study of the past, and never has the past had less meaning in shaping the real life of our present. Art and religion and the passion for justice will continue, but they will be more and more cut off from the rationality the universities should offer them. Technological excellence plus museum scholarship are not enough. When they are considered sufficient, the mass of students will become listless. Scholarship is a means to thought, not a substitute for it.

LETTER 12 (extract)

When Grant returned to Dalhousie he found that it, too, had changed in the twenty years since he had taught there. Canadian universities, he concluded, had come to terms with modernity and its imperatives. He had not. Even when he retired in 1984, he still cared deeply about higher education and the role of the philosopher as teacher.

8 January 1985

Dear William [Christian],

... The Dalhousie faculty are taking a strike vote tomorrow. I hope they fail in getting a majority, but doubt it. The union seems dominated by two types of opinion. (a) A large number are not from here, let alone Canada, and, therefore, have little sense (or care) about the place they teach. (b) They are held by that kind of vague mixture of marxism and liberalism which gives them little picture of what the modern world is really like. Very unfair to the students, if they strike, for salaries that are more based on competing for staff with Ontario, rather than apposite to the lower standard of living here.

LETTER 13 (extract)

4 February 1985

Dear Joan [O'Donovan],[27]

... I am very glad to be retired and try to write things down. I was particularly glad to be retired because the faculty union called a strike. I do not think faculty have the right to strike against students and would have gone on teaching. Luckily the strike collapsed. I would never feel this about strikers who are badly paid, but here it was a lot of greedy people, who are highly paid for Nova Scotia.

... I was very glad to hear that you were teaching. Teaching is not only good because of what is taught, but it is so good for the teacher because when he or she gets to his feet he finds out how clear or unclear he may be on the matter at hand because he hears what he is saying in relation to the taught people. There is no bluffing in teaching because, when it is present it is exposed, more so than in one's writing.

Over fifty years, from his review of Hutchins's book in 1938 until his death in 1988, George Grant confronted the forces that sought to turn the universities into the servants of society's short term and secular interests. Although he had few illusions about the likelihood of success, he fought with courage. It was better, he often said, to go down with guns blazing and flags flying than to give up hope.

NOTES

1 George Grant, Review of R.M. Hutchins, *The Higher Learning in America, Queen's University Journal*, 18 June 1938, 3. R.M. Hutchins (1899–1977), president of the University of Chicago and educational reformer. In 1954 Hutchins founded the Center for the Study of Democratic Institutions.
2 John Dewey (1859–1952), American philosopher and educational theorist. Grant later attacked his views on progressive education.
3 John Dewey, *Educational Essays* (1910). Dewey was also author of *The School and Society* (1900).
4 Maude Grant (1880–1963), Grant's mother.
5 Gerald Graham (1903–90), history professor and family friend.
6 Classics.
7 A.E. Kerr (1898–1974), United Church clergyman who served as president of Dalhousie University in 1945–63.
8 'In the context of eternity.'
9 George Grant, 'Philosophy,' in *Royal Commission Studies: A Selection of Essays Prepared for the Royal Commission on National Development in the Arts, Letters and Sciences* (Ottawa: King's Printer 1951), 119–31.
10 Fulton H. Anderson (1895–1968), head of the University of Toronto's philosophy department in 1945–62.

11 Anderson wrote a forceful critique of Grant's royal commission study. See Fulton Anderson, 'Introduction,' in J.A. Irving, ed., *Philosophy in Canada: A Symposium* (Toronto: University of Toronto Press 1952), 1–5.

12 C.N. Cochrane (1898–1945), later Professor of Classics, University College, University of Toronto. Grant very much admired his *Christianity and Classical Culture* (1940).

13 George Grant, 'Pursuit of an Illusion: A Commentary on Bertrand Russell,' *Dalhousie Review* 32, no.2 (summer 1952), 97–109.

14 George Grant, 'Popper and Plato,' *Canadian Journal of Economics and Political Science* 20, no.2 (May 1954), 185–94.

15 Murray G. Ross (1910–), founding president, York University.

16 Denis Smith to George Grant, 10 February 1960 (Grant papers, Halifax).

17 'In the status of a student,' that is, of a subordinate.

18 Marcus Long, *The Spirit of Philosophy* (1953).

19 Leo Strauss (1899–1973), German-born American political philosopher.

20 Derek Bedson (1920–89). Educated at the University of Manitoba. Joined the Canadian Army in 1942. Balliol College, Oxford, 1945–7. Bedson was principal private secretary to federal Conservative leaders George Drew and John Diefenbaker in 1954–8. In 1958 he became clerk of the Manitoba executive council and secretary to the premier of Manitoba, positions he held under four successive Manitoba premiers, both NDP and Conservative.

21 Most Rev. W.F. Barfoot (1893–1978), primate of all Canada in 1951–8.

22 St John's College in Winnipeg.

23 William Sibley (1919–), chairman of the University of Manitoba's philosophy department.

24 Douglas J. Hall (1928–), principal of St Paul's United College, University of Waterloo in 1962–5. Rhoda (Palfrey) Hall was a friend from Halifax.

25 Charity Grant (1913–), Grant's sister, formerly dean of women at University College, University of Toronto.

26 R.C. McIvor (1915–), dean, Faculty of Social Science, McMaster University.

27 Joan E. O'Donovan wrote the first monograph about Grant, *George Grant and the Twilight of Justice* (Toronto: University of Toronto Press 1984).

Index